EURIPIDES
10 Plays

Misunderstood in his own time, Euripides was a genius whose plays explore the inequalities of society, the agonies of war, the conflicts of faith and reason, and the cruelty of human nature. His most famous play, *The Bacchae,* is often cited by scholars as one of the key texts of Western civilization. The enduring significance of Euripides' themes and the power of his poetry ensure that he remains one of the most widely read of the ancient Greek dramatists.

Paul Roche, a noted English poet and scholar, is the author of *The Bible's Greatest Stories* (Signet) and the translator of *The Oedipus Plays of Sophocles* and *The Orestes Plays of Aeschylus* (both Meridian).

EURIPIDES
TEN PLAYS

TRANSLATED BY
PAUL ROCHE

𝒞

SIGNET CLASSICS

SIGNET CLASSICS
Published by New American Library, a division of
Penguin Group (USA) Inc., 375 Hudson Street,
New York, New York 10014, USA
Penguin Group (Canada), 90 Eglinton Avenue East, Suite 700, Toronto,
Ontario M4P 2Y3, Canada (a division of Pearson Penguin Canada Inc.)
Penguin Books Ltd., 80 Strand, London WC2R 0RL, England
Penguin Ireland, 25 St. Stephen's Green, Dublin 2,
Ireland (a division of Penguin Books Ltd.)
Penguin Group (Australia), 250 Camberwell Road, Camberwell, Victoria 3124,
Australia (a division of Pearson Australia Group Pty. Ltd.)
Penguin Books India Pvt. Ltd., 11 Community Centre, Panchsheel Park,
New Delhi - 110 017, India
Penguin Group (NZ), 67 Apollo Drive, Rosedale, North Shore 0632,
New Zealand (a division of Pearson New Zealand Ltd.)
Penguin Books (South Africa) (Pty.) Ltd., 24 Sturdee Avenue,
Rosebank, Johannesburg 2196, South Africa

Penguin Books Ltd., Registered Offices:
80 Strand, London WC2R 0RL, England

Published by Signet Classics, an imprint of New American Library,
a division of Penguin Group (USA) Inc.

First Signet Classics Printing, October 1998
25 24 23 22 21 20

Introduction copyright © Paul Roche, 1998
All rights reserved

(See page 579 for permissions information.)

 REGISTERED TRADEMARK—MARCA REGISTRADA

Printed in the United States of America

Contents

Introduction

Of the nineteen extant plays of Euripides, out of the more than
ninety that he wrote, nine are about women. If we add his first play,
the lost *Daughters of Pelias*, presented in 455 B.C. when Euripides
was about thirty, the number becomes ten. Women, war, and God
were his perennial themes. And of course, the human condition.

As to the first, he was appalled by the low status of women
even in hypercivilized Athens. They had no vote, they were
expected to stay at home, they could not engage in commerce—
and of course not war—and they were barred from the dramatic
festivals.

In spite of this, we must be on our guard against supposing that
their prestige and influence were nil, as they would be with us
under similar trammels. Euripides, without being a feminist,
showed in play after play that women were powers in society,
and though he does not approve of the henpecked husband or of
giving a child the mother's surname, he takes almost more care in
the delineation of their characters than he does in those of men.

As to war, three of his plays, *Iphigenia in Aulis*, *The Trojan
Women*, and *Helen*, inveigh against the cruelty and stupidity of
war. Indeed, at every possible turn in his plays he underscores
the monumental folly of war, which wrecks and demoralizes
both victors and vanquished.

When it comes to God, there are those who see a problem and
accuse Euripides of being an atheist. This premature and unjust
assumption is, I believe, based on his apparent dismissal of the
gods and his distrust of Apollo. The truth is that a sense of divine
presence and omnipotence is taken for granted in all his plays.
His "dismissal" of the gods was a plea to look further and deeper
than a wine-bibbing Bacchus, an inept Apollo, or a rollicking
Heracles.

He was not understood, even by the clever Aristophanes, who lampooned him mercilessly. People did not realize that Euripides was propounding great moral problems, demanding a new analysis of human nature, its instincts, passions, and motives. He deals with the cornered human heart of the individual, at bay against the tyranny of a false theocracy. He deals with the cruelty and selfishness of man.

Euripides, in his seventy-third year, disappointed possibly by the public's lack of appreciation (he had won first prize only four times, and even his masterpiece the *Medea* took only third prize), accepted an invitation from King Archelaus of Macedon to come and live with him. So he was able to escape from being "baited incessantly by a rabble of comic writers, and of course by the great pack of the orthodox and the vulgar."*

In Macedon he wrote three more plays, including his greatest, *The Bacchae*, which was presented after his death in Athens in 406 by his son, and took first prize.

The happy endings of Euripides' plays may seem to us silly after all the horror that precedes them. They must have seemed silly to Euripides too: the rescue out of the blue of a murderous Medea; the return of Alcestis from Hades to Admetus, who did not deserve her; the marriage of Electra to Pylades, who deserved something better. In all these quasi-deus-ex-machina escapes from reality it is as though Euripides were saying: "You want a happy ending, but can't you see that the ending would not have been happy? Very well, I'll give you an ending that you can't believe in."

Tradition has it that Euripides was taciturn and retiring. We know that he sought solitude for his work in a cave on the island of Salamis near Athens. Recently a clay pot inscribed with his name has been unearthed in a cave at Peristeria in the south of the island. The pot has been dated between 440 and 430 B.C. and only the first six letters of his name are inscribed. Experts say that the inscription was applied later by an admirer of the poet. It seems to me just as likely that the inscription was on the pot because the pot was his, and the pot was in the cave because that was the cave Euripides wrote in.

*   *   *

*Gilbert Murray.

I have based my translation on two Greek texts: that of the Harvard University Press and William Heinemann in the Loeb Classical Library, edited by Arthur S. Way, and that of the Collection des Universités de France, edited by Léon Parmentier and Henri Grégoire. When line numbers are given in the footnotes, they refer to the numbers in the Greek text of the Loeb Classics series.

I owe an enormous debt to Moses Hadas and John McLean, whose translation in the Bantam Classic edition steadied me throughout. I found it a masterpiece of direct, simple, and scrupulously faithful rendering. If I have lifted a phrase or two it is because they could not be bettered.

In compiling the glossary I am indebted to Professor J. E. Zimmerman for his small but comprehensive *Dictionary of Classical Mythology* (1965 edition), published by Bantam Books.

I am also greatly beholden to my patient editor at Penguin Putnam, Hugh Rawson, who has guided me throughout.

Translator's Preface

One of the features of my endeavor to render Euripides faithfully is that I keep strictly to the structure of his plays, which varies very little.

He begins with a Prologue spoken by one of the characters, which is followed by the Parados (entry song of the chorus) or sometimes by the First Episode. Occasionally a lyric monologue or dialogue stands in for the chorus. After which comes the First Choral Ode or Lyric (I use the terms Choral Ode and Choral Lyric interchangeably), followed by the Second Episode, followed by the Second Choral Ode, followed by the Third Episode, and so on till the final chorus.

The advantage, if there is an advantage, of giving headings to this structure is that it stresses Euripides' procedure. There is this to it, too, that with signposts pointing the way it is easy for a student or an actor to pick exactly any passage that he or she wants to study or rehearse.

Lastly, I must make clear that this version is a translation, not an adaptation or a paraphrase. I might almost boast that it could be used as a crib by that little band of people that still studies classical Greek.

There are no stage directions or divisional headings in the Greek text. These are my additions.

The Prosody of Euripides

Many years ago in my first attempts to translate Greek drama (it was Sophocles), I wondered how I could transcribe the iambic trimeter of the Greek, which is a twelve-syllable line set out in two sets of three. If read naturally and not with the theoretical quantities imposed on it by grammarians, the line reads with six basic stresses.*

I discovered (as I say elsewhere) that the pace of Greek is faster than English, and this would make a twelve-syllable line in English (hexameter) too slow for the Greek and not at all its aesthetic equivalent. This made me cast my first translations in the shorter line of iambic pentameter; but I came to realize that pentameter was too much of a straitjacket for the fluidity of the Greek, so I invented a line I called "Compensated Pentameter." In this, the length of the line could vary, so long as the overall count was the same. For instance, if I went into a hexameter, I would compensate the next line by making it a tetrameter.

This worked fairly well, but though I sprinkled around a goodly smattering of dactyls, anapests, trochees, and spondees, I found that the line was still too rigid to reflect the limpid flexibility of the Greek. Then I thought: different though Greek is from English, both tongues love iambs. Indeed, iambs are natural to English in verse and prose, though in prose one should not strive for a musical line unless the emotion requires it.

The upshot of all this was that I alighted on what I christened the "Freewheeling Iambic," and that is what I use now. The Freewheeling Iambic reads very naturally and I have arranged the lines exactly as they should be spoken.

The choruses, whether in Aeschylus, Sophocles, or Euripides, are another matter: especially in Euripides, who wrote almost as if he were composing hit tunes. I have generally attempted at least to echo his meters, taking trouble to make the strophes and antistrophes strictly correspond.

The Challenge of Translating

I have spoken at length in my translations of Aeschylus and Sophocles about the problems of the translator and my attempts to solve them. It has always struck me as ironic that one begins

---

*It must not be thought that I imply that quantity and stress are the same thing, they are not, but because it is not so much sound that differentiates them but silences and pauses, and because in Greek, Latin, and English the natural value of words takes precedence over quantity, the overall effect is the same.

to be equipped to translate a Greek play only when one has completed it; though complete it one never does—at least not until it is acted. Only then do the weak lines, the impossible lines, embarrassingly scream for another attempt. I would willingly put all my translations in the wastepaper basket and try again.

When Crossroads Productions was filming my translation of *Oedipus Rex* for Universal Pictures, I kept the Greek text in my pocket and would whip it out to accommodate some unhappy, and usually recalcitrant, actor or actress.

I shall never forget the horrific day in the old theater of Dodona when Orson Welles, as Tiresias, was being filmed. He had spent the night combing through his lines and removing most of the stichomythia (line by line) dialogue. He no doubt did a good job so far as meaning went, but what he did not realize was that he had blurred the gradual crescendo of feeling propelled by the antithetic rhythm of the lines. The result was that when Oedipus and Tiresias had finished their great set-to, Oedipus, far from being demolished (as Sophocles intended) was as cocky as ever.

Ezra Pound made the same mistake in his otherwise remarkable renderings. It is the mistake of someone who has confused logical succinctness with the power of poetry. And yet the world of pop and rock has proved over and over again, from errand boy to archbishop, that rhythm bypasses the meddling intellect and goes straight into the bloodstream of intellectuals no less than that of the most bovine.

My own endeavor in translating is to find out as nearly as possible what the great playwright said and how he said it. This is very different from adapting or paraphrasing in the manner of Jeffers, Anouilh, Lowell, and Hughes. Such "imitations" have their value and can be masterpieces in their own right (vide Dryden's *Virgil* and Pope's *Homer*), but as scholarly transcriptions of what was actually said and meant, they are virtually useless.

If then the translator intends to be faithful to the text and is not merely using it as a vehicle for his own invention, how does he find the words which not only denote and connote neither more nor less than they do in the original, but at the same time bring over the emotive power locked in the sonic texture? It is a question both of unearthing the right words with the right meaning, association, color, timbre, and valence, and of putting them in the right order with the right tones, rhythms, and cadences.

As an illustration, a phrase of the *Agamemnon* of Aeschylus comes to mind. Clytemnestra, in her exultant speech explaining how a relay of beacons flashed the news of the fall of Troy to Greece, says: "with a leapfrog over the sea the strong light skipped with joy." Her words in the Greek for "a leapfrog over the sea," are *hupertelēs te pontou hōste nōtizai*, which translated literally mean: "leaping over the sea like a back flip." But one cannot pronounce *hupertelēs te* without it being onomatopoeic: the very rhythm of the seven syllables does the leap for one. Therefore in English I found a similar rhythm of seven syllables, "a leapfrog over the sea." Of course, "somersault" would have done as well.

Let us take a simpler example in another language. How does one translate the two words *Italia mia*? Nothing easier: "My Italy." But "My Italy" gets nowhere near the emotional blend of pride, fondness, and gentle defiance that emanates from the Italian. Pronounce the syllables with a good round mouth and think of Italy. The whole phrase purrs and sings. What can be done about it in English? Very little. I would venture "Italy, my Italy!" This at least begins to capture the magic.

Take another example: Horace's witty remark *"Quidquid dicam aut erit aut non,"* which translates literally into "Whatever I may say either is or is not," which doesn't sound particularly aphoristic or clever. What if we use the rhythm of his *aut . . . aut* but don't actually translate it and say: "Whatever I may say certainly is or certainly isn't"? Now some of the sharpness begins to tell.

I once lived in Mexico near a village called Santo Thomas de los Platanos. How poetic and evocative! How can I possibly turn this into St. Thomas of the Bananas? Or what if we put into French Tennyson's famous lines "Break, break, break on thy cold grey shores, O sea!", and have him say (as Edith Hamilton, that great classicist, acutely pointed out): "Cassez-vous, cassez-vous, cassez-vous sur vos froids gris caillous, O mer!"?

And, as a last absurdity, let us consider Xenophon. He tells us in his *Anabasis* (*The March Up-country*) how the ten thousand Greek mercenaries after months of fumbling their way through the wilds of Mesopotamia climb their final hill, and as each wave of soldiers hits the summit, the ones below hear a roar: *"Thalassa! Thalassa!"* ("The sea! The sea!"). What if we render this immemorial yelp semantically correctly as: "A vast expanse of salt water! A vast expanse of salt water!"? It is unthinkable.

But even among the synonyms of our own tongue we cannot ignore the imaginative charge of words without being monstrous. You might, for example, be excused for declining an invitation to dinner when the menu offered was dead calf with fungus in heated dough, scorched ground tubers, and cabbage stalks, all swilled down with rotten German grape juice, and topped off with the dust of burnt berries in scalding water diluted with congealed oozings from the udders of a cow. You might well decline such a bill of fare, but you would miss an excellent meal of veal and mushroom pie, roast potatoes and spring greens, chased by a bottle of hock, and finished with a steaming cup of coffee and cream. What's in a name? Just about everything.

When it comes to Greek drama, the pace is surprisingly fast. The dialogue is written in iambic trimeter, a twelve-syllable line which (as I point out earlier in this preface), scans as six feet divided into two sets of three. "Aha!" says the incautious translator, "the English equivalent is another twelve-syllable line, none other than the iambic hexameter." He slaps it into that and has fallen into the trap. He may be a genius, but he will never know why his lines begin to pall and drag. They do so for the reason that twelve syllables of English ordinarily take more time to say than twelve syllables of Greek.

I puzzled over this and it was only when analyzing the opening lines of Sophocles' *Antigone* that the truth struck me. English uses twice as many consonants as Greek and it is the consonants that delay. Take a two-syllable word like *sophos* and put it against a two-syllable word like *knowledge*. How swift is the Greek! How slow and stodgy the English! And this in a mere two syllables. What of twelve? Multiply the extra seconds needed in line after line and no matter how brilliant the translation, it will drag. The effect is something like looking at a film in which every shot is several seconds too long.

Listen, for instance, to the late eminent scholar Moses Hadas (for whom I have enormous respect) falling into exactly this mistake in his translation of the *Antigone*.

Sister Ismene, my own dear sister, do you know
Of any ill of those bequeathed by Oedipus
That Zeus does not fulfill for us two while we live?
There is nothing painful, nothing fraught with ruin,
No shame and no dishonor that I have not seen
In your woes and mine.

               And now what is this new
Edict of which men speak our captain has just published
To all the Thebes? Have you any knowledge of it? . . .

Alas, this is not the only way of slowing down the Greek. Here
is Agamemnon replying to Clytemnestra's fraudulent welcome
in the *Oresteia* on his return from Troy.

Off-spring of Leda, of my household warder,
Suitably to my absence hast thou spoken.
For long the speech thou dids't outstretch! But aptly
To praise—from others ought to go this favour.
And for the rest—not me, in woman's fashion,
Mollify, nor—as mode of barbarous man is—
To me gape forth a groundward-falling clamour!
Nor, strewing it with garments, make my passage
Envied, for a mortal on these varied beauties
To walk—to me, indeed, is nowise fear-free.
I say—as man, not god, to me do homage.

Believe it or not, this is the great Robert Browning, one of my
favorite poets. He has supposed that the best way to be faithful to
Aeschylus is to reproduce Greek word order and syntax. The
result is a translation that needs a translation.

My own principle of faithful re-creation (for re-creation it
must be if it is to live) is that one language best translates another
when it is least like it and most true to its own genius. One language cannot take a photograph of another.

This does not mean that they cannot share parallel qualities
of sound. Indeed, they must if they are to engender the same
emotions—even to the illusion, where possible, of a common
rhythm. Greek and English, though etymologically so different,
both love many of the same things. There is a preoccupation with
cadence, which shows itself in a predilection for alliteration and

assonance and the associative power of similar sound; there is attention to the well-timed pause and the break in the middle of a line; a love of antithesis of both sound and sense; there is a feeling for the symmetrical phrase as well as the asymmetrical as a means of emphasis; the use of repetition and parallelisms of speech for pointing up a phrase or creating pathos; there is joy in twists of expression, telling paradoxes, oxymora, litotes, and a whole host of figures of speech that put salt on the tongue and blood in the veins. And finally, Greek and English both insist on economy and clarity. (I have heard it said that in Greek drama there is no rhyme. This is not true. There is end rhyme and internal rhyme. However, in polysyllabic words rhyme often goes undetected.)

One last and fundamental point: though Greek drama depended for its effect on an amalgam of the arts—spectacle, music, poetry, song, and dance—the most important element of all was speech. And it is through the ear ultimately that these great plays enter the psyche.

The Choruses

Though the choruses in Euripides are far less integral to the action of the drama (except in *The Bacchae*) than they are in Aeschylus and Sophocles, they are nonetheless important and a production that fails to make them effective will be irretrievably marred.

Unfortunately some directors seem to find them an embarrassment to be got rid of as soon as possible. The key to success is to realize that the function of the chorus, psychologically, is to relieve the audience of dramatic tension after each episode and introduce a new tension, a lyric tension—one that hits below the belt.

To accomplish this it is no more necessary that the words should be understood than it is, say, for us to understand a poem of Mallarmè, or Hopkins, or Dylan Thomas the first time we hear it; remembering always that poetry begins to communicate long before, or at least beyond the point at which, it is understood. I would even hazard a guess that the Greeks themselves understood very little of a chorus the first time they heard it. Which is not to say that it did not bowl them over.

That is what a chorus must do. Though commenting on,

recording, and condensing the action of the play,* the chorus must transcend it, lift it to a new plane of experience. This it can only do if it is poetically different from the realism of each episode. The chorus should be emotionally convincing and sweep the audience off its feet in the way that music, dance, and mime can do.

My own instinct is to turn the choruses into ballet. One has only to experience Martha Graham's *Oresteia* to see how overwhelming that can be. The difficulty is, how does one train dancers to speak the lines superbly as they dance? The Greeks would not have dreamed of undertaking such a task without six months' or a year's training—and they were dealing with people who had sucked in poetry and dance with their mothers' milk. I hardly think it possible.

SOME SUGGESTIONS

1. Make the size of the chorus as large as is compatible with the size of the stage, remembering that twelve people are generally more impressive than three.

2. The chorus must be trained in mime and dance.

3. Rarely allow the chorus to speak directly (except of course when it takes part in the dialogue).

4. Though there may indeed be occasions when voice-in-unison can be attempted, recitation in unison is difficult to bring off convincingly without being self-conscious and "arty." The danger of splitting the chorus into different voices is that this too easily degenerates into mere dialogue, thus jeopardizing the incantatory power of the words.

5. I favor having the words come "voice-over" the mime and dance, live or recorded, magnified and impeccably delivered.

6. Choral dialogue, that is, lyric dialogue, must not be confused with the chorus used as dialogue. In choral dialogue the verbal orchestration of the words must function as verse given its full prosodic value.

7. The verses of the chorus should be beaten out rhythmically

---

*Sir Arthur Packard Cambridge in his monumental *The Dramatic Festivals of Athens* goes so far as to say that the audience could probably have followed the action of the play by watching the chorus alone. It mimed throughout.

with little attempt to make them sound "natural." The design of the poetry must not be turned into prose. The design must be allowed to appear.

8. All sorts of sonic experiments in the speaking or chanting of the choruses are not only permissible but to be encouraged. For instance, after a first straight hearing, the words can be fragmented into various patterns of repetition, cross-cutting, overlapping, truncation and so on. They can echo liturgical prayers and litanies, the English perhaps played off against the Greek, or conversely, turned into wounded animal sounds. Remember always that the aim is to make the chorus—both in sound and sight—breathtaking.

9. The choice of music is crucial. There should be music throughout the drama: introducing scenes, repeating themes, coming in and out of both dialogue and choruses. Care must be taken, however, that whenever the words are pitted against the music, the words be given first place. The audience must not have to strain to catch the words above the music. As to instruments, I favor drum, flute, and lute, or guitar and harp, as coming nearest to the Greek timbal, flageolet, and lyre. (I once made a successful recording of the *Antigone* with the music of Moon Dog from the streets of New York with flute and drum; also a powerful performance of *Oedipus Rex* against the strident music of Varesi.)

10. In general, let the director have enough faith and courage to cut himself off from being merely rational. The choruses must exhibit the beauty and surprise of their own design. They must be aesthetically irresistible.

EURIPIDES
10 Plays

ALCESTIS

— ✦ —

ΑΛΚΕΣΤΙΣ

For Erica Lindgren and Raffaella Smith

When *Alcestis* was performed in 438 B.C., Euripides was already an experienced poet and playwright with seventeen years of writing behind him. He placed the play, as if it were a comedy or satyr play, after the usual three preceding tragedies. Certainly he has tongue in cheek throughout, even though the question he asks strikes at the roots of male and female assumptions in fifth-century-B.C. Athens. Can a man, a provenly decent man, let his wife die for him? To us, Admetus' bland assumption that he can seems astonishing chauvinism, but among the Athenians watching the play for the first time and untouched by feminist enlightenment, the behavior of Admetus would have met with a certain sympathy. Euripides, however, has layered the action with so much pathos and irony that even they, surely, would have come away with questions.

CHARACTERS

APOLLO
DEATH
CHORUS, elders of Pherae
MAIDSERVANT
ALCESTIS, wife of Admetus
ADMETUS, king of Pherae
EUMELUS, son of Admetus and Alcestis
SISTER OF EUMELUS
HERACLES
PHERES, father of Admetus
BUTLER TO ADMETUS
ATTENDANTS, guards, servants, citizens of Pherae

TIME AND SETTING

The past: The god Apollo in punishment for a misdemeanor was once constrained by his father, Zeus, to tend the cattle of Admetus in the plains of Thessaly. To reward Admetus for being

a kind and just master he extracted from the Fates the promise
that they would let Admetus off death when his time came provided someone else died for him. The only one willing to do this
was his own wife, Alcestis.

The present: The fatal day for Admetus' death has come. As
arranged, Alcestis is dying in his stead. People ask, "Is there no
hope?" Apollo arrives to plead with Death for the queen's life.
Splendidly dressed as an archer, with bow and quiver, he steps
into the city square of Pherae outside the palace.

PROLOGUE

APOLLO: Ah! house of Admetus where I was a lowly servant
once,
   yes, I a god, and all because
   Zeus slew my son Asclepius,
   hurled lightning through his heart,
   and I in my rage slaughtered his one-eyed giants,
   the Cyclopes who forge his thunderbolts.
For my punishment
   the Father made me flunky to a mortal man.
So here I came, my host's cattleman
   and staunch supporter of his house until this day.
An upright man myself, I found an upright man,
   and by tricking the Fates I saved him from his time of death.
Those ladies made this bargain with me:
   "We'll let Admetus off his dying, for now,
   if he'll exchange one body for another down below."
Well, he importuned and canvassed all his near and dear,
   including father and old gray-haired mother,
   and found absolutely no one
   to give up the light for him and die:
   no one, that is, except his wife.
She's limp in his arms this moment in the house,
   gasping out her last.
Today's the day she has to die and flit from life.
But I've come outside the house, these friendly halls,
   I don't want death's contagion smeared all over me in there.

[*He sees* DEATH *emerge, drably and mournfully dressed with a drawn sword*]

Ah! no less than Death himself, the great undertaker,
    itching to take her down to the house of Hades . . .
Right on time too!
He's been watching for this day—the day she dies.

[DEATH *lumbers forward with a snarl*]

FIRST EPISODE

DEATH: Ha! You, Apollo!
What are you doing here,
    prowling about outside the palace?
Up to no good again, eh?
Purloining the privileges of the powers below
    and canceling their privileges?
Weren't you satisfied with undoing Admetus' death—
    tricking the Fates with a lowdown trick?
Now you come armed with a bow
    to protect this woman, this daughter of Pelias,
    when it was all agreed with her husband
    that she should lose her life to save his.
APOLLO: Say what you like, I've got my reasons—fair ones too.
DEATH: Fair ones? With bow and arrow?
APOLLO: You know I always carry these.
DEATH: Just as you always cheat and help this house.
APOLLO: No—just as I'm always sad to see a friend of mine in
                                   trouble.
DEATH: So you do mean to cheat me of this second body too?
APOLLO: I never forced you to give up the first.
DEATH: Then why is he on earth, not under sods?
APOLLO: Because he swapped life with the woman for whom
                                you've come.
DEATH: Exactly so, and soon I'll drag her down below.
APOLLO: Take her, then, and go . . . I doubt I can dissuade you.
DEATH: Dissuade me from killing? Why, that's my work.
APOLLO: You should restrict it to carrying off the ripe.
DEATH: I see what you're leading up to with such warmth.

APOLLO: Yes. Is there no way Alcestis can reach old age?
DEATH: Certainly not. I enjoy some rights as well, you know.
APOLLO: It's only one single life you're carrying off.
DEATH: Ah, but young lives are more valuable.
APOLLO: But think of the gorgeous funeral if she died old.
DEATH: Tut tut, Apollo! Legislating for the rich!
APOLLO: What, you a sophist too? I'd never have thought it.
DEATH: Who would not buy Death off until old age?
APOLLO: So you won't oblige me with this little favor?
DEATH: Of course not. You know my principles.
APOLLO: I do indeed: loathsome both to men and gods.
DEATH: You can't just suit yourself in everything, you know.
APOLLO: And you, ruthless though you are, you shall be stopped.
A man is coming to the house of Pherae,
    sent by Eurystheus to fetch a team of horses
    from the wintry plains of Thrace.
He'll be a welcome guest in the palace of Admetus,
    and he'll wrest that woman from you by sheer force.
You'll have no thanks from me in this, just my dislike,
    and yet you'll do it.

[APOLLO *strides off as* DEATH *shouts after him*]

DEATH: Rant away. It'll do no good.
This woman *shall* go down to Hades.
I'm on my way. My sword is ready.
Every head of hair this blade has shorn
Is dedicated to the nether gods forlorn.

[DEATH *slinks away as the old men of Pherae, the* CHORUS, *march slowly in. They divide into groups, chanting back and forth to each other*]

PARADOS OR ENTRY SONG

[*In a mood of consternation and bewilderment the old men ask one another if there is any hope of saving* ALCESTIS]

STROPHE I

1: What is this hush inside the palace?

Why is Admetus' house so quiet?
2: There is no friend at hand to tell us
Whether we ought to weep for our queen
As dead, or whether our lady yet
Lives and looks upon the light:
Alcestis, child of Pelias,
Who seems to me and all of us
The best of wives a man could get.
3: Can you hear a keening note—
Beating of hands inside the home?
Or solemn wail of requiem?
4: No one stands outside the gate.
5: O come, Apollo through the foam
Of seething woe and fate.

ANTISTROPHE I

1: They'd not be silent if she'd passed.
2: She's dead and cold.
3: No cortege yet has left the house.
4: How do you know? I wish I had your hope.
1: Would Admetus have denied
His noble bride
The proper pomp?
3: Nor do I see outside
The vase of water from a spring,
The lustral offering
Put beside
The portals of the dead;
Or the clipped tresses in the hall
Which mourners should make fall,
Or the beating hands of girls.

STROPHE II

2: Yet this is the fatal day . . .
3: Can you be sure?
2: On which it is decreed for her
To pass down below, to pass away.
3: You break my heart, you bruise my soul.
1: When the best of us so fade
We who are loyal to the core

Mourn for her shade.
2: Nowhere on earth could one sail,
   Lycia or the vale
   Of rainless Ammon, where
   We could retrieve the soul
   Of this dying girl.
3: The cliff of doom is sheer;
   What altars shall I near
   Or sacrifice prepare,

ANTISTROPHE II

What god could hear my prayer?
4: Asclepius alone
   Were he alive again
   Could make her leave the gloom
   And portals of the night
   To come into the light.
1: Yes, he could raise the dead
   Even if lightning sped
   From Zeus and struck him down.
   But now what hope is left
   For a life so bereft?
2: Admetus has performed
   All the rites he can.
   All the altars fume
   With sacrifice and none
   Can bring the slightest balm.

[A MAIDSERVANT *has come out of the palace*]

CHORUS LEADER: Look, here comes a woman from the palace,
a servant maid in tears . . . what shall we be told?

[*Addressing the* MAIDSERVANT]

Are we to mourn? Would that be right?
We must know.
Is our mistress alive or is she dead?

SECOND EPISODE

MAIDSERVANT: You might say she is living and she's already dead.
LEADER: Deceased yet seeing the light? That makes no sense.
MAIDSERVANT: She's sinking now, breathing out her last.
LEADER: Poor Master! Such a man deprived of such a mate.
MAIDSERVANT: The loss, the shock—he does not feel it yet.
LEADER: Is all hope gone of saving her?
MAIDSERVANT: Her hour has come: her destiny is sure.
LEADER: Is all that is necessary being done?
MAIDSERVANT: Her husband has done everything to dress her for
the tomb.
LEADER: Tell her she dies splendid. The noblest consort under
the sun.

MAIDSERVANT: The noblest, yes. Who could deny it?
What paragon could hope outdo her?
How could a woman show
    more devotion to her man than die for him?
This is common knowledge in the town,
    but wait till you hear how she behaved at home.
When she knew that her final day had come,
    she bathed her milk-white body in water from the stream,
    then chose from the cedar chests her jewels and best apparel
    and decked herself becomingly.
Then standing before the hearth she made this prayer:
"Hestia, lady,
    as I prepare to go down into the dark,
    I kneel before you.
Be a mother to my little ones.
Give my son a loving bride;
An upright husband to my daughter.
Keep my children from untimely death,
Not like their mother's,
And bless them with a full and happy life
Lived in their native land."

Then she went with sprigs of myrtle* she had plucked

*myrtle: a fragrant evergreen shrub; a very different plant from the periwinkle
(Vinca), a trailing plant which came to be called myrtle in America.

to every altar in Admetus' halls,
  garlanded them and prayed.
There was no sighing and no sobbing.
The doom she walked towards
  did not dim the sweet tenor of her face.
Then to her room she flew and to the bed.
There her tears began to flow.
"Bed, my bed," she cried,
  "where I unlocked my maidenhood
  for this very man for whom today I die—farewell.
I do not hate you—see—
  though you caused my death . . . but only mine.
I shall not fail you, nor my man. That's why I die.
Some other bride will own you soon:
  not more chaste than I, but luckier perhaps."

Falling on the bed, she kissed it
  and let the tears that swept her eyes bestrew the coverlet.
And when she had wept her fill,
  tearing herself away from the bed
  she wandered dismally off, then back again—
  over and over again—throwing herself on the bed.
Meanwhile, the little children sobbed,
  clinging to their mother's skirts.
She took them each in turn,
  hugged and fondled them
  as one about to die.
All the women in the house were crying
  in pity for their lady mistress.
She held out a hand to each,
  none too low for her to greet and wait for a reply.
These are the tragic happenings going on now
  inside Admetus' house.
If he had died it would be over and done with.
As it is, his escape
  has brought him such pain he never will forget.
LEADER: He must be calling out in anguish at the loss of such a
                                               wife.

MAIDSERVANT: Yes, he holds his beloved in his arms,
  weeping and beseeching, "Do not desert me,"

asking the impossible,
for she droops, she wilts, she sinks in her decline.
Weak as she is,
scarcely able to draw breath,
she trails her hand as if it were a weight,
yet wishes still to face the sun and let her eyes
go feasting on its rays one last time.

[*The* MAIDSERVANT *pauses, surveying the dismal looks of the old men*]

Now I'll go inside and say that you are here.
Such loyalty as yours is rare:
To rally to the great ones in their need.
But you have been friends to my master
For many a year.

[*The* MAIDSERVANT *goes into the palace. The old men of the* CHORUS *huddle in groups, hoping still that there may be a way of saving* ALCESTIS]

SECOND CHORAL LYRIC

1: What escape, O Zeus, is there
   For our sovereigns from despair?
2: What smallest chink of hope is left?
   Or must I tear my hair?
   Put on mourning dress?
3: Friends, it's clearly all too clear
   But let us offer prayer:
   The gods have power.

All: Lord Apollo, healer,
   Find a way to help Admetus.

1: Procure, provide, a plan.
   You did before. We know you can.
   Snatch her from Death's door.
   Keep murderous Hades back.
4: Son of Pheres, overwhelming
   Will you find your consort's going:

The lack! The lack!
2: Enough to make a person loose
   His very life with knife or noose.
3: More than loved one, most beloved,
   He will see her dead today.
1: Look, she comes, she comes
   With her husband from her home.

All: Wail it out, O shout in groans,
     You land of Pherae:
     The perfect woman
     Sick and sinking down
     Towards the world of Hades.

LEADER: Without a doubt a wedding brings much more pain than
                                                           joy.

Look at the past
   and now at the sufferings of our king:
   bereft of his wife, his nonpareil,
   he will live an unlivable life of gray.

[*The doors of the palace are thrown open and* ALCESTIS, *half
carried by* ADMETUS, *sways down the steps. The little boy*
EUMELUS *and his sister cling to their mother. The servants set
up a couch as* ALCESTIS *and* ADMETUS *chant to each other*]

CHORAL DIALOGUE

ALCESTIS: The sun and the day's clear light;
   The clouds in the wheeling sky . . .
ADMETUS: Have us two unhappy beings in sight;
   We did no wrong that you should die.
ALCESTIS: The sweet earth and this high-roofed home,
   And the land I came from as a bride . . .
ADMETUS: Bear up, my darling, do not leave me alone.
   Ask, and the mighty gods cannot turn aside.
ALCESTIS: I see the boat with its brace of oarblades—
   The ferry of corpses—
   And resting his arm on an oar, Charon is calling:
   "Quick, get aboard, you waste my time."

He harasses, he hurries me to come.
ADMETUS: Oh, what a bitter passage you envisage!
Our agony, my woebegotten one, is savage.
ALCESTIS: I am dragged . . . someone is dragging me . . .
Can you not see? . . . to the halls of the dead.
His eyes are grim and they glower on me.
He is winged . . . He is Hades . . . What is he doing?
Stop it, let go . . . Bleak is the road . . . I am coming.
ADMETUS: A heartbreaking road for those who love you:
For me most of all and the children that had you.
ALCESTIS: Let me go, let me go, lay me down now.
My legs give way . . . Hades is on me.
The black of night seeps into my eyes.
O my children, my babies, your mother is dying.
Children, farewell . . . The light! The light!
May you look at it long.
ADMETUS: These are the heaviest words to hear:
Worse than death are these words to me.
By all the gods, I beg you, don't leave me;
For the sake of the children you hold dear.
Look up, resist! Once you are gone
I no longer exist.
In you we are not, or in you we are.
For you are the love we adore.

[*End of Choral Dialogue*]

[ADMETUS *walks* ALCESTIS *to the couch and lays her down.
She takes his hand*]

ALCESTIS: Admetus, you see how matters stand with me,
so let me tell you my last wish before I die.
I have cherished you
and though it cost me my own life
have set your eyes to gaze upon the sunlight still.
I die for you, though had I wished
I could have wed again and made a prosperous royal home.
But I had no wish to live apart from you,
with these children fatherless,
even though it meant the sacrifice of youth and all its gifts—

which I so enjoyed.
I did this even though your father
    and the mother who gave you birth abandoned you.
They were ripe enough to die with grace—
    yes, die gracefully and praised—
    for their own son's sake: an only son at that,
    with no prospect of a further heir when you were gone.
We could have lived our days out to the end,
    you and I; you no weeping widower
    with children who were motherless.
Well, some destiny has planned things as they are;
    so be it, but remember always what you owe to me:
    something I can never ask you to repay,
    for nothing is so valuable as life—
    as you yourself will readily admit.

[ALCESTIS *turns her head and rests her eyes on the two children, who stand by with their nurse*]

These children you will love no less than I,
    if your heart be right;
    so bring them up as masters in my home.
Do not remarry and impose on them
    some vicious stepmother who through jealousy of me
    takes her hand to them—
    these your little ones and also mine.
Do not do that, I beg you—oh, not that!—
    a second wife loathes the children there before she came . . .
    is about as tender as an adder.
A boy's bulwark is his father:
    he goes to him and waits on his advice;
    but a girl, you my little daughter,
    what kind of girlhood can you have?
    What kind of woman would you find your father's second
                               wife?
Not one—I can only pray—
    who blasts your maiden prime away with vicious gossip
    and blights all hope of marriage.
There'll be no mother at your wedding to see you through,
    and none to cheer you at your lying-in,

just when a mother is so comforting.
I must die,
   and not tomorrow or the following day:
   the ordeal is now;
   in a moment I'll be reckoned with the dead.
Farewell. Be happy.
You, my husband, can be proud
   you married such a wife as I;
   and you, my children, to have had me as your mother.
LEADER: Madam, be consoled.
   I do not hesitate to speak for him:
   all this he'll do—or else be raving mad.

[ADMETUS *kneels beside his wife and presses her hand*]

ADMETUS: All shall be as you say. Have no fear.
   As in life you alone were mine,
so in death no one else shall be called my wife.
No Thessalian bride shall ever claim me after you.
None is so nobly born,
   none so beautiful—not one.
As for children, I have no need of more.
May ours bring some happiness to me,
   seeing all joy in you is dead.
I shall weep for you—not just one year
   but as long as life shall last.
Yes, my love, forever.
And I'll hate her who gave me birth,
   and curse my father.
Their love was only words; but you,
   you gave me the most precious thing you had,
   to save my life.
The loss—the loss of one like you—
   how can I not cry out in pain?

[ADMETUS *turns towards the elders and citizens*]

All celebrations I disallow, all drinking parties:
   no more song and garlands in my house;
   never again shall I touch the lyre
   nor gladden my heart with a song to the flute.

For you, you take my heart away.
I'll have a sculptor make an effigy of you
   and lay it sleeping in my bed.
I'll fall on it and fondle it,
   calling out your name,
   and think I have my darling in my arms
   whom I have not.
Cold comfort, certainly,
   but still a way of lessening the load upon my soul.
In dreams perhaps you'll come to me and make me glad.
It's sweet to see our loved ones, even in the night,
   even for the moment that they last.
Had I the tongue of Orpheus and his mellifluous strains
   and by song could cast a spell
   on Persephone and her spouse to wrest you out of hell,
   I should go down
   and neither Pluto's hound
   nor the spirit-ferrying Charon at his oar could stop me:
   not till I'd brought your soul up into the light.
Wait for me down there. Wait for me to die.
Prepare the home where you and I shall live as one.
For I shall make them lay my bones side by side with yours:
   stretched out with you in the selfsame cedar box.
Not even in death would I be apart from you—
   my one and only faithful love.
LEADER: We too shall share as friend with friend
   your heaving grief for her—who is owed so much.

[ALCESTIS *raises herself and beckons the two children*]

ALCESTIS: Children, you have heard your father's promise
   never to dishonor me and marry another woman.
ADMETUS: Yes, I say it again and shall do as you say.

[ALCESTIS *takes the children's hands*]

ALCESTIS: On these terms, then, receive these children from my
                                      hand.
ADMETUS: I do. A lovely gift from a hand so loved.
ALCESTIS: Be these children's mother now, in place of me.

[ADMETUS *takes the children's hands in his*]

ADMETUS: I must be that, now they don't have you.
ALCESTIS: Dear children,
    just when I should be most alive, I leave you to go below.
ADMETUS: And me? What shall I do when I am left and you are
                                  gone?
ALCESTIS: Time will heal you . . . The dead are nothing.
ADMETUS: By all the gods, take me with you. Take me down
                                  below.
ALCESTIS: No, my dying is enough: my dying for you.
ADMETUS: O destiny, what a wife you wrench from me!

[ALCESTIS *sinks back*]

ALCESTIS: My eyes . . . so heavy now . . . weighted with the dark.
ADMETUS: Wife, my wife, you leave me—leave me lost.
ALCESTIS: Say I am nothing, no longer here.
ADMETUS: Lift up your head. You cannot let your children go.
ALCESTIS: I must, against my will . . . My little ones . . .
                                  Goodbye.
ADMETUS: Just look at them! Look!
ALCESTIS: I am . . . going.
ADMETUS: What? No . . . not slipping from us?
ALCESTIS: Farewell.

[*Still in* ADMETUS' *arms,* ALCESTIS *falls back dead*]

ADMETUS: It's all over . . . I am lost.
LEADER: She is gone. The wife of Admetus is no more.

[EUMELUS *tears himself from his nurse and throws himself on his dead mother with a wail*]

CHORAL DIALOGUE

EUMELUS: Aaah! Mother is gone, gone down below:
    She is no longer in the sun . . .
    O Father!
    Mamma has left me—poor Mamma!
    Now I live without a mother.

Look, her eyelids; look, her fingers
All gone limp now . . . Listen, Mother.
O Mamma, please listen to me.
It's me, it's me, Mamma, that calls you:
Your little chick falls on your lips.

[ADMETUS *gently disengages him*]

ADMETUS: She can't see you, she can't hear you.
    You two and I are crushed by fate.
EUMELUS: I am all alone and little,
    Deserted, Father, by my mother,
    My mother darling . . . Oh what anguish!
    And you, my little sister,
    Know this anguish too.
    It failed, Father, failed:
    Your marriage never lasted
    Till old age with her.
    She has gone before you.
    And, Mother, now without you
    Our home is over.
LEADER: Admetus, you must live through this catastrophe.
You're not the first and not the last
    to lose a noble wife.
Accept that every one of us must pay
    the debt of death.
ADMETUS: I do accept.
Nor did this evil swoop without a warning.
The threat of it has tormented me for long.

[*End of Choral Dialogue*]

[*He rises slowly from the couch on which* ALCESTIS *lies*]

I need your help.
I must arrange the cortege for the dead.
Stay here and chant the dirge
    to the implacable lord of the underworld.
Every Thessalian in my realm,
    draped in black with shaven head,
    I summon in mourning for this lady.

You harness grooms of single horse or chariot-in-four,
    see all manes are sheared.
In all the city let there be no sound of pipe or lyre
    till full twelve moons have run their course.
Never shall I lay beneath the sod
    the body of one more loved and generous.
Rightly I salute her, for she died,
    and she alone, in my stead.

[*The servants and attendants gather up the body of* ALCESTIS
to prepare it for burial. The old men of the CHORUS *group
themselves around and chant a dirge of both mourning and
celebration*]

THIRD CHORAL LYRIC

STROPHE I

Fare you well, O daughter of Pelias,
    In your passage down to the halls of hell,
    There to live in a sunless home.
    Let Hades that god of midnight hair
    And that other, the grisly man
    Who sits and steers the ferry for the dead,
    Know that he has sped
    In his two-oared skiff
    The most excelling wife of all.

ANTISTROPHE I

Much shall the music-makers, the Muses,
    Sing of your fame on the seven-stringed shell
    Of the mountain tortoise, or chant it sole
    In Sparta when the moon rides high
    All through the night in the month of Apollo,
    And in Athens, the blessed, shining Athens.
    Your death bequeaths
    A theme for songs
    For us, and lays for endless singers.

STROPHE II

I wish it were in my power to ferry you back

Across the River of Sorrows,* the crying waters.
Row you into the light from the halls of Hades.
Only you, most beloved of women
Had the valor to ransom your spouse from Pluto
By giving your life. Let the dust lie light on you,
Lady. And if your husband should ever select
A new wife, your children and I should hate him.

ANTISTROPHE II

His was the mother who would not inter her body
  Under the earth, oh, for the sake of a son!
Nor would his ancient sire. They lacked the spirit,
Crassly, to rescue the son they bore; their hair
Was white as hoar. But you in your youth and bloom
Willingly left your life and quenched your light.
Could I be paired with so loving a wife (most rare!)
Blissfully would I cling to her through life.

THIRD EPISODE

[*Hardly has* ALCESTIS' *body been carried into the house, followed by* ADMETUS *and the children, when* HERACLES *with lion skin and club approaches. He is bluff, hail-fellow-well-met, hearty*]

HERACLES: Friends, natives of this realm of Pherae,
  Do I happen on Admetus in his home?
LEADER: Yes, Heracles, Admetus is at home.
  What brings you into Thessaly and the town of Pherae?
HERACLES: I have a labor to perform for King Eurystheus of
                                                    Tiryns.
LEADER: On your way to where, and on what errand?
HERACLES: To round up the four-horse team of Diomedes, king
                                                   of Thrace.
LEADER: And how will you manage that?
  Have you no inkling of the reception you will get?
HERACLES: Not really . . . I've never put a foot in his domain.

---

*River of Sorrows: the river Acheron—one of the five rivers flowing through the underworld.

LEADER: You'll not win those steeds without a fight.

HERACLES: And I'll not flinch before a task in hand.

LEADER: Kill or be killed, then; stay or come back quick.*

HERACLES: It's not the first time that I've run that risk.

LEADER: And when you've overthrown their keeper—what next?

HERACLES: I'll drive off the horses in a team to Tiryns.

LEADER: It's not an easy thing to put the bit between their teeth.

HERACLES: Why? Do they snort out fire?

LEADER: No, but with their teeth they tear men into tatters.

HERACLES: Horses don't eat flesh, only beasts of the mountains
do.

LEADER: Wait till you see their mangers splashed with gore!

HERACLES: Their keeper—whose son does he proclaim himself?

LEADER: Son of Ares, and master of the Thracian shield of solid
gold.

HERACLES: Phew! Another test of strength—that's what you
mean . . .

hard going always—uphill work,
if I have to take on *all* the sons of Ares.
First it was Lycaon, then Cycnus, and now a third ordeal:
I have to grapple with those horses and their master.
But no one shall ever see
Heracles, Alcmena's son, cowering before some strong-armed
bully.

LEADER: But look, the master of this realm himself comes out:
Admetus from the palace.

[*Enter* ADMETUS *with shaven head and dressed in black, followed by attendants similarly accoutered*]

ADMETUS: Welcome, son of Zeus and scion of Perseus.

HERACLES: And joy to you, Admetus, king of Thessaly.

ADMETUS: Ah, if joy were possible! But thank you all the same.

HERACLES: It seems you are in mourning. Why the shaven head?

ADMETUS: [*hedging*] I have to go and bury someone . . . someone
dear.

HERACLES: Nothing's happened to one of your children? Heaven
forbid!

ADMETUS: My children are alive and well inside the house.

quick: in the sense of "the quick and the dead."

HERACLES: Your father, then? . . . But he was ripe to go.

ADMETUS: He's quite himself, Heracles. So is my mother.

HERACLES: It's not your wife, is it? Not Alcestis gone?

ADMETUS: Well now . . . about her . . . there are two things to say.

HERACLES: What do you mean? Is she alive or is she dead?

ADMETUS: She is alive and she is not. It's most disturbing.

HERACLES: I'm none the wiser. You talk in riddles, man.

ADMETUS: She has a special rendezvous with Fate. Didn't you know?

HERACLES: I knew she'd pledged herself to die for you.

ADMETUS: So cannot . . . go on living . . . if she gave her word.

HERACLES: Well then, keep your tears for when it happens.

ADMETUS: The doomed are dead. The dead are not alive.

HERACLES: Naturally! To be or not be: there is a difference.

ADMETUS: Put it your way, Heracles. I'll put it mine.

HERACLES: But whom *are* you mourning? Some dead friend?

ADMETUS: A lady. A lady . . . much in our thoughts just now.

HERACLES: Some remote acquaintance or a relative?

ADMETUS: Remote in origin but—very close to home.

HERACLES: How did she come to die inside your house?

ADMETUS: Her father was dead. She found a haven here.

[HERACLES *gathers his lion skin about him and prepares to leave*]

HERACLES: Sad, sad! Admetus, I wish I'd found you less in mourning.

ADMETUS: [*apprehensively*] What do you mean? What are you getting at?

HERACLES: I mean to propose myself as guest in some other house.

ADMETUS: [*embarrassed*] My good sir, God forbid! That would be a disgrace.

HERACLES: But guests are a nuisance to a house in mourning.

ADMETUS: The dead are dead. Please step inside.

HERACLES: Make merry while friends mourn? It's unthinkable.

ADMETUS: We'll take you to the guest wing. It's quite separate.

HERACLES: A thousand thanks but . . . just let me go.

ADMETUS: To lodge with someone else? Out of the question.

[*He turns to a servant*]

Escort this gentleman to the guest wing by the palace
    and tell those in charge to lay out food in plenty.

[*As* HERACLES *begins to move off after the servant,* ADMETUS
summons his butler]

Make sure the doors are shut of the palace court.
A guest's enjoyment mustn't be spoilt
    by sounds of mourning.
LEADER: What are you doing, Admetus?
    Overwhelmed by catastrophe, and you think of entertaining?
    Are you out of your senses?
ADMETUS: You mean, you'd think much more of me if I turned
                                him out:
    expelled a guest from house and town?
Surely not! My being unfriendly
    would do nothing to reduce my woes.
It would simply add the evil of inhospitality
    and my house would get the name of Unfriendly Hall.
I find this fellow the best of hosts
    whenever I visit the thirsty land of Argos.
LEADER: Maybe, but why do you hide your misfortune
    from a man who comes here—you say yourself—as friend?
ADMETUS: Because if he had the slightest inkling of my sorrows
    he'd not put a foot inside the house.
I daresay some would think me foolish and give no credit,
    but to be discourteous and turn a guest away
    is unheard of underneath my roof.

[*Exit* ADMETUS *into the palace*]

FOURTH CHORAL LYRIC

[*The old men of the* CHORUS *sing in praise of* ADMETUS' *hospitality, amply proven when in spite of his bereavement he lets nothing spoil the entertainment of his guest* HERACLES]

STROPHE I

Guest-blest home of the great, everlastingly free,
    Graced with a visit no less than lyric Apollo's.

In your fields with his lyre he consented to be
A herdsman, and piped on the slopes of the hills
Wedding songs to shepherds with their sheep.

ANTISTROPHE I

The parded leopard in love with his music agreed
   To mingle with them, and the ambery lions to feed
   Forsaking their dens; and the milk-speckled fawns
   On their neat little feet tripped out from the pines
   And danced to the zest of the tunes of your lyre, Apollo.

STROPHE II

Thus does this monarch hold sway over lands
   Rich with cattle along the shores
   Of Boebia, that rippling lake.
   His arable fields and his prairies spread
   As far as the shadowy stables of the sun god's steeds
   In the deep Molossian range. The Aegean Sea
   Is the term of his sway
   And the harborless shores of Mount Pelion.

ANTISTROPHE II

And now again though with eyelids wet
   He has opened his door wide to his guest
   Yet keens in his palace over the corpse of his wife
   So dear, so lately dead. For the gentle-born
   Cannot err but in generous wise. All wisdom resides
   In the noble. It sets me to thinking. Deep in my soul
   A faith abides
   That the reverent man will always fare well.

FOURTH EPISODE

[*Amid the sound of funeral music, a procession of attendants led by* ADMETUS *and carrying the bier of* ALCESTIS *issues from the palace. They are followed by servants bearing offerings for the late departed. In the distance the old man* PHERES *can be seen approaching.* ADMETUS *turns to a group of citizens of Pherae*]

ADMETUS: Men of Pherae, it's good of you to come.
You see my people carrying
    the body of Alcestis raised aloft,
    all decked for burial and the tomb.
Salute the dead, as custom is,
    and speed her on her final way.
LEADER: I see your father coming, with his old man's shuffle.
His servants carry offerings for your wife:
    adornments for the dead.

[ADMETUS *halts the procession, and* PHERES *accosts him, while his servants stand by with their loads*]

PHERES: I have come here full of sympathy for you, my son.
You have lost a noble wife, a virtuous wife—
    and nobody can deny it.
But such sufferings must be borne,
    grievous though they be.

[PHERES *holds out an offering to* ADMETUS]

Accept these ornaments,
    and let them go with her into the grave.
We must pay our homage to the corpse of her
    who died instead of you, my son,
    and saved me too from being deprived of you
    and doomed to a sad and doddering old age.
Her life, the sheer courage of her act,
    is a shining light to womankind.

[*He stretches out a hand towards the bier*]

Fare you well, you savior of this man,
    who raised us up when we were down.
May you be blessed in Hades realm.

[*He turns back to* ADMETUS]

This is the kind of marriage, to my mind,
    that does the most for humankind . . .
Otherwise why marry?

[ADMETUS *pushes away the proffered offering*]

ADMETUS: Unasked by me, you come here to this burial,
    and quite emphatically not my friend.
These offerings of yours she'll never wear.
Nothing of yours is needed for her tomb.
There was a time for you to feel for me,
    when I was at the point of death;
    but you stood aside and let another die:
    the young die for the old.
Now you come whining over this dead body.
Can you really be my father standing there?
Can she really have brought me forth, that woman
    who said she did and is called my mother?
Or was I born of slave's blood:
    put to your woman's breast and suckled secretly?
You showed your true self when it came to the trial.
I count myself no son of yours.
Oh, you are a master coward!
    Senile, on the very fringe of life, yet lacking the heart—
    oh no, the guts—to lay your life down for your son.
You let this woman do it—outsider to our blood.
She is the one, and she alone,
    I have the right to look upon
    as both my mother and my father.
And yet it would have been a lovely thing
    to win the battle for my life
    by dying for your child.
How brief a fraction, after all,
    was left for you to live.
You have enjoyed every happiness a man could ask:
    kingship in your prime,
    me for son and heir
    to save you dying without a child,
    your unprotected house the prey of strangers.
Nor can you say
    it was because I disrespected your gray hairs
    that you abandoned me to die.
I always honored you. I made a point of it.
This is the thanks I get from you and from my mother.

Well, lose no time:
    spawn some offsprings to pamper your old age,
    deck you out and wind your shroud when you are dead.
For I shan't lift a hand to bury you.
To you I am already dead,
    and if in fact I look upon the light
    it is because I found salvation from another.
I am that person's child, I say:
    devoted to that person till the end of life.
Dotards' prayers to die are insincere:
    they grumble of old age and life's long span,
    but once·let death come near,
    not one desires to go, and age becomes quite dear.
LEADER: Admetus, stop!
There is enough unhappiness as things are.
Do not drive your father to a fury and too far.
PHERES: My boy,
    whom do you imagine you berate:
    one of your bought Lydian or Phrygian slaves?
I am a Thessalian, don't you know:
    a true son-and-free of a Thessalian sire.
You overreach yourself.
You fling your adolescent words at me to hurt.
You shall not get away with it.
I brought you into the world. I brought you up:
    you to be master of this house.
Ought I now to die for you?
Is this the custom handed down—
    that fathers die for sons? The Greek tradition?
It was never handed down to me.
You were born for your own good or ill.
Whatever is your due from me, you've had.
You enjoy wide power,
    and wide acres I shall leave to you,
    just as my father left the same to me.
Do I harm you? . . . How?
Do I rob you? . . .Of what?
Don't you die for me and I shan't die for you.
You enjoy the light of day.
Do you think your father doesn't?

Oh yes, he reckons life is sweet
   just because it is so short
   and eternity below so long.
You struggled without a blush to hang on to life.
And now you only live because you killed this woman
   and went beyond your span.
Yet *I'm* the coward, you say, you—you prince of cowards:
   shown up by a woman who died for you—oh, fine young man!
   so smart you've found a way to live forever
   if you can wheedle the current wife to die instead.
But don't revile your friends
   if they won't do the same.
So keep your mouth shut, coward, and remember:
   if you love your life, so does everybody.
If you speak ill of us,
   you'll hear ill of you—and true.
LEADER: Ill—there's been too much already.
Please stop, old man, railing at your son.
ADMETUS: Let him rant. I've said what I had to say.
If it hurts him to hear the truth,
   he shouldn't have hurt *me*.
PHERES: It would have hurt much more to die for you.
ADMETUS: So a young man's and an old man's death are worth
                       the same?
PHERES: We each have a single life to live, not two.
ADMETUS: And you'd make yours longer than Zeus's, wouldn't you?
PHERES: Must you insult your blameless father?
ADMETUS: Yes, because I see a glutton for longevity.
PHERES: Aren't you the one that's burying this body that should
                       be you?
ADMETUS: Precisely. Which shows how pusillanimous you are.
PHERES: Say what you like—she didn't die for me.
ADMETUS: One of these days you'll need my help, I hope.
PHERES: Meanwhile, keep up the wife supply—with more to die.
ADMETUS: And more disgrace to you—who refuse to die.
PHERES: The light of day is lovely: lovely and god-given.
ADMETUS: What a little soul you have! How cowardly!
PHERES: At least it's not old me you're carrying off with glee.
ADMETUS: What a shabby death it'll be when your turn comes!
PHERES: It won't concern me what men think when I am dead.

ADMETUS: See how the senile have no self-respect whatever!
PHERES: Self-respect? Had she? Or was she just a simpleton to you?
ADMETUS: Will you kindly leave and let me bury my dead.
PHERES: I am going. You murdered her and you can bury her.
    You will answer to her kin for it.
If Acastus is half a man
    he will require something for his sister's blood.

[PHERES *gathers himself together and departs with his servants as* ADMETUS *shouts after him*]

ADMETUS: Go, you and that woman who lives with you.
    Grow decrepit together as you deserve:
    a barren pair though your son still lives.
Never come under my roof again.
If I needed town criers to shout out my break with you and yours
    wouldn't I just use them now!

[*He turns back to the bier*]

Let us move on and bear our burden of the dead,
    and lay this body on its funeral bed.

[ADMETUS *moves off with the cortege while the elders of the* CHORUS *chant a short dirge for* ALCESTIS]

CHORUS: Go, poor blighted lady.
    Great and best of ladies, go.
    Farewell to you! May gentle Hermes
    Pilot you; Pluto receive you.
    And if down there the good have merit,
    Sit beside the bride of Hades.*

[*Enter* BUTLER, *disgusted*]

FIFTH EPISODE

BUTLER: Every sort of visitor, from every sort of land,
    I've known and waited on in Admetus' house,
    but this guest today

bride of Hades: Persephone.

is the worst ruffian I've ever had to serve.
First, though he sees our master is in mourning
   he strides right in and makes himself at home without a blush.
Then, with no consideration for our feelings,
   he isn't satisfied with what we have to offer
   but hollers out for what we haven't brought.
He grabs the loving cup with ivy round it
   and swills it down neat like so much grape juice.
Of course the wine's black fire smothers him
   and he's in a blaze.
He thrusts twigs of myrtle on his head
   and bellows hideously.
A double discord hits the ears:
   his unstaunchable cacophonies
   (oblivious of Admetus' sorrows),
   and our household lamentations for our mistress.
Even so, in accordance with our master's wishes,
   we did not let him see our brimming eyes.
And here I am now regaling him and making him at home—
   this robber bandit, probably—
   when from this home my lady's gone
   and I didn't even follow her last walk
   or lift my hand to say farewell.
She was like a mother to me
   and all us servants.
She fended off a thousand ills
   and calmed her husband down.
Am I not right to abominate
   this insensitive, intruding man?

[HERACLES *lurches in, garlanded, cup in hand, drunk*]

HERACLES: You there,
   why that glum and priggish look?
A servant shouldn't show a guest a vinegary face:
   he should beam and serve.
You see before you your master's pal,
   and you greet him with a scowl and a face like doom,
   sunk in some private trouble of your own.
Come over here and learn a thing or two.

Do you understand the secret of mortality?
I don't suppose you do. How should you?
But listen to me. Take death.
All men have to pay that debt,
 yet not one man jack of them can tell
 if he'll be around tomorrow.
Fortune is mysterious: the march of events.
It can't be foreseen or taught or caught by any trick.
There you have it!
 I've told you now and now you know and now cheer up.
Have a drink and think:
 each day is yours to live—just as it comes—
 the rest is luck.
And one thing more:
 pay homage to the sweetest power of all,
 Aphrodite,
 mankind's most gracious goddess.
For the rest, forget it . . .
 but don't forget my words.
They do make sense—do they not?
I think they do.
Go on, let your heartache go, it's overdone.
Put a garland on and move off from that door,
 and take a swig with me.
I have no doubt the wine splashing in your cup
 will change your mood
 and free you from your dumps.
We are but human. We should keep a human mind.
You solemn scowling worriers—if you ask me—
 do not lead lives at all but plain catastrophes.

BUTLER: [*stiffly*] I know all this, but our position here
 hardly calls for merriment and gaiety.

HERACLES: But the dead woman's an outsider, isn't she?
 why overdo the grief?
Your lord and lady are alive.

BUTLER: Alive? So you know nothing of our sorrows here?

HERACLES: Well, no . . . unless your master lied to me.

BUTLER: He's just too considerate, too hospitable.

HERACLES: Considerate? When I'm neglected for some dead
             outsider?

BUTLER: Oh, she's an outsider now, all right.

HERACLES: So there's something that he didn't tell me, eh?

BUTLER: [*hedging*] Please . . . go in peace.
  Our master's woes are our concern.

[BUTLER *turns to go, but* HERACLES *seizes him*]

HERACLES: So it wasn't really all about some dead outsider?

BUTLER: No. That's what so upset me when I saw you rollicking.

HERACLES: So I've been deluded by my host?

BUTLER: You came at a time inopportune for guests.
  We're in mourning black—as you see.
  Our heads are shaven.

HERACLES: Who is dead, then? One of the children? Surely not! . . .
  His old father?

BUTLER: [*reluctantly*] If you must, sir . . . it's Admetus' wife.
                          She's gone forever.

HERACLES: [*slowly putting down his cup*] What are you saying? . . .
  And he went and welcomed me!

BUTLER: He was embarrassed to turn you away.

HERACLES: Unhappy man—what a soulmate he has lost!

BUTLER: And we are lost—not she alone.

HERACLES: Yes, I felt it. I saw it in his eyes—the brimming—
  the shaven head, the drawn face.
But when he said it was a stranger's funeral,
  I was convinced
  and against my deeper instincts passed in through these doors,
  then made merry in this kind man's house—
  this stricken man.
And here I am in my cups and garlanded! . . .

[HERACLES *throws his cup down and tears off his garlands*]

The whole house laid flat and you didn't say a thing!
  Where is he burying her? Where can I find him?

BUTLER: Straight along the road that takes you to Larissa . . .
  You'll see a hewn sepulcher outside the city.

HERACLES: Come, reckless heart and sturdy hand,
  and show what sort of son Alcmena bore—
  she queen of Tiryns and Electryon's child—
  bore to Zeus.

I must go at once and save this lately dead,
    restore Alcestis to this home of hers,
    and make Admetus some return.

[*He begins to fasten his lion skin securely and picks up his club*]

I'll go and hunt out Death,
    that gloom-draped king of corpses;
    and I think I'll find him knocking back libations near the tomb.
I'll leap out from an ambush, grab him,
    weld my arms around him,
    and no matter how he heaves and strains
    no man alive shall prize him from my bone-crushing vise
    until he has handed back this woman.
But if by chance my quarry balks me,
    doesn't come to get his bait of blood and porridge,*
    I'll take myself below
    to the sun-starved halls of Persephone and Pluto
    and do my asking there.
I am sure I shall fetch Alcestis up
    and put her in the arms of my most generous host,
    who made me at home and did not turn me out
    though he was struck to the heart with grief:
    yes, hid his feelings, heroic man, and did me honor.
Is there anyone in Thessaly more hospitable than he?
Anyone in Greece?
Never let him say that such nobility
    was answered by a lack of generosity.

[HERACLES *stomps out followed by the* BUTLER *just as the funeral procession is heard returning.* ADMETUS *enters with his train*]

CHORAL DIALOGUE

ADMETUS: Oh, my return to my home, return to lament!
    Oh, the emptiness in these unwelcoming rooms!
    Go where? Be where? What say? What not?

porridge: Euripides uses the word *pelanos,* a kind of gruel which was a mixture of meal, honey, and oil offered to the gods.

I wish I were dead.
  What doom-laden doom, what mother produced me?
  I yearn for the shade. I lust after phantoms.
  Theirs are the homes I crave to indwell.
  The joy in my eyes is a light gone dim.
  The joy in the tread of my feet is gone.
  Death has cleft me from half my life—
Traded to Hades.

LEADER: Take a step forward! Go into the house!

ADMETUS: Aiai! Aiai!

CHORUS: You've suffered enough to make you wail.

ADMETUS: Weep—aiai! Aiai!

LEADER: Your agony—I understand.

ADMETUS: Aiai! Aiai!

CHORUS: It is no help to her below.

ADMETUS: Aiai!

LEADER: Bitter indeed never more to behold
  The face of your loved one.

ADMETUS: The mere recall of it batters my heart.
  What greater pain can any man face
  Than suffer the loss of a faithful wife?
  I wish I had never married or lived
  Inside this house with her I loved.
  I covet the ones who never wedded:
  The childless ones; their single life
  Only a measured grief begets.
  The ills of children, the nuptial bed
  Blasted by death, are all a scourge
  Compared to lives that can be led
  Without a child and still unwed.

CHORUS: Fate has struck, ineluctable fate!

ADMETUS: Aiai!

LEADER: Your lamentations have no limit.

ADMETUS: Aiai!

LEADER: It is a bitter load to bear but . . .

ADMETUS: Aiai!

LEADER: You're not the first to lose . . .

ADMETUS: Aiai! Aiai!

LEADER: A wife . . .

Disaster strikes at many in many a guise.

ADMETUS: The lasting sorrow, the long lament
For those underground . . . Oh why did you
Hold me back from the leap in the grave
That gaped, to lie along her side,
Dead with her that had no peer?
Hades would then have been able to take
Two devoted souls, not one,
To cross the land of the nether lake.

LEADER: There was in my own family a man
Whose only son died in his home:
A stripling worthy of his tears.
Yet he tempered his grief, this childless man,
Although his hair was turning white
And he gone far into life.

[ADMETUS *stops in front of the house, unable to proceed inside*]

ADMETUS: Ah! palace, my home, how shall I go in?
How dwell in you with all my luck reversed?
Everything is changed from what it was at first.
Once, by torchlight to the strain of wedding songs,
Holding her beloved hand, I went in.
And after us trooped a merry shouting throng
Cheering my dead one, cheering me:
A comely and noble couple we were seen to be.
But now instead of the wedding march and glittering dress,
I am led to a lonely deserted bed.

CHORUS: [*severally*]

1: Sorrow was strange to you, yours a happy life.
2: Then sorrow struck . . . nevertheless . . .
3: It saved your life, and though your consort has gone,
    Leaving her beloved behind, is this so rare?
4: Many a man has death severed from his wife.

[*End of Choral Dialogue*]

ADMETUS: Friends, although it might not seem to be,
I think my wife's fate is happier than mine:

She never can be hurt again.
For her a thousand cares are over—she is sublime.
But I, who have no title to be living
   and have overstepped my mark,
     must go on and on—most melancholy—alive.
Too late, too late I learn this now!
How shall I enter my empty home?
Whom shall I greet inside? By whom be greeted?
Which way to look?
The wilderness there will drive me,
   the empty bed, her favorite chairs,
   the unswept floors throughout the house,
   the children clinging to my knees and crying for their mother,
   the servants all in tears
   for the tender queen this house has lost.
Thus will it be at home,
   but, oh, in the world outside!
Young unmarried women with weddings in their eyes
   will frighten me away—
   buzzing around in female swarms . . .
No, I shall not be able to brave the sight
   of my wife's compeers.
And any man who does not like me
   will seize his chance and jeer:
     "Look at the cheap coward, alive and well,
   who ran away from death—
   so small he got his wife to die instead.
   Do you call that a man?
   He execrates his parents but could not die himself."
Yes, that's the charming reputation I shall earn
   on top of all my sorrows.
Tell me, dear friends,
   is there any point in going on,
   with such a stigma and a life so wrong?

FIFTH CHORAL LYRIC

[*The old men of the* CHORUS *sing first of the inescapable
weight of the bleak goddess Necessity; and then they chant a
panegyric of* ALCESTIS, *who will be famous forever*]

STROPHE I

High as the Muses I
    Have sung and searched the sky
    Where great ideas lie
    But have never found as yet
    A stronger thing than Fate;
    Nor any drug in Thrace
    Prescribed by Orpheus
    Listed and engraved
    On tablets; nor his voice,
    Nor what Apollo gave
    Asclepius and his race:
    No anodyne that can
    Cure the fate of man.

ANTISTROPHE I

Necessity alone
    Although she is divine
    Is accessible to none
    Through effigy or shrine.
    She heeds no sacrifice.
    O Mistress, do not move
    To make me less alive.
    Even mighty Zeus
    Needs you to fulfill
    His work, and so his will . . .
    Chalybian steel
    Is far less hard, for she'll
    Bend to none or feel
    Soft for us.

STROPHE II

And now in the clamp of her grip, Admetus, she
    Holds you fast; but bear it, for never will weeping
    Raise the dead from the dead. Even the children
    Of gods Death fades into his shades.
    Loved she was among us; loved she will be
    Even though dead: the noblest woman you could
Hold to your bed.

ANTISTROPHE II

Never think of her tomb as the same as the mounds
    Of the dead gone by, but more like a shrine of the gods
    And a pilgrim's place to pray. Climbing the path
    That winds along, a passerby will say:
    "Here lies she that saved her consort. Now
    She is a hallowed spirit . . . Lady, I
    Salute you. Bless us." Thus will pilgrims cry.

LEADER: Look, Admetus,
    I think I see Alcmena's son—Heracles—
    heading for your home.

[*Enter* HERACLES, *leading a woman heavily veiled*]

SIXTH EPISODE AND DENOUEMENT

HERACLES: One should be candid with a friend, Admetus,
    not keep grudges smoldering within.
Coming upon you in your house of sorrow
    I might have thought to share it like a friend.
Why then did you never tell me
    that the body which you had to bury was your wife's?
You made me at home and welcomed me
    as if the one you mourned were just a far-off friend.
I garlanded my brow deliriously
    and tossed libations to the gods—
    all in a stricken home.

[*He wags a finger*]

That was reprehensible of you—reprehensible!—
    but I shall not tax you with it
    seeing how great your sufferings are.
Well, what I've come back to tell you is:
    take this woman and keep her for me, please,
    till I return here with the Thracian thoroughbreds,
    having done to death the Bistonian king.
If I fail to come back safe and sound,
    as I certainly hope and pray I do,
    the woman's yours to fetch and carry in your house.

She came into my hands after quite a struggle.
It was at a public tournament
   organized by people that I met:
   a real test of strength for athletes.
I won her as a prize. That's her origin.
The winners in the lighter heats led horses off,
   but in the major events—boxing and wrestling—
   the prize was cattle, and a woman was thrown in.
To decline such a splendid offering once I'd won it
   seemed to me a shame.
So, as I said,
   I place this woman in your hands.
She isn't something I just grabbed:
   I won her with my sweat and blood.
In time, perhaps, you'll even come to thank me.
ADMETUS: It was not to snub you, Heracles,
   nor because I was embarrassed,
   that I hid my poor wife's fate from you,
   but simply that—had you gone off to stay with someone else—
   it only would have added one anguish to another.
There were tears enough for the sorrows that I had.
As to this woman, I beg you, sir,
   if it is remotely possible,
   ask some other Thessalian man,
   who hasn't had to face what I have faced,
   to care for her.
You have many friends in Pherae.
Don't bring home my grief to me.
I could not see her in the house and keep from tears.
I am sick to the heart, weighted down with sorrow.
Do not make me sadder.
Where, moreover, in my house
   could a young woman properly be lodged? . . .
   for young she seems to be, from her pretty style and dress.
Is she to be housed under the same roof as men,
   and she remain untouched lodging with young men?
For it is not easy, Heracles,
   to check a young man in his prime . . .
   I'm only thinking of what's suitable.

Or am I to intrude her into my dead wife's room,
    lodge her there?
But how could I? . . .Give her my own wife's bed?
I recoil from a double accusation that might bring:
    first the charge from some citizen
    that I was being unfaithful to one who saved me,
    falling into bed with another woman—and a young one too;
    then from the deceased herself,
    who merits my adoration . . .
Oh, I must be circumspect!

[ADMETUS *turns towards the veiled figure with a start*]

Young lady, whoever you are,
    know that you have the build and figure of Alcestis.

[*He turns his back*]

By the gods,
    remove this woman from my vision!
Don't trample on a man that's down.
For when I look at her it seems I see my wife;
    my heart is in a turmoil,
    my eyes brim.
Stricken to the soul, at last I taste
    the full peculiar bitterness of fate.
LEADER: There's nothing good about your lot that I can say.
    Heaven's visitations we must shoulder as we may.
HERACLES: I wish I had the power to march
    your consort from the mansions of the dead
    into the day and give you some delight.
ADMETUS: I'm well aware you would. There is no way, however.
    The dead once dead never come into the light again.
HERACLES: Bear up! Don't overdo your grief.
ADMETUS: Oh, it's easier to advise the sufferer than to suffer!
HERACLES: Maybe, but what is the good of endless mourning?
ADMETUS: None, I know. It is love compels me.
HERACLES: Yes, love for the departed compels our tears.
ADMETUS: Oh, she has undermined me to the core!
HERACLES: You've lost a perfect wife, there's no denying.
ADMETUS: So perfect, I'll not enjoy this life again.

HERACLES: Time softens pain . . . Your grief is young.

ADMETUS: Time, you say. If only time spelt death!

HERACLES: A new bride could change all that: the love of a woman.

ADMETUS: Stop it! What a thing to say! How could you?

HERACLES: And why not? You'll not remarry? Will hug an empty bed?

ADMETUS: No woman alive shall ever bed with me.

HERACLES: And you imagine this will profit your deceased?

ADMETUS: I must revere her . . . wherever she may be.

HERACLES: Fine! Fine! But simple, men will say.

ADMETUS: All right! But make no bridegroom out of me.

HERACLES: I admire this dedication to your wife.

ADMETUS: I'd rather die than be disloyal, even though she's dead.

HERACLES: In which case, take this woman now into your noble home.

ADMETUS: No, by Zeus, your own father! I implore you.

HERACLES: You'll be making a mistake if you say no.

ADMETUS: And I'll be wounded to the heart if I say yes.

HERACLES: Trust me. This little favor may win a great reward.

ADMETUS: I wish to God you'd never won that competition.

HERACLES: But I did, and now you're going to share my winnings.

ADMETUS: Kind of you, I'm sure, but the woman has to go.

HERACLES: If she must, she must, but let's consider *if* she must.

ADMETUS: She must. Unless of course it makes you hate me.

HERACLES: In which case, I insist. I know what I am doing.

ADMETUS: All right, you win. But it doesn't give me pleasure.

HERACLES: One day you'll thank me. Just trust me now.

[ADMETUS *turns to the servants*]

ADMETUS: Take the woman in, since I have to have her in my house.

HERACLES: I'm not putting her in any servant's hands.

ADMETUS: Then take her in yourself, if that's what you would rather.

HERACLES: I'd rather place her in *your* hands.

ADMETUS: And I'd rather keep them off her . . . Can't she just walk in?

HERACLES: Only in the security of your own right hand.
ADMETUS: Sir, you are forcing me against my will.
HERACLES: Just take the risk. Put out a hand and touch her.

[ADMETUS, *gingerly with the tips of his fingers and looking
away, touches the veiled figure*]

ADMETUS: My hand is out.
HERACLES: You look as though you were beheading a Medusa.
Have you got her?
ADMETUS: I have.
HERACLES: Then hold on to her.
One day you're going to say that Zeus's son
was a most rewarding guest to entertain.

[HERACLES *steps towards the veiled figure and lifts her veil*]

Take a look at her.
Does she strike you like . . . anything like your wife?

[ADMETUS *staggers back*]

Let your tears give place to joy.
ADMETUS: O you gods, what shall I say?
An apparition beyond the wildest dreams!
Am I really looking at my wife? Really her,
not some hallucination from the shades?
HERACLES: No delusion, truly. You really see your wife.
ADMETUS: Are you sure she's not some ghost rising from the
shades?
HERACLES: That would make your guest a spirit-raiser.
ADMETUS: But is she—do I really see—the wife I buried?
HERACLES: You do indeed . . . I don't wonder that you doubt
your luck.
ADMETUS: Can I touch her? Can I speak to her . . . my living
wife?
HERACLES: By all means, speak. You have your heart's desire.
ADMETUS: Sweet wife! Sweet face! Sweet form!
Beyond all hope I hold you,
whom I never thought to see again.
HERACLES: You hold her, yes: and may no deity be jealous.

ADMETUS: Most illustrious son of mighty Zeus,
   be blessed forever. Your father keep you.
You alone have raised me up . . .
   but how ever did you bring her back from shadows into light?
HERACLES: By battling with the Lord of Ghosts.
ADMETUS: Battling with Death, you mean? Where was that?
HERACLES: At the tomb. I darted out and locked him in my grip.
ADMETUS: [*suddenly apprehensive*] Why does she stand here
                                                without a word?
HERACLES: She is forbidden to talk with you
   until three days have passed and she be purged
   of her consecration to the powers below.
But now take her into the house.
And, Admetus, for the future,
   go on being kind to guests . . . Farewell.
There is a labor that I have to deal with,
   set by that king the son of Sthenelus.
ADMETUS: No no, stay and make your home with us.
HERACLES: Another time . . . I must be going.
ADMETUS: The best of luck, then. Come this way again.

[HERACLES *moves off and* ADMETUS, *holding* ALCESTIS' *hand,
addresses the citizens of Pherae*]

ADMETUS: In every province and township of my realm
   I proclaim a festival of choruses and dance
   to celebrate this happy happy happening.
Let altars fume with sacrifice of kine.
We have our former state reversed
   to a better kind of life.
I shall not disavow that I am happy now.

[*As* ADMETUS *leads* ALCESTIS *into the palace; the whole* CHORUS
chants the envoi]

CHORUS: Many the forms of divine intervention,
   Many the marvels the gods entertain.
   What was expected was never perfected
   And God found a way for the unexpected.
So ends this story today.

HIPPOLYTUS

⬥⬥⬥

ΙΠΠΟΛΥΤΟΣ

For Tobit Roche and Nancy Oakley

Euripides was fifty-five when he produced *Hippolytus* in 429 B.C. It was one of his five plays to win first prize at the dramatic festival. The manner and theme of the play are typical of Euripides, beginning with the Prologue, spoken by Aphrodite, which sets out the plot. We know what is going to happen but we do not know how it is going to happen. Virtue is pitted against virtue, and by a twist of fate virtue is betrayed by virtue. Phaedra, in spite of her passion for her stepson, would rather die than declare it, let alone give way to it. Finally, when she involves the object of that passion in her own destruction, the motive is not simply vindictiveness for thwarted love but terror that the boy will reveal her secret. Hippolytus, for his part, has too much respect for his father, even if he were tempted, to dishonor his father's bed. But there is a flaw in the young man's nature that makes it impossible for him to give rein to love at all. He has turned against love on principle because it was love—free love—that got him born a bastard. His withdrawal from something so central to human life is what Euripides castigates. He is not suggesting that Phaedra and her stepson should succumb to an affair, but he *is* saying that to have a horror of love itself is devastatingly unnatural.

CHARACTERS

APHRODITE, goddess of love
HIPPOLYTUS, natural son of Theseus and the Amazon queen
CHORUS of Huntsmen, companions of Hippolytus
OLD RETAINER of the palace
CHORUS of Women of Troezen
NURSE of Phaedra
PHAEDRA, wife of Theseus
THESEUS, king of Troezen and Athens
MESSENGER from the country
ARTEMIS, goddess of hunt
SERVANTS and ATTENDANTS of the palace

TIME AND SETTING

It is morning outside the royal palace of Troezen in southern
Greece, where Theseus—grandson of the old king Aegeus and
sometime ruler of Athens—now lives with his young wife,
Phaedra, daughter of the king of Crete, and his stripling bastard
son, Hippolytus, whose chief enjoyments are hunting with his
companions and training his stable of thoroughbred chariot horses.

The central palace doors are shut. The exit on the right hand of
the palace leads to the open country and is flanked by a statue of
Artemis. That on the left leads to the main highway and is
flanked by a statue of Aphrodite, who now appears aloft.

PROLOGUE

APHRODITE: Mighty am I on earth, and mighty in heaven,
    named by many a name—I Aphrodite,
    who have under my sway
    every living soul in the light of the sun:
    from the Euxine seashores to the Atlantic main.
I honor those who reverence my power,
    but the proud and resistant heart
    I bring to the ground.
Even the gods, you see,
    delight in the homage of mankind.
Let me show you the truth of what I say.

Hippolytus, son of Theseus and the Amazon,
    and brought up by Pittheus, that pure-hearted man,
    has defamed and blasphemed me:
    treats me as the most despicable of gods.
He alone in all Troezen
    spurns love,
    turns his back on the very idea of sex.
He worships Artemis, Zeus's daughter,
    reveres her above all deities;
    ranges with her in continual partnership
    as he sweeps through the woods with his swift hounds
    emptying the green wild.

I do not begrudge him that—why should I care?—
   but for this, his slight to me,
   I mean to punish Hippolytus today.
Indeed, his road to ruin is already cleared;
   it needs but little more.

Once when he came from the home of Pittheus
   to the land of Pandion,*
   to see and to be sealed in the holy Mysteries,
   Phaedra, his father's highborn wife,
   laid eyes on him and her heart caught fire:
   just as I had planned.
She, even before she came to Troezen,
   had built a shrine to Aphrodite
   near the rock of Pallas that overlooks the land:
   a shrine for her faraway love,
   named after Hippolytus and sacred to the goddess
   for ages to come.

But ever since Theseus bade farewell to the land of Cecrops
   (fleeing from his guilt for the murder of the sons of Pallas)
   and sailed with his wife to these shores,
   banishing himself for a single year,
   his wretched consort goaded by a silent passion
   moans out her heart and begins to waste away:
   her malady a mute mystery to her maids.
But this love-itch of hers is not to end just there.
Oh no! I mean to make it known to Theseus
   and everything will be blazed abroad.
This young man, this enemy of mine,
   shall be driven to his death by his father's curses:
   something made possible by the three wishes
   granted Theseus by Poseidon, king of the sea.
Phaedra, therefore, has to die,
   though she saves her good name.
Yes, she must die.
Her present agonies are not enough

land of Pandion: Attica.

to outweigh the penalty I must exact
   from those who do me wrong.

But I see Hippolytus swaggering in, hot from the chase,
   so I must go.
How his fellows throng around him shouting and singing
   in praise of Artemis!
Little does he know that the gates of Hades
   gape wide open for him,
   and that his last gaze
   on the day's light . . . is today's.

[*As* APHRODITE *fades from view,* HIPPOLYTUS, *surrounded by
shouting young* HUNTSMEN, *strides in garlanded. They lay
down their spears and nets and advance to the statue of*
ARTEMIS, *pointedly ignoring the statue of* APHRODITE]

CHANTED DIALOGUE

HIPPOLYTUS: Come, follow me, fellows, hymning to Artemis
   Throned in the sky, daughter of Zeus:
She is our friend.
HUNTSMEN: Hail, great goddess and queen.
   Hail, daughter of Zeus, and child
   Of Leto . . . Without compare
   Among the undefiled
   Who dwell in the heavenly halls
   Of your noble father's court—
   The golden palace of Zeus.
   Hail, most beautiful lady
   Of Olympus' beautiful ladies:
Artemis, hail!

[*End of Chanted Dialogue.* HIPPOLYTUS *steps up to the statue
of* ARTEMIS, *takes off his garland, and places it on her altar*]

HIPPOLYTUS: Lady, Mistress, here I bring you
   this garland chain of flowers:
   flowers from a meadow none have trampled,
   a pasture never pastured
   by any shepherd with his flock:

a spot no sickle comes to
  but only the winging bee in spring;
  a purlieu watered like a garden by the deity Devotion.
There the pure of heart, they only,
  the naturally clean of living, may gather flowers.
So, my lady, sweetest queen,
  deign to take from my worshiping hand
  this garland of mine
  to bind into your golden hair.
Only to me among all mortals
  has this grace been given to be with you and talk with you:
  to hear your voice though never to see you face to face.
As I have begun my coil of life,
  so may I never cease.

FIRST EPISODE

[*An* OLD RETAINER *who has been listening steps forward*]

RETAINER: Prince, when it comes to calling upon the gods, our lords,
  will you take a little advice?
HIPPOLYTUS: Of course, or else I am a fool.
RETAINER: Are you aware of the way of the world?
HIPPOLYTUS: Not I . . . What are you hinting at?
RETAINER: The avoidance of aloofness and arrogance.
HIPPOLYTUS: And rightly so. The inconsiderate are odious.
RETAINER: And there's grace in friendliness.
HIPPOLYTUS: There certainly is. And earned with so little effort.
RETAINER: But do you think this is also true of the gods?
HIPPOLYTUS: Of course, if mankind gets its codes from the gods.
RETAINER: Then why are you above saluting a certain august
                                                   goddess?
HIPPOLYTUS: Which? Be careful of a slip of the tongue.*
RETAINER: Her statue stands right by your gates—Aphrodite.
HIPPOLYTUS: I'm not interested in sex—I keep aloof.
RETAINER: Indeed! But she's a hallowed goddess, a glory for
                                                   mankind.

---

*It was considered dangerous to name the "august goddesses," the Erinyes or
Furies, who were later renamed the Eumenides (Kindly Ones).

HIPPOLYTUS: I know, but like the gods, some choose one thing,
         some another.
RETAINER: That's good judgment—may it guide you to good
         luck.
HIPPOLYTUS: I don't like deities that flourish after dark.
RETAINER: All the same, my boy, it pays to show respect.
HIPPOLYTUS: [*turning to his entourage*] Into the house, fellows,
         and see to our dinner.
    There's nothing like a full board when the hunt is done.

[*Signaling to a groom*]

You there, rub my chargers down.
    When I have eaten well I want them harnessed to my chariot.
    I mean to give them a thorough workout on the track.

[*Addressing the* RETAINER]

As for this Aphrodite of yours,
    I wave her a long farewell.

[HIPPOLYTUS *strides into the palace followed by his companions, leaving the* OLD RETAINER *standing alone. He lifts his arms towards the statue of* APHRODITE]

RETAINER: Aphrodite, my lady,
    we must not copy young men in thoughts like these.
In such words as a slave may use,
    allow me to bow in prayer before your image here.
Overlook a young hothead's foolish prattle.
Pretend you never heard.
After all, you gods should show more clemency than men.

[*The* OLD RETAINER *shuffles into the palace as the* CHORUS *of Troezen women enters chanting. They express perplexity and concern at* PHAEDRA*'s disturbing behavior and try to find reasons for her wasting away*]

PARADOS OR ENTRY SONG

STROPHE I

There by a certain boulder splashed
   With droplets Ocean distills and spills,
   There where pitchers are plunged and filled,
   A girl I know was dipping clothes:
   Royal purple in the stream.
   She spread them out on the hot rocks
   Under the blaze of the sun.
   She was the one who told me first
   About our mistress, how she lay

ANTISTROPHE I

Strewn on her bed inside the house
   Ravaged with fever, hiding her golden
   Head in the flimsiest of veils.
   This is the third day, they say,
   She has shut her lips to every morsel.
   Her body is purified, refined by fast,
   Ready—as she would have it—to steer
   Beyond the boundaries of pain at last
   Into the dismal haven of death.

STROPHE II

One group: Young woman, has your spirit been seized
   By the frenzy of Pan or Hecate's spell?
   Or perhaps by the sacred Corybants,
   Or even mother Cybele who rules
   The hills? Did you offend Artemis
   Queen of the wild and are wasting away
   Because you neglected her sacrifice . . .
   She with her power to range over lakes
   And over savannahs to the ends of the earth,
   Walking the waves over swirl of the sea?

ANTISTROPHE II

Another: Perhaps a rival lurks in your home,
   Seduces your lord, Erechtheus' scion*

---

*Erechtheus' scion: Theseus.

(That hero prince so nobly sprung)
With a secret passion hidden from you.
Another: Or has a sailor put in from Crete,
   Happy to be in this favored port
   But bringing our queen some dreadful news,
   Clamping her spirit with pangs of grief,
   Chaining her to her couch, where she lies
   Prostrated in the bitterest sorrow?

EPODE

All: The agonized grip, the helplessness,
   The spasms and the delirium
   Of bearing a baby are common enough
   In the fiber of woman. I have felt it all:
   The thrill and the chill deep in the womb.
   I have called out to Artemis, queen of the arrow,
   Goddess of childbirth, desperately needed,
   Who always comes by the grace of heaven.
Leader: But here at the door is the queen's old nurse
   Helping to lead her mistress out.
   Oh what anxiety clouds her face!
   I long to know what makes it so.
   What is the canker working there,
   Eating the queenly frame away?

[PHAEDRA, *supported by the* NURSE, *slowly enters while servants carry a palliasse for her to lie on*]

CHANTED DIALOGUE

NURSE: [*testily*] Oh what damnable diseases blight this life!
   And now what is it I must do with you?
Or what not do?

[*She steers* PHAEDRA *towards the palliasse*]

See, here is the sunshine, here the air.
   We've brought your sickbed out from the palace.
You clamored for that.
   But soon you'll be hurrying in again.

It all comes to nothing. Nothing is right.
You don't like *this,* you don't like *that.*
I'd rather be sick any day than nurse the sick.
It's one thing simply to suffer,
But nursing the sufferer quite another:
One's nerves are taut, one's hands are full.
Oh, the life of mortals is a general mess,
With never a gap in their throng of woes.
And if there is a better life beyond,
It's all wrapped up in a misty black—
So we cravenly cling to the life we have.
That at least we know: the brightness of light.
What's after that we certainly can't . . .
And the myths are bent.

PHAEDRA: [*stirring helplessly*] Lift me up. No, hold my head.
I'm so limp, my friends, my muscles are gone.
Women, take my hands—my pretty hands and arms . . .
Oh this tiara, it weighs a ton.
Off with it. Let my hair fall down.

NURSE: Bear up, dear child, stop tossing and turning.
Relax; you'll bear your sickness better.
Your class should show some self-control.
Every mortal has to suffer.

PHAEDRA: O . . . h!
I wish I could drink from a crystal spring,
Spring water fresh as dew,
Lying on a grassy bank
Under the poplars' leafy shade.

NURSE: Hush, child, you're talking wild.
Do you want everyone to hear?
Crazy words just flying about!

PHAEDRA: [*clutching* NURSE] Take me to the mountains:
I'm off to the forest pines.
Oh to run with the hounds in the hunt
Flying after the dappled hinds!
God, what a thrill to hulloo them on,
Gripping my Thessalian spear
Held above my yellow hair
Flaming as I hurl!

NURSE: Child, you're raving! You and the chase!

And hankering after mountain streams!
  If it's water you want, why, right here
  Next to the palace is a well.
Drink some of that.
PHAEDRA: [*taking no notice*]
Oh, Artemis, queen of the sea along Limna's shores,
  Where the thunder of hooves beats on the flats,
  What wouldn't I give to race on your tracks
Breaking in my Enetian colts!
NURSE: You're out of your mind. What nonsense is this?
  One minute hankering after hills and the hunt,
  And next to race on the level sands?

  [*There is a pause.* PHAEDRA *shakes herself and seems to come
  to her senses*]

PHAEDRA: It's all hopeless. What have I done?
  Where been blundering? Where gone wrong?
  I was possessed, crazy, under a spell.
  Nanna, cover my head again.
  I am ashamed of what I've mouthed.
  Go on, cover it. My tears pour down.
  My eyes are ashamed for very shame.
  To come to one's senses is to come to pain.
  Madness is terrible but at least it's blind.
NURSE: There, I've covered you.

  [NURSE *leans back, talking as if to herself as she holds* PHAE-
  DRA'*s hand*]

And I wish Death would cover *me*.
  My long life has taught me many a lesson.
  We ought to be careful when we make friends:
  Not pin our hearts to the pith of a soul.
  Cords of affection ought to be flexible,
  To tighten or loosen—easy to pull.
  When a single soul suffers for two
  It's a heavy burden . . . as I do for you.
  Too clinging a bond brings more pain
  Than pleasure, they say, as well as being

The ruin of health.
  So for me it's not "Nothing's enough"
But rather "Nothing too much."
So say the wise and so say I.

[*End of Chanted Dialogue.* PHAEDRA *sinks back on her bed*]

SECOND EPISODE

LEADER: Old woman, you are indeed a faithful nurse
  of Phaedra our queen.
Her turbulent state is all too clear
  but the cause of the malady is a puzzle.
What do you think? We'd like to hear.
NURSE: I've asked her but she refuses to say.
LEADER: When did this whole turmoil begin?
NURSE: The answer's the same: she won't speak.
LEADER: How weak she is! She's wasting away.
NURSE: It's been three days since she touched a thing.
LEADER: Is she mad, or is she trying to die?
NURSE: Both. She's starving herself to death.
LEADER: It's strange that her husband lets her do it.
NURSE: She hides her problem; denies she's sick.
LEADER: Doesn't he guess? One look at her face!
NURSE: He's not here; he's gone abroad.
LEADER: Then you must force her to divulge
  the sick cause of her unhinged mind.

[*During this colloquy* PHAEDRA *has been dozing. Now she
begins to stir*]

NURSE: I've done my best but get no further.
  Even so I won't give up.
  And you are witness to my devotion.

[*Stroking* PHAEDRA's *brow*]

Come, precious child,
  let us both forget the things we said.
Let a sweeter mood be yours.
Smooth out that frown.

Let go those wayward thoughts.
And I, I shall be more patient in my turn.
If your sickness dare not be named,
    there are women here to help you.
If it is something that can be told to men,
    why then, speak out and a physician will prescribe.

[*The* NURSE *waits for a reply*]

What, silent? You should not be silent, child.
    Scold me if I've said something wrong;
    or answer me, if to the point.
One little word. Look at me.

[*She pauses again, then turns to the* CHORUS]

Women, our efforts are a waste of time.
We're as far away as ever.
She wouldn't listen then, and she won't listen now.

[*Looking down at* PHAEDRA, *who still reclines*]

Very well, be stubborn as the sea,
    but know this: if you die
    you'll be a traitor to your children
    and they will never inherit their father's house . . .
    not a chance, with the bastard son
    of that flaming chariot Amazon queen.
He'll lord it over yours, and he's far from a bastard.
You know who I mean—Hippolytus.

[PHAEDRA *sits bolt upright*]

PHAEDRA: O God!
NURSE: So that touched you?
PHAEDRA: [*grasping* NURSE'*s hands*] Nanna, you're killing me.
By all the gods, I beg you,
    do not speak of that man to me again.
NURSE: So now you see!
But seeing straight is not enough,
    unless you're willing to save your children by saving your life.

PHAEDRA: I do love my children . . . That is not the storm in my heart.

NURSE: What then? Your hands aren't dripping with blood, are they?

PHAEDRA: My hands are clean. It is my soul that's fouled.

NURSE: Under the spell of some destructive power?

PHAEDRA: Under the spell of a friend, and not his choice or mine.

NURSE: You mean, Theseus has hurt you, done you wrong?

PHAEDRA: No, no! If only I could not wrong *him*.

NURSE: Then, what is this dread driving you to die?

PHAEDRA: Oh leave me to my sinning! My sin is not for you.

NURSE: Never! And only you can stop me.

[NURSE *seizes* PHAEDRA'*s hands*]

PHAEDRA: You've imprisoned my hand: confession by force!

NURSE: And your knees . . . I'll never let go.

PHAEDRA: Then, poor woman, you'll have to share my doom.

NURSE: What doom could be worse than losing *you*?

PHAEDRA: Dying would, though for me that's the only hope.

NURSE: Your only hope? For my sake, tell me what it is.

PHAEDRA: Very well. Out of evil I'm trying to wrest some good.

NURSE: Don't hide it, then. Let good be manifest.

PHAEDRA: Off with you! By all the gods, let go my hand.

NURSE: No, not till you grant me what I ask.

PHAEDRA: [*after an agonized pause*]
So be it! I cannot resist the holy pressure of your hands.

NURSE: I'll say no more. It's up to you to speak.

PHAEDRA: It begins with my poor mother. How freakish was her love!*

NURSE: You mean for the bull, child? . . . Or what?

PHAEDRA: Then my unhappy sister—bride of Dionysus.

NURSE: Child, why harp on family tragedies?

PHAEDRA: Because I'm the third to be destroyed.

NURSE: I am baffled. Where is the story heading?

PHAEDRA: Nowhere new. The same fate wrecks us all.

NURSE: I'm no nearer hearing what I want to know.

---

*Her mother was Pasiphaë, on the island of Crete, who fell in love with a bull and gave birth to the Minotaur—half man, half beast.

PHAEDRA: [*with a groan from the depths*]
    A . . . h! If only you could say what I must say!
NURSE: I'm not a prophet. I can't unravel the unknown.
PHAEDRA: What do people mean when they speak of love?
NURSE: Dear child: the sweetest and the bitterest thing on earth.
PHAEDRA: For me it is agony. That is all I know.
NURSE: So you're in love, my baby? Who's the man?
PHAEDRA: [*hedging*] The man? . . . Well, whoever . . . he's the
                                    Amazon's . . .
NURSE: No? Not Hippolytus?
PHAEDRA: Your lips have uttered it, not mine.
NURSE: [*jerking away her hands*]
    Child, what are you saying? It tears me apart.
    Women, this cannot be borne. I can't go on.
Cursed the light of this cursed day!
I'll hurl myself down, fling headlong this body,
    get rid of life; my life is done—farewell! . . .
The virtuous in love with vice . . .
    maybe not willingly but still—in love.
If this can be, then Aphrodite
    is not just a goddess but something more.
She has ruined her and me and all this house.

[*The* NURSE *takes a seat as the* CHORUS *divides into several
groups of dumbfounded women*]

CHANTED DIALOGUE

CHORUS: *1st group:* Did you hear? Did you listen
    To that unbearable
    Wail of a dire confession
    From our mistress queen?
2nd group: I'd rather die, dear lady, than needle
    My heart with a problem like yours.
3rd group: Poor pitiable victim of pain!
    Pitiable mortals, fodder for horror!
4th group: As good as dead . . .
    Dragging your crisis into the light!
All: Something awful will hit this house.
    Writ large is the aphrodisiac fate

Of this unhappy girl from Crete.

[*End of Chanted Dialogue*]

THIRD EPISODE

[PHAEDRA, *mustering her resources, rises from her couch and stands erect*]

PHAEDRA: Women of Troezen,
   who dwell on the fringes of Pelops' land,
   how often in the sleepless reaches of the night
   have I mused on the ways our human life is wrecked.
It seems to me this penchant for disaster
   is not something we were born with
   (witness the good sense of many)
   but something to be explained another way.
We know what is right, we understand it,
   but do not do it . . .
   partly from laziness, partly
   from allowing pleasure to swamp our sense of duty.
Life has so many aimless charms:
   long conversations, idleness
   (sweet but so seductive);
   then there is that two-edged sense of self-respect:
   harmless on one side and a curse on the other . . .
   we ought to call these two by different names.
This being so,
   as soon as I saw my problem, my compulsion,
   I knew at once that nothing could cure it,
   nothing could make me change my mind.
So let me tell you the road my reason trod.

The moment love smote me
   I cast about for a way to handle it.
I determined to keep quiet and hide my sickness.
One cannot trust the tongue:
   so glib at bringing others to heel,
   so bad at coping with troubles of its own.
Next, I made up my mind to master this madness

through sheer self-control.
Thirdly, when this attempt to quell love's power failed,
  I began to see that death was the only way out—
  none can deny it.
I would rather have my virtue than my shame
  blazoned forth for all to see.
For the scandal, I knew, would be just as great
  to own the passion as to give it rein.
Besides, I realized that as a woman
  I was the ready butt for hate by all.

Oh, a plague on the woman
  who first shamed her marriage vows
  and made love with another man!
It was from noble families, too,
  that this evil first sprang up;
  and when the higher classes misbehave
  the lower take it as their code of excellence.
How I hate those women who extol chastity
  but secretly indulge their flagrant affairs!
I ask you, Aphrodite, Sea-born One,
  how can they look their husbands in the face
  and not quake with dread
  that one day the conniving dark,
  the very bedroom walls
  will find a voice and shatter their deceit?

So, dear women, you see now why I have to kill myself:
  to save my husband from disgrace and save my children.
I want them to grow up in this home of theirs,
  our glorious Athens, unfettered in speech, unfettered in act,
  and honored in their mother.
Even the most upright man is reduced to groveling
  if confronted with a mother's or a father's turpitude.
As everyone knows,
  only an untrammeled consciousness, good and just,
  can stand up to the pressures of life.
Time in its own good time,
  like a young girl with a looking glass,
  shows up baseness to the base.

Among such may I never find a place.

LEADER: Fair is virtue everywhere
And the fruit of it: a name as fair.

[*The* NURSE *rises from her seat and approaches* PHAEDRA]

NURSE: Mistress, when this news of yours first shattered me,
my response—I see now—was all too shallow.
Second thoughts are usually more balanced.
What you are going through is neither uncommon nor strange.
Aphrodite has swooped upon you.
You are in love. What wonder in that?
You are one of hundreds.
Would you, for loving, throw away your life?
Are all lovers today and tomorrow to die for it?
What good is that?
When Aphrodite swoops there's no defense.
Only to the docile does she gently come.
When she finds the stubborn of heart, the arrogant,
she takes him by the scruff of the neck—and what do you
think?—
boxes the pride out of him.
Aphrodite permeates the air;
she's in the waves of the sea;
everything that is comes out of her.
She scatters her love; she gives it in largesse;
and from that love every one of us on this earth is sprung.

Those who know their legends
and the stories of the Muses
know how Zeus once lusted after Semele;
how lightsome and lovely Dawn, all for love,
snatched Cephalus to heaven—
there to dwell with him among the gods
and, I would say, enjoy his victimhood.

So you now, will you not yield?
If you reject the way the world runs,
your father should have begotten you by a special dispensation
subject to a different set of gods.
How many men, do you think, and wise ones too,

look the other way when cuckolded?
How many fathers, do you think,
    play the pander for their lovelorn sons?
Sensible mortals follow a rule:
    not to dwell on what disturbs them.
Don't try too hard to square life's paradoxes.
Why, even the carpenter has a job
    getting the measurements of your roof beams right.
You've fallen into the deep,
    do you really expect to come out high and dry?
You're only human,
    and if you have more good than evil in you
    you're doing fine.

[*Taking* PHAEDRA *by the hand*]

Come, precious child,
    cease your suicidal thoughts;
    stop being so presumptuous.
For this is presumption running wild,
    this wanting to outsmart the gods.
Trust in your love: a god has willed it.
You are sick, but you can find a cure.
There are incantations and healing formulas.
Some remedy surely will be found for this disease:
    tardily, I grant, if left to men,
    but not to the sagacity of us women.
LEADER: Phaedra, given your plight,
    this woman's attitude is more commonsense than yours.
All the same, it's you that I applaud,
    though my approval, I dare say,
    is less welcome than her palliatives
    and certainly more painful.
PHAEDRA: [*disengaging herself from* NURSE]
    And precisely what makes fine cities and happy homes
    tumble down? . . . sweet but specious double-talk.
Words should not be used to seduce,
    but to foster virtue.
NURSE: Oh what a lot of pious twaddle!
It isn't platitudes you want but a man.

We have to find out what *his* feelings are.
This is no time to quibble.
The blunt truth about you must be told.
If you hadn't gotten your life into such a muddle
    and really were a levelheaded woman,
        I'd not be urging you to a course of lust and pleasure,
        but we're fighting for your life:
        there's nothing ignoble in that.
PHAEDRA: Rotten to the core—the things you are saying.
Will you please stopper your mouth.
Don't start that vicious, vicious talk again.
NURSE: Vicious, but able to save your life more than virtue.
Better a behavior that saves
    than a highfalutin principle that damns.
PHAEDRA: For the gods' sakes, don't go on. Please don't.
It's too disgusting, and you're too persuasive.
I'm already undermined by love,
    and if you go on eulogizing evil,
        my last resistance will be gone.
NURSE: Very well then, if you are determined not to sin,
    things being what they are,
    listen to the next best thing.
I have at home a formula—I've just remembered it—
    a soothing love-drug.
It will solve your problem
    and won't hurt either your reputation or your mind.
But you must not be a coward.
I'll need some item from the man you sigh for:
    a lock of his hair, a scrap of clothing . . .

[*Spoken in an aside*]

    something that will knit two loves in one.
PHAEDRA: And your drug: is it an ointment or a potion?
NURSE: I'm not sure. Don't try to know everything, child. Just be
                             helped.
PHAEDRA: I am nervous. You may prove to be too clever by half.
NURSE: What a bundle of nerves you are! You are frightened of
                               what?
PHAEDRA: That you will blurt out my secret to Theseus' son.

NURSE: Forget it, child, I know how to bring this off.

[*She turns to the statue of* APHRODITE *and murmurs a prayer out of the hearing of* PHAEDRA]*

Sea-foam goddess, be my ally.
As to the rest of my plan,
I'll fix that as best I can
With our friends within.

[*The* NURSE *hurries into the palace*]

SECOND CHORAL LYRIC†

[*The women of the* CHORUS *launch into a nervous encomium of* APHRODITE, *fluctuating between a craven adoration of the beauty of love and a horror of its destructive power, citing examples from the legendary past*]

STROPHE I

Eros, Eros, clouding our eyes
    With a mist of yearning when you sweeten the hearts
    Of those against whom you plan your attack.
    Please never show yourself to wound me.
    Please never turn everything upside down.
    Neither lightning nor the fall of a star
    Wreaks more havoc than Aphrodite's
    Lance when loosed from the hand of Eros,
Zeus's boy.

---

*These lines are omitted from some mss. as seeming to promote the match. There is no need to omit them. They are illustrations of Euripides' subtlety in delineating character. The Nurse is playing a Machiavellian game. She has cleverly called her charm a *thelktēria erōtos*, which I have correctly translated "love-drug." She knows that Phaedra will take this to mean an antidote to love, whereas she means something that will promote love. The fact that she doesn't even know whether her love-drug is an ointment or a potion suggests that she intends to use much more direct methods to stir up some enthusiasm from Hippolytus. This is in line with her earlier encouragement of the match and it also explains why she rebukes her mistress for asking questions.
†In this instance the Chanted Dialogue on p. 60 stands in for the First Choral Lyric.

ANTISTROPHE I

Useless, useless, the pouring of blood
   That Greece has shed of slaughtered kine
   On the banks of Alpheus or Apollo's shrine:
   Useless, if Eros isn't adored.
   Dictator of men, the keeper of keys
   To Aphrodite's beds of love—
   He is the prime wrecker of mortals,
   The bringer of catastrophe
When he attacks.

STROPHE II

There was a girl in Oechalia
   A filly unbroken by man:
   Unbedded, unbridled, unfettered,
   Who was driven by Love, Aphrodite,
   And fled like a flame or a Bacchant
   Far from her home; and was given
   As a bride to Alcmena's son
In a wedding most gory.

ANTISTROPHE II

You hallowed Theban ramparts
   And mouth of Dirce's stream,
   You can tell how gently
   Aphrodite comes.
   But the mother of Bacchus she flared
   To bed with bloody Death.
   Over the earth she breathes:
A bee, she hovers.

[PHAEDRA, *who has been listening, suddenly runs to the door of the palace and stoops to hear*]

PHAEDRA: Dear women, be quiet . . . O . . . h! My life is over.
LEADER: What is it, Phaedra? Is something happening in the
                                 house?

PHAEDRA: [*bending to the door and listening*]
Hush! I want to hear what they are saying in there.
LEADER: I am mum . . . But something bad is happening.

PHAEDRA: [*in a wail of anguish*]
A . . . h! I can't bear it . . . It's too much!

CHANTED DIALOGUE

[*In which* PHAEDRA *speaks and the* CHORUS *chants*]

CHORUS: What is she wailing for? Why are you shrieking?
   Tell us what you have heard with such dismay.
PHAEDRA: I am ruined. Just stand by the door yourselves and
                                                      listen
   to the uproar in the house.
LEADER: You are nearest the door.
   You can hear it best.
   Tell us, oh, tell us
   What is going on.
PHAEDRA: The son of the horse-loving Amazon, Hippolytus,
   is hurling insults at my nurse.
LEADER: I can hear a rumpus
   But cannot catch the words.
   Surely you heard it all
   From behind the doors?
PHAEDRA: All too clearly, yes:
   he's calling her the go-between of sin—
   the adulterer's accomplice.
LEADER: Mercy! You are betrayed, dear lady,
   What can I say? Your secret is out.
You are destroyed.
PHAEDRA: O . . . h!
LEADER: Betrayed by one who loves you.
PHAEDRA: She has destroyed me: divulged my obsession,
   and done it with love: damned me by her cure.

[*End of Chanted Dialogue*]

FOURTH EPISODE

LEADER: What now? What can you do, poor helpless thing?
PHAEDRA: There's only one course left, one cure for my disorder:
   to die as soon as possible.

[HIPPOLYTUS *bursts through the doors, followed by the* NURSE.
PHAEDRA *shrinks into the shadows*]

HIPPOLYTUS: O Mother Earth, and you bright sun,
  what a hideous suggestion have I just heard!
NURSE: Hush, hush, boy! Don't shout it out.
HIPPOLYTUS: It's too disgusting to keep quiet.
NURSE: Please, you must, by your fine right hand.

[*She tries to seize his hand, then his tunic*]

HIPPOLYTUS: Take your hands off me, and off my clothes.
NURSE: I'll clasp your knees, then. Don't destroy me.
HIPPOLYTUS: How can I if, as you say, you've done no wrong?
NURSE: Please, my son, the story's not for every ear.
HIPPOLYTUS: [*with bitter sarcasm*]
  As many ears as possible if it's a good story.
NURSE: My child, you will not repudiate your oath?
HIPPOLYTUS: Sworn by my tongue, never my soul.
NURSE: What, boy, you'd do it—destroy your own?
HIPPOLYTUS: I spit out "my own" if they are bent on vice.
NURSE: Forgive! To make mistakes is human, son.
HIPPOLYTUS: Great Zeus,
  why ever did you give a place to women under the sun:
  that pestilent tribe, that curse to man?
Was it to perpetuate the human race?
That could have been done without womankind.
In your temples you could have produced offspring
  to be bought according to their price in gold, iron, or copper;
  then men could have lived an untrammeled life
  in houses free of women.

Woman is a plague, and here's the evidence.
The father who begets her and brings her up
  then pays a gross dowry to get her out of the house
  and be rid of the baggage.
The man who takes home this noxious package
  is then thrilled to bedeck his idol with every kind of frippery.
He dolls her up in expensive gowns.
He fritters away—poor fool!—his heritage.

And he is in a bind:
>he may have got himself excellent in-laws but an impossible
>>>wife,
>or an excellent wife but insufferable in-laws.
He has to juggle with profit and loss.
The luckiest man is he who wins a nobody for a wife,
>a brainless nincompoop who just sits at home.
A brainy woman I abhor,
>and in my house, at least, I hope there'll never be
>a woman of above-average brains.
It's the clever ones that go in for Aphrodite's fun and games.
The dullards are kept in check by their own ineptitude.
And don't let maids near wives;
>let their company be animals—preferably those that bite—
>which can't talk scandal and can't talk back.
As it is,
>worthless women hatch their plots in closets
>and their maids broadcast them abroad.

So, you despicable old crone,
>you have the nerve to come to me
>promoting incest in my own father's bed.
I'll flush this obscenity away,
>splash running water on my ears.
How could I be so vile
>when the very suggestion of it makes me feel defiled?
Reflect on this, old woman,
>it's only my piety that saves you.
If you hadn't tricked me into a solemn oath
>I'd go straight to my father now and tell him everything.
As things stand I'll stay away from home
>until Theseus comes back from abroad,
>and I'll keep my lips tight shut.
But when I rejoin my father
>I'll watch the way you meet his eyes—
>you and that mistress of yours.
Then I shall know exactly how far you have gone
>in your shamelessness.

>>>>>>>>>>*   *   *

Meanwhile, my curses on you!
My hatred of women is inexhaustible.
I don't care if people say: "He has a one-track mind."
Theirs is too and the track is vice.
Either let them learn a little modesty
    or me go on in my antipathy.

[*As* HIPPOLYTUS *stomps off into the palace,* PHAEDRA *emerges from the shadows, and it is the nurse's turn to make herself scarce—perhaps behind a pillar*]

CHANTED DIALOGUE

LEADER: Oh what a pitiful miserable fate
    Is our unbearable doom as women
Once we have fallen!
    What tricks, what coaxing, what cunning
Can unloose us from scandal?
PHAEDRA: You Earth, you light of the Sun,
    I have brought this on myself.
    How can I elude my plight?
    How can I—oh you my friends!—
    Conceal my ruin? What god
    Will succor me? What mortal
    Will come anywhere near
    To take my part in this
Unfair affair?
    My life is overwhelmed,
    There is no breaking through
    For me most damned of women.

[*End of Chanted Dialogue. The* NURSE *nervously comes forward*]

FOURTH EPISODE

LEADER: Alas, Mistress, alas! The die is cast.
    Your nurse's scheme went wrong and all is lost.

PHAEDRA: [*wheeling on the* NURSE]
　You most monstrous of
women, destroyer of your friends,
　　may Zeus the Father tear you up by the roots and shatter
　　　　　　　　　　　　　　　　　　　　　　　　you
　　and blast you to a cinder!
Did I not tell you—did I not have forebodings—
　　not to breathe a word, not a word,
　　of what is now manifest disgrace?
But, oh no! you went right ahead,
　　and now I cannot even die with honor.
I must think afresh.
That boy's disgust is honed to frenzy.
He'll tell his father I am to blame for your mistake . . .
　　oh yes, and old Pittheus too.
He'll fill the realm with the foulest slander.
Damn you! and all those do-gooders
　　who meddle their way uninvited to the ruin of friends.
NURSE: Madam, it is not surprising
　　that you round on me for the harm I've done:
　　the wound is all too raw just now for you to think objectively.
But I too have something to say, if you will listen.
I reared you. I cherished you.
I tried to find a cure for your disease,
　　and I failed.
If I had succeeded
　　you'd think me now a genius.
So much for success as our criterion of esteem!
PHAEDRA: So this makes everything all right?
　　Assassinate me first and then admit it?
NURSE: We're going round in circles . . . Yes, I made a mis-
　　　　　　　　　　　　　　　　　　　　　　　take;
　　there *is* a way out, child.
PHAEDRA: Speak no more to me. Your first advice was bad,
　　and your first attempt to help disastrous.
Get out of my way and look to your own concerns.
I'll handle my affair as best I may.

[*The* NURSE *goes sadly into the palace.* PHAEDRA *turns to the*
CHORUS]

And you, my noble women of Troezen,
   all I ask is this:
   that you draw a curtain of silence across everything you've
                                     heard.

LEADER: By the holy maiden, Artemis, child of Zeus,
   I swear never to bring to light
   any inkling of your trouble.

PHAEDRA: Good . . . I've been thinking . . .
   There's only one solution to this problem:
   one way of leaving my children some honor to live by
   and at the same time salvaging something for myself;
   for I refuse to disgrace my Cretan heritage,
   and I refuse to face Theseus on such a hideous charge
   just to save one paltry life.

LEADER: So you are bent on some irrevocable folly?

PHAEDRA: To die . . . But how? . . . I must work this out.

LEADER: Don't even speak of it.

PHAEDRA: You would lecture me too!
   But Aphrodite will be pleased, my destroyer,
because this very day I shall rid myself of life,
a victim to remorseless love.
But once dead,
   I'll bring a curse on someone else.
He shall not gloat on my demise,
   and when he comes to share my tragedy,
   perhaps he'll learn a little modesty.

[PHAEDRA *walks slowly into the palace*]

THIRD CHORAL LYRIC

[*The women of the* CHORUS, *citing legendary places of grief,
wish they could fly in sympathy like a bird to those parts. They
lament* PHAEDRA*'s having left her happy Crete. Her heart has
been infected and broken by* APHRODITE. *The lament turns into
a dirge for her coming death*]

STROPHE I

Bury me under the earth's
   deepest recesses

Or turn me into a bird
   amongst feathered fellows
And let me go soaring over
   the Adriatic's
Wave-beaten shores to the river
   Eridanus in whose
Purpureal waters the daughters
   of the sun god drip
Tears like drops of amber
   for Phaëlthon their brother.

ANTISTROPHE I

To the gardens of the apple-hung shores
   surely I'd wing:
To where the Hesperides sing
   and the lord of the deep
Blocks the path of the sailor
   and Atlas the giant
Holds up the verges of heaven,
   and where ambrosial
Fountains brim beside Zeus's
   couch and divine
Mother Earth showers largesses
   and bliss for the gods.

STROPHE II

You white-pinioned galley from Crete, through the boom
   And surge of the salty sea, you carried
   My lady away from her happy home
   To a fatal unhappy marriage. How doomed
   Was the vessel's departure as it flew from Crete
   To glorious Athens, for there ill fortune
   Was waiting right on the quay of Munychia
   As the mariners knotted their twisted hawsers
   And sprang on the firm earth of the mainland.

ANTISTROPHE II

The sinister omens were proven true: she was struck
   To the heart by the wound of incestuous love—

Aphrodite's. Swamped by sorrow she'll arrange
The dangling noose in the nuptial chamber
Around the white of her neck, unable
To face the shame of a life overflowing
With loathing, choosing instead the fame
Of an unspotted name, ridding thereby
Her heart of all the tortures of loving.

[*The voice of the* NURSE *is heard screaming within*]

FIFTH EPISODE

NURSE: [*from within*] Help! Help! Is nobody near? Come running.
　　She hangs from a halter—Theseus' wife.
LEADER: It's over! It's over! The queen our lady is no more.
　　She has hanged herself.
NURSE: [*still within*] Hurry, hurry! Someone bring a sharp knife.
　　We must sever the knot around her neck.

[*The* CHORUS *breaks into confused groups*]

CHORUS
　　1: Women, what shall we do? Break through the doors?
　　2: We've got to loosen the queen from the halter.
　　3: Why *us*? Aren't there any servants around?
　　　　It never pays to meddle.
NURSE: [*within*] Lay her out. Her poor crumpled body!
　　What a bitter duty for this house!
LEADER: She must be dead, unhappy soul.
　　They're already laying out the corpse.

[THESEUS, *in traveling clothes and crowned with a laurel
wreath, bursts in from the side, accompanied by retainers*]

THESEUS: Women, what is the meaning of this uproar in the
　　　　　　　　　　　　　　　　　　　　　　palace?
　　A piteous sound drifts on my ears, like servants wailing.
　　And why aren't the doors of the house flung open in welcome—
　　especially since I come crowned—straight from the oracle?
Is there bad news about my father, old Pittheus?
His passing, old as he is, would weigh me down with sorrow.

LEADER: Theseus, it is not from the old that bad news has struck.
    Your grief comes crushing from the young.

THESEUS: No? Not my children? Not a young life snatched?

LEADER: They live. It is their mother, sadly, that is dead.

THESEUS: What are you talking about? My wife dead? How
                        could she be?

LEADER: She strangled herself: put a halter round her neck.

THESEUS: What? Numbed by longing? What else could it have
                        been?

LEADER: That is all I know.
    We've only just heard the news ourselves
    and are here to mourn your loss.

THESEUS: [*snatching the wreath off his head*]
    Away with this crown of plaited leaves,
    stricken pilgrim that I am!
Servants, slide back the bolts, unbar the doors,
    and let me gaze on the bitter sight of my dead wife,
    who destroys me, dying.

[*The doors are thrown open to reveal the body of* PHAEDRA
surrounded by weeping servants and retainers. The CHORUS
splits into groups]

CHORAL DIALOGUE

CHORUS: *Group 1:* Pity, oh pity! You agonized woman!
    The hurt you have done to yourself, to this house!
Group 2: Breaching death with unholy courage.
    How sad a victory over yourself!
Group 3: Unhappy one, what was the shadow cast on your life?

STROPHE

THESEUS: O . . . h! O . . . h! my city, my sorrow!
    the worst I have suffered.
Fate, fate you have trodden me down,
    trampled my house:
A victim caught by some sleuth of a fiend,
    a canceled life—
Swamped in an ocean of sorrow so wide,
    wretch that I am,

Never to make the shore again,
   never to rise
Above this flood of disaster . . . O . . . h!
   Oh, my beloved,
There are no words to equal the weight
   of this terrible fate.
Out of my hands, little bird, you have slipped
   in a headlong leap
And flitted to Hades . . . Oh! Oh,
   the pity, the loss!
The bitterest pity, the sorrow, alas!
   Long long ago
Some ancestor sinned and today the gods
   have brought it home.
LEADER: King, you are not the only one to suffer such.
   Many another has lost a perfect wife.

ANTISTROPHE

THESEUS: Under the earth among the shades,
   yes, under the earth,
Wretchedly dead let me abide.
   Shorn of your presence,
My best beloved, I've died a death
   more than your own.
How did this black disaster creep
   into your heart,
My stricken wife? Can anyone tell me? . . .
   Oh, what is the use
Of a palace of menials harbored for nothing?
   My wife! My wife!
The anguish that looms large in my halls
   cannot be spoken,
Cannot be broken. All is destruction,
   a desolate home,
Children orphaned . . . You have gone, gone,
   beloved and best
Of women that starry-eyed night or the sun
   ever beheld.
CHORUS: You poor, poor blighted man,
   what immeasurable grief

Rules your house! My eyes are brimming,
    blinded with tears.
But now a dreaded evil I feared
    is about to begin.

[*End of Choral Dialogue.* THESEUS *approaches* PHAEDRA'*s body and sees a letter in her hand*]

SIXTH EPISODE

THESEUS: Ah, what is this?
    A letter clutched in her dear hands.
Is it to tell me something left unsaid?
My poor darling perhaps has written down her wishes:
    concern for the children, or about my remarrying.
Bear up, dear heart, there is not a woman alive
    I'd intrude into this house or let lie down in Theseus' bed.

[*He stoops and takes the letter from her hand*]

See, here is the stamp of her golden seal . . .
    oh my departed wife, how it tugs at my eyes!
But come, let me undo the ribbon and seal
    and read what she tells me.

[*He opens the letter and reads*]

CHORAL DIALOGUE

CHORUS:

[*severally*]

1: No, not again! One horrible evil,
    Demon-propelled, close on another?
2: What has occurred has made my life unlivable.
3: And the house of my masters, alas, alas, a ruin!
4: Oh, is there any way, dear God, to avert what is coming?
    I plead, for I see like a prophet a further blow.
THESEUS: [*crying out in anguish*]
    A . . . h! Another nightmare crowding on the old:
    past enduring, past imagining.

LEADER: What now, may I ask? Oh, tell me!
THESEUS: It shrieks. The letter shrieks. Its lips shout perfidy.
   An avalanche of woe I can't escape. It obliterates.
   The letter speaks, it speaks.
   The letter has a tongue.

[*End of Choral Dialogue*]

LEADER: Sire, your words fill me with alarm.
THESEUS: The choking obscenity. I cannot contain it. It must out,
   break through the portals of my mouth . . .
My city, my city!
   In the full glare of Zeus's holy eye
   Hippolytus has ravished my wife.

[*Flinging his arms out*]

Father Poseidon, hear me.
You promised me once three curses,
   let me have one of them now—to destroy my son.
If there is power in them,
   let him not escape this very day.
LEADER: For the sake of the gods, King, cancel that prayer.
   Believe me, you'll come to know in time the mistake you have
                                                         made.
THESEUS: Never. But this I'll add:
   I'll drive him out of the realm, and then
   one of two fates shall strike him down:
   either Poseidon will honor my curse
   and hurtle him dead through the gates of Hades,
   or, as a banished wandering derelict on foreign soil,
   he'll drink to the dregs life's bitter cup.
LEADER: Sire, here he is: your son comes, Hippolytus.
   Let go your terrible anger, King Theseus.
Consider only what best serves your house.

   [HIPPOLYTUS, *dressed in hunting gear, enters with a group of
   young companions and moves briskly towards* THESEUS]

HIPPOLYTUS: Father, I heard your cry of anguish and have hur-
                                                    ried here.

I can't imagine what has caused your groans.
Tell me, please.

[*Suddenly seeing* PHAEDRA's *body*]

Ha! What is this? Your wife's body?
Phaedra dead? I can't believe it.
I left her only moments ago.
Yes, in the full blaze of day.
What could have happened? . . . Father, how did she die?
You must tell me. I must hear it.

[*He waits for a reply*]

You say nothing.
Silence is no help in time of sadness.
Your very life is close to my heart,
    and that includes your sorrows.
To hide your tragedies from your friends
    is not right, Father . . . Oh much more than friends!
THESEUS: What a waste of human effort
    in this world of errors are ten thousand skills
    and all the ingenious discoveries of man,
        when one thing is missing—undetected, unresearched—
    how to teach wisdom to a fool.
HIPPOLYTUS: That would need a master craftsman, sir:
    to make fools wise by solemn force.
But such speculations, Father, are not fitting here.
I fear your grief has made your tongue run wild.
THESEUS: Confound it!
    Mankind should have some touchstone somewhere,
    some yardstick of the heart
    that registers false friends from true.
Every man should have a double voice:
    the voice of honesty and the voice of opportunity;
    that way the opportunist voice could immediately be parted
    from the voice of honesty
    and we would not be so easily deceived.
HIPPOLYTUS: Has some aquaintance infected your ear against
                                                              me?

Am I infected, unspotted as I am?
I am stunned.
Your insinuation quite astounds me.
It is wildly out of line.
THESEUS: What brashness has the human heart!
How far will it push?
Is there any limit to its brazen nerve?
If it continues to spawn in each new age,
    son outsmarting father in depravity,
    the gods will have to double the earth
    to make room for the crops of seedling rascals.

[*Turning to the horrified bystanders*]

Look at this fellow,
    my own son, yet he has tried to rape my wife:
    his heinousness laid bare in the handwriting of the dead.

[HIPPOLYTUS, *stupefied, covers his face with his hands*]

Sirrah, show your face.
You've already shown how you could pollute me,
    so show your father your face—
    you, you colleague of the gods,
    you so modest man, so uncontaminated.
I am not so easily convinced by all your highfalutin cant.
I am not so stupid as to link the gods with your wrong-headedness,
So go on bragging.
Promote your vegetarian diet like a charlatan,
    with Orpheus* your hero-model, and rave away in your devotion
    to those portentous tomes and their gaseous nonsense.
You have been caught out.

[*Turning to the bystanders*]

Let me warn you all to keep away from such hypocrites.
They go hunting souls with sanctimonious sophistries
    when all the while they plot obscenities.

Orpheus: poet, magician (as well as musician), and master of the Orphic mysteries, is said to have encouraged an ascetic diet free of animal flesh.

[*Thrusting the letter at* HIPPOLYTUS]

She is dead. Do you imagine that will save you?
No, it seals your doom.
What solemn affidavits, what sworn defense,
    can outbalance the allegations in this letter?
"She hated me," you'll say,
    "bastards and true-born are natural antagonists."
What a fatuous bargainer that makes her,
    bartering her life—the dearest thing she had—
    simply out of hate for you!
Or perhaps you'll go on to say
    that this kind of hysteria is not in men
    but women are born with it.
Let me tell you,
    I have known young men
    not one whit less vulnerable than women
    when Aphrodite stirs the hot sap of youth.
They're just as helpless for all their manliness.

But why should I bandy arguments with you
    when here her body lies,
    the most clinching argument of all?
Go from this land. Go to your destruction. Go at once,
    and never come near our celestial Athens,
    nor any region where my spear holds sway.
Were I tamely to pass over your enormities,
    why, Sinis of the Isthmus would swear I never slew him
    but only bragged about it,
    and the rocks of Sciron that fret the sea
    could say I never was the scourge of pirates.
LEADER: There is no such thing as a happy human being,
    and those are last who once were first.
HIPPOLYTUS: Father, this diatribe of yours, this frenzy of soul,
    is strange and terrible.
It might seem plausible at first
    but at bottom is pure calumny.
I'm no good at public speaking.
I am more convincing among my friends,
    and not too many of them; which is natural enough. ·

Besides, among the intelligent,
    the glib demagogue ranks low enough.
Nevertheless, caught as I am in this predicament,
    I am forced to loosen my tongue.

Let me begin my defense with your original indictment—
    which you think so irrefutable.
This light that you see, this earth,
    they do not enshrine a chaster heart than mine,
    deny it though you may.
And one of the first lessons I ever learnt
    was to serve the gods;
    next, never to cultivate criminals as friends
    but only such as would be appalled at the very suggestion of
                                       evil,
    let alone of carrying it out.
I don't make fools of my comrades, Father,
    but am the same loyal friend whether they are with me or not.

If there is one thing of which I am absolutely guiltless,
    it is that which you think you've caught me at.
To this day my body is pure.
I know nothing of the act of intercourse
    except what I've heard in talk or seen in pictures.
These things leave me cold, for I have a virgin soul.
If you won't believe I'm chaste
    it's up to you to show how exactly I became unchaste.
Did I find the body of this woman irresistible?
Or did I hope to take over your establishment
    by taking over your rich wife with her fine dowry?
What a senseless fool I'd be!
Ah, but "it's so sweet to be a king!"
Not at all! Not to the unambitious man;
    only to those whom the lust for power has undermined.
I might aspire to come in first at the Hellenic Games,
    oh yes, but in politics I am content to come in second,
    and so live contentedly with the best people as my friends.
That way one enjoys the free unpressured life,
    with none of the risks of being king.

*   *   *

You've heard my arguments,
    but one thing remains to be said.
If I had a witness to my innocence,
    if this woman were alive to face me at my trial,
    a cross-examination would expose the guilty one.
As it is, I can only swear by Zeus the god of oaths,
    swear by the gravity of Mother Earth,
    that I have not so much as touched your wife,
    never wished it, never given it a thought.
Were I that kind of scoundrel
    I am ready to die for it:
    yes, die, nameless, fameless, cityless, homeless—
    a vagabond on the face of the earth,
    a rejected carcass disowned by land and sea
    till finally I am claimed by death.

If it was fear that drove this woman to end her life,
    I have no idea.
I may say no more.
She sought to save her virtue, but by vice,
    and I the virtuous have had to pay the price.
LEADER: You have said enough to overturn the charge.
    You have sworn by the gods—no paltry pledge.
THESEUS: What a wizard with words! What a trickster the
                                            fellow is!
He cuckolds his father,
    then blithely thinks cajolery will better him.
HIPPOLYTUS: And you, my father, you amaze me too.
    If you were my son and I your father,
    and you had laid a finger on my wife,
    I'd have killed you on the spot—not just banished you.
THESEUS: An excellent suggestion,
    but you'll not just die.
That's too nice a sentence you've proposed.
Death is swift and easy for a man in misery,
    but banished from your land and home,
    as you so well described,
    to wander abroad dragging out your sorrows . . .

HIPPOLYTUS: Don't tell me! You wouldn't, would you,
just hurl me from the realm,
and not even wait to hear the testimony?

THESEUS: Hurl you, yes, beyond the Atlantic Ocean if I could,
so thoroughly do I hate the sight of you.

HIPPOLYTUS: Without a trial? Without examination?
Without respect of pledge or oracle?
You'd throw me out?

THESEUS: This letter needs no prophet's seal.
It is testimony enough.
Let the birds of augury go flapping in the sky:
I wish them luck.

HIPPOLYTUS: Dear gods, must my lips be sealed
when the sacred seal of secrecy I put on them for you
is killing me?
Yes, I cannot break it
unless I break the oath I swore . . . and for no good:
it would not persuade the one I should.

THESEUS: What, not again?
Your sanctimoniousness is murdering me.
Leave this land. Just get out and go.

HIPPOLYTUS: Go where? What host would welcome me:
a wretch banished on such a charge?

THESEUS: A fellow criminal, no doubt:
one who likes to entertain wife seducers in his home.

HIPPOLYTUS: A . . . h! You stab me to the heart and brim my tears:
that I should appear to you obscene, and you believe it.

THESEUS: This sniveling—you should have done it earlier,
before you had the shameless gall to rape your father's wife.

HIPPOLYTUS: [*throwing his arms out towards the palace*]
You noble halls,
can you not shout out in my defense
and tell them I am not a sinful man?

THESEUS: A neat trick you have of sheltering behind dumb
witnesses.

[*Pointing to* PHAEDRA'*s corpse*]

Your handiwork, however, needs no voice to proclaim your
crime.

HIPPOLYTUS: Ah! if I could only stand aside and see myself,
    such tears I'd see to see such sorrow.
THESEUS: And you have a gift for worshiping yourself
    rather than for being a dutiful and filial son.
HIPPOLYTUS: Oh, my poor mother! What a bitter birth!
    Let no one I love ever be a bastard.
THESEUS: [*turning to his attendants*]
    Servants, drag the fellow away.
    Did you not hear my word of banishment?

[*Two servants advance*]

HIPPOLYTUS: Touch me if you dare, just one of you, and you'll
                                                regret it.

[*to Theseus*]

Throw me out yourself—if you have the nerve.
THESEUS: [*stalling*] Yes, I'll do just that if you won't go.
    I feel no pity for your banishment.

[THESEUS *turns on his heel and walks into the palace. The
great doors are shut as* HIPPOLYTUS *moves towards the statue
of* ARTEMIS]

HIPPOLYTUS: The verdict's fixed, my ruin's complete.
I know the truth yet know I cannot make it known.

[*Lifting his hands in prayer*]

Great daughter of Leto, virgin goddess, my favorite god,
    I am banished from Athens, that glorious city.
Farewell my town! Farewell the land of Erectheus
    and the plain of Troezen—that happy terrain
    where young men train.
I see and salute you for the last time.

[*Turning towards his entourage*]

Come, dear fellows, comrades of my age,
    godspeed me and escort me from this soil.
You'll never see a man more innocent,

though my father thinks the opposite.

[HIPPOLYTUS *leaves with his companions*]

FOURTH CHORAL LYRIC

[*The* WOMEN OF TROEZEN *are now joined by a chorus of young* HUNTSMEN. *After a halfhearted attempt to believe in the benevolence of divine providence, they give themselves over to nervous platitudes, then to despair, and finally to full-throated grief*]

STROPHE I

HUNTSMEN: A soothing thing it is to believe
   in the care of the gods
     when grief overwhelms,
And I hold in my heart the hope
   of a guiding will;
Yet when I survey the fortunes of mortals
   and how they fare
     my confidence wavers:
Everything shuttles backwards and forwards
   in the life of man.

ANTISTROPHE I

WOMEN: If heaven would only grant this prayer
   and Fate oblige it:
     riches and success,
A heart untrammeled with anguish, a mind
   not shallow but strong,
And an easy spirit that takes each day
   just as it comes
     and shapes it to each morrow;
Ah, wouldn't I then have attained the summit
   of lifelong bliss!

STROPHE II

HUNTSMEN: But I've lost, alas, my wholesome hope:
   all is frustration
   When I see the star of Athens,

that shining city,
   Cast away to an alien land
by the wrath of a father.
   Farewell for him to the sands
of my native shores;
   Farewell to the oak-green slopes of the hills
where he flew with his hounds
   Along with Artemis, the blessed,
after the quarry.

ANTISTROPHE II

WOMEN: Nevermore will he drive his trained team
   of Enetian coursers,
   Reining them in as they strain
thundering round
   The chariot tract of the course at Limna.
Nevermore will be heard
   The tireless Muse on the strings of his lyre
in his father's house.
   Nevermore will the grottoes of Artemis, deep
in the green, be decked
   With garlands. His flight has canceled the struggle
of girls for his love.

EPODE

A SINGLE WOMAN: So shall I weep tears for your ruin
and lead a lifeless life.
   And you, his sorrowful mother, how grim
was the birth you gave birth to!
   I'm incensed with the gods, oh yes!
and you three arm-linking Graces,
   How could you have let so blameless a man
be thrust from his home and his country?
LEADER: Look, I see one of Hippolytus' men hurrying to the
                                 palace.

   His face is dark.

[*A* MESSENGER *bursts in from the countryside, breathless and distraught*]

SEVENTH EPISODE

MESSENGER: Which way, ladies, should I go to find your ruler
                                                    Theseus?
Tell me if he's here. Is he in the palace?
LEADER: He is here . . . and coming out.

[THESEUS *in mourning emerges from the palace*]

MESSENGER: Theseus, I bring you news, momentous news,
    affecting you and all the citizens of Athens
    right to the ends of Troezen.
THESEUS: News? What news?
    A fresh disaster striking our twin cities?
MESSENGER: Hippolytus is dead—or as good as dead.
    He still sees the light, but all is in the balance.
THESEUS: Killed by whom?
    Doubtless by another outraged cuckold
    whose wife he ravished, as he did his father's.
MESSENGER: Destroyed by his own team of chariot thorough-
                                                    breds,
    and by those curses from your lips
    which you hurled down on your son:
    curses your ancestor granted you, Poseidon, lord of the deep.
THESEUS: Great gods! Poseidon!
    So you are my father after all: you heard my prayers . . .
But tell me, how did he die?
How did Justice club him down
    for his injustice to his father?
MESSENGER: We were combing out his horses' manes
    by the surf-battered shore, and we were weeping.
A messenger had come to tell us
    that never again would Hippolytus set foot in this land
    because most unhappily you had banished him.
Then Hippolytus himself arrived
    bringing the same tearful story to us by the sea,
    and with him was a crowd of young companions.
At length he ceased lamenting, saying:
    "What is the point of these outpourings?
My father has to be obeyed.

Harness the horses to my chariot.
This city is no longer mine."
Every man of us snapped into action,
   and hardly sooner said than done we'd harnessed the horses
   and led them to their master.
He took hold of the reins at the chariot rail
   and planted his feet in the foot rests firmly.
Then, before proceeding,
   he stretched out his open palms in prayer to the gods:
"Zeus, if I am a perfidious man
   I'd rather not live.
May my father come to know how he has wronged me—
   if not while I behold the light,
   at least when I am dead."

Then taking the whip in his hand
   he touched each horse in turn.
We servants near the chariot
   kept pace with our master, holding on to the bridles
   till we came to the Argos-Epidaurian road.
Just as we entered a deserted stretch
   where the shoreline beyond the Troezen border
   dips down to the Saronic Sea,
   a growl like Zeus's thunder broke from the ground
   in a petrifying rumble.
The horses' heads jerked up, their ears pricking.
We were seized with foreboding—
   quite unable to place the sound.
Then with our eyes fixed on the sea-crashing shore,
   we saw a towering tidal wave columning up into the sky.
It blotted out the Scironian headland.
It hid the Isthmus and the cliff of Asclepius.
Rearing up higher and higher and snorting with spume
   it swelled along the shore in a mist of spray
   to where the four-horse chariot was.
As the giant wave broke
   it belched from its surge a bull:
   a paralyzing monster whose bellowing
   thundered and reverberated over the countryside.

The apparition was too terrible to see.

Panic, uncontrollable panic, seized the animals,
    but their master, experienced horseman as he is,
    reined them in hard with both hands,
  . straining like an oarsman at the oar
    and leaning his whole weight backwards
    with the reins twisted round him.
But the horses, biting down on their steel bits,
    bolted away with him,
    responding neither to their driver's hand
    nor to the tight traces and the hard-braked car.

Each time that he managed to rein them in
    towards smoother ground, the bull loomed up in front
    and headed him off, maddening the four-horse team with
                                                    terror.
In their frenzied career
    the horses veered towards the rocks,
    but the bull sidled alongside the chariot
    and finally pressed it into a crash.
The wheels struck a rock and the chariot overturned.
Pandemonium followed:
    the axles with their linchpins exploded into the sky.
The unfortunate youth,
    inextricably entangled in the reins, was dragged along—
    his dear head battered against the rocks and his body shredded.
He was screaming piteously:
    "Halt, halt, you thoroughbreds of my own stable,
    don't dash me to pieces . . . Oh, that curse of my father!
    Save me, someone, save me! I am innocent."

Of course we tried to save him, but many were left behind.
He had cut himself loose somehow
    from the tight coil of the reins
    and lay where he had fallen, breathing still a little life.
As to the horses—they had vanished;
    so too that monster freak of a bull . . .
    vanished somewhere in the rocky plain.

[*The* MESSENGER *gathers his cloak around him, preparing to go*]

I am only a slave in your household, Sire,
    but there is one thing you can never make me do:
    believe your son was guilty of that vile charge;
    no, not even if the whole race of womankind
    goes and hangs itself;
    not even if somebody pins indictments up
    on every pine tree on Mount Ida.
I know no nobler man.
LEADER: This is the consummation of bad news.
    There's no escape from doom when doom's ordained.
THESEUS: Bad news that pleases me:
    sufferings of the man I've come to hate . . .
    and yet, and yet, I mustn't forget
    my filiality to the gods and that he was my son;
    which leaves me neither glad nor sad.
MESSENGER: Well then, are we to bring the poor victim here?
    What do you want us to do with him?
If you will allow me to say it, sir,
    you should not be heartless towards your stricken boy.
THESEUS: Bring him here to me.
    I want with my own eye to see the man
    who would not confess to ravishing my wife.
I want to pronounce over him
    the ineluctable sentence of the gods.

[*The* MESSENGER *goes off*]

FIFTH CHORAL LYRIC

[*The* CHORUS *of Troezen Women, crushed by* APHRODITE*'s ruthless assault on an innocent victim—and all because of* PHAEDRA*'s thwarted passion—are nevertheless forced to pay homage to the universal power of love*]

CHORUS (Troezen Women):
    O Aphrodite you
    shape the immalleable hearts
       of gods and of mortals:

                    *   *   *

You and that imp with diaphanous wings,
   flitting around his quarry
      hovering over the earth
         and the salty musical boom of the sea.

Yes, Eros the goldenly-winged one
   ever ready to madden
      and enchant the hearts he attacks.

He enthralls young beasts in the mountains
   and creatures of the deep:
Whatever this earth gives life to,
   whatever the sunbeams strike,
      including man.

You reign over all, Aphrodite,
   you alone have sovereign sway.

   [ARTEMIS *appears aloft*]

              LYRIC MONOLOGUE

ARTEMIS: [*chanting*] I call on you, noble son of Aegeus.
   I daughter of Leto address you.
   Listen to me closely.

Theseus, you miserable man,
Why do you gloat over slaying your son
   Utterly wrongly,

Believing the unproved lies of your wife?
Terrible now is the proof that is proven.
Why are you not in Tartarus, hiding
Under the earth, cringing in shame?
Why not be turning into a bird
And fly away from this vale of calamities?
For there isn't a place for you anywhere now
   Among men of goodwill.

   [*End of Lyric Monologue*]

EIGHTH EPISODE

Theseus, hear this exegesis of your sorrows.
I promise no salve, only pain.
I am here to show you the pure heart of your boy
    and so let him die with honor.
And I must explain to you the fevered impulse of your wife
    and in sort her noble character.

Spurred on by that deity
    whom those of us who love virginity cannot abide,
    she was goaded into passion for your boy.
Through sheer self-control
    she tried to vanquish Aphrodite
    but was foiled by the unwitting machinations of her nurse;
    who under an oath of secrecy
    revealed her mistress' love-pangs to your son.
But he, being an honest man,
    neither yielded to her scheming
    nor broke his pledge of secrecy when victimized by you,
    for he is a godly man.
But she,
    dreading the charge of adultery,
    penned that fraudulent letter
    and through deceit destroyed your son—for you believed her.
THESEUS: Great God!
ARTEMIS: Stung to the heart, eh, Theseus?
    Then listen quietly to what happened next
    and let your lamentations swell.
Those curses of Poseidon—remember them?
Well, one you leveled at your child—
    you monstrous man,
    when it could have been against an enemy.
Your father, Poseidon, king of the deep,
    with only good intentions to honor his word, consented.
But both of us, he and I, consider your action wrong.
For you proceeded, without examination, without proof,
    without auguries and without waiting for the revealing hand of
                                           time,

to release curses against your son and kill him.
THESEUS: Great mistress, I deserve to perish.
ARTEMIS: What you did was criminal,
    nevertheless, there is a way for you to be forgiven.
It was Aphrodite, after all, in a splurge of hate,
    who made this whole disaster come to pass;
    but according to divine protocol
    no god can go against the fixed purpose of another:
    we have to stand aloof.
Were it not for this and my respect for Zeus,
    I never would have sunk so low as to allow a man to die
    who was my favorite among mortals.

As to your vicious blunder, first this:
    ignorance acquits you.
Next, your wife by dying made it impossible
    to disprove her charge, and so she forced your credence.
Finally, in all this tragedy,
    you are the one who suffers most, though my grief too is great.
For godhead in nowise delights in the demise of the good.
It is the wicked we wipe out—
    with their children and their homes.

[HIPPOLYTUS *is half-carried in between two men*]

CHANTED DIALOGUE

CHORUS: See here comes the stricken one,
    His stripling flesh in shreds,
    His battered golden head.
    What misery for this house!
    What pangs of double grief
    Suffered in these halls,
    Suffered from on high!
HIPPOLYTUS: A . . . h! the pain!
    I am shattered, piteously shattered,
    Wronged by the curse of a father so wrong:
    O . . . h! my head, the shooting spasms!
    Deep in my head the splitting twinge.
    Let me rest this sinking frame.

I detest you now, my chariot team:
You who were fed by my own hands,
You who have smashed me, killed me. Oh!

Tenderly, servants, by the gods, I beg,
Hold up this mangled carcass of mine . . .
Who's on my right? Be careful, you.
Gently, don't jar me. Hold me up:
The blighted cripple lost and cursed
By his father's mistake. Zeus, Zeus,
Are you witnessing this: me the modest,
Me the pious one, I who excelled
In temperance? Do you see me going
Down into Hades, my life ground down?

How uselessly I tried to respect
The rights of mankind . . . Oh! Oh!
The terrible pain is on me again.
Put me down. Let me go. Ah! Aah!
Come, Death, come, beautiful healer!
Finish my misery . . . Give me a sword
To slash my life and put it to bed.

Oh, that inexorable curse of my father!
And the evil spell bred by some bloody
Family sins of long, long ago—
It has hatched again now, refuses to wait,
Hurries towards me: I who am innocent.
How sad! How sad! How can I sever
My life from this ruthless saddle of pain?

Come, Death, somnolent comrade!
Come with your black necessary night!

[*End of Chanted Dialogue.* HIPPOLYTUS *collapses into the arms of his companions.* ARTEMIS, *still aloft, moves nearer*]

ARTEMIS: Poor blighted boy, yoked to disaster!
    Destroyed by your own nobility.
HIPPOLYTUS: Ah, the fragrance of divinity!

Sweet breath and balm to my dying body.
Is Artemis the goddess really here?

ARTEMIS: She is, dear suffering one.
She loves you most of all the gods.

HIPPOLYTUS: Lady, you see me as I am—a broken man.

ARTEMIS: I see, but as a god may not shed tears for you.

HIPPOLYTUS: Your master of the hunt, your worshiper, is gone.

ARTEMIS: Gone, but to me most precious in his going.

HIPPOLYTUS: Your steeds will miss their groom, your effigies
their guardian.

ARTEMIS: Aphrodite, the unscrupulous, has done it all.

HIPPOLYTUS: Now I know. I know the power that cut me down.

ARTEMIS: She blamed your neglect of her. She loathed your
chastity.

HIPPOLYTUS: In a triple ruin, I see now, how Aphrodite triumphs.

ARTEMIS: Yes, your father and his wife and you.

HIPPOLYTUS: So now I mourn my father's ill fate too.

ARTEMIS: He was duped by a scheming deity.

HIPPOLYTUS: Ah, unhappy father, so engulfed in sorrow!

THESEUS: [*stepping towards* HIPPOLYTUS]
In ruin, my son. Life has no more joys for me.

HIPPOLYTUS: A tragic error! I mourn for you more than for
myself.

THESEUS: Would that I were dying, my child, instead of you.

HIPPOLYTUS: What a bitter gift your father, Poseidon, offered
you!

THESEUS: Curse that cursed prayer! I wish it had never left my
lips.

HIPPOLYTUS: In your white-hot rage you would have killed me
anyway.

THESEUS: I would. The gods had undermined my mind.

HIPPOLYTUS: If only mortals could cast spells on gods!

ARTEMIS: Enough!
Though you be buried in the gloom below
you shall not go unavenged against the goddess Aphrodite.
From this good right arm of mine
I shall loose my unerring arrows,
loose them on some other mortal, some pet of hers,
and avenge myself through him.

And you, sad victim, to make up for your sufferings,
   on you I shall bestow the highest honors in the town of Troezen.
Unwedded girls before their bridal night
   shall shear their locks for you, and in ages to come
   you shall reap a bountiful harvest of tears for you.
Young girls ever afterwards
   shall sing their elegies in memory of you,
   and the story of Phaedra's love for you
   shall never fade into mute oblivion.

   [*She turns to* THESEUS]

And you, son of ancient Aegeus,
   take your boy into your arms and clasp him to you.
Unwittingly you killed him.
Mankind led on by gods err all too easily.

   [*Turning to* HIPPOLYTUS]

You, Hippolytus,
   I urge you not to hate your father:
   this death of yours was destiny . . . And now, farewell.
I may not look upon the dead,
   nor smudge my eyes with the death throes of the dying:
   for I see that you are close to going.

   [ARTEMIS *fades from sight*]

HIPPOLYTUS: Farewell, blest virgin, as you go,
   our lasting friendship so easily released!
My father, as you bid me, I forgive.
I have always responded to your bidding.

   [THESEUS *steps towards* HIPPOLYTUS, *and gently removing*
   him from the support of his companions, takes him into his
   arms]

A . . . h! the dark is curtaining my vision.
Hold me, Father, lift me up.
THESEUS: No, my son, you must not go. Would you leave me
                                 lost?

HIPPOLYTUS: I am slipping. I see the portals of the dead.
THESEUS: And you would leave me with murder on my soul?
HIPPOLYTUS: No, not that . . . I absolve you from my death.
THESEUS: You mean that? You acquit me of all blood?
HIPPOLYTUS: By Artemis, I swear it—goddess of the bow.
THESEUS: Best beloved, how noble to your father you have
proved!
HIPPOLYTUS: Pray for legitimate sons as loyal as I am.
THESEUS: I weep for your great soul: devoted and so good.
HIPPOLYTUS: Farewell, my father—forever and farewell.
THESEUS: No no! Do not leave me, son. Bear up!
HIPPOLYTUS: It's over, Father . . . I am . . . gone. Quickly cover . . .
my face.

[HIPPOLYTUS *expires in* THESEUS' *arms*]

THESEUS: O glorious Athens, Kingdom of Pallas,
what a man you have lost and how great my loss!
Aphrodite, the evil you have done
shall never in my life be gone.
CHORUS: Out of the blue a blow has struck:
A common sorrow for all the city.
Many shall be the tears that fall.
The tragedies of the great ones after all
Are the most compelling tales of all.

[THESEUS *with his retinue, together with the* CHORUS *of Troezen Women and the* CHORUS *of Huntsmen, moves away in a
slow lugubrious march, to the strains of a dirge, carrying the
body of* HIPPOLYTUS]

ION

—⁓⁓⁓—

IΩN

For India and Duncan-Krishna Roche

The date of *Ion* is uncertain, but it comes possibly after *Heracles*, which would put it between 420 and 410 B.C., when Euripides was in his middle sixties.

We have here the picture of an attractive young man brought up since babyhood in the temple precincts—as sheltered, we might say, as a convent girl—who in the course of the story grows up. Without repudiating his open, ingenuous nature he changes from a sweet, honest stripling into a mature human being: indeed, one hardened enough to contemplate murder.

The play is sometimes considered tragicomedy and is perhaps unique in Greek drama in the way it breaks with the tradition of a grandly simple structure and pursues a plot almost Shakespearean in its complexity. As to the gods, Euripides as usual levels them down to the ordinariness of mortals. Apollo in particular, far from exhibiting the type of moral excellence one expects, and though he escapes the stricture of being something of a feisty bungler like Heracles in the *Alcestis*, nevertheless has to be rescued in the end from obloquy by the special pleading of Pallas Athena. He is in fact not present during the play.

CHARACTERS

HERMES
ION, son of Creusa and Apollo; caretaker of Apollo's shrine at Delphi
CHORUS, women attending Creusa
CREUSA, wife of Xuthus and queen of Athens
XUTHUS, king of Athens
OLD MAN, retainer of Creusa
SERVANT of Creusa
PYTHIAN PRIESTESS
PALLAS ATHENA
TEMPLE GUARDS
SERVANTS of Xuthus

TIME AND SETTING

Some nineteen years ago, Creusa was seduced by Apollo and bore a son, whom, for fear of her father, she abandoned in a cave. Hermes rescued the baby and put him in charge of the temple priestess at Delphi, where he was reared and came to serve in Apollo's shrine. Meanwhile, Creusa has married Xuthus, but the couple are childless and determine to go to Delphi and ask for offspring.

It is dawn outside the temple at Delphi. Hermes strides into the arena.

PROLOGUE

HERMES: Atlas, who carries the heavens—
    the dwelling of the gods—
    on his bronze-strong back,
    sired my mother Maia from a goddess
    and she bore me to Zeus the Great.
I am the divine ones' errand boy
    and I've come here to Delphi, where Apollo has his seat
    at the very navel of the earth
    and gives forth oracles to man,
    uttering without number
    those things that are and those that are not yet.

In Greece there is a city not without renown
    called after Pallas Athena—she of the gold-tipped spear—
    and there it was that Apollo
    forced his love on Creusa, Erechtheus' child:
    forced it in a cave under the hill of Pallas,
    near those northerly crags in the land of the Athenians
    which the Attic rulers call "the Beetling Cliffs."
Never telling her father,
    who was a friend of the god,
    she carried to conclusion
    the fruit of her womb.
And when her time was come
    she bore at home a baby boy,
    then took him to the very cave where she and the god had lain,

and exposed the infant there to die (or so she thought)
   recessed in the lightly rocking enclave of a cradle.

Even so, she kept up one ancestral custom
   which dated back to Erichthonius,
   the earth-born one,
   whom Athena furnished with a brace of snakes
   to be his bodyguard
   when she handed him over
   to the daughters of Aglaurus to look after.
That is the origin of the Erechthid tradition
   of putting gold-hammered snakes in nurseries.
So did Creusa hang around her boy
   such trinkets as a girl might have
   and left him there to die.

It was then that Apollo, who is my brother, said:
   "Go, brother, to the people of glorious Athens—
   you know Athena's city well—
   and there from the hollows of a rock
   rescue a newborn baby.
Take him with his cradle and all his baby gear
   to my oracle at Delphi, and dump him on my doorstep there.
You may as well know—the child is mine.
   As to the rest, I'll take care of it."

I did everything my brother Loxias* asked:
   went and got the basket and put the baby
   on the very steps of this selfsame shrine,
   flipping open the cradle lid
   so that the baby could be seen.

Now the priestess enters the temple of the god
   just as the disk of the sun begins to ride,
   and when she beheld the newborn babe
   she was outraged that some Delphian slut
   had had the nerve to toss out her secret brat
   onto the god's own temple steps.

Loxias: Loxias, Phoebus, and Apollo are all the same.

At first she was all for flinging it away—
    away and out of the holy precincts—but compassion
    cast out callousness . . . (the god, of course,
    was not about to let his child be jettisoned from his own
                                 house),
    and she picked the baby up and began to care for it.
She had no inkling, naturally, that Apollo had engendered it
    nor who his mother was;
    and the boy now has no idea who his parents are.

The lad romped and played
    among the altars of his temple home,
    but when he grew to manhood the Delphinians
    appointed him custodian of Apollo's gold
    and trusted him with care of everything.
So he continues to this day
    within the god's temple leading a pious life.

Meanwhile Creusa, the mother of this young man,
    has married Xuthus . . . This is how it happened.
A fierce war had broken out
    between the Athenians and the people of Chalcedon
    (those who hold Euboea), and because Xuthus
    supported Athens and helped them on to victory
    he was honored with the reward of Creusa's hand,
    though he was not of their race but Achaean-born:
    son of Aeolus son of Zeus.
But he and Creusa, though they've tried and tried,
    are childless. That is why they've come to Apollo's oracle
    to plead for children.
Apollo is directing their destiny in this.
His plan is obvious, as you'll see.
For when Xuthus comes into the temple
    he'll hand his own son to him and say
    Xuthus is the father.
The boy accordingly
    will come into his mother's house
    and Creusa will acknowledge him.
This way Apollo keeps his love affair a secret
    and the boy regains his rights.

Ion is the name he has given him—
     founder of Ionia in the East—
     a name he will be called by throughout Hellas.

But now I'll slip away into that laurel thicket
     and watch how the boy's destiny unfolds.
I see him coming with branches of sweet bay,
     this, Apollo's son,
     to decorate the portals of the temple.
Of all the gods I am the first to call him Ion:
     the name that shall be his.

[*As* HERMES *slips into the bushes, the temple doors open and*
ION *steps jubilantly into the arena, followed by servants car-*
rying his bow and arrow. He is lightly dressed in a short
chiton, and his head is crowned with laurel. He turns into the
rays of the early sun as it breaks through the twin peaks of
Parnassus]

PARADOS OR ENTRY SONG

ION: Gaze on the blazing car of the sun
     Whose rays go streaming over the earth
     And burn the stars' light from the skies
     In flight until mysterious night.
     Parnassus' lonely peaks are tinged,
     Shining on mankind with spokes of sun.

     From the aromatic desert drifts
     The scent of myrrh to Apollo's courts
     As on the sacred tripod sits
     The Delphic priestess poised to chant
     For the pilgrim Greeks the oracles
     Apollo whispers in her ears.

     But come, you Delphians, Apollo's devout,
     Go to Castalia's silver springs
     And dip yourselves in its crystal dews.
     Then enter the shrine with lips all purged
     Of hurtful converse. Set your tongues

As paragons of gracious speech
To those who would consult the god.

And I for my part shall fulfill
Those duties I have since childhood held:
With sprays of bay and sacred wreaths
I'll sweeten the pathway of Apollo.
I'll sprinkle his floor with water drops.
I'll aim my arrows and chase away
Those flocks of birds that foul his offerings.
Mother or father I have none:
I serve my nurse—Apollo's shrine.

[*The rhythm changes into verses of strophe and antistrophe as*
ION, *in a kind of dance, begins to sweep, arrange, clean the
temple precincts, singing as he does so*]

STROPHE I
You brush of newly plucked bay
   You serve him too,
Come, sweep the temple threshold
   Of Apollo's shrine:
You who throve in perennial
Gardens where chrismed waters
Brim in living rills
Bedewing the holy leaves
   Of myrtle groves:
Day after day I use you
   Just when the sun
Beats with his lifting wing
   And I begin
    My daily task—
To sweep Apollo's shrine.

Healer, Apollo, Healer!
Thrice-blessed son of Leto,

ANTISTROPHE I
How I bless this duty
I do before your temple!

Oh yes, Apollo,
How I honor
Your home and oracle
And glory in my task!
My dedicated service
   Is not to mortals
   But immortals:
   A blessed work
   That never tires.
For Phoebus is like a father,
   So I praise him,
So I call him "father":
   Phoebus Apollo,
   Lord and master
   Of this temple.

EPODE

Healer! Phoebus! Healer!
Thrice-blessed son of Leto!
Now I've finished sweeping
With my bay-sweet broomstick
Let me sprinkle water
From a golden ewer:
Water pure as dewdrops
Brimming from Castalia's
Spring and chaste as I am.
   Oh may my service
     To Apollo
Never cease; or cede
Only to further bliss.

[*Suddenly* ION *thrusts away his broom and urn of lustral waters and, snatching up his bow and arrows, runs through the temple gardens waving his arms and shouting. In an exuberant mime he makes a show of warding off the various birds that begin to alight*]

STROPHE II

Bah! the feathered hordes are back, swarming
   From their roosting on Parnassus. Stop it!

Get off those cornices; these gilded courts
Are not your lavatories . . . And you, you eagle
Of Zeus—are you back too? Just wait, you
Talon-tearing snatcher, strongest of birds,
I'll have an arrow at you. And what's this?
A swan cruising down towards the altar.
Get those crimson feet of yours away
Or your swan song, be it as melodious
As Apollo, will not save you from my arrows.
So, off with you! Away—away
To the lake of Delos, or else your blood
Will flow as musically as your final melody.

ANTISTROPHE II

Ha! What's this new bird arriving?
No doubt you want to make your nest of sticks
And straw under the eaves for your fledglings. Yes?
The twang of my bow will make you keep your distance.
Are you listening? Go and do your breeding
Among the deltas of Alpheus or
Somewhere on the wooded Isthmus, not
Here, besmirching the sacrificial offerings
And temple of Apollo; though to shoot you
Is against my principles, because you birds
Let us know the will of the gods. But I,
Apollo's servant, have my duties and
Am dedicated to my tasks, especially
To one by whom I get my living here.

[*End of Parados. From the road that leads into Delphi a congeries of young women appears: they are* CREUSA's *attendants. As they scurry about excitedly, commenting on the beauty of the temple buildings,* ION *with folded arms stands aloof in the shadows, smiling*]

CHORAL CONVERSE

STROPHE III

LEADER: So not in holy Athens only
Do the gods have lovely courts with noble

Columns or pay homage to Apollo
As patron of roads,
  He features here as well
Does Leto's son
  Gleaming on this twin facade.

[*The* LEADER*'s astonishment is echoed severally by the rest of
the* CHORUS]

One: Take a look at this, Zeus's son
  Slaying the monstrous snake of Lerna
  With a golden scimitar . . .
    Over there, dear.

ANTISTROPHE III

Another: Yes, and next to him is someone
  Lifting up a blazing torch.
Another: Is that the story I embroidered:
  Iolaus,
  Pal of Heracles, Zeus's son,
  Who shared . . .
Another: With him his several labors—yes?
Another: Oh, do look at this: a man
  Astraddle a winged horse, cutting
  Down a fire-breathing monster
    With three bodies.

STROPHE IV

Another: My eyes are stretched in every direction.
  Just look at that battle of giants in marble!
    Girls, we could stare forever.
Another: And that woman standing over Enceladus
  Shaking her shield of Gorgons' heads—
      See it?
Another: I'm looking at my goddess, Pallas.
Another: Why, so it is!
  And isn't that Zeus with the mighty thunderbolt
    Flaring at both ends?
Another: It certainly is—
  With Mimas, that nasty man,

Being frizzled to a cinder.
Another: And there's orgiastic Bacchus
   Slaughtering yet another earth-child
   With his thyrsus, ivy-crowned
     And never meant for battle.

[*The women become aware of* ION *surveying them from the porch of the temple, and they accost him*]

ANTISTROPHE IV

LEADER: Sir, you standing by the temple,
   Is it all right to enter the sanctuary
With bare feet?
ION: No, my friends.
LEADER: And sir . . .
ION: Yes, say what you have to say.
LEADER: Is it true that this
Shrine of Apollo
   Houses the navel of the earth?
ION: Yes, smothered in garlands
And guarded by Gorgons.
LEADER: That's what we've always been told.
ION: If you have offered some blessed cake
    At the temple entrance and have questions
   For Apollo, you may approach
   The altar steps, but you may not pass
   Into the shrine itself unless
You have sacrificed a sheep.

LEADER: I understand. And the rules of the god
   we are not about to disobey.
   Our eyes can feast on what's outside.
ION: Yes, let them feast on everything.
LEADER: Our mistress allowed us to come out here
   and gaze at this god's sanctuary.
ION: You are the servants of—what particular house?
LEADER: She is a queen, our mistress, and
   was born and lives in a palace in Athens.
   But here she is, the one you ask of.

[CREUSA, *with attendants, walks with heavy steps into the*

temple arena towards ION. *She wears a traveling dress and a broad-brimmed hat and is veiled.* ION *takes a step forward, bowing*]

FIRST EPISODE

ION: Lady, whoever you are you have distinction:
a poise that reveals your character . . .
One can always tell if someone's wellborn just by their bearing.

[*Taking a closer look*]

But what's this? You surprise me.
Why the downcast eyes, and tears on the noble cheeks?
What troubles you, my lady?
Why, when other eyes rejoice to see this sanctuary,
do yours fill with tears?
CREUSA: My friend, I think it no rudeness in one like you
to be astonished by my tears.
The truth is, the sight of Apollo's house
jerked my memory back down an ancient path.
I stood here but my thoughts were back at home.
Ah, what we women endure when the gods go sinning!
Indeed, to whom shall we plead our cause
when our own masters are our ruin?
ION: Such strange sadness, lady! Why?
CREUSA: It's nothing . . . I just let loose my smart . . .
I'll be quiet now. Think no more of it.
ION: But who are you? Where do you come from?
What's your family, and what must we call you?
CREUSA: My name is Creusa. Erechtheus was my father.
The city of Athens is my home.
ION: A famous city and noble parentage!
I'm in awe of you, my lady.
CREUSA: That is where my blessings end, my friend.
ION: Please then tell me this: is the story true that . . . ?
CREUSA: What exactly do you want to know, my friend?
ION: Well, did your father's father really spring from Earth?
CREUSA: Erichthonius? Yes. Though little good that does me.

ION: But did Athena really lift him out of the Earth?
CREUSA: She did: into her virgin arms. She did not give him birth.
ION: That's the way he's usually shown; but did she hand him
over . . .
CREUSA: . . . to the daughters of Cecrops? yes, provided they did
not look at him.
ION: But the girls went and opened the cradle—so I've heard.
CREUSA: And died for it. The rocks ran red with blood.
ION: [*pondering this*]
Really! . . . And another thing: is it true or false that . . .
CREUSA: Go on. I have time to spare.
ION: . . . that your father Erechtheus sacrificed your sisters?
CREUSA: Without a qualm: for his country's sake.
ION: How were you the sister that survived?
CREUSA: I was a baby in my mother's arms.
ION: Then did the Earth really gape and gulp your father down?
CREUSA: Yes, in one stroke the sea god's trident finished him.*
ION: [*after further thought*]
Is there a place there called the Beetling Cliffs?
CREUSA: [*drawing in her breath*] What makes you ask? . . .

[*Aside*]

Oh the memory!
ION: It's a spot honored by the Pythian wild fire of the Pythian
god.†
CREUSA: Honored, indeed! I wish I had never seen the place.
ION: How can you abhor a place the god holds dear?
CREUSA: Let it pass . . . That cave and I are privy to a shameful
story.
ION: You are married to a man of Athens, madam, are you not?
CREUSA: Yes, but my husband is no citizen. He's from abroad.
ION: Who then? He must be of noble birth.
CREUSA: Xuthus, son of Aeolus and descended from Zeus.
ION: But an alien. How could he marry a native?
CREUSA: Well, Euboea is a city-state neighboring Athens and . . .
ION: I know: separated so they say by a sleeve of sea.

---

*The sea god Poseidon was also the patron of earthquakes.
†*Pythian god:* Apollo.

CREUSA: . . . and Xuthus sacked it with the help of Cecrops' sons.

ION: So he came as an ally, and your hand was his reward?

CREUSA: A war dowry, yes: the prize won with his spear.

ION: Is your husband with you or have you come to the oracle alone?

CREUSA: I'm with my husband but he's visiting the oracle of Trophonius.

ION: As a sightseer or gone to ask a question?

CREUSA: He has a single question for both Trophonius and Apollo.

ION: Is it about fields and crops or about children?

CREUSA: We've long been married but we have no children.

ION: No children? So you've never had a child?

CREUSA: [hedging] A childlessness of which Apollo is aware.

ION: Unhappy woman, blest and then unblest by fate!

CREUSA: [surveying him] And you—who are you? Your mother must be proud.

ION: Slave of the god they call me, and, madam, so I am.

CREUSA: A city's offering, or sold by someone?

ION: All I know is: I belong to Loxias.

CREUSA: Then it's my turn to pity you, my friend.

ION: For what? Not knowing my parents or where I am from?

CREUSA: Do you live in the temple here or under your own roof?

ION: The god's house is my home, all of it: I can sleep anywhere.

CREUSA: Did you come to this shrine as a boy or as a young man?

ION: A baby, they say—those who seem to know.

CREUSA: What woman of Delphi suckled you?

ION: I never had a breast to suckle. The woman who cared for me . . .

CREUSA: Yes, poor baby, who? [Aside] How sadness and the sad find each other!

ION: The prophetess of Apollo. I think of her as mother.

CREUSA: But how did you subsist before you came to manhood?

ION: The altars and the stream of pilgrims kept me fed.

CREUSA: And your wretched mother—who on earth was she?

ION: Probably some poor discarded woman.

CREUSA: But you make a living, and you are well dressed.

ION: My clothes come from the god I serve.

CREUSA: And you never set out to find your parents?

ION: Lady, I don't have a single clue.

CREUSA: How sad! . . . I know another woman who was cheated
like your mother.

ION: Who was she? She might help me to bear with things.

CREUSA: She is the reason I came here before my husband did.

ION: So what is your question? I am at your disposal, madam.

CREUSA: I want to ask Apollo an oracle in private.

ION: Just tell me, and leave the rest to us.

CREUSA: This is my story, listen . . . No, no, I am ashamed.

ION: Then nothing can be done. Shame is a hopeless deity.

CREUSA: [with a pause to muster courage]
    I have a friend, and Phoebus lay with her she says.

ION: Phoebus seduced a woman? No, my friend, don't tell me
that.

CREUSA: And she bore the god a child without her father knowing.

ION: It cannot be. Some man got her into trouble and she's
ashamed.

CREUSA: She insists, and what she went through was pitiable.

ION: How so, if her lover was a god?

CREUSA: But the baby she bore she threw out from her home.

ION: Threw out? Then where's the baby now—still alive?

CREUSA: Nobody knows. That's what I want to ask the oracle.

ION: If he no longer exists, how did he perish?

CREUSA: Poor mite. Wild beasts killed him—or so she suspects.

ION: What evidence is there for that?

CREUSA: She went to the spot she left him at and found him gone.

ION: Were there any drops of blood along the path?

CREUSA: None, she says, though she scrutinized the ground.

ION: How long ago was the baby killed?

CREUSA: He'd be about your age if he were alive.

ION: It was not fair of the god, and I feel for the mother.

CREUSA: I know. She never had another child.

[There is a pause while ION wrestles with his unwillingness to
believe Apollo guilty]

ION: What if Phoebus took him and brought him up in secret?

CREUSA: That would be unjust: to hug that pleasure to himself.

ION: Sad! Sad! And so very like my own plight.

CREUSA: And I expect your poor mother also pines for you.

ION: Don't revive a long-forgotten sorrow.

CREUSA: I'll say no more . . . Now, about my question . . .

ION: Which contains a serious flaw, you know.

CREUSA: What was not a serious flaw for that unhappy woman?

ION: But how can the god's oracle undo the god's own secret?

CREUSA: Isn't his tripod without reserve meant for every Greek?

ION: But you'd only embarrass him—broadcast his shame.

CREUSA: Which is nothing to the shame of the woman he
wronged.

ION: No one at this oracle will answer that.
If Apollo were proved guilty in his own house
he'd quite naturally exact some penalty from his critic.
So, my lady, do not proceed.
There cannot be an oracle against the god of oracles.
Any attempt to pressure unwilling gods
to reveal what they do not want to reveal—
whether by the sacrifice of sheep upon their altars
or by the flight of birds—
would be the height of foolishness.
Reluctant gods, my lady, can only give reluctant gifts.
They give nothing well if not willingly.

LEADER: Innumerable the number of human woes
no matter how they differ in their form:
you would be lucky if you found a single happy human being.

CREUSA: [lifting up her arms towards the temple]
And you, Apollo,
how you have misbehaved and misbehave
towards her who is not here herself but pleads!
You did not save your son as save you should.
And you the prophet will not prophesy
and let the questing mother know about her boy,
so raise a monument to him if he no longer lives;
and if he is alive . . . Ah! I must not dwell on that:
the god himself is set against my learning what I want to
know.

[CREUSA turns in the direction of the road from the country,
where a man is seen approaching]

My friend, I see my noble husband Xuthus coming
   after his visit to the cavern of Trophonius.
Breathe not a word of what we've talked about
   or I shall be put to shame for meddling in hidden things
   and our whole design would be misinterpreted.
How hard it is for woman to deal with men!
They lump the good and the bad together
   and find us all a pest . . . It is our lot.

[XUTHUS, *followed by servants and retainers, strides in. He
has the erect resolute bearing of a soldier, and with his handsome himation thrown over the left shoulder and fastened with
a large gold brooch on the right, he cuts something of a
swashbuckling figure. Raising his hand in salute to the temple,
he then bows to his wife*]

XUTHUS: All greetings first to the god,
   as is his due, and then of course to you, my wife . . .

[*He pauses as he sees the anxiety in* CREUSA*'s eyes*]

But has my late coming made you anxious?
CREUSA: No, but you were in my thoughts.
   Now tell me, what revelation do you bring
   from the oracle of Trophonius?
   What hopes of children have we from our seed?
XUTHUS: He did not think fit to anticipate the god,
   but this he said: that neither you nor I
   would leave the oracle without a child.
CREUSA: [*throwing open her arms in appeal*] O Lady Mother of
                                Apollo,
   vouchsafe success to this our coming.
   May our former dealings with your son
   bring about a happier ending soon.
XUTHUS: Amen to that! . . . But who here represents the oracle?
ION: [*stepping forward*] Outside the temple, I do;
   inside, the duty falls on others:
   those, sir, who are seated round the tripod—
   the noblest citizens of Delphi, chosen by lot.
XUTHUS: Good! That is all I want to know.

Now I'll go inside,
   for I hear that the sacrificial victim for all the pilgrims
   already has been felled before the altar.
This day, this auspicious day,
   I want to hear the god's response, the oracle.

[*Turning to* CREUSA]

You, my wife,
   with sprigs of laurel in your hands,
   must visit all the shrines
   and pray the gods that from Apollo's house
   I shall return with happy promise of children.
CREUSA: It shall be! It shall!

[CREUSA *watches* XUTHUS *enter the temple, then extends her
hands in supplication*]

If Loxias will redress his former wrongs,
   though he can never entirely be my friend,
   I shall accept whatever he foretells, for he is a god.

[CREUSA *with one or two attendants walks away*]

ION: What makes this woman
   so full of dark and damaging hints against the god?
Is it because she loves the woman for whom she is consulting
   or does she hide some guilty secret?
But what concern of mine is Erechtheus' daughter?
She is nothing to me. No.
So let me go with these golden ewers
   and fill the stoops with holy water.
But I must scold Apollo.
What *is* the matter with him?
Ravishing girls and then deserting them!
Sneakily making babies, then leaving them to die!
That's not you, Apollo, surely!
You have the power, so follow virtue.
Wicked men the gods punish,
   so how can you yourselves flout the laws
   you've made for mortal man?

If the day ever comes
   (I know the notion is absurd)
   when you gods must pay the price to human beings
   for all your rapings and your whorings,
   you and Poseidon, yes and Zeus himself the king of heaven,
   will bankrupt every temple to meet the bill.
To chase your fancies without thought is wrong.
One simply can't go on blaming human beings
   for copying the glorious conduct of the gods:
   blame the setters of example.

   [ION *goes into the temple. The women of the* CHORUS *address
   an impassioned eulogy and plea to Pallas Athena and
   Artemis as patrons of childbirth to use their influence to get
   a favorable oracle. Then they sing of the joy of children,
   ending with an address to Pan, in whose cave* CREUSA *was
   raped*]

FIRST CHORAL ODE

CHORUS: You, Athena, our own Athena,
   Born without the need of birth pangs,
   You we beseech, blest Lady of Triumph,
   Whom from the lofty forehead of Zeus
   Prometheus the Titan brought to birth:
   Come from Olympus' golden mansions .
   To this shrine of the Pytho, come wafting down
   To the town where Apollo's hearth at the navel
   Of earth gives forth infallible futures,
   And choristers dance around the tripod.
   Come with Leto's daughter, Artemis:
   Both of you, goddesses; both of you, virgins,
   Both sacred sisters of Apollo:
   Maidens, beseech that the ancient line
   Of Erechtheus may have at last
An oracle's forecast of children.

ANTISTROPHE
What a perennial human joy
   Are children to the parental home!

Lighting the rooms with youth and promise,
Passing on their father's stock
To offspring of the following age.
They are our strength when times are hard,
They are bliss when all is well.
They are their country's shield in war.
More precious than riches, far more rare,
To me are children to care for and raise
In the ways of virtue. Life without children
Is to me a life that is lacking.
I censure anyone choosing such.
Let me be modest in possessions
But happily blessed with children.

EPODE

O the hidden haunts of Pan:
   The secret cave by the Beetling Cliffs
   Where the daughters of Aglaurus dance
   On the emerald sward in front of the shrine
   Of Athena to the musical sound
Of your panpipes, Pan,
   When you play in your sunless caverns.
   In these caves a virgin became
   A mother; poor derelict girl
Who bore to Apollo
   A baby in these caves
   And left him to be fodder for birds
   And a gory banquet for beasts.
   Bitter the sufferings from that rape,
   And never has loom or legend spun
A felicitous story
   Of children born of gods to mortals.

[ION *enters from the temple*]

SECOND EPISODE

ION: Good women of Creusa who keep watch here
   by the steps of this fragrant shrine,
   has Xuthus left the oracle and holy tripod

or is he still inside waiting for an answer?
LEADER: Sir, he is still inside
and has not crossed the threshold yet . . .
Wait! I hear the creak of gates:
someone is coming out; yes, it is my master.

[XUTHUS *in a state of excitement emerges from the temple and attempts to fling his arms around* ION]

XUTHUS: My son! my son! Heaven bless you! How wonderful to greet you so!
ION: [*trying to withdraw*]
Greetings too, but do be sensible and all will be well with us.
XUTHUS: Your hand, dear boy, and let me hug you.
ION: [*backing away*]
Sir, are you out of your mind? Has some demon struck you mad?
XUTHUS: Mad? When I've found my dearest and will not let him go.
ION: Stop it! Stop clutching! You're crushing the god's garlands.
XUTHUS: Of course I'll clutch you. I'm no robber and I've found my precious own.
ION: Will you let go or do you want an arrow through your ribs?
XUTHUS: Trying to escape me, eh, just when you've found your dearest?
ION: Now I don't like giving lessons to unhinged boorish strangers, but . . .
XUTHUS: Go ahead, kill me. Burn the body and be your father's murderer.
ION: You—my father—how? Am I to think this joke is funny?
XUTHUS: Wait and you'll see. I have a long story to tell.
ION: To tell me what? Begin.
XUTHUS: I am your father and you are my son.
ION: Who says so?
XUTHUS: Loxias: he who reared my son.
ION: We've only got your word for that.
XUTHUS: No: straight from the mouth of the oracle.
ION: A riddle, and you've got it wrong.
XUTHUS: Then I'm not hearing right.
ION: What did Phoebus actually say?

XUTHUS: He said that the first man I met as I . . .

ION: Met?

XUTHUS: . . . as I came out of the god's temple . . .

ION: Well, what about him?

XUTHUS: . . . would be my own born son.

ION: Your son? Really? Or just a present from someone?

XUTHUS: A present, yes, but still my very own.

ION: And you walked straight into *me*?

XUTHUS: None other, my child.

ION: [*pausing in wonderment*] How is this possible?

XUTHUS: I ask myself that as much as you do.

ION: Yes . . . but who was the mother you had me of?

XUTHUS: That I cannot say.

ION: But didn't Phoebus tell you?

XUTHUS: I was so excited I forgot to ask.

ION: Born from Mother Earth perhaps.

XUTHUS: The ground spawns no offspring.

ION: How exactly am I yours?

XUTHUS: I do not know. I leave that to the god.

ION: [*after long thought*] Let's tackle this another way.

XUTHUS: That would be better, my son.

ION: Have you ever had affairs?

XUTHUS: Only when I was young and had no sense.

ION: Before you married Erechtheus' daughter?

XUTHUS: Yes, but never since.

ION: So that was when you begot me?

XUTHUS: The time fits.

ION: But how on earth did I get here?

XUTHUS: I'm at a loss.

ION: I must have come from far.

XUTHUS: That too puzzles me.

ION: Did you ever come to Delphi before?

XUTHUS: Once for a torchlight festival of Bacchus.

ION: And you put up in the public inn?

XUTHUS: Where I was introduced to some girls from Delphi
                                                           and . . .

ION: Introduced to their rites, you mean?

XUTHUS: Yes, they were Bacchanalian maenads.

ION: Were you sober or in your cups?

XUTHUS: Well, there was good Bacchic cheer.

ION: That's it then. That's how I got begotten.

XUTHUS: And destiny has discovered you, my son.

ION: But how did I come to this shrine?

XUTHUS: Exposed there by the girl, probably.

ION: At least I can't be slave-born.

XUTHUS: And you have a father, my child.

ION: I suppose I must not doubt the god.

XUTHUS: Now you are being sensible.

ION: What more could I wish for than . . .

XUTHUS: And you are seeing things rightly.

ION: . . . than being born the son of a son of Zeus!

XUTHUS: And how it becomes you!

ION: So I can touch my progenitor?

XUTHUS: Yes, if you believe the god.

ION: [*throwing himself into Xuthus' arms*]
Dear, dear father! . . .

XUTHUS: What a joy to hear you say it!

ION: Oh, bless this day!

XUTHUS: How happy you have made me!

ION: [*as they separate*]
And now, my dear mother, shall I ever see your face too?
Whoever you are, I long to see you more than ever.
Perhaps you are dead and I never shall.

LEADER: We also have a part in this house's happiness.
If only my mistress could be blessed with children too,
and the whole house of Erechtheus.

XUTHUS: My son, I have found you just as the god has promised:
you and me he has brought together;
and you have found at last the closest to your heart.
As to your other yearning, so natural, I feel it too,
but how shall you, my child, discover your mother
and I discover what sort of woman bore you?
We'll find out no doubt in time.
Meanwhile, leave this compound of the god,
this rootless life and join your father.
Come to Athens where great wealth and royalty are yours
and the double slur of bastardy and beggary are not.
Quite the contrary,
you'll lead a rich and distinguished life.

[*He waits for an answer*]

What, silent? Withdrawn in thought and your eyes cast down?
This change from gaiety casts gloom upon your father.
ION: Things seen from a distance are different
from things seen close at hand.
I thank providence for finding me a father,
but, Father, if you'll listen, what worries me is this:
Athens, they say, that famous city,
springs from her own soil, she is indigenous,
but I an intruder will face twin handicaps:
a bastard with a foreign father.
Under such scorn and in this weak position
I shall count for nothing—a nobody.*
And if I force myself to the forefront in the realm,
I shall be hated by the second-rate—
as the elite are always hated;
while by the sincere and competent
who wisely keep their peace
and do not plunge into the public gaze,
I shall be branded as a nincompoop
who could not keep quiet in a nervous city.
Or if I seek my rightful place
I shall be blocked by the power of the demagogic lobby
which plays fast and loose with the commonwealth.
That is what always happens, Father.
Those who control cities and dignities
are ruthless to rivals.

I shall be intruding into a strange house
whose childless chatelaine shared with you
her disappointment in the past,
but now, alone with her broken hopes,
she will feel the full bitterness of her lot.
How can I escape her hatred
when still without a child
she sees me standing by your side
and gazes with resentment at your happiness?

*This line is missing from many mss.

You will either have to look to her, your wife,
    and throw me out,
    or respect my position and break up your home.
How many murders, how many deaths by poison,
    have wives not effected for their husbands?
I do feel sorry for your consort, Father,
    she is getting older and has no child.
It's a sad thing for the last of a noble line
    to be scourged with infertility.

As to kingship, it's not worth considering:
    fair of face, full of anguish within.
Who can be happy, who can be envied,
    eking out his days in fear of the sidelong glance?
    Give me the simple contentment of the common man
    and not the cares of power,
    in which, for fear of the assassin,
    one must fawn upon the unscrupulous and shun the honest.
You may say that gold outweighs these obstacles
    and that it's pleasant to be rich,
    but I have no wish to cling to wealth
    tense with foreboding at every sound I hear.
    Give me a modest role instead, free from worry.

Father, listen to the blessings I have had here.
Leisure first of all,
    that greatest gift to human beings;
    then freedom from turmoil,
    without some oaf pushing me off the road
    or my having to step aside for some nobody.
I spent my time in prayer to the gods
    and converse with my fellow men.
The people I served were cheerful, not cantankerous.
Hardly had I sent one batch of pilgrims on their way
    when another would arrive.
There was a gracious intercourse,
    with one fresh face following another.
Worship, willy-nilly, is the right thing for man,
    and both by duty and by temperament
    I was drawn to serve the god.

* * *

When I mull these matters over, Father,
   I think I am better off here than there.
   So let me stay here.
Pleasure is sweet pleasure
   whether enjoyed in great or little things.
LEADER: You have chosen well;
   may those I love find happiness in those you love.
XUTHUS: Enough of this talk.
   Learn to go with your good fortune.
Let us begin with a celebration here
   right where I found you:
   a dinner together, one of many to come.
I shall offer up those thanksgiving sacrifices
   for your birthday that I never made.
I'll wine and dine you
   like some loved one I was bringing home.
I shall take you with me to Athens
   pretending you're a sightseer, not my beloved son.
Like this I'll not upset my childless wife
   with my own happiness.
In time I'll find a way to win her
   and give you title to my scepter in the land.
I name you Ion*, to match the event,
   for it was on my way to the god's shrine
   that our paths crossed.
Now call in a crowd of your comrades
   for this sacrifice and happy farewell party
   so they can say goodbye to you
   on the eve of your leaving Delphi.

[*Turning to the women of the* CHORUS]

Don't you women breathe a word of this.
It's death to you if you tell my wife.
ION: All right, I'll come.
   But one thing lacks in all my luck:
   finding the mother who gave me birth.

_____
*Ion means "going" or "coming."

Father, unless I do,
　　life will not be tolerable.
If I may express a prayer:
　　may my mother be a woman of Athens
　　so that on my mother's side
　　free speaking is my right.
An alien entering a city of pure blood,
　　though he be technically a citizen,
　　does not enjoy free speech—his lips are fettered.

[XUTHUS *and* ION *go off arm in arm*]

SECOND CHORAL ODE

[*The women of the* CHORUS *in devotion to their mistress have
taken a dislike to* XUTHUS: *somewhat illogically, it would
seem, for they imagine that she will be distressed to discover
that her husband now has a son while she remains childless.
They extend their vicious condemnation of* XUTHUS *to* ION,
whom they wish dead]

STROPHE

CHORUS: Tears, recriminations, pangs of grief
　　Are what I foresee when my queen discovers
Her husband is blessed with a son while she is
　　Without issue and barren.
Prophet Apollo, child of Leto,
What is this prophecy you have chanted?
Where does this boy you have raised in your temple
　　Stem from? Who is his mother?
　　I distrust the oracle and I suspect
　　　　A cover for something infamous.
　　I fear the outcome. How will it end?
Weird is the word of the god and weird his story.
　　It smacks of fraud—something fortuitous—
　　This tale of a child of unknown blood.
　　　　Who will gainsay it?

ANTISTROPHE

[*Voices speaking severally*]

1: Girls, ought we to blurt it out
   In our mistress' ear? Shouldn't we tell her
   That the husband who was her life and soul,
     The associate of her hopes . . .
2: Unhappy woman whose life is ruined!
3: While blissfully he dishonors his wife,
   Who is sinking now into gray old age . . .
4: Despised, and yet she loves him.
5: Miserable man, he came from outside
    Into this prosperous house . . .
6: He doesn't deserve his luck, the wretch!
7: He cheated my queen; may the gods when the altars flame
   Cancel his prayers . . . Let her know that I am
   Loyal to my lady . . . They're feasting now,
8: This new father and son.

EPODE

You pinnacles of Parnassus and you crags,
  With your sky-high tower, where Bacchus at night
With his maenads holding aloft his two-headed torches of pine
Prances—may that boy never come
To my city, but die on the morning day
    Of his new life.
Only if our city were harassed
Would it be right to allow foreigners in:
    As was Erechtheus the king
    Our leader of old.

THIRD EPISODE

[CREUSA *and an* OLD MAN—*a family retainer—begin labori-ously climbing the incline to the sanctuary*]

CREUSA: Come along, old man,
  you my father Erechtheus' lifelong guardian,
  brace yourself for the climb up to the god's sanctuary.
You'll share my joy if Loxias foretells the birth of children.

Joy shared with friends is double joy,
  and hard times—God forbid!—are halved.
How sweet it is to look
  into sympathetic eyes . . . Your mistress I may be
  but I feel for you as for a father
  as you once felt for mine.
OLD MAN: [*stopping to get his breath*] My daughter,
  how true you are to the fine traditions of your forebears!
Never do you disgrace your ancient line
  sprung from Earth itself.

  [*Resuming the climb*]

Now give me a hand. Help me along.
Up, up, what a climb the oracle is! . . . That's for sure!
You must support me, be nurse to my decrepitude.
CREUSA: Step after me . . . careful . . . step by step.
OLD MAN: My poor fumbling feet, but, oh, a nimble heart!
CREUSA: Lean on your stick, and watch those twists.
OLD MAN: [*nearly stumbling*] I'm so shortsighted—walking
                                                    blind.
CREUSA: I know you are, but don't give up.
OLD MAN: Not willingly . . . but I don't have full control.

  [CREUSA *and the* OLD MAN *arrive at the plateau where the*
  women of the CHORUS *are*]

CREUSA: Good women of mine,
  you trusty associates of my web and spindle,
  what news did my husband take away from here?
Was there hope of children:
  the reason for our coming to this place?
Do tell me.
If the news is good you'll make your mistress happy
  and she won't forget.
LEADER: Doom!
CREUSA: A bad opening!
LEADER: Tragedy!
CREUSA: A baleful oracle?

LEADER: [*looking at her colleagues*]
   What can we do? It's death if we . . .
CREUSA: What is this? This terror?
LEADER: Shall we say it or be silent? . . . What can we do?
CREUSA: Say it: the bad news you have for me.
LEADER: Very well, I'll tell you, though I die a double death.
   Madam, you'll never have a baby in your arms or at your
                                                          breast.
CREUSA: [*sinking to the ground*] O . . . h! I'd rather die.
OLD MAN: My child!
CREUSA: I'm shattered, my friends. I can't go on. I'm crushed.
OLD MAN: My child!
CREUSA: No no! It's agony—stabbed to the heart.
OLD MAN: [*putting his arms round her*] There there! Don't cry
                                                     until you . . .
CREUSA: I am swept by grief.
OLD MAN: . . . until you know whether . . .
CREUSA: What's left to know?
OLD MAN: . . . whether the master shares your plight or only you
                                                     are stricken.
LEADER: Old man, Apollo has given him a son
   and she is not included in the celebrations.
CREUSA: What you have just said caps everything, crowns my
                                                          sorrow.
OLD MAN: This child? Is he still to be born
   or did the oracle say he was already born?
LEADER: He's born, all right! A strapping young man!
   That's what Apollo's given him . . . I was there.
CREUSA: What did you say? No! It's outrageous. I won't listen.
OLD MAN: Nor I. What is the sense of the oracle? Explain. Who is
                                                        this boy?
LEADER: Apollo gave as son to your husband
   the first person he met on leaving the temple.
CREUSA: [*with a bitter cry*]
   I am finished. What is left for me? . . .
A lonely childless life in a barren house.
OLD MAN: But whom did the oracle mean?
   Who was he that my poor lady's husband met?
LEADER: Dear mistress, do you recall the youth who was sweeping
                                                     the temple?

He is the child.

CREUSA: [*breaking into verse*] I wish I could fly through the
liquid sky
To the farthest western stars
Far from the land of Hellas:
So great is my pain, my dears.

OLD MAN: What name did his father give him?
Do you know, or must that remain a mystery?

LEADER: The name Ion, because he was the first person he met
when going.

OLD MAN: And the mother? What sort of woman is she?

LEADER: I cannot tell. All I know, old man,
is that her husband has gone off secretly
to the sacrificial tents to offer up thanksgivings
and birthday celebrations for the boy.
He sits down to feast with his new son.

OLD MAN: Mistress, we have been cheated,
and I grieve with you—cheated by your husband.
It is abominable:
a plot to get rid of us from the courts of Erechtheus.
I say this not out of hatred for your husband
but out of love for you.
He came an alien to the city,
married you and took possession of your house and heritage.
Now his secret is out:
his tricking you with a child by another woman.
Let me tell you how the trick was worked.
When he found that you were barren,
scorning to shoulder the burden of this fate with you,
he took some slave girl to his bed
and furtively begot this child,
then gave him to some acquaintance at Delphi to bring up.
There the deception was continued
and the boy was reared in the god's house—free of it all.
When Xuthus learnt that his son was a grown young man,
he persuaded you to come here to consult about your barrenness.

It was not the god that lied but he.
He has been rearing the boy all these years.

His plan was this:
> if discovered, to make the deity responsible for all,
> but if the plot succeeded,
> to invest the boy with royal status
> and put him beyond all criticism.

As to the fancy name of Ion,
> that was a ruse to fit the story of their meeting as he went.

LEADER: How I dislike those rascals
> who camouflage the wrong they do with lies!
> I'd rather have an honest dullard as a friend
> than a brilliant scamp.

OLD MAN: [*turning to* CREUSA] And you, you must put up with
>   something worse:
> take into your house a motherless nonentity—
> the whelp of some female slave.

It would be bad enough
> if he'd intruded into your home the son of a decent mother,
> using your barrenness as excuse and asking your permission.

If this were not to your taste,
> he should have gone and married someone from Aeolia.*

So now, what you have to do
> is steel yourself to an act worthy of womanhood.
> Seize a sword, think of a trick, concoct a poison,
> and dispatch your husband and the boy
> before they do you.

Otherwise you'll lose your life.

Two antagonists in the same house cannot exist:
> one or other of them must go under.

As for me,
> I am ready to take part with you in this:
> to go into the house where he is junketing
> and murder the boy.

That will repay you, my mistress,
> for all you have done for me.

Only the name of slave is a slave's shame.

---

*This remark is probably sarcastic. Aeolia in northeastern Greece was remote and,
to the Athenians, uncivilized. So the Old Man is saying: "He should have gone and
got a woman from the sticks." Also, Aeolia was where Xuthus came from.

In all else honest slave
   and freeman are the same.
LEADER: I too, dear mistress, am ready to share your lot:
either to live with honor, or die without a blot.

LYRIC APOSTROPHE

CREUSA: O my soul, how can I be quiet?
   Yet to uncover that dark affair
   Is to say goodbye to honor.
   What obstacle remains to stop me?
   What point anymore pursuit of virtue?
   A husband false, I stripped of home,
Stripped of children.
   Hopeless was that struggle to keep
My liaison hidden
   And hide that birth so damning.
But I could not.

   So, by the star-spangled seat of Zeus,
   By the goddess of our mountains,
   And by the sacred shores of Triton's lake,
   I vow no longer to keep my lover hidden.
What a relief
   To lift the burden from my heart!
   Let then the tears drop and the agony rage:
Mortals and immortals
   Have schemed against me.
   Let me show them up for what they are:
Unsavory bedroom lechers.

   You who pluck song from the lifeless horns
   Of bullocks on the seven-tongued lyre,
   You melody-making son of Lêto,
You Apollo:
Your disgrace I shall drag
Into the glaring light of day.

   With the gleam of the sun in your golden hair
   As gold as the flowers I was gathering there
Into the folds of my skirt,

You swooped and drew me by my white wrists
And pulled me away to that rock cave bed
As I was screaming: "Mother! Mother!"
Ravisher divine, you forced me there
And shamelessly you worked your will:
Aphrodite's ecstasy.

Miserable me, I bore your son,
But fear of my mother drove me
To toss him on that bed of yours:
That ruthless couch for ruthless rape
Of me poor blighted stricken girl.

But, oh, my boy is gone, is gone.
The birds of the air have rent and eaten
Him my boy, my boy and yours—
You cruel god, you lyre player,
You singer of exultant songs!

Apollo son of Leto, listen:
I call you seated on your throne
Dispensing sanctimonious answers
From earth's navel . . . I will shout it
Into your ear, you, you
Despicable seducer!

To my husband you have given
A son and heir though you owe him nothing.
For me, you heartless one,
You've let our child—yes, yours as well—
Be snatched from his swaddling clothes
To be the prey of carrion birds.

Delos your very birthplace hates you.
The laurel and the sweet bay hate you
In that spot where Leto bore you
The seed of Zeus in a holy birth
Under the tender palm trees.

[CREUSA *sinks to the ground by the temple steps weeping and*

exhausted. *The women of the* CHORUS *and the* OLD MAN *begin
to comfort her*]

FOURTH EPISODE

LEADER: Alas, the lid is lifted
on a casket of tragedies!
Who would not shed a tear?
OLD MAN: [*reaching down to help her up*] My daughter,
I see nothing in your glance to reassure me.
My mind boggles.
Hardly had I bailed out from one billow of sorrows
when a surge at the stern swamps me with your story.
Just when you had surmounted one tribulation,
a new avenue of horrors has opened up.
Do you really mean what you say:
this charge against Apollo? . . . And a child you gave birth to?

[*He pauses for a reply*]

Where in the surroundings of this city
did you say you put him:
this welcome dinner for wild animals?
Explain it all to me again.
CREUSA: Old man, you heap my shame upon me, but I shall tell
you.
OLD MAN: The sorrows of a loved one have all my sympathy.
CREUSA: Then listen.
You know the cave to the north of Cecrops' rocks,
called the Beetling Cliffs?
OLD MAN: I do. Nearby stands the altar and shrine of Pan.
CREUSA: It was there that I suffered the appalling outrage.
OLD MAN: Outrage? Let my tears in full measure flow.
CREUSA: Against my will I . . . coupled with Apollo.
OLD MAN: My daughter, was that when I began to notice some-
thing?
CREUSA: I don't know . . . Speak quite openly and so shall I.
OLD MAN: You were stifling your sighs against some mysterious
ill.
CREUSA: Exactly that: the tragedy I am revealing to you now.

OLD MAN: But how did you keep hidden this union with Apollo?

CREUSA: I gave birth . . . but wait, old man, before I tell you . . .

OLD MAN: Where was it? Who delivered you, or did you go
through this alone?

CREUSA: All by myself: in the very cave where I was raped.

OLD MAN: But the baby? Where is he now?
He could be the answer to your barrenness.

CREUSA: Dead, old man: exposed to beasts of the wild.

OLD MAN: Dead? And that cad Apollo did nothing to help?

CREUSA: Nothing. The boy is in Hades now, eking out his days.

OLD MAN: Who exposed him? Surely it was not you?

CREUSA: It was . . . in darkness . . . swaddling him in the clothes
I wore.

OLD MAN: But the exposure—was no one privy to the secret?

CREUSA: Only wretchedness and furtiveness.

OLD MAN: But how could you bear to leave your baby in a
cave?

CREUSA: I know, how could I! Bitter the cries that sprang from
my lips.

OLD MAN: How wretched and how reckless! But the god was
even worse.

CREUSA: If you'd seen how the little thing stretched out his hands
to me!

OLD MAN: Searching for your breast . . . to curl up in your
arms . . .

CREUSA: Where he belonged. And I deprived him of it.

OLD MAN: What good did you imagine could come of tossing out
your child?

CREUSA: I thought the god would rescue his own son.

OLD MAN: How sad! What a winter has fallen on your house!

[*There is a pause and* CREUSA *surveys the* OLD MAN *with concern*]

CREUSA: But what's this? Your head droops, old man, and you
are crying.

OLD MAN: Yes, to see you and your father brought so low.

CREUSA: It is the way of mortals. Nothing good endures.

OLD MAN: My daughter, let us not cling to these adversities.

CREUSA: Then what must we do? There's no escape from hopelessness.

OLD MAN:

[*sweeping his hands over the whole temple scene*]

Revenge yourself on the god who started it all.
CREUSA: But how can I a mortal take on stronger powers?
OLD MAN: Burn down Apollo's holy oracle.
CREUSA: I am afraid. I have troubles enough already.
OLD MAN: Have the courage . . . you can . . . kill your husband.
CREUSA: But I revere the wonderful love that once was ours.
OLD MAN: At least kill the boy who has come into your life.
CREUSA: But how? If that were only possible I'd give anything to
                                                            do it.
OLD MAN: Put swords into your attendants' hands.
CREUSA: Very well! But where is it to be done?
OLD MAN: In the hallowed tents where he banquets with his
                                                        friends.
CREUSA: Blatant murder! And such weak support from slaves!
OLD MAN: [*throwing up his hands*] Oh dear! Oh dear! So faint-
                                                        hearted!

[*After a pause*]

What would *you* devise?

[CREUSA *leads the* OLD MAN *to the temple steps and sits him
down. Breathlessly she begins to spell out her scheme*]

CREUSA: Yes, a ruse . . . I have it. And I think it will work.
OLD MAN: [*pointing to his head and displaying his hands*]
    Both these are at your service.
CREUSA: Listen then. Do you recall the Battle of the Giants?
OLD MAN: I do. The battle they waged with the gods at Phlegra.
CREUSA: When Earth gave birth to Gorgon—a terrifying freak.
OLD MAN: To come to the aid of her sons and topple the gods?
CREUSA: Yes, and the goddess Pallas, Zeus's daughter, killed her.
OLD MAN: What was she like, that fearsome Gorgon?
CREUSA: Her bosom was armed with crawling snakes.
OLD MAN: Is this the story I heard so long ago?
CREUSA: Yes, and Athena wears the hideous creature's skin over
                                                    her breast.

OLD MAN: Is that what is called the "Aegis": Athena's breast-
                                                        plate?

CREUSA: It is: because she *charged* with the gods into battle.*

OLD MAN: My daughter, how can that help us against our
                                                        enemies?

CREUSA: You know Erichthonius? ... Of course you do, old
                                                        man ...

OLD MAN: Your first forebear, whom Earth gave birth to?

CREUSA: Yes, and when he was just a baby, Pallas gave him ...

[*She breaks off*]

OLD MAN: Well, why are you waiting?

CREUSA: ... gave him two droplets of the Gorgon's blood,
                                                        which ...

OLD MAN: Have some potency over human beings?

CREUSA: Yes: one is deadly, the other heals.

OLD MAN: And she armed the child with these? But how?

CREUSA: On a gold chain which Erichthonius gave my father.

OLD MAN: And when he died it came to you?

CREUSA: Exactly ... Look, I wear it on my wrist.

OLD MAN: But how does this gift from heaven do its double
                                                        work?

CREUSA: The droplet from the open vein at the killing ...

OLD MAN: Yes yes, but how do you use it? How does it work?

CREUSA: It keeps disease away and sustains life.

OLD MAN: And the other drop? What does that do?

CREUSA: It kills. It is poison from the Gorgon's snakes.

OLD MAN: Are they together or do you keep them separate?

CREUSA: Separate. Good and evil do not mix.

OLD MAN: Dearest child, you have all you need.

CREUSA: [*holding out one of the phials*]
    This is the one to kill the boy, and you will do it.

OLD MAN: Where and how? Just tell me and I shall.

CREUSA: In Athens, when he comes into my house.

OLD MAN: [*after a pause*]
    That's not such a good idea ... My turn to find fault.

---

*Aegis: aigis, from *aïssō*, to rush, move violently, charge. There is a play on
words impossible to reproduce in English, unless perhaps "chargeplate."

CREUSA: Why not . . . Ah yes, I think I know! . . .

OLD MAN: Because you'd be thought to have killed the boy, even
                                        if you didn't.

CREUSA: You have a point. Stepmothers are notorious children-
                                        haters.

OLD MAN: Kill him right here, and now; then deny it.

CREUSA: That would get me a sweet satisfaction faster.

OLD MAN: And you'll snare your husband in his own snare.

CREUSA: [rising] So you know what to do?
    Here is Athena's golden bauble,
    a trinket of great age, take it,
    and go to the place where my husband furtively
    is having his sacrificial feast,
    and when the banqueting is done and the libations start,
    slip it from under your gown and drop it deftly
    into the young man's cup—but only his, no one else's,
    and make sure his drink is on its own—
    this young man who would be master in my house!
Once he swallows it
    he'll never reach our glorious Athens.
    He'll remain right here—a corpse.

OLD MAN: Go your way then to the pilgrim's guest house
    and I shall carry out my assignment.

[The OLD MAN watches CREUSA walk away, then, rising slowly
from the steps, he jauntily addresses his feet]

Come on, old decrepit foot, get young:
    there's work ahead in spite of your years.
    Full march against the foe!
    Help your mistress kill her enemy and rid her home of him.
It's a fine thing to be law-abiding when things go well
    but when it comes to enemies the law's an obstacle.

[As the OLD MAN plods off, the women of the CHORUS chant for
divine help in furthering the murder of ION. He has no more
right to the beauty of Athens than the Muse of poetry has to
broadcast the sins of women. For the sins of men are far
worse: witness the infidelity of XUTHUS]

THIRD CHORAL ODE

You, Enodia, Demeter's daughter, queen
Guiding the spirits of night and day,
Guide the cup that my dearest mistress
    Has filled with the deadly drops
From the slashed throat of the earth-spawned Gorgon:
    Guide it towards the man
Who reached for the house of Erechtheus.
Never let an alien from an alien home
    Reign over my city.
    Let none but the noble clan
    Of Erechtheus rule it.

ANTISTROPHE I

If this murder misses its mark and my mistress
Misses her aim and all the hopes
Of this business falter, then will there enter
Her soul a compulsion to stab
Her throat with the keen blade of a sword
Or hang her neck in a halter,
So end her sorrows but only to suffer
Others on her way to another
World . . . Never, oh, never
On this light-filled earth will she
Let a stranger lord her house.

STROPHE II

I blush for Bacchus that many-hymned god
Should ever this youth be allowed among those
Who go to the springs and beautiful dances
Where all through the night they wait for the day,
That twentieth day when the torches flare
    And the stars in the holy empyrean
Prefigure the dance with the moon taking part,
And the fifty daughters of Nereus swirl
In the deeps of the sea, the ripple of streams,
Dancing to honor the goldenly crowned
        Maid and her mother.*

---

*I.e., Enodia and Demeter.

How dare he aspire to be there as king,
   Usurping the labor of others:
      Phoebus' vagabond.

ANTISTROPHE II

All you poets that follow the Muse
With your slanderous songs about the passions
And sinful lusts of woman, acknowledge
That we are far more virtuous than
Brutish and lascivious man;
   So Muse sing us
A canceling ode that shows the damage
Which men do to women. Look at this son
Of a son of Zeus: his perfidy
And his begetting not in the bed
     Of my mistress, an heir.
He charmed his way with another woman
   And made for himself
    An illegitimate son.

[*A distraught* MANSERVANT *of* CREUSA *hurries in*]

FIFTH EPISODE

SERVANT: Good women, where can I find our mistress, Erech-
                     theus' daughter?
  I have searched the city everywhere and cannot find her.
LEADER: Good slave-mate, is something wrong? .
  What are you in such a hurry to tell us?
SERVANT: They're hunting for her.
  The country's rulers want to stone her.
LEADER: That's terrible!
  Has someone divulged our plot to kill the boy?
SERVANT: Exactly so,
  And you'll not be the last to pay for being involved.
LEADER: How was our dark plan discovered?
SERVANT: The god let it out, to prevent his temple being defiled.
LEADER: What happened?
  On my knees I beg you tell me.
  If die I must, I'll die more happily for knowing . . .

unless, of course, we are let off.

[*The women press round the* SERVANT *in a circle*]

SERVANT: When Creusa's husband left Apollo's shrine,
  taking with him his newfound son
  to celebrate with feast and sacrifice to deity,
  he was on his way to the double crags of Dionysus,
  where the consecrated fires of Bacchus leap,
  to sprinkle a victim's blood
  in thanksgiving for the present of his son.
Then Xuthus said:
  "Stay here, my boy,
  and have the workmen set up a spacious tent.
If I am gone long,
  sacrificing to the gods of birth,
  proceed with the feasting for our friends that come."
At which he left, together with his heifers,
  while the young man conscientiously
  set up the poles that hold the canvas tent walls,
  taking particular care to keep the face of the tent
  away from the fierce glare of the sun
  from noon till sundown.
He marked out a hundred feet
  for each side of a quadrangle,
  making—according to those who know—
  a space of ten thousand square feet;
  for he wanted to invite all the people of Delphi to the feast.
Then he hung a series of religious tapestries
  from the treasury as backdrops.
They were amazing.

To begin with,
  stretching over the tent's ceiling was the drape
  dedicated to the god by Heracles son of Zeus
  as part of the spoils from the Amazons.
On it were woven designs
  such as Uranus herding the stars in the vault of the sky,
  with Helios driving his coursers into the sunset,
  trailing Hesperus behind him, the bright evening star.

There was Night, swathed in black,
   hurtling onwards in her chariot
   drawn by two untraced horses, the stars her escort;
and the Pleiades in mid-heaven pursuing their path
   with Orion and his sword, and over all the Bear
   rearing around with his golden tail;
and the disc of the full moon,
   dividing the months and beaming out her arrows of light;
and the Hyades, the sailors' guide,
   and Dawn, forerunner of day, stampeding the stars.

Then on the walls he hung tapestries from abroad:
   ships bristling with oars bearing down on a Greek flotilla;
   freakish creatures half-man, half-beast;
   horsemen pursuing stags or stalking ferocious lions.
In the vestibule he hung a tapestry given by some Athenian:
   Cecrops with his daughters,
   his limbs coiling with snakes.
In the center of the banquet table
   he laid the golden mixing bowls.

When a herald strode in
   announcing that any native of Delphi who wanted
   was welcome to the feast,
   the pavilion filled with people,
   who decked themselves with garlands
   and helped themselves sumptuously from the rich board.
When they had replenished themselves to their heart's content,
   an old man came forward
   and stood in the middle of the floor.
He made the guests laugh at his punctiliousness:
   for out of the urns he solemnly poured water
   for washing the hands;
   he swung thuribles of incense;
   he busied himself over the golden cups—
   a self-appointed majordomo.

When the feast had reached the point when the flutes start up
   and the communion bowl is set out for all,
   the old man said: "Away with these puny wine cups

and bring out larger ones,
then you gentry can get merry sooner."

There was much bustle fetching and carrying
the gold and silver goblets,
and he, grasping a distinctive chalice
in a gesture of service to his new master,
handed it to Ion filled to the brim,
having first however dropped into the wine the lethal drug
which—so it is said—our mistress gave him
with a view to killing her husband's new son.

Of course nobody knew this,
but just as the newly disclosed son
and all the company were poised with their cups,
one of the servants made a suspicious remark
and the young man, trained in the temple
among professional diviners,
interpreted this as a bad omen
and insisted on a fresh filling as he poured his drink
onto the floor at the first libation,
bidding everyone to do the same.

So, in a hushed solemnity,
we filled the ritual bowls with water, and wine from Byblus.
But as we were doing this
a flutter of tame doves descended
(doves are at home in the temple precincts)
and they began to dip their beaks in the libations
poured on to the ground by the guests—
greedily sucking them up into their feathery throats.

The god's libations did the birds no harm,
except for one.
This dove alighted on the spot
where Ion had drained his cup,
and no sooner had she imbibed the wine
when a shudder went through every feather of her frame.
Screeching, she hobbled
in an uncanny cacophony of pain,

leaving the whole assembly of banqueters stunned.
Finally, in convulsions, she expired:
  her pinkish claws and feet all limp.

Ion, the oracle child,
  flinging his cloak back from his shoulders,
  vaulted over the table shouting:
  "Who is the one that wanted to kill me?
  Say it, old man—you who were so attentive.
  Yes, it was from you that I took the cup."
At which, grabbing the old wrinkled arm,
  he began to search and caught the old man with the poison on
                                                           him.
He, thus detected,
  was compelled willy-nilly to disclose
  Creusa's dastardly ruse of poisoning the cup.

At once the young man,
  he whom Apollo's oracle had revealed,
  ran off with all the banqueters
  and stood before the Delphinian authorities.
"O hallowed Earth," he exclaimed,
  "a foreign woman, the daughter of Erechtheus
  has tried to murder me with poison."
The rulers of Delphi, by a majority vote,
  decreed that my mistress, for attempting to kill the temple
                                                         child
  and commit murder in the sanctuary,
  be thrown from the precipice.
The whole town is searching for her now:
  a woman whom sheer sorrow has reduced to this.
She came to Apollo's temple with children as her quest.
All hope of children she has lost, and her life not least.

[*The* SERVANT *turns and walks dolefully away as the women of
the* CHORUS *begin a lament for the tragedy about to befall
their mistress, and they bemoan a penalty they themselves
cannot escape*]

FIFTH CHORAL ODE

None! None! There is no way
   For us to escape from dying.
   Wide, wide open—the secret is out:
   The lethal draft discovered—
   The juice of the Bacchic grape
   Infused with the viper's venom.
   Our bribes to the gods below
   Are known and lead to disaster
   For us, and death from the rock for our mistress.
   Oh for the wings to fly far away!
   Oh for a cranny deep in the earth
   To evade a stony destruction!
   Set me in a chariot propelled by chargers,
   Set me in a ship to sail afar.
   There's nowhere to hide unless
   A deity deigns to hide us.
   And for you, poor mistress, what horror
   Lies in wait for your spirit?
   Does it mean that those who attempt
   To damage a fellow human
Must rightly suffer?

[CREUSA, *heavily veiled and distraught, rushes in*]

SIXTH EPISODE

CREUSA: Women, they're hunting me down.
   They mean to butcher me.
   The Pythian vote condemns me:
   I am marked for extinction.
LEADER: Alas, we know your doom, unhappy lady!
CREUSA: Where can I find shelter? . . . Hardly was I out of the
                                                  house
   before the lynchers got there . . . I gave them the slip and here
                                                      . I am.
LEADER: Shelter? Where but the altar.
CREUSA: What good is that?
LEADER: To kill in the sanctuary is sacrilege.

CREUSA: Not if I die by law.
LEADER: And only if they catch you.
CREUSA: O . . . h! Here they come charging, swords at the ready.
What a cruel race we run!
LEADER: Sit on the altar. If they kill you there
your blood will be on your killers . . .
With fate we must take our chances.

[CREUSA *hurriedly seats herself on the altar and crouches by
the effigy of Apollo.* ION *bursts in with a band of armed sup-
porters. At first he does not notice or recognize the heavily
veiled woman*]

ION: O father Cephisus,* you bull-shaped avatar,
what viper have you begotten?
What dragon with eyes of burning murder! . . . She . . .
She—ready for any crime:
venomous as those beads of Gorgon's blood
she would have used for my extinction.

[*He sees and recognizes* CREUSA]

Seize her.
Fling her like a discus down the ravine
and let the crags of Parnassus comb her pretty hair.

[*Taking a step towards her*]

How lucky that this took place before I came to Athens,
before I fell into a stepmother's clutches.
When I found out how dangerous you were
my friends were with me, but trapped in your house
you would have sent me packing down to Hades.
Neither Apollo's altar nor his shrine will save you.
I pity you,
but my feelings are for my mother and for myself.
She is not here in person, but her image is.

---

*Cephisus, here a synonym for Athens (Creusa's town), was the chief river of
the Athenian plain.

[*He turns to the bystanders and points derisively at* CREUSA]

Just look at her: she stops at nothing—
    trick after tricking . . . cringing at the altar of the god,
    hoping this will get her off due punishment
    for all her machinations.

[ION *signals to the guards to seize her.* CREUSA *lifts her veil
and speaks, not without a certain dignity and doomed authority*]

CREUSA: I warn you not to kill me.
    I speak in my own name.
    I speak in the god's name where I stand.
ION: Phoebus? What do you have in common with *him*?
CREUSA: My body. I give it to the god.
ION: Really? After attempting to poison his servant!
CREUSA: Servant you are no longer. You are your father's.
ION: Born from my father, yes, but belonging to Apollo.
CREUSA: And now no longer. It is I who belong.
ION: Minus the true devotion that was mine.
CREUSA: You were death to my house. I had to kill you.
ION: Why? I was not marching in arms against the house of
                                            Erechtheus.
CREUSA: You were, and you would have made a bonfire of it.
ION: Where were my torches? Where were my firebrands?
CREUSA: You meant to seize my house by force.
ION: A land in the gift of my father, which he had earned.
CREUSA: His? What fraction of the soil of Pallas do Aeolians
                                            own?
ION: He saved it with his arms, not with his tongue.
CREUSA: A common mercenary has no rights to ownership.
ION: You planned my death because you were afraid.
CREUSA: Yes, afraid for my life: if the chance came your way.
ION: A childless murderess all because a father finds a child!
CREUSA: Just because I'm childless must my house be plun-
                                            dered?
ION: You should offer me at least my father's heritage.
CREUSA: A buckler and a javelin—that's your heritage.
ION: [*angrily*] Get off that altar. Leave the hallowed seat.
CREUSA: Go give lessons to your mother, wherever she may be.

ION: And let you go scot free after trying to murder me?
CREUSA: Then why not put an end to me right here in this sacred
spot?

[CREUSA *seizes the flowers and garlands adorning the altar
and drapes them round her*]

ION: Will dying in the god's garlands make you happy?
CREUSA: It will strike a blow at the god who struck at me.
ION: [*in accents of impatience and despair*]
The world is mad:
    the divine dispensation neither good nor wise.
It ought not to be religiously correct
    for criminals to find sanctuary at altars:
    criminals should be rooted out.
It is not right that gods be touched by dirty hands.
Only the innocent should sit on sacred altars.
Instead, good and bad are made one and the same:
    equal treatment to the gods' acclaim.

[*As* ION *advances on* CREUSA, *the* PYTHIAN PRIESTESS *enters
from the temple carrying a cradle swathed in bands of wool.
She wears a long white alb reaching down to her ankles and
her head is crowned with bay leaves and a chaplet of ribbons.
Her demeanor is one of solemnity, wisdom, and age*]

PRIESTESS: [*lifting a hand in admonition*]
Hold there, my son! I have left the tripod and the oracle
and stepped across the boundary line:
I Apollo's prophetess, I the chosen one
from all the women of Delphi to maintain
the venerable rubrics of the tripod.
ION: [*bowing*] Welcome dearest mother, though not my mother!
PRIESTESS: But call me that: a name I do not shun.
ION: Are you aware this woman hatched a plot to kill me?
PRIESTESS: I am, and that you are sinning too by ruthlessness.
ION: But surely murder must be met with murdering?
PRIESTESS: Stepmothers are always harsh to stepchildren.
ION: And so are we when they treat us badly.

PRIESTESS: Enough of this . . . Now when you leave the sanctuary
for your native land . . .

ION: Leave? What do you mean?

PRIESTESS: . . . you must go to Athens with unsullied hands,
fruitful auguries.

ION: Hands are quite unsullied that strike an enemy down.

PRIESTESS: Not so. Now listen. I have something to tell you.

ION: Speak on. I know you'll only tell me what is for my good.

PRIESTESS: Do you see this basket I am carrying?

ION: I see an antique sort of cradle, all beribboned.

PRIESTESS: The cradle I took you from so long ago—a newborn
babe.

ION: What do you mean? I've never heard this news before.

PRIESTESS: A secret once, but now to be divulged.

ION: A secret? How could you keep it all these years?

PRIESTESS: The god designed you for service in his house.

ION: And now no longer, is that it? How can I know?

PRIESTESS: Having revealed your father, he is sending you from
here.

ION: But these items you hold, were you commanded to keep
them? Why?

PRIESTESS: Apollo put the idea into my head to . . .

ION: To do what? Tell me. Please go on.

PRIESTESS: . . . to preserve this curious find until today.

ION: For my good . . . or is it for my bad?

PRIESTESS: In it are the swaddling clothes in which you were
wrapped.

[CREUSA, *still seated on the altar, thinks she has seen the
basket before. She listens, riveted*]

ION: Are these clues to help me find my mother?

PRIESTESS: Precisely that, for the god now wishes it but not before.

ION: Oh what a blessed day that will be!

PRIESTESS: [*handing him the cradle*]
So take this now and go and find your mother.

ION: For that I'll comb all Asia and all Europe.

PRIESTESS: It's up to you.

[*She pauses as if wondering whether to say more*]

My son, on behalf of the god I reared you
   and now I return these things to you
   which he asked me—without commanding it—to take and
                                         keep.
Why he wanted this, I cannot tell.
   No living human being knew I had them nor where they were
                                     hidden.

[*She advances and takes* ION *in her arms*]

Goodbye . . . I give you a mother's kiss.

[*She begins to walk away, then turns*]

This search for your mother,
   you must go about it in the proper way.
First inquire whether it was a girl from Delphi
   who gave you birth and left you in this shrine,
   or if not, was she at least Greek.
That is all you will hear from me or from Apollo.
He is interested in your destiny.

[*The* PRIESTESS *moves into the temple.* ION *walks forward a
few steps uncertainly, then stops.* CREUSA *watches fascinated
and perplexed. She sees him break down in tears as he fondles
the cradle*]

ION: Strange! Strange! My eyes well with tears
   when I picture the woman who bore me,
   her clandestine affair
   and her getting rid of me unsuckled at her breast.
My life and home have been under the god's roof
   and I a nameless servant.
Fate was cruel but the god good.
All those years I might have had the happiness
   of nestling in a mother's arms
   but was cheated of her love and care.
And she was cheated too, she who gave me birth:
   bereft of the joy of a son.

[*Carrying the basket,* ION *walks towards the temple thinking aloud*]

I shall take this cradle now
    and consecrate it to the god.
    I don't want it to reveal something shattering.
    What if my mother turned out to be a slave?
    It's better not to pry than to unearth such a mother.

[*He turns towards the statue of Apollo, holding out the still unopened basket*]

"To your shrine, O Phoebus, I dedicate this . . ."

[*He stops and scrutinizes the basket, trembling*]

What is the matter with me?
I am evading the god's design.
He kept these tokens of my mother for me.
I must open them. I must have the courage.
One cannot sidestep fate.

[*He begins to undo the ribbons and bands that enclose the basket.* CREUSA *watches, spellbound with premonition*]

Yes, holy laggings and holy bindings,
    what secret have you locked away from me?
Look, a wicker cradle—and marvelously preserved!
After being stowed away all these years
    there's not a spot of mildew on the braiding.

[CREUSA *springs to her feet, shouting*]

CREUSA: A miracle! A miracle! beyond my wildest dreams.
ION: [*surprised and annoyed*]
    Oh be quiet! You've just shown that you can.
CREUSA: No no, I can't be quiet. Don't scold me,
    for what I see is the very cradle in which I left you—
    O my boy, my baby—abandoned you
    in Cecrops' cave under the ceilings of rock
    hard by the Beetling Cliffs.
I'll leave this altar now. I don't care if I die.

[*She runs to* ION *and throws her arms around him*]

ION: Grab her. She's raving,
and she's left the effigies and altar. Bind her arms.
CREUSA: Slay me, don't hesitate, but I'll not let go
of this cradle or you and these scraps of all your secret.
ION: This is outrageous. I'm being jibbered off my course.
CREUSA: No, my love, you're being found by those who love you.
ION: You, you love me? And you tried to kill me?
CREUSA: You are my child: a mother's supremest love.
ION: [*attempting to free himself*]
Stop clinging . . . I'm going to deal with you.
CREUSA: Oh please do! That's why I'm here, my son.
ION: [*wrenching the basket from her*]
Is this basket empty? What does it contain?
CREUSA: The swaddling clothes in which I left you once.
ION: Then itemize them, and don't look inside.
CREUSA: If I cannot list them, I agree to die.
ION: Go on, name them . . . Your confidence is strange.

[ION *opens the basket and* CREUSA *turns her head away so as
not to look*]

CREUSA: Item one, check: some fabric that I wove while still a girl.
ION: What sort of fabric? Girls weave lots of things.
CREUSA: It's unfinished: a beginner's effort on the loom.
ION: But the design? You won't catch me there!
CREUSA: A Gorgon, woven at the center of the cloth which . . .
ION: [*shaken*] Great Zeus! the hounds of destiny are on me.
CREUSA: . . . is fringed with snakes—like the aegis.

[ION *pulls out the fabric so that* CREUSA *can see it*]

ION: The weave—take a look. [*Aside*] Things seem to be coming
together,
like an oracle.
CREUSA: [*fingering the material*]
How wonderfully it has kept the work of my girlhood!
ION: What else is there? Was that a lucky guess?
CREUSA: Snakes in gold—an antique—a present from Athena.
She likes children to have them in memory of Erichthonius.

ION: What is it for, tell me? This golden bauble? What use is it?
CREUSA: To hang around the necks of newborn babies, my son.
ION: [*pulling it out of the basket*]
Here it is . . . Now what about the third thing inside?
CREUSA: A chaplet of the olive I crowned you with
    from the one Athena first planted on our rock.
If that is here
    it will not have lost its greenness;
    it'll still be vigorous
    because it comes from a holy tree.

[ION, *amazed, brings the fresh-looking olive chaplet out of the
basket, then flings himself into his mother's arms*]

ION: My own dearest mother, what bliss to see you!
    And what bliss I see in the face I kiss!
CREUSA: My child, my light, more dazzling to a mother than the
                                                                    sun
    (as the god will know),
    I hold you in my arms,
    the treasure I never hoped to find,
I thought you had gone long ago
    to dwell among the shades with Persephone.
ION: Instead, dearest mother, here I am and in your arms:
    you see one resurrected from the dead.
CREUSA: [*breaking into verse*]
    O bright heavenly spaces,
    What words can I find to shout?
    Where did this happiness spring from,
This rapture and surprise?
ION: An impossible undared for hope, to discover I am yours.
CREUSA: I am still trembling.
ION: Lest you don't have me, but you do.
CREUSA: I'd banished every hope from me.

[*Turning to the* PRIESTESS]

Madam, how did you, how ever did you
    Come to take my baby in your arms?
    By what hand did he come to Loxias?
ION: By providence divine : . . Oh may our future

be as happy as our past was sad!

CREUSA: My son, in tears were you born,
And from me in tears were you torn.
But now against your cheek
Blessed and blissful, I breathe.

ION: What you say of yourself you say for me.

CREUSA: No longer childless or sonless
My house has a spark, a flame.
My country has a prince,
Erechtheus is young again.
His halls are loosed from night
And fixed on the shine of the sun.

ION: Mother, let my father share our happiness.

CREUSA: My son, you don't know what you say ... The truth
must out.

ION: What?

CREUSA: You came from ... someone else ... someone very
else.

ION: No, don't tell me: not a bastard born?

CREUSA: Not with dancing and the flaring of torches
Were you conceived, my dear one;
Were you born, dear son.

ION: O ... h! I am baseborn, then, Mother—but of whom?

CREUSA: Think of the Gorgon-killer,* whose ...

ION: Meaning what?

CREUSA: ... whose seat on the hill of olives
High above my house ...

ION: You're talking in riddles ... I don't follow.

CREUSA: ... near the Rock of the Nightingales
Where Apollo ...

ION: Apollo? Why speak of him?

CREUSA: ... with me lying on a hidden couch ...

ION: Go on. This presages good news for me.

CREUSA: After a ten-month passage
I bore you in secret to Apollo.

ION: Oh tidings of joy, if what you say is true!

CREUSA: Afraid of my mother, I wrapped you around
In these swaddling clothes so rough-and-ready,

---

*Gorgon-killer: Pallas Athena.

A young girl's fumbling.
> No mother's breast to give you milk,
> No mother's hands to bathe you:
> Tossed into a derelict cave,
> A morsel for birds to tear and eat,

You were left to die.

ION: What appalling bravery, Mother!

CREUSA: No, dread, my son
> It was dread that made me cast you out:

I was your unwilling killer.

ION: And I yours.

CREUSA: Dire indeed was our destiny then
> And dire our destiny to follow:
> Flung to and fro, baubles of fate
> Sometimes fair, sometimes foul.

But winds veer.
> May a fair wind stay—
> A calm after storm, my child.

We have suffered enough.

LEADER: Never let anyone suppose,
> in view of what has happened then,
> that something good can't happen now.

ION: Oh the topsy-turvy vicissitudes of chance,
> twisting between failure and success!

How nearly did I kill my mother
> unwittingly and face disaster!

What nightmare!

How in the space of a single day can we make sense
> of the sun's golden and unrolling scroll?

[*He turns to* CREUSA]

Be that as it may, in you, my mother,
> I have unearthed a treasure, and as to my birth,
> I cannot quarrel with that.

[*He pauses, then beckons* CREUSA]

There is however something I must say to you alone.
Come closer, Mother.

Let me whisper it in your ear and swaddle it in dark.
Are you certain
    that like any fragile girl
    you did not succumb to a secret lover
    and then lay it on the god?
Could you perhaps be trying to escape the disgrace
    of bearing me by claiming that Apollo,
    no mortal man, had sired me?
CREUSA: No, by Athena goddess of victory,
    who in days of old fought side by side with Zeus
    in her chariot against the Giants,
    no living mortal is your father
    other than he that reared you,
    the lord Apollo.
ION: Why then did he hand over his son to another father
    and declare that I was the born son of Xuthus?
CREUSA: No, not born son but given son: born of Apollo, given to
                                                                Xuthus;
    just as a friend might give a friend his son to be a son and heir.

[ION *pauses, as if seeking courage to ask the next question*]

ION: Is the god genuine or are his oracles a fraud?
    I am troubled, Mother, and with good reason.
CREUSA: Listen, my son, this is what I've come to think.
    It was for your good that Loxias established you in a noble
                                                                house.
Had you been known as the god's
    you wouldn't have inherited a home or father's name.
How could you, when I myself kept the union secret
    and slyly tried to kill you?
For your well-being he bequeathed you to another father.
ION: This cannot be passed so lightly. I must pursue it.
    I shall walk into the temple and question Loxias.
    Either I am from a mortal man, or from Apollo.

[ION *strides towards the temple but halts amazed, for above the
temple buildings* PALLAS ATHENA *has appeared in majesty,
riding in a small chariot. Some fall to their knees, some cower,
some prepare to run*]

Oh look! a godlike vision more brilliant than the sun.
Mother, we must fly,
    not gaze on deity without the given grace.

[PALLAS ATHENA *signals to all to stay*]

ATHENA: Do not run away. I am no adversary
    that you should run from me.
I am your friend here as I am in Athens.
I am Pallas who has come to you,
    I who gave your land my name.
I hasten here on Phoebus' behalf,
    who did not think it fitting to confront you both
    lest bickerings about the past be tossed back and forth,
    so he sent me to give his message. To whit:

[*Directing her gaze on* ION]

This lady *is* your mother,
    and Apollo *is* your father.
He bequeathed you to another not your father
    just to let you have a noble home.
Once the truth was out and Creusa knew,
    he feared you might die by your mother's hand
    or she be killed by you,
    and so he set himself to save you.
The lord Apollo meant to keep this quiet
    until you went to Athens,
    then tell you that this woman is your mother
    and that you are her and Apollo's son.

[ATHENA *waits for this statement to sink in*]

Now to complete my errand:
· listen, the two of you, to the god's oracles,
    which I harnessed my chaise just to bring you.
Take this boy, Creusa, and go to the land of Cecrops*
    and set him on the kingly throne.
Scion of the sons of Erechtheus,

---

land of Cecrops: i.e., Athens.

he is fit to rule my land.
His fame shall spread through all Hellas.
And the four sons born to him,
    stemming from a single stock,
    shall give their names to the four clans of my country:
    those natives of my tableland:
The Gelions first, then come the Hoplites,
    followed by the Argades, and last the Aegicores:
    clan-named from my aegis.
Their children in due time
    shall colonize the island cities of the Cyclades
    and the mainland coasts, thus strengthening my land.
On opposite sides of the straits
    they shall occupy the terrains of two continents—
    Europe and Asia's territories—
    and be called the Ionians after this young boy here,
    and they shall achieve fame.

[*Looking at* CREUSA]

To you and Xuthus shall be born two sons:
    Dorus, from whom in the land of Pelops,
    the glory and renown of the Dorian nation
    shall take its rise;
and Achaeus,
    who shall rule over the coastal lands of Rhion,
    whose people will take their name from him and their distinc-
                                                         tion.

Apollo has arranged all things well.
First, he gave you an easy lying-in,
    which kept all your friends from knowing;
    then, after you had given birth to this boy
    and wrapped him in his swaddling clothes,
    he had Hermes gather him up
    and waft him here in his arms,
    feed him and not let his life go out.
Now, as to his being yours, say nothing.
Let Xuthus enjoy his wishful thinking,
    as you your blessings.

*   *   *

So, farewell,
   after this relief from your ordeals
   I predict for you a happy time.
ION: O Pallas, daughter of Zeus Supreme,
   we lack no faith in what you tell us.
I firmly believe that my father is Apollo
   and this lady is my mother.
Even before you said it I wanted to believe it.
CREUSA: And from me, hear this:
   I now praise Apollo, whom I would not praise before,
   because he gives me back the child he once ignored.
Beautiful now are the portals that I face,
   and the god's shrine—once so loathsome.
Now I pay homage before his gates
   and clasp with joy the knocker on these doors.
ATHENA: And I praise your change of heart
   now that you praise the god.
Oh yes, the gods act slowly,
   but finally with power and surely.
CREUSA: [*turning to* ION] Let us go home, my son.
ATHENA: Go. I shall be with you.
CREUSA: The champion guardian of our way.
ATHENA: And your city's friend.

   [*To* ION]

Yours is to sit on the ancient throne.
ION: A priceless possession.

   [*There is a reverent hush as* ATHENA *fades from view.* CREUSA
   and ION *and all their attendants begin to move away. The
   women of the* CHORUS *muster for the exodus march*]

EXODUS

WHOLE CHORUS: Praised be Apollo, son of Zeus and Leto.
   Those whom misfortune undermines
   Should reverence the gods and take courage.
   The virtuous in the end will win,
   The wicked, by their nature, not:
Because of sin.

ELECTRA

ΗΛΕΚΤΡΑ

For Clarissa and Cordelia Roche

If one can overlook her exaggerated hatred of her mother for having murdered her contemptible father, Electrà is a well-meaning enough woman who genuinely cares for the peasant to whom she is married in name only: a marriage forced on her by her mother and Aegisthus to render her powerless. Though she conceives it her duty to avenge her father, she would rather think of marriage, nurses, and babies, and is motivated as much by envy of her mother as by devotion to her father.

As to Clytemnestra, if murder is ever justified, she is not nearly so evil as her daughter makes out. True, she took a lover during the ten years her husband was away at Troy, but he had already irredeemably blotted his copybook by sacrificing her daughter Iphigenia.

Their son, the young man Orestes, who expatiates about nobility and is no doubt personally attractive, comes over as something of a prig and a fumbler, alternately self-pitying and self-important. But he is handicapped from the beginning by a senseless oracle of Apollo telling him to avenge his father and murder his mother. His simplemindedness in trying to follow these instructions is almost endearing. But he needs a lot of bolstering before he can play his part in the murders, which when done merely reveal the predictability and ineptitude of human beings. Euripides seems to be saying: "Take supposedly great characters and push them into the arena of the real world and see how they expose themselves."

Because of his determination to depict people as they are and not as they could or ought to be, Euripides was sniped at from the beginning. Even after writing his masterpiece *The Trojan Women*, there were those who said the work clearly showed that he didn't know how to write a play.

Nevertheless, his plays increasingly disclosed how tellingly they dealt with the human scene, and by the time of Alexander the Great (mid-fourth century B.C.) they were being mounted wherever Greek was spoken—from Athens to the borders of India.

Apart from the verbal beauty of this play, we are given elements of pleasure open and simple enough to appeal to the sensitivity of the most ordinary mortal: in scenes and vignettes, costumes, movements and groupings, presenting a living tableau unexpected and varied.

CHARACTERS

PEASANT, honest countryman of Mycenae
ELECTRA, daughter of Agamemnon and Clytemnestra
ORESTES, brother of Electra
PYLADES, lifelong comrade of Orestes
CLYTEMNESTRA, wife of Agamemnon and Queen of Argos
OLD TUTOR, servant of Agamemnon
MESSENGER, servant of Orestes
CASTOR AND POLLUX, brothers of Clytemnestra
CHORUS of Argive women
ATTENDANTS of Orestes and Pylades (who are both princes)
HANDMAIDS of Clytemnestra

TIME AND SETTING

A little before dawn outside a peasant's cottage and within sight of the royal palace of Mycenae, near the town of Argolis in Argos, where some eighteen years ago Clytemnestra and her lover Aegisthus slew Agamemnon in his silver bath. Orestes, who was a baby and was saved from the slaughter, is now a young man and has returned to the scene with his friend Pylades, hoping to find his sister, and because of an oracle of Apollo telling him to kill his mother.

PROLOGUE

[*The* PEASANT *comes out of the cottage and gazes over the plain*]

PEASANT: Dear old Argos with your streams of Inachus,
    from where Agamemnon King once launched
    a thousand ships against the land of Troy
    and killed Priam, king of Ilium,

sacking Troy, that Dardanian city . . .
He came back here in triumph to Argos
    heaping its lofty temples with loot from abroad.
Fortune smiled on him at Troy.
Not so in his own house,
    where he was tricked to his death by his wife Clytemnestra
    and the hand of Aegisthus, Thyestes' son.

When King Agamemnon sailed to Troy
    he left behind a boy, Orestes, and a girl, Electra.
Of these two, Orestes
    was saved from the murdering hand of Aegisthus
    by his father's old tutor,
    who gave him to Strophius
    to be brought up in the land of Phocis.
But the girl, Electra, stayed on in her father's house
    and in the first delicate bloom of her youth
    was courted by suitors, princely men,
    from all over Hellas.

Aegisthus, nervous that she might bear one of these a son,
    who one day would avenge the murdered king,
kept her closeted
    well out of the sight of any bridegroom.
This however did not rid him of his fear,
    and terrified she might secretly bear a child,
he made up his mind to kill her.
    But her mother—coldhearted woman that she was—
saved her from Aegisthus.
Killing her husband was one thing:
killing children, quite another.

Aegisthus then alighted on another plan.
He offered a prize in gold
    to anyone who would kill Agamemnon's son,
    who had fled the land;
meanwhile giving me Electra as my wife.
Well, I am a true-bred Mycenaean
    and though a poor man, by no means ignoble.
Nobility however does not cancel poverty.

*   *   *

Aegisthus abated his anxiety
  by giving her to a nobody,
  knowing that if a man of power married her
  the murder of Agamemnon would be roused from slumber
  and heavy retribution fall on Aegisthus' head.

Here let me make quite clear
(with Aphrodite as my witness)
  that not once have I taken advantage of her bed.
She is a virgin still.
I would count it a disgrace
  to deflower the child of a noble house . . .
  I am so far beneath her by birth.
But I blush for Orestes as if he were my brother
  should he ever come to Argos and look upon
  his sister's humiliating marriage.

In the eyes of many I may be a fool, ·
  taking a young girl into my house and not touching her.
Such a one provides a prurient yardstick
  by which he should himself be measured,
  and is exactly what he thinks of *me*.

[ELECTRA *walks out of the cottage carrying a pitcher on her head. She is solemn and drably dressed, and stands for a moment gazing over the lightening plain—though it is still dark*]

FIRST EPISODE

ELECTRA: I salute you, black-winged Night,
  nurse of the golden stars,
  each dawn that I fill my pitcher at the spring,
  bearing it on my head.
I am not forced to do this menial work.
I choose to do it
  to show the gods Aegisthus' wickedness
  and raise a lamentation for my father.
My mother, that evil daughter of Tyndareus,

has, to please her husband, turned me out of the palace.
She has borne Aegisthus other children,
 so Orestes and I count for nothing.
PEASANT: [*approaching her*] My poor girl,
 why must you toil and moil for me
 even when I beg you not to—
 you who have been nurtured royally?
ELECTRA: My friend,
 I look on you as I would a god,
 for you have not taken advantage of my wretchedness.
Blessed are those mortals
 who find physicians such as you when they are in trouble.
I count it my duty to ease your life
 and share your burden as far as I can.
You labor in the fields hard enough.
It is only fair that I should keep the house.
How sweet it is for a man coming in from toil
 to find a smiling home.
PEASANT: Please yourself then:
 our cottage is not far from the spring
 and it is almost dawn.
I must drive the cattle to the pastures and sow the fields.
Idleness and pious prating
 never earned a livelihood.

[*As the* PEASANT *goes off into the fields and* ELECTRA *walks
with her pitcher to the spring, two young men appear along
the coastal road:* ORESTES *and* PYLADES. *They are clad in
loose tunics worn over a kind of kilt, with woollen capes
thrown over their shoulders. Their feet are shod in heavy sandals laced up the calf, and broad-rimmed hats hang at their
sides*]

ORESTES: You know, Pylades,
 in loyalty and love I count you my dearest comrade.
Of all Orestes' friends you are the only one
 who stood by me in my ordeal
 when the foul Aegisthus and my ever-evil mother
slew my father.
Now by Apollo's oracle I am bidden to Argos secretly

to pay back the assassins of my father.
Last night I went to my father's tomb
  and with my tears left there a lock of hair
  and poured the blood of a sheep upon the grave:
  all without the knowledge of this country's rulers.
I shall not set foot inside the walls
  but stay on the doorstep here—and for a double reason.
If discovered I can slip over the border,
  and secondly to find my sister.
Rumor has it she is married
  and a maid no longer.
I must get in touch with her
  and ask her help in this act of vengeance.
I must find out exactly what is going on
  inside these walls.

But already the pale face of dawn is lightening.
Let us step off this path awhile
  till some plowman or some servant woman comes
  whom we can ask if my sister lives anywhere near.

Ah! I see a servant girl
  carrying a heavy pitcher of water on her cropped head.
Crouch down, Pylades;
  let us see if we can learn from this servant girl
  what we came here to discover.

[ORESTES *and* PYLADES *slip behind some trees as* ELECTRA,
returning from the spring, balances a full pitcher on her head.
The meter changes into those of strophe and antistrophe]

LYRIC MONOLOGUE

STROPHE I

ELECTRA: Foot walk faster, time is pressing.
  Keep on keeping on though you be weeping.
  Sad, how sad!
  Agamemnon sired me, Clytemnestra,
  Tyndareus' hateful daughter, bore me.
  Unhappy Electra is what they call me

In this town here.
I hate my burdens, I hate my life.
Father, do you lie in Hades,
Cut down by your wife and by Aegisthus?
Oh Agamemnon!

MESODE

Stir up the tears again
 Only tears relieve the pain.

ANTISTROPHE I

Foot walk faster, time is pressing.
 Keep on keeping on though you be weeping.
 Sad, how sad!
 What town my brother—in what haven
 Do you linger in your wandering,
 Far from that unhappy sister
 You said goodbye to at the palace
 Leaving her to untold sorrows.
 Come now save me from these sorrows.
 Zeus, O Zeus, avenge my father's
 Bloody murder: come to Argos.

STROPHE II

Set down the pitcher, lift it from your head.
 Salute the dawn with lamentations
 As you saluted night
 With dirges for your father, dirges
 For my dead father under sods.
 These lamentations are my occupation
 As into my tender neck I dig my nails
 And buffet my shorn head for your dying.
 And like some doleful swan
 Calling forlornly by the flooding river
 For her lost sire
 Tangled in the meshes of a net,
 So do I call for you—with tears, my father.

ANTISTROPHE II*

Oh that last and fatal bath of yours
   As you splashed with death
   And lay down dying there.
   It is unbelievable:
   The bitter double blade, the bitter plot,
   That ambushed you when you came back from Troy.
   It was not with wreaths and garlands, no,
   That your wife saluted you,
   But with the two-edged sword of Aegisthus.

[*The* CHORUS, *composed of fifteen young peasant women, in a
slow march, enters*]

CHORAL DIALOGUE

STROPHE

Daughter of Agamemnon,
   I have found your rustic home.
   A man came by from the mountains,
   A milkman from Mycenae,
   With news that the Argives have proclaimed
   A three-day festival,
   And all the young girls are to go in procession
   To the temple of Hera.
ELECTRA: No splendid raiment,
   No necklaces of gold,
   Stir the heart of this wretch that I am.
   I shall not take my place among the Argive girls
   To trip and twirl,
   But pass the night in tears—
   As I pass the day.
   Look at my snarled hair†
   And the rags I wear . . .
   How do they suit a princess—
   Agamemnon's daughter?
   How do they match
   My father's sack of Troy?

---

*This antistrophe does not correspond in number of lines with the strophe.
†Euripides seems to have forgotten that he has just described her hair as cropped.

ANTISTROPHE

CHORUS: Great is the goddess, so come.
 I'll lend you a beautiful gown
 And glittering jewels of gold.
 Do you think that tears can quell
 Your foes if you do not honor the gods:
 Not with moaning but with prayers
 For happy days, my child?
ELECTRA: Not one of the gods
 Will listen to the cries
 Of this wretched girl
 Or recall her sacrifices for her father.
 But I grieve for him, he that is gone,
 And he that wanders
 A slave at someone's hearth
 In an alien land—
 And he sprung from a king,
 While I live in a hovel
 Pining in the cliffs,
 Banished from my home.
 My mother shares with another
 A bed blotched with murder.
LEADER: Your mother's sister, Helen, is the cause
 of so much the Greeks have endured.

[ORESTES *and* PYLADES *show themselves, together with their servants in the background*]

SECOND EPISODE

ELECTRA: God help us, women, I must cease my dirge.
 Strange-looking men from near the cottage have ambushed us.
Take to the road and fly.
I shall run into the cottage to escape these blackguards.

[ORESTES *puts out a hand to stop her*]

ORESTES: Stay, unhappy woman . . . Don't tremble at my touch.
ELECTRA: God Apollo, please, don't let me be killed.
ORESTES: I'd rather kill someone that I hated.
ELECTRA: Let go. Don't handle what you should not touch.

ORESTES: There is none I may touch with better right.

ELECTRA: What, with drawn sword right outside my house?

ORESTES: Wait, hear me out and you'll not say no.

ELECTRA: I have no choice. I am in your power.

ORESTES: I have news for you from your brother.

ELECTRA: Oh my friend, is he alive or dead?

ORESTES: Alive. Let me give you the good news first.

ELECTRA: Blessings on you for your sweet words.

ORESTES: Blessings on us both, to share together.

ELECTRA: Poor forlorn! Where does he live his forlorn days of
                                                    banishment?

ORESTES: He roams abroad. He has no single city.

ELECTRA: But does he have enough to live on day by day?

ORESTES: In truth, no. But exile cuts down a man's appetite.

ELECTRA: What is the message you bring from him?

ORESTES: He wants to know if you live and how you are.

ELECTRA: Well, to begin with, see how my body has withered.

ORESTES: Indeed, so wasted with grief it makes me cry to see.

ELECTRA: And cropped head—like a Scythian slave.

ORESTES: The loss of your brother and father are eating your
                                                    heart away.

ELECTRA: I know, I know! Who can be dearer than they?

ORESTES: How sad! And what do you feel about your brother?

ELECTRA: A dear one far away when he should be near.

ORESTES: What makes you live here, so far from town?

ELECTRA: My friend, I am married. A marriage like death.

ORESTES: To a lowly Mycenaean? I pity your brother.

ELECTRA: Hardly the kind of man my father had in mind.

ORESTES: Say whom, so I can tell your brother.

ELECTRA: This is my husband's cottage—far from the city.

ORESTES: Fit dwelling for a ditch-digger or a cowman.

ELECTRA: He is a poor man but kind, and he respects me.

ORESTES: How does this husband of yours show respect?

ELECTRA: Not once has he taken advantage of me.

ORESTES: Through some scruple of religion, or do you not appeal
                                                    to him?

ELECTRA: He thinks it wrong to dishonor my parents.

ORESTES: Surely he was thrilled to make a match like this?

ELECTRA: He thought the man who gave me had no right to.

ORESTES: And he was fearful of the wrath of Orestes?

ELECTRA: Fearful maybe, but he is also naturally good.

ORESTES: A generous character . . . He must be rewarded.

ELECTRA: Yes, if Orestes ever reaches home.

ORESTES: And your own mother allowed you to be treated so?

ELECTRA: My friend, women love their husbands, not their children.

ORESTES: But Aegisthus, why did he treat you so abominably?

ELECTRA: He wanted my children to be nonentities.

ORESTES: I see . . . Who would never be avengers?

ELECTRA: That's what he had in mind. May he be punished for it.

ORESTES: Does Aegisthus know you are still a virgin?

ELECTRA: He does not. I have kept it from him.

ORESTES: [glancing at the CHORUS]

These women listening here—are they your friends?

ELECTRA: Yes, they will not divulge our conversation.

ORESTES: But if Orestes came to Argos, what could he do?

ELECTRA: Your question surprises me. He'd act, of course!

ORESTES: If he did return, how would he kill your father's murderers?

ELECTRA: He'd dare what those assassins of his father dared.

ORESTES: And would you dare with him to kill your mother?

ELECTRA: I would . . . using the same ax that destroyed my father.*

ORESTES: Shall I tell Orestes this? Is your mind made up?

ELECTRA: Let me die, so long as I kill my mother.

ORESTES: If only Orestes was here to hear you utter this!

ELECTRA: My friend, I should not know him if I saw him.

ORESTES: Of course! You were both children when you parted.

ELECTRA: Only one of my friends would recognize him.

ORESTES: The one, they say, who stole him away from murder?

ELECTRA: An old man from long ago who brought my father up.

ORESTES: Is your father buried in a tomb?

ELECTRA: Yes, of sorts—he was flung out from the palace.

ORESTES: A sorry sorry tale!

How even the troubles of strangers can wring the human heart.
But continue

so that I may report your story to your brother . . .

---

*Euripides seems uncertain about the instrument. Sometimes it is an ax, sometimes a two-edged sword.

Not a matter to celebrate but to attend to all the same.
Compassion is an attribute of the cultured man
    that the dolt knows nothing of:
    but compassion and understanding exact their price.
LEADER: I feel what this man feels,
    but living far from the city
    have no idea what goes on there.
I should like to know.
ELECTRA: Since I must, let me speak out,
    but be it to a friend.
Let me tell of the disasters
    that have fallen on me and my father.
And I ask you, my friend,
    since it is you who have prompted me,
    to relay to Orestes the horrors that have happened to me and
                                  Agamemnon.

Tell him first
    of the rags I wear in this rustic hovel.
Tell him of the filthy sight I am,
    living in a hut—I that stem from royal palaces.
I weave my own clothes with my own hands,
    else would be naked.
I fetch water from the spring.
I take no part in festivals:
    no part in dances.
I flee the society of matrons,
    virgin that I am.
I blush when I think of Castor my cousin,
    to whom I was engaged before he joined the gods.
My mother lords it on a throne,
    weltering in the captured wealth of Troy
    and surrounded by captive ladies from the Orient
    whom my father won:
    all clad in gorgeous Oriental robes
    fastened with brooches of gold.
And all the time my father's blood
    rots and blackens in the palace
    while his murderer mounts his chariot,
    the very chariot my father rode,

and rides out in public
proudly holding in his criminal hands
the scepter that once marshaled the whole of Hellas.

Agamemnon's tomb, neglected and unhonored,
has received neither libations nor sprigs of myrtle.
It is bare of ornament,
and that magnificent man, called my mother's consort,
sodden in wine cavorts on the grave
and pelts my father's monument with stones,
shouting out insults like:
"Where is Orestes, that fine lad?
How zealous he shows himself
in protecting your tomb!"
So by Orestes' absence is he ridiculed.

[*Going down on her knees*]

My friend, I beseech you, tell him this.
I speak for the many who summon him . . .
my hands, my lips, my blighted heart, my shaven head,
and the father that begot him.
It is unthinkable that the son of a father who dismembered Troy
should not cut down in single combat his mortal enemy.
LEADER: I see the man who is called your husband
approaching the cottage, his day's work done.

[*The* PEASANT, *looking a little weary after his digging and with mud clinging to his boots, approaches with a look of concern at seeing* ORESTES *and* PYLADES *together with* ELECTRA]

PEASANT: Holla! Who are these strangers coming towards my
house?
What brings them to my rural doors?
Is it me they want?
A woman should not stand around talking with young men.
ELECTRA: [*taking his hand*] Dear friend, do not be suspicious.
Let me tell you what this means.
These visitors have brought me tidings of Orestes.

[*Turning to* ORESTES *and* PYLADES]

Sirs, forgive his abruptness.

PEASANT: Do they say he lives and sees the light?

ELECTRA: According to their story, yes—and I believe them.

PEASANT: Does he know what you and your father have been through?

ELECTRA: Let us hope so. But a man in exile has little power.

PEASANT: What was the message from Orestes that they brought?

ELECTRA: He sent to find out what I was suffering.

PEASANT: Your sufferings are obvious, and you will tell the rest.

ELECTRA: They already know. There is nothing left to tell them.

PEASANT: Then shouldn't you open your doors and welcome them in?

[*The* PEASANT *turns to* ORESTES *and* PYLADES, *beckoning*]

Come into the house.
　　In exchange for your good news accept my modest hospitality.

[*Turning to the young men's servants*]

Take their baggage into the house, men.

[*Seeing the hesitation of* ORESTES *and* PYLADES]

Please do not refuse me.
　　You are friends coming from a friend,
　　Poor as I am, I shall not be niggardly.

[*As the* PEASANT *leads the way into his cottage, followed by* PYLADES, ORESTES *and* ELECTRA *pause on the threshold*]

ORESTES: Great gods! So this is the man that lets you thwart his marriage—
　　the man who will not shame Orestes.

ELECTRA: Yes, the man known as unlucky Electra's husband.

ORESTES: Ah, one can never foretell a manly spirit,
　　so full of variety is the nature of men.
I have met a nonentity, the son of a fine man,
　　and I have seen cultured children born of humble parents.
I have seen a millionaire with a shriveled heart,
　　and a generous spirit in the heart of a pauper.

By what measure can one truly judge and discriminate?
By riches?
   That would be no better gauge than poverty,
   and poverty's even worse:
It teaches men to do wrong through need.
What about skill at arms?
   Just to see a man with a spear is no guarantee
   that he is a brave man . . .
Best not try to unravel these paradoxes.

Look at this man:
   he has no standing among the Argives,
   is not swollen-headed because of his line,
   is a man of the people,
   yet whose humanity blazes forth.
So learn some wisdom
   and avoid the pitfall of hasty judgment.
Only by conduct and by character
   should you judge the quality of a human being:
   those that make contented states and happy families.
The mere muscled hunk
   with not a thought in his head
   is an effigy fit for the marketplace.
Bulging biceps succumb to the shock of the lance
   no less than the puny arm.
In all, it is the spirit that matters.

So let us honor the hospitality of this cottage,
   in the name of Agamemnon's son whether here or not—
   him for whom we have come.
Slaves push inside . . .
Give me a poor man for a host rather than a rich one:
   a poor man with a heart.

   [*Turning to* ELECTRA]

I thank this man for his invitation,
   but I wish your brother were here
   bursting with prosperity
   to lead me into a prosperous home.

Perhaps he will come.
The oracles of Apollo can't go wrong
   and human guesswork's not worth a damn.

   [ORESTES *and his servants enter the cottage, leaving the* PEASANT
   and ELECTRA *still outside*]

LEADER: Some joy, Electra, more than ever,
   should rekindle our hearts.
Fate is softening its hardness
   and unfolding a little happiness.
ELECTRA: [*to* PEASANT] My dear friend,
   you know the poverty of your hearth,
   why must you strain your resources for these guests?
PEASANT: Why ever not?
If they are as noble as they seem
   they will surely be content with my provision,
   meager or otherwise.
ELECTRA: Well, since you have made your mistake, poor as you
                             are,
   go to the good old man who brought my father up.
You will find him pasturing his flocks
   near the river Tanais
   which separates Argos from Sparta,
   for he has been banished from the city.
Ask him to come here
   with some provender for the guests that have arrived.
He will be overjoyed and thank heaven to hear
   that the boy he once saved is still alive.
From my mother's home, my father's palace,
   we would not get a scrap:
   and our news that Orestes is alive
   would come as a deathblow to that wretched woman.
PEASANT: So, if you please,
   let me go and take your message to the old man.
Meanwhile, get things ready in the cottage
   as quickly as you can.
Women are magic improvisors when it comes to food.
Even now there's enough in the house
   to take care of these men for a single day.

[ELECTRA *goes into the cottage. The* PEASANT *pauses on the
threshold as if some great thought had struck him*]

When I come to think it over,
  it occurs to me that wealth is almost everything.
One can entertain,
  or provide for a sick body:
  though for one's daily bread
  it's much the same rich or poor:
  a full stomach is a full stomach.

[*As the* PEASANT *goes off to find the* OLD MAN, *the women of
the* CHORUS *celebrate in retrospect the arrival of Achilles and
Agamemnon on the shores of Troy. They describe with wonder
Achilles' famous shield with its Gorgon's head and chariot of
the Sun: also Achilles' golden helmet depicting the Sphinxes
carrying off their victims. Finally, they turn on* CLYTEMNESTRA,
the traitoress of all this glory, and prophesy her death.
ELECTRA *stands listening*]

FOURTH CHORAL ODE

STROPHE I

CHORUS: You glorious ships that sailed to Troy
  Bristling with oars and pounding the main
  Where the Nereids danced
  And the music-besotted dolphins bounded
  Teasing the prows as they forged along:
  You ships that escorted spring-footed Achilles,
  Agamemnon too,
  To the shores of Simoïs at Troy . . .

ANTISTROPHE I

The Nereids skirting the Cape of Euboea
  Carried the shield Hephaestus shaped
  On his anvil of gold.
  Past Mount Pelion, past the lonely glens of Ossa,
  They came for Achilles, the stripling son
  Of Thetis, reared by a gentle father
  To be the glory of Greece and champion

Challenger for the sons of Atreus.

STROPHE II

Achilles, son of Thetis, one day
   I heard in the port of Nauplia,
   From one rèturning from Troy, of your famous shield
   Whose design itself was enough to frighten the Trojans.
   Its rim showed Perseus winged with sandals
   Hovering over the sea and holding
   The head of the Gorgon with sliced throat.
   With him was Hermes, Maia's son:
   A god of the fields.

ANTISTROPHE II

In the center of the shield the sun blazed
   Drawn by a chariot of flying chargers.
   There too the Pleiades danced with the Hyades
   To tell Hector his sun was about to set.
   On the gold of the helmet Sphinxes clutched
   In their talons victims failing the riddle.
   On the breastplate a fire-breathing
   Lioness with open claws was leaping
   On a colt from Pirene.

EPODE

On his murderous lance a four-horse chariot
   Careering on, and a cloud of black dust
   Rolling along behind their backs . . .
   But the leader of these warriors was cut down
   For your illicit love, perfidious child of Tyndareus.
   Therefore the gods above one day
   Shall send you to your slaughter,
   And I shall see, oh, I shall see
   The steel piercing your throat
   And the spurt of blood.

[*The* OLD TUTOR *enters. He is dressed in a homespun mantle that reaches to his knees, and his loose trouser legs are lagged with hessian. Around his shoulders he carries a lamb, and a*

*basket hangs full of provisions. He walks carefully over the
uneven ground, talking to himself.*

THIRD EPISODE

TUTOR: Where, where is the young woman, the princess my
                                     mistress,
  daughter of Agamemnon,
  whom long ago I reared?
My word, how hard this path is to her house!
  Hard for the feet of this shriveled old man.
No matter, I must reach my friends:
  push on this bent old back,
  these quaking knees.

[*He sees* ELECTRA *coming out of the cottage*]

Ah, there you are, my daughter, by the house.
Look, I've brought you a suckling from my flock
  just taken from its mother,
  and wreaths of flowers,
  and cheese fresh from the frame,
  and last, not least, this ancient wine, this gift of Bacchus,
  with its smooth bouquet.
There is only a little
  but enough to transform a weaker draft.

[*Clapping his hands*]

Come, servants,
  and carry all this into the house—
  it is for the guests . . .
I must wipe away my tears with this ragged old sleeve.
ELECTRA: What's this, old man, your eyes are brimming?
  Have my old sorrows mingled with your own?
Or is your sadness for Orestes' banishment
  and for my father whom you dandled in your arms and nur-
                                         tured?

A lost delight to you and to your friends.
TUTOR: Lost indeed!
  But that is not what made me sad.

It was that as I passed the tomb
    and found it abandoned, I knelt and wept.
Then I undid the plug of the wineskin
.   that I've brought your guests and poured libations,
    placing sprigs of myrtle on the tomb.
Nearby the pyre
    I saw a slaughtered sheep with black fleece,
    its blood but newly spilt,
    and locks of golden hair from a blond head.
It made me wonder, child,
    who in the world would approach that tomb?
Certainly no Argive would.
Could your brother have arrived by stealth and passed
    paying this honor to your father's tomb?
Put this lock of hair against your head
    and see if its hue is like yours.
Offspring of the same father
    often manifest similarities.
ELECTRA: What nonsense you talk, old man,
    if you imagine that my courageous brother
    would slink into this land in terror of Aegisthus.
Besides,
    how could a lock of his hair match mine:
    the hair of a man exposed to manly sports
    with the hair of a woman
    softened by brush and comb?
No, the comparison does not hold.
Besides, old man, one often comes across
    people with similar hair
    who are not related at all.
TUTOR: Then step into his footstep
    and see if the print of his sole
    matches your foot, my child.
ELECTRA: Footprints on this rocky terrain? Hardly,
    and even if there could be,
    the feet of brother and sister, of male and female,
    are not the same. The male is larger.
TUTOR: If your brother did come here
    is there any piece of cloth of yours on him
    that you could recognize—

such as the clothes he wore when I stole him away from
death?

ELECTRA: Don't you know I was only a child
   when Orestes was banished from the land?
If I had woven garments for him
   how could he still be wearing
   clothes he wore as a child . . .
   unless his clothes grew with him?
No, some visitor passed and took compassion
   and made an offering of his hair,
   or he himself did by means of spies.

TUTOR: Who are these strangers?
   I'd like to question them about your brother.

ELECTRA: Here they come briskly from the house.

   [ORESTES *and* PYLADES *emerge from the cottage*]

A good-looking couple, sure!
   but one cannot always go by that.
   A noble facade can hide a villain.

ORESTES: Greetings, old man. . . Electra,
   who among your friends is this ancient relic?

ELECTRA: He was the one who brought my father up, sir.

ORESTES: You mean the one who stole your brother away?

ELECTRA: Yes, the one that saved him . . . if he is still alive.

ORESTES: Why is he staring at me like that—
   as if he scrutinized a newly minted coin?
Is he comparing me with someone?

ELECTRA: It delights him perhaps to see a comrade of Orestes.

ORESTES: A very dear comrade . . . Why is he circling me?

ELECTRA: That surprises me, too, my friend.

TUTOR: [*taking her hand*]
   Electra, noble child, say a prayer to the gods.

ELECTRA: For what? Something gone, something coming?

TUTOR: Something—a treasure—the god is about to reveal.

ELECTRA: See, I do say a prayer, though I don't know what
                                    you're talking about.

TUTOR: Take a second look, my child, at this beloved man.

ELECTRA: I've been staring at him a long time and I fear you've
                                    lost your wits.

TUTOR: Lost my wits when I see your own brother standing
there?

ELECTRA: Do you really mean it? . . . I can't believe it.

TUTOR: Yes; I am looking at Orestes, Agamemnon's son.

ELECTRA: How can I believe you? What evidence do you offer?

TUTOR: The scar on his eyebrow from a fall long ago
when chasing a fawn with you in your father's palace.

ELECTRA: Are you sure? . . . I do see the mark of a fall.

TUTOR: But still hesitate to run into his arms?

ELECTRA: [*flinging herself on* ORESTES]
No no no, old man, I am convinced . . .
At long last, Orestes, beyond all hope you have appeared.

ORESTES: At long last held by me.

ELECTRA: Never to be expected!

ORESTES: Never to be hoped!

ELECTRA: You are really he?

ORESTES: Yes, your only champion . . .
But now to close the net I have come to cast and shall—
or give up belief in gods if the good can be undone by evil.

[*Brother and sister remain in each other's arms while the
women of the* CHORUS *burst out in celebration*]

THIRD CHORAL ODE

CHORUS: You have come, you have come, at last you have come
As bright as a flare flooding the city.
Long was his exile . . . Far from the hearth of his fathers
He has roamed in disconsolate misery.
Some deity, some powerful god
Is making us triumph, oh yes.
So lift up your hands, lift up your voice,
Hurl your thanksgiving high into heaven,
That fortune, good fortune in his own country,
May follow the steps of your brother.

FOURTH EPISODE

ORESTES: So be it.
I thank you for your generous welcome.

Someday I shall make a return.
Meanwhile, old man,
  you have appeared in the nick of time.
Tell me what I must do
  to avenge my father's murder.
  Is there anyone in Argos, my friend,
  sympathetic to me,
  or am I—like my fate—a shattered man?
Whom shall I ask to help me?
Shall I do it by night or day?
What is the way to go against my foes?

TUTOR: My son, in failure no one is a friend:
  rare indeed is it to be accepted regardless of success or failure.
Now, listen to me.
You are not sustained by friends or wishful thinking.
The regaining of your ancestral home and city
  depends entirely on yourself—and a little luck.

ORESTES: Well, what do I have to do?

TUTOR: You must kill Aegisthus and your mother.

ORESTES: I have come for exactly that. But how shall I achieve
it?

TUTOR: Not by going inside the walls, even if you were willing
to.

ORESTES: Are they guarded by sentries and armed patrols?

TUTOR: Precisely. He's frightened of you. He cannot sleep.

ORESTES: So . . . what's the next move, old man?

TUTOR: Listen carefully. I have a plan.

ORESTES: A good one, I hope . . . I am all ears.

TUTOR: I caught a glimpse of Aegisthus as I stole here.

ORESTES: I follow you, but where exactly was it?

TUTOR: In the paddocks adjacent to these fields.

ORESTES: What was he up to? . . . I see a gleam of hope.

TUTOR: It looked as though he was preparing a banquet for the
nymphs.

ORESTES: For an infant's birthday, or a baby on its way?

TUTOR: I only know he was preparing to slay an ox.

ORESTES: How many were with him . . . just his servants?

TUTOR: No Argives were there—only people from the palace.

ORESTES: Was there anyone, old man, who could recognize me?

TUTOR: No, they are slaves. They have never seen you.

ORESTES: Would they side with me if I succeeded?

TUTOR: Yes. That is the nature of a slave—luckily for you.

ORESTES: How could I manage to get near him?

TUTOR: Let him see you at the spot where he celebrates.

ORESTES: Near his fields along the road, you mean.

TUTOR: When he sees you he'll invite you to the feast.

ORESTES: Please God, I'll be the bitterest of guests.

TUTOR: Just watch for your chance.

ORESTES: I will . . . Where is my mother at this moment?

TUTOR: In Argos. Her consort expects her later at the feast.

ORESTES: Why don't my mother and her husband go together?

TUTOR: She is embarrassed and fears derision.

ORESTES: I see. She's aware of the people's hatred.

TUTOR: Just so . . . An evil woman is abhorred.

ORESTES: But how can I kill her at the same time as him?

ELECTRA: [*stepping forward*] Leave my mother to me. I'll manage her death.

ORESTES: And fortune will arrange the rest.

ELECTRA: [*pointing to the* TUTOR] He can be a help to both of us.

ORESTES: Good . . . How do you mean to kill our mother?

ELECTRA: [*pauses in thought*]
Go to Clytemnestra, old man, and tell her . . . tell her
I have given birth to a boy.

TUTOR: Delivered some time ago or just now?

ELECTRA: Ten days ago . . . the normal time for a mother's purification.

TUTOR: How can this lead to your mother's demise?

ELECTRA: She will come when she hears I am not well and with a baby.

TUTOR: What makes you think she cares for you, my child?

ELECTRA: Mark my words, she'll come—to moan over the low birth of my baby.

TUTOR: Perhaps . . . But the main question is . . .

ELECTRA: The main question is: if she comes, she dies.

TUTOR: Then I hope she'll come right in at the door.

ELECTRA: Which is only a step from the entrance to Hades.

TUTOR: It would give me joy to see it.

ELECTRA: But first, old man, be Orestes' guide.

TUTOR: To the spot where Aegisthus is offering sacrifice?

ELECTRA: Yes, then deliver my message to my mother.

TUTOR: Straight as if it came from your own lips.
ELECTRA: [*to Orestes*] Go to work. Yours the privilege of first
blood.
ORESTES: So I do, following my guide.
TUTOR: Right here to escort you most willingly.

[*All three lift their hands in prayer*]

ORESTES: Great Zeus, God of Fathers, be god also of avengers.
ELECTRA: Pity us, for pitifully have we suffered.
TUTOR: Have compassion on the offspring of your blood.
ORESTES: Hera, Queen, who reigns over the altars of Mycenae . . .
ELECTRA: Grant us victory if our cause be right.
TUTOR: Let them avenge the murder of their father.

[*All three fall to the ground rapping the earth with their knuckles*]

ORESTES: You, my father under the earth and foully wronged . . .
ELECTRA: Awesome Earth whom I batter with my hands . . .
TUTOR: Fend, oh forfend your darling children.
ORESTES: Come with the hosts of the dead as allies.
ELECTRA: Those whose lances smashed the Trojans.
TUTOR: All those who hate sacrilege and perfidy.

[*They rise*]

ORESTES: Do you hear us—you whom my mother mangled?
TUTOR: Your father hears everything . . . but it is time to go.
ELECTRA: Let me shout it out: Aegisthus has to die.
But should you succumb in the duel, I too am dead—spoken
of no more as living.
I shall drive a two-edged sword into my heart.

Now to make ready in the house.
If I hear the best, the house will yell with joy.
But if you die . . . how different!
This I must tell you.
ORESTES: I know, I know.
ELECTRA: Then play the man.

[ORESTES *and the* TUTOR *walk towards the fields.* ELECTRA
turns to the women of the CHORUS]

ELECTRA: Women, blaze out the outcome of this contest.
I shall keep watch with weapon in hand
for never shall I deliver my person for revenge
should I not win.

[ELECTRA *retires into the cottage. The women of the* CHORUS
*sing the story of the Golden Lamb, which was a talisman of
power for whoever got hold of it. Thyestes (Aegisthus' father)
did, with awesome consequences*]

FOURTH   CHORAL   ODE

STROPHE I

Ancient tradition tells
    That Pan the god of meadows and fields,
    With the trilling music of his pipes,
    Tempted a lamb with golden fleece
    Away from its mother on the Argive hills.
    High on the stone steps the herald
    Stood and cried:
    "Mycenaeans,
    To the marketplace, the marketplace . . .
    Come see the miracle that foretells
    A prosperous reign for him who has the lamb."
    The house of Atreus won it. The people danced.

ANTISTROPHE I

The gilded temples opened
    And fire blazed on the Argive altars.
    The master of the lotus flute
    Breathed out the most bewitching airs
    And song after song celebrated
    The Golden Lamb—now Thyestes'
    (Who had seduced Atreus' wife
    Into covert bed with him). He took
    The prodigy into his own house; then
    He went to the Assembly and declared he owned

The horned phenomenon with the golden fleece.

STROPHE II

That was the moment Zeus
   Reshaped the glittering stars in their courses,
   The glory of the sun and the silvery visage
   Of dawn and bathed the western savannas
   In a wash of divine fire. The clouds,
   Lumbered with water, fled to the north.
   With no refreshing showers from Zeus,
   Ammon* in Africa shriveled.

ANTISTROPHE II

There is a legend, which
   Frankly I do not believe, that
   The Sun averted his golden face,
   Canceled his rays and let the world
   Go down in misery, because
   Of a single human being. Religion
   Cultivates these tales of fear.
   But when *you* killed you had forgot.

FIFTH EPISODE

LEADER: A . . . h! my friends, did you hear a shout,
   or am I imagining it . . .
   Like Zeus rumbling underground?
But now a calming breeze is blowing
   and Electra, my lady, issues from the house.

[ELECTRA *comes out of the cottage, distraught with anticipation*]

ELECTRA: My friends, how does it go? How do we stand in the
                                                    struggle?
LEADER: I know only that I heard a death cry.
ELECTRA: [*straining her ears*]
   I hear it too . . . far away . . . but still I hear it.
LEADER: Yes, unmistakable—though a long way off.

*The seat of a famous oracle of Zeus.

ELECTRA: The shriek of an Argive, is it? Is it my friends?

LEADER: I cannot be sure . . . the shriek is a jumbled sound.

ELECTRA: Then you sentence me to death. Why do I wait?

LEADER: Wait, till you find out how things lie for you.

ELECTRA: It is useless. We are done for. Where are his messengers?

LEADER: His messenger will come. It is not easy to kill a king.

[*A moment later a* MESSENGER *bursts on the scene. He is the servant who attends* ORESTES]

MESSENGER: Women of Mycenae, victory!
    To all who love Orestes I announce that he has won.
    Aegisthus, Agamemnon's murderer, lies dead upon the field.
Let us thank the gods.

ELECTRA: Who are you? What evidence do you have that this is true?

MESSENGER: You know me, madam—remember?—the servant
                                                of Orestes.

ELECTRA: My friend, I was too frightened to recognize your face.
    Do you really mean the hated butcher of my father is no more?

MESSENGER: Since you insist, I'll say it twice: he is dead.

ELECTRA: O you gods, and you all-seeing Justice who has struck
                                                at last . . .
But tell me exactly—I must know—
    how he killed Thyestes' son.

MESSENGER: After we had marched off from this house
    we followed the noisy chariot route
    till we came to the spot where the prestigious king of the
                                                Mycenaeans was.
He was plucking tender sprigs of myrtle for a wreath
    in his well-watered park.
On seeing us he called out:
"Greetings, strangers!
    Who are you and where do you come from?
    What is your country?"
Orestes replied:
    "We are Thessalonians on our way to the river Alpheus
    to sacrifice to the Zeus of Olympia."
To which Aegisthus replied:
    "You must be my guests and share this banquet with me:
    I am making offerings to the Nymphs.

Tomorrow if you rise at dawn
    you can make up for lost time.
Deign to enter my domain."

Saying this, he took our hands and led us in.
We could not refuse.
    "Servants, on the double," he ordered,
    "bring water for our guests,
    that they may stand near the altar by the lustral bowls."
"My lord Aegisthus," Orestes answered,
    "we have just bathed in the clearest-running streams,
    so if it is permitted for strangers
    to take part in the sacrifice of citizens, we are ready."

That is the way their conversation went.
Then, laying down the spears with which they guard their
                                                        master,
    one and all set their hands to work.
Some fetched the blood-letting bowls,
Others got receiving baskets ready.
Still others lit the fire
    and lined up the cauldrons round the hearth.
The whole house was in a turmoil.

Then taking the barley grains, this bedfellow of your mother
    scattered them on the altar, uttering:
"Nymphs of the grottoes,
    grant that I may offer up many a bull,
    and that my Tyndarid wife and I
    continue to flourish—as we do—in our home:
    that, and destruction to our enemies."
He meant, of course, Orestes and you.
My master for his part quietly whispered the opposite:
    that he should regain his ancestral house.

Then Aegisthus took a sharp flat knife from the basket
    and sheared off a tuft from the bullock's head,
    throwing it on the sacred fire with his right hand.
The slaves heaved the bullock onto their shoulders

and he killed it, saying this to your brother:
"The Thessalonians brag about their prowess
at dismembering a bull and at breaking horses.
Take this well-hammered hunk of steel, my friend,
and prove that reputation true."

Orestes, gripping the tempered Dorian blade,
tossed from his shoulders his elegant cloak,
brooch and all, pushed away the slaves,
and beckoned Pylades to be his second.
Grasping the bullock's foot,
he swept down his outstretched arm
and flared open the glistening flesh,
flensing the hide off faster than a sprinter at the hippodrome
finishes two laps.
Then he split apart the flanks.

Aegisthus, scooping up the entrails in his hands,
stared at them in some dismay:
they were devoid of liver lobes
and the rigid bladder forewarned him of evil to come.
As Aegisthus glowered, my master asked him:
"What makes you so downhearted?"
"Stranger," he said, "I suspect the guile of an outsider:
the man I most hate,
the enemy of my house—the son of Agamemnon."
Orestes replied:
"You fear the resources of a banished man,
you who reign over the city?
No matter, let us proceed to the feast . . .
If someone will bring me a Phthian cleaver
instead of this inept Dorian blade,
I shall plunge it through the thorax."

He was given one and he cut right through.
Aegisthus meanwhile rummaged among the entrails,
staring at them as he drew them apart.
He was bent low, and your brother
raising himself on his toes
struck through his back, smashing through the vertebrae.

His whole frame jolted
   and he bawled out, convulsing, in the bloody agony of death.

Seeing this, the slaves ran for their weapons:
   a crowd to fight against a couple.
But Pylades and Orestes with drawn swords
   confronted them like men.
"I come not as an enemy,
   against this city and my subjects.
I have avenged the murder of my father.
I am Orestes, the distressed one.
Do not kill me.
You were my father's servants long ago."

Hearing this they held back their spears,
   and when Orestes was recognized by an old man
   who had long served the house,
   they crowned your brother with garlands,
   cheering and shouting:
"He is on his way here
   bringing you not a Gorgon's head
   but the Aegisthus that you hated.
Blood for blood, the dead has paid with interest
   the debt he owed."

[*As the* MESSENGER *bows out, the women of the* CHORUS *begin
to celebrate, inviting* ELECTRA *to the dance*]

FIFTH CHORAL ODE

STROPHE

Set your footsteps to our dance, dear friend,
   Just like a fawn
   That lightly bounds in the air for joy.
   Your brother has won:
   More wreathed in triumph
   Than an athlete coming from Olympia.*

---

*The Greek has ". . . an athlete coming from the banks of Alpheus." See glossary for a fascinating note about Olympia.

Sing a song of victory while we dance.
ELECTRA: O glorious light, you hurtling chariot of the Sun,
    O Earth and Night that held my gaze till now:
my eyes open wide and free,
for Aegisthus has fallen,
the assassin of my father.
Let me go at once, my friends and fetch
    the jewels I used to dress my hair with,
    locked up in the cottage,
    to adorn the head of my victorious brother.

[ELECTRA *hurries into the house while the* CHORUS *sings another burst of celebration*]

SIXTH CHORAL ODE

ANTISTROPHE

Yes yes, bring out your jewels to dress his head
    While we dance away
    Delighting the Muses. The dynasty
    Of old has been
    Restored: to reign over the land
    Justly. The unjust are abolished.
    Shout it out with all the music of joy.

[ELECTRA *emerges from the cottage as* ORESTES *and* PYLADES *arrive with servants carrying the body of* AEGISTHUS]

SIXTH EPISODE

ELECTRA: Hail, Orestes, beautiful conqueror
    sprung from a conquering father—the hero of Ilium.
Receive this wreath to crown your head of curls.
In the athletes' heats you've run a winning race
    and slain your enemy, Aegisthus—
    murderer of your sire and mine.
And you, Pylades, his ally,
    reared by a gentle man,
    accept from my hands this wreath,
    for you had an equal share in the struggle.

Be blessed always in my sight.
ORESTES: But first, Electra,
    salute the gods, the authors of this outcome,
    then praise me.
I am only the pawn of fate and heaven,
    who have in a battle of deeds not words destroyed Aegisthus.
So all should know it, I bring you the corpse itself.
Expose it if you will for beasts to ravage
    or impale it on a stake for vultures to rend.
He is your chattel now, once called your king.
ELECTRA: I blush to speak but am forced to say it . . .
ORESTES: Say what? Speak out. All fear is past.
ELECTRA: . . . that gloating over the dead invites reprisals.
ORESTES: You are blameless. No one can find fault.
ELECTRA: But the city and our people are querulous and censure-
                                    prone.
ORESTES: Then, sister, say your say.
    Between this man and us, there's nothing blocks us now.
ELECTRA: [*addressing the corpse of Aegisthus*]
    But where can I even begin my indictment?
Where can I end it, and how fill the middle?
    In truth every morning I have gone over it again and again.
    What to say to you face to face if I were free from fear.
Well, I am free now,
    So I shall whip you with the words
    I wanted to let fly while you were alive.

You wrecked my life,
    orphaned me of my dear father—Orestes and me—
    though we had never hurt you.
You made a disgusting marriage with my mother,
    having murdered her spouse.
Though you never set foot in Troy
    you destroyed the commander of the Greek armada;
and having befouled my father's nuptial bed,
    you were fool enough to imagine
    that in my mother you would have a virtuous wife.
Ah! when a man plays around with another's wife,
    seduces her and is forced to marry,

he is an idiot if he thinks she will be faithful to *him*
    when she was not to her first husband.

You led a miserable life, unconscious of it.
You knew you had married a sacrilegious woman
    and she knew her husband was a fraud.
Both of you were criminals, each infecting the other.
    She took on your dishonesty, and you her reputation.
"Clytemnestra's husband," the Argives called you,
    never "Aegisthus' wife."
I think it disgraceful when the woman rules the house,
    not the man.
Nor am in favor of children being called by their mother's name,
    and not the father's.
When a man marries a woman of high station
    the husband counts for nothing, only his wife.
In your simplicity you made a fatal mistake,
    imagining you'd be someone just because you were rich.
Wealth is something transient—on the side.
Character not money is the true gauge.
Character is permanent: it excludes evil.
Mere wealth by itself is grotesque—
    fit servant of oafs—
    and after a brief flowering, scatters.

As to your sins with women,
    it is not for me, a virgin, to speak,
    so I'll say no more—though I can hint.
Possessing a regal house and fetching features
    went to your head.
But I'd rather have a real man—
    not a girl-faced husband—
    one whose sons are potential warriors.
The merely pretty is decoration—
    fit for the dance.

[*Approaching the corpse*]

Be forever cursed, you blind, crookèd man,
    found out at last and punished.

Let no miscreant ever think
  that if he has got away with the first lap
  he has outrun Justice.
Let him wait till the finishing line
  when he completes his course.
LEADER: [*to the corpse*]
  Enormous were your misdeeds, enormous the price you paid—
  to him and her. Mighty is the competence of Justice.
ORESTES: Come, slaves, carry the body into the house,
  enshroud it in shadow.
My mother when she comes must not see the corpse
  before she is cut down.

  [*While slaves take the body of* AEGISTHUS *inside, the sound of
  a carriage can be heard in the distance*]

ELECTRA: Listen, we must secure the next phase of our plan.
ORESTES: Do you see reinforcements coming from Mycenae?
ELECTRA: No, my mother—the woman who gave me birth.

  [CLYTEMNESTRA's *horse-drawn carriage, capacious and sump-
  tuous, hoves into view*]

ORESTES: How she glitters in the luxury of her chariot and dress!
ELECTRA: Primed for the meshes of our net.
ORESTES: Our mother . . . what are we to do . . . murder her?
ELECTRA: Have you gone soft at the sight of your mother?
ORESTES: No, but to kill the one who bore me, gave me suck!
ELECTRA: The one who butchered your father and mine.
ORESTES: Apollo, what a blunder your oracle has made!
ELECTRA: If Apollo blunders, who on earth is wise?
ORESTES: But to have me kill my mother—against all nature!
ELECTRA: How does it hurt you to avenge your own father?
ORESTES: But to be branded as a matricide—I who was innocent!
ELECTRA: Be branded as sacrilegious, then, if you don't succor
                                   your father.
ORESTES: I'll have to pay the blood-price of my mother.
ELECTRA: But if you do not avenge, what price for your father?
ORESTES: It was a demon telling me to do it, pretending to be a
                                       god.

ELECTRA: Sitting at the holy tripod? I think not.
ORESTES: I'll never be persuaded that this oracle is wholesome.
ELECTRA: So you'll turn coward? Be no more a man?
ORESTES: [*after a long pause*]
  Very well then, how do I do it? Lay the same trap for *her*?
ELECTRA: Exactly: the snare that trapped and killed Aegisthus.
ORESTES: Sheer horror is this enterprise, and horror if I succeed.
  But if it please the gods, so be it: a bittersweet ordeal.

  [*As* ORESTES *and* PYLADES *go into the cottage,* CLYTEM-
  NESTRA, *riding majestically in her carriage with her captive
  Trojan ladies-in-waiting, halts, while the* CHORUS *sings a
  short but dubious and subservient welcome*]

SIXTH CHORAL ODE

Queen of the land of Argos, welcome,
  Tyndareus' child,
  Sister of the handsome twins, the sons of Zeus,
  Who dwell in the empyrean among the stars
  And safeguard mariners at sea:
  I bow before you as to a goddess
  For your great wealth and blessedness.
  To revere such blessedness is right.
  Salutations, Queen!

SIXTH EPISODE

CLYTEMNESTRA: My ladies of Troy, descend from the carriage . . .
  Take my hand and help me down.

  [*To herself as she descends*]

The temples here are loaded with Trojan loot,
  and these women from Phrygia
  are assigned for my household use:
  A paltry reward for my lost daughter—Iphigenia—
  but very acceptable.
ELECTRA: Mother, let me take your blessed hand.
  After all, I too am a slave,

cast out from my father's home and living in misery.

CLYTEMNESTRA: [*waving her away*] Don't trouble yourself.
                              Leave it to the slaves.

ELECTRA: Why should I? . . . I am a slave:
   torn from my home when my home was torn from me.
I was made a captive like these women,
   and left without a father.

CLYTEMNESTRA: Only because of the plots your father was hatch-
                                                              ing
   against his nearest and dearest.
Now, I know I am a woman saddled with a bad reputation,
   but bitterly criticized as I am—and unjustly—
   let me explain.
Once you know the truth,
   if you still think I am worthy of hate, then hate away,
   but if not, where is the hate coming from?
Tyndareus gave me to your father
   not to be slain, nor slain those I bore.
But Agamemnon tricked my child from home
   with the promise of a wedding to Achilles.
He enticed her far away from the palace
   to the blocked naval base at Aulis.
There he lay her on the sacrificial altar pyre
   and shore through her tender white throat.

If he had been seeking to defend Mycenae,
   or bolster up his house, or save his other children,
   and had sacrificed one for the many,
   it would not be past forgiving.
But no, it was all done
   because of that harlot Helen
   and a husband unable to curb her lust.
It was for that my daughter was immolated.
Even so, though I was outrageously wronged,
   I did not storm and fume, nor would I have killed my hus-
                                                              band.
But he came home with that crazy Cassandra for his bed,
   and there we were two brides under the same roof.

                    *   *   *

Women are silly creatures, I grant you,
    all the same, when the husband goes a-roaming
    and neglects his nuptial bed,
    the wife is apt to copy her husband and get herself a lover.
Then what a burst of scandal flares up around her,
    while the real culprit, the man, goes off without a blotch.
If Menelaus had been kidnapped from his palace,
    would I have had to kill Orestes
    to save my sister's husband?
Would your father have allowed such a thing?
If after killing my daughter
    he did not deserve to pay with his life,
    did I deserve to pay with mine
    if I laid a hand on his son?

Yes, I killed him. There was no other way.
I turned to his enemies,
    for who of your father's *friends*
    would have helped me in his murder?
Speak if you wish. Feel free to explain
    why you think your father died unjustly.
ELECTRA: You plead justice,
    and your plea is a sham—utterly unjust.
A woman, in everything, if she has any sense,
    should yield to her husband.
Women who think otherwise
    are for me beyond the pale . . .
Bear in mind, Mother, what you last said:
    that I was to speak with complete freedom.
CLYTEMNESTRA: I repeat that, daughter, and take nothing back.
ELECTRA: Yes, Mother, but will you listen, then castigate?
CLYTEMNESTRA: Not at all. I shall be gentle with your senti-
                                 ments.

ELECTRA: Then I shall speak, and my prelude is:
    I wish, Mother, you had more compassion.
It is all very well to praise
    your and Helen's beauty—and rightly so,
    you are a handsome pair, but profligates both,

unworthy of your brother Castor.
She, torn from home and longing to be ravished,
   You, on the plea that you must destroy a husband for the sake
                                                    of a daughter,
   Murderess of the noblest man in Hellas.
Nobody knows you as I do.
Why, even before your daughter's sacrifice,
   when your husband had just left home,
   you sat primping before a looking glass,
   sleeking your shining hair.
Any woman who dolls herself up
   when her husband is far from home,
   can be dismissed as a profligate.
There is no call for her to make herself up for display
   unless she is up to no good.
You were the only woman I know
   who became ecstatic when the Trojans were winning
   but quite downcast when they were not.
You did not want Agamemnon back from Troy,
   and yet you had every reason to be a faithful wife:
Your man was not one whit inferior to Aegisthus.
He was chosen by Hellas to lead her armada.
And you, in contrast to your sister Helen's disgrace,
   you could have shone;
   for wrongdoing is a foil for the beauty of the right.

If, as you say, my father killed his daughter,
   how does that make me and my brother reprehensible?
Why, when you killed your husband,
   did you not give to Orestes and me our ancestral home,
   but instead intruded an outsider—bought with it your lover,
   the price of shame?
Your lover was not banished for the sake of your son,
   nor put to death for the sake of me—
   I who have suffered a death far worse than my sister's,
   a living death.
And justice? If it comes to blood for blood,
   only by your death can Orestes and I avenge our father.
If the first murder was right, so is the second.

[*She turns to the* CHORUS]*

He is an idiot who marries a woman because of birth and wealth.
A loyal if lowly wife is best.
LEADER: The marriage of woman depends on luck.
    It's a toss-up whether it all goes well or dismally.
CLYTEMNESTRA: Dear girl, you always loved your father,
    which is natural enough: some are father-lovers,
    some are drawn more to mothers.
I can forgive you . . . and to tell the truth,
    I am not proud of everything I've done, my child.

[*Looking her up and down*]

But why are you so dirty and in rags,
    considering the turmoil of giving birth is over? . . .
Oh, I'm so sorry for all my plottings:
    I drove my husband to resentment and went too far.
ELECTRA: Your regrets come too late. They cannot be redressed.
    My father is dead.
    But why do you not bring back your banished vagabond son?
CLYTEMNESTRA: Because I am afraid,
    and must think of myself not him.
He is angry, they say, about his father's death.
ELECTRA: Why is your husband so antagonistic towards us?
CLYTEMNESTRA: It is his way . . . and you are stubborn too.
ELECTRA: Because I am hurt. But I'll let my anger go.
CLYTEMNESTRA: In which case he'll stop oppressing you.
ELECTRA: He puts on airs living in my palace.
CLYTEMNESTRA: There you go again—adding fuel to the
                                                    quarrel.
ELECTRA: I'll keep quiet, and fear him as I fear him.
CLYTEMNESTRA: Enough of this. What made you call me, child?
ELECTRA: I expect you've heard about my baby.
    Will you make the offering for me—
    I haven't an inkling what—

---

*I was very tempted to omit lines 1097–1101 (in both Greek and English).
They smack to me (and to others) of interpolation. On the stage they should
certainly be omitted: they wreck the edge between Clytemnestra and
Electra.

the usual tenth-day offering for a newborn.*
I've never had a child and I'm at a loss.
CLYTEMNESTRA: This is the duty of the midwife: the woman who
                      helped to deliver you.
ELECTRA: I was my own midwife. I bore my child alone.
CLYTEMNESTRA: Do you live far from friends and neighbors?
ELECTRA: Friends? No one wants the poor for friends.
CLYTEMNESTRA: Let me go and pay the dues for your child's birth.
  After this service to you
  I shall go to the pastures where my husband
  is making offerings to the Nymphs.

[*Turning to her attendants*]

Put away my carriage, servants,
  and take the horses to their stalls.
When you think I have finished my devotions
  come for me.
I must consider too my husband's wants.
ELECTRA: Enter my humble abode.
  Be careful the sooty beams don't soil your dress.
  Offer whatever sacrifice you think is proper.

[CLYTEMNESTRA *enters the cottage.* ELECTRA *pauses on the threshold*]

The basket is ready to receive.
The blade that slew the bull is whetted.
By his side, struck down you'll lie,
and in Hades you shall be the bride
of him you loved in the light of day.
That is the most that I can do for you,
and for my father's death the least repayment due.

[*As* CLYTEMNESTRA *goes into the cottage unwittingly to her death, the* CHORUS *recapitulates the revolving story of horror*]

*The tenth day after a child's delivery, invitations were sent out to family and friends to a sacrifice and a banquet, at which the infant was given its name.

SEVENTH CHORAL ODE

STROPHE

Revulsion relived, full cycle the evil's return
   Like a gale that veers on this house.
   Yesterday it was my king cut down,
   My dear king killed in his bath.
   Steeped in the ceiling, the cornice blocks,
   Are his last shrieks: "Surely not, wife?
   How miserably sad to kill me the day
   I come back to my dear country
   After ten years away!"

ANTISTROPHE

And now full cycle the evil returns to punish
   The bad woman untrue to her marriage
   Who slaughtered her husband, swinging
   An ax in her hands when he came home
   After a long time away:
   Home to the Cyclopean walls that tower
   Into the sky . . . You poor man,
   What a woman you got yourself!
   What ruin in her redressing a wrong!

SEVENTH EPISODE

[*The cries of* CLYTEMNESTRA *can be heard inside the cottage*]

CLYTEMNESTRA: No no, children, by the gods, do not kill your
                                     mother.
LEADER: Do you hear that shriek coming from within?
CLYTEMNESTRA: No no, I beg.
LEADER: My heart goes out to her—slain by her children.
CHORUS: God when the right time comes does right.
   Though pitiable your fate
   It was your fault to perpetrate
   A crime yourself, you doomed woman.
LEADER: Look, they are coming back,
   all smeared with the fresh blood of their mother:
   they have achieved undoubtedly their slaughter.

No house exists, no house ever was
    more blighted than the house of Tantalus.

[ORESTES, ELECTRA, *and* PYLADES *emerge from the cottage.
The ekkyklema, a customary stage device, opens the scene to
reveal the bodies of* CLYTEMNESTRA *and* AEGISTHUS *stretched
out side by side*]

LYRIC DIALOGUE

STROPHE I*

ORESTES: O Earth and Zeus who see everything
    That mortals do, see these things too,
    Bloody and horrible:
    Two corpses stretched out on the ground
    By the swipe of my hand
    To pay for all my wrongs.
ELECTRA: What a fall of tears, my brother,
    And I am the cause.
    My anger was a furnace
    Against this my mother:
    Yes, my own mother.
CHORUS: What a fate, what a fortune
    For the mother who bore
    In her children avengers.
    Nevertheless it was right
    To atone for their father's murder.

ANTISTROPHE I

ORESTES: It was you, Phoebus, who commended
    This revenge. You've dragged into day
    Deep sorrows asleep.
    Me you have branded to roam far
    From Hellas. For, what city,
    What honest man,
    What host could bear to face
    A matricide?
ELECTRA: Gone, gone . . .

*Two lines are missing from Strophe I.

What dances to join?
What wedding ever, or what husband
Will let me near a marriage bed?
CHORUS: A change of heart!
   How you have veered with the wind!
   Now tender thoughts—not then:
   A ghastly act and a forced brother.

STROPHE II

ORESTES: Did you see how the stricken thing threw open
   Her bosom as she was being murdered? Ah!
   Those limbs, my mother's limbs,
   Strewn on the ground
   And her hair, which I . . .
ELECTRA: I can understand the agony
   You felt when you heard those cries of hers,
   Your own mother.

ANTISTROPHE II

ORESTES: Her hand touched my chin. "O my child,"
   She pleaded as she hung on my neck
   And I let go the grip on my sword:
   It dropped to the floor.
CHORUS: [to ELECTRA] Poor woman, how could you bear
   To watch the blood oozing from
   Your dying mother?

STROPHE III

ORESTES: I threw my cloak over my eyes
   And did the thing, forcing the steel
   Through my mother's throat.
ELECTRA: I was urging you on.
   My hand was on the sword with yours.
CHORUS: What you have done is heinous beyond all words.

ANTISTROPHE III

ORESTES: Lift her up. Staunch her wounds.
   Cover my mother's limbs with a gown.
   The children born to you

Have become your murderers.
ELECTRA: Shroud her whom we hated and loved
In this robe, and end the curse of this house.

[*With a rumble of thunder and flash of light,* CASTOR *and*
POLLUX *appear above the scene*]

CHORUS: What is this vision flooding over the housetops?
Am I seeing demons or gods from heaven
Who come by no earthly path?
Why have they made themselves visible?

EIGHT EPISODE

CASTOR: Daughter of Agamemnon, listen.
We the twin brothers of your mother, sons of Zeus, address
you:
I Castor and this my brother Pollux.
After calming the shipwrecking sea
we have just arrived in Argos
having witnessed the killing of your mother, our sister.
Her punishment was just, but you did wrong.

[*Turning to* ORESTES]

And Phoebus Apollo . . . Ah. Phoebus Apollo! . . .
But I can't say a thing against my king.
He may be wise
but his oracle for you was not . . . We must accept,
and you must do whatever Zeus and Fate lay out for you.

You Electra,
let Pylades take you as his wife into the palace.
But you, Orestes, must depart from Argos.
You may not walk her streets because you killed your mother.
The fearful ugly sisters, the dog-eyed goddesses, the Furies,
will hunt you into a lunatic and a vagabond.
Go to Athens,
throw your arms around the effigy of Pallas,
who will turn aside their snakelike rage

and stop them hurting you.
Shelter your head under her Gorgon shield.

There at the hill of Ares
    where the gods first sat in judgment on the blood that flowed
    when ferocious Ares slew Halirrothius,
    the sea god's son—slew him in anger
    because he had raped his daughter.
That tribunal ever since
    stands sacred in the sight of the gods.
So there you must go for your murder trial.

Your death sentence shall be quashed because of equal votes
    and Apollo will take the blame
    for having told you to kill your mother.
Ever afterwards this law will stand:
    that equality of votes equates acquittal.
The outraged Furies will collapse
    into a rift of earth near the same hill,
    ever to be revered as an oracle.
You must live in a town on the banks of the Alpheus
    in Arcadia near the shrine of Zeus the Lycenaean.
The town shall take your name.

To you, Electra, let me say this:
    the people of Argos will cover the body of Aegisthus in a
                                                            tomb.
As to your mother,
    Menelaus, who recently arrived in Nauplia from Troy,
    will bury her—he and Helen:
Helen who never went to Troy
    but has just come home from Proteus' palace in Egypt.
It was Zeus who sent a phantom Helen to Ilium
    for he wanted strife and slaughter among mankind.*

Let Pylades take his virgin wife
    away from the land of Achaea and go home.†

*Because he'd decided that there were too many human beings.
†Pylades came from Phocis in northern Greece.

[*Turning to* ORESTES]

And let him go with you his brother-in-law-to-be
  to the land of Phocis, there to laden him with riches.
But first travel by way of the neck of the Isthmus
  to Athens and the holy hill of Cecrops.
And when you have annulled your guilt for murder,
  you will live a happy life there freed from all these toils.

CHORAL TRIALOGUE

CHORUS:

[*to* CASTOR *and* POLLUX]

Children of Zeus, is it all right for us to address you?
CASTOR: It is, for you are free from pollution of murder.
ORESTES: Sons of Tyndareus, may I join in the conversation?
CASTOR: You may, for I blame Phoebus for the act of blood.
CHORUS: How is it that you, gods and brothers of the deceased,
  Did not ward off the powers of death from her house?
CASTOR: Karma and fate propelled her to her downfall:
  That, and the careless utterance of Apollo.
ELECTRA: What Apollo, what oracles, made me kill my mother?
CASTOR: It was a joint compulsion, with a joint result:
  A single ancestral curse has ruined you both.
ORESTES: Dear sister, after all this time, as soon as I see you
  I must leave you, lose the magic of your presence.
  I am lost to you and you to me.
CASTOR: She has a husband and a home.
  She is not pitiable but for leaving Argos.
ELECTRA: But what is more pitiable than to leave behind
  The land of one's birth?
ORESTES: And me? I have to leave the palace of my father
  And be sat upon in judgment by utter strangers
  To extenuate the murder of my mother.
CASTOR: Bear up! When you come to the holy city of Pallas
  All will be well, so have courage.
ELECTRA: Then let us hug each other, beloved brother,
  We shall live separate lives, apart

From our paternal home, and be haunted
By the strictures of our murdered mother.

ORESTES: [*flinging his arms around her*]
Hold me tight while your tears flow:
Tears like the dirges for the dead.

CASTOR: Sad it is,
Bitter even for us gods to hear.
For I and the denizens of heaven
Have compassion on human misery.

ORESTES: [*still embracing* ELECTRA] I shall never see you
again.

ELECTRA: Nor I look into your shining eyes.

ORESTES: So this is the last time we talk together.

ELECTRA: Goodbye to my city, goodbye to my city's women.

ORESTES: Dear faithful sister, must you leave already?

ELECTRA: I go, my eyelids sodden with tears.

ORESTES: Pylades, goodbye, your lot is happy.
Take Electra whom you are to marry.

[PYLADES *and* ELECTRA *walk away arm in arm, and* CASTOR
turns to ORESTES]

CASTOR: They have a wedding before them, but you must flee
From these bitches from hell who are on your track.
Hurry to Athens, for they come at a furious pace
To throw themselves on you with their serpent arms.
Their flesh is black: they batten on human pain.

[ORESTES *rushes away, and* CASTOR *and* POLLUX *turn to the*
CHORUS]

As for us, we must hasten away
Over the Sicilian seas to save the galleys
Battling through the brine, as we traverse
The spacious vacuum of the sky. We shall not come
To help the wicked but only those who live
Lives that show themselves devout and just.
We ease their days, preserve them from distress.
Let no one, therefore, live in wickedness
Or fellow-travel with a perjured liar.

    I am a god: it is mortals I address.*
CHORUS: Welcome then, to him who while
    Never enduring a cruel ordeal,
Lives happily and well.

*Euripides ends both this speech and the envoi of the CHORUS with rhyming triplets. A rare occurrence, perhaps unique, in Greek drama.

IPHIGENIA
AT AULIS

❧

ΙΦΙΓΕΝΙΑ Η
ΕΝ ΑΥΛΙΔΙ

For Vanessa and Carl Lindgren

Iphigenia at Aulis, together with, possibly, the *Orestes* and *Cyclops* and certainly *The Bacchae*, is among the last plays that Euripides wrote towards the end of his life when he was the guest of King Archelaus of Macedon. The *Iphigenia* proved to be his very last and was left unfinished when he died in 406 B.C. It is thought to have been completed by his son, who produced it shortly afterwards at the City Dionysia in Athens together with *The Bacchae* and a lost play, the *Alcmaeon*. It appears to be this trio for which Euripides was posthumously awarded first prize: for the fifth time only, compared to thirteen times for Aeschylus and eighteen for Sophocles.

Iphigenia at Aulis marks the culmination of Euripides' career as playwright and poet—not because this is his greatest play but because it is in many ways his most interesting, for in it he pushes to an extreme his disdain for the heroics of Greek tragedy and shows his characters to be pathetically, and almost endearingly, human.

The mighty Agamemnon, stripped down to his naked pomposity, is no more than another well-meaning but fumbling politician. His sidekick and brother, Menelaus, fares no better. The swashbuckling Achilles—answer to a maiden's prayer—is a flashy commonplace juvenile who could be waiting in his Porsche for his date at the high school gates. Even Clytemnestra, though a queen, is the kind of queen who rides a bicycle to the supermarket and trundles her trolley like any suburban housewife. Only Iphigenia, in her courage and simplicity, rises above the mediocrity and vulgarity of the rest of them.

In this reduction of the heroic to the ordinary, Euripides focuses on the psychology and probabilities of human beings as they are, and so opens the door to all we know about modern drama.

The text of this play is in many places uncertain, and the conclusion obviously spurious. In the mss. the Prologue is mysteriously sandwiched between the lyric dialogue of Agamemnon and the retainer that runs between lines 1–48. What is also odd is that this whole passage is cast in the verse form of lyric dialogue.

CHARACTERS

AGAMEMNON, commander in chief of the Argive forces
OLD RETAINER of Agamemnon
MENELAUS, brother of Agamemnon and husband of Helen
CLYTEMNESTRA, wife of Agamemnon
IPHIGENIA, daughter of Agamemnon and Clytemnestra
ACHILLES, Greek prince and soldier
MESSENGER, officer of the Greek army
CHORUS, women of Chalcis who have come to Aulis to see the
                                                    fleet
SECOND MESSENGER, a Greek soldier

Attendants and guards and the infant Orestes (son of Agamemnon and Clytemnestra with his nurse)

TIME AND SETTING

Helen, wife of Menelaus, has been abducted—all too willingly—by the good-looking Trojan prince Paris. The outraged Menelaus, assisted by his brother, determines to bring her back by force of arms. The Greeks muster a formidable armada at the naval port of Aulis on the east coast of Boeotia. The fleet, however, is unable to sail for lack of breeze. Day after sultry day passes, and the idling army grows dangerously restless.

The scene is the Greek camp just before dawn. A light burns in Agamemnon's tent, and he steps outside with a letter in his hands.

FIRST EPISODE AND LYRIC DIALOGUE

AGAMEMNON: Come on out, old man, here by my tent.
RETAINER: [*emerging from a hut*] I'm coming, Agamemnon.
    What's up, my king?
AGAMEMNON: But hurry.
RETAINER: I'm hurrying. I'm wide awake.
    Too old to sleep much. On the watch!
AGAMEMNON: What is that star in the night sky?
RETAINER: Sirius, rising high in the heavens,

Next to the seven Pleiades.
AGAMEMNON: [*gazing around the sleeping camp*]
    Not a sound anywhere. No, not a bird.
    Not even a whisper from the sea,
    And along the Eripus the breeze is still.
RETAINER: And you fretting outside your tent!
    Why, Agamemnon king, when all
    Aulis is quiet. The watch on the walls
    Hasn't yet stirred . . . Let's go in.
AGAMEMNON: I envy you, old man, as I envy
    Anyone who's lived a quiet life,
    Unrenowned. How little I envy
    Positions of power!
RETAINER: But that's where all the glory is.
AGAMEMNON: A dangerous glory, and ambition
    However sweet lies close to grief.
    A little irreverence and the gods
    Swoop; and sometimes human beings
    Through prejudice and misconception
    Tear one apart.
RETAINER: This sort of pessimism, sire, won't do—
    Not in a leader. No, Agamemnon,
    You're not Atreus' son for nothing.
    You'll have joy and you'll have sorrow
    Just like an ordinary mortal man . . .
    By divine arrangement, like it or not.

    You've written a letter by the light of your lamp.
    You're carrying the tablet* in your hands.
    You've been wiping it clean again and again,†
    Sealing it, unsealing it,
    Throwing it on the ground and crying.
          *   *   *

---

*Letters were often incised in a waxed tablet with a stylus.
†One must presume that Old Retainer had been watching Agamemnon before retiring to his hut.

There isn't a symptom I can think of
That doesn't declare you raving mad.
What's the trouble? What has happened?
Come, Agamemnon, confess to me:
Confess to a good and loyal man.
Ages ago Tyndareus sent me
As a bridal present for your wife—
Part of her dowry.

[AGAMEMNON *walks to a rock and beckons the* OLD RETAINER *to sit beside him. Looking into the distance and speaking almost to himself as if to clarify his mind,* AGAMEMNON *explains*]

PROLOGUE

AGAMEMNON: Leda daughter of Thestius had three girls:
   Phoebe, my wife Clytemnestra, and Helen.
For Helen's hand
   the richest and noblest young men of Hellas came abiding.
However, there was such rivalry among them
   that they hurled threats of murder at each other
   and Tyndareus her father was in despair.
Then he hit on a plan:
   let all the suitors come together,
   grasp their right hands in pledge,
   seal it with burnt offerings,
   then drink to the following treaty.
Whoever became the husband of Tyndareus' daughter,
   him they were to protect;
   and if any man wrested her from home and husband's bed,
   they would march against him
   and raze his city to the ground
   no matter who he was—Greek or alien.

After old Tyndareus had cleverly tricked them to this pledge,
   he allowed his daughter to be guided in her choice
   by the sweet winds of love.
She chose—and what a fatal choice!—
   she chose Menelaus.

Then who should come prancing into Sparta
   but the one legend says
   judged the beauty contest of three goddesses,
   Paris, dressed up like a flower,
   glittering in gold, stunning in un-Greek finery.
He fell in love. She fell in love,
   and he carried her off to his ranch in the Idan hills.

All this while Menelaus was away;
   who came storming back, scorching his way through Greece
   and clamoring for action:
   fulfillment of the Tyndarian treaty against aggression.
The whole of Hellas flared up in arms.
They came with their ships and their shields,
   their cavalry and chariots, and—
   as a gesture to Menelaus my brother—
   chose me as their general:
   an honor I heartily wish someone else had won.

So here we are,
   the whole army mustered at Aulis
   with not a thing to do.
There isn't a breath of breeze for the fleet.
We are at a loss.
And now the seer Calchas has declared:
   my own daughter, Iphigenia, must be sacrificed
   to Artemis, the goddess of this place.
In no other way shall we set sail to sack Troy.

Hearing this, I've told Talthybius the herald
   to broadcast my decision to disband the army;
   for it is out of the question for me to kill my daughter.
But now my brother, Menelaus,
   with the most pathetic pleas,
   has constrained me to a horrible dilemma.
So I've written a letter to my wife
   telling her to send our daughter here
   for a wedding to Achilles.
I've extolled his manliness

and told her that he's refused to sail
unless he has as bride a daughter from our family
for his home in Phthia.
This fictitious prospect of a wedding
    was a trick I knew my wife would fall for.
There're only four of us Achaeans that know the truth:
    Calchas, Odysseus, Menelaus, and I.
But now I am trying to repair my mistake.
    I've written another letter—the one you saw me opening—
    yes, old man, opening and sealing up again in the gloom of
                                                              night.
Here, take it,
    and off with you double-quick to Argos.
Wait.
    You're such a loyal servant of my wife and me,
    I'll tell you word for word the secret of the message.

LYRIC DIALOGUE

RETAINER: Yes, better speak it just in case
    It differs from the written word.

[AGAMEMNON *unwraps the letter and reads*]

AGAMEMNON: Daughter of Leda, I write again
  Canceling what I wrote before:
    Do *not* send your child here
    To this lazy enclave of Euboea,
This placid port of Aulis.
    We must postpone our daughter's wedding
Till another time.
RETAINER: Yes, but how do you propose
    To deal with the fury of Achilles?
    If you deprive him of his bride
    His rage against you and your wife
    Will be uncontrollable—
    Awesome—please tell me that.
AGAMEMNON: Achilles only lends his name.
    He knows nothing about a wedding,

Nothing about what we've plotted.
He has no inkling yet of a proposal
To surrender our girl to his embrace in wedlock.
RETAINER: You've been playing with fire, my lord Agamemnon,
Even to think of bringing your daughter here
For the Greeks to slaughter
On the pretext of a marriage with Achilles,
Son of an immortal.
AGAMEMNON: I know, I know. I'm out of my mind.
I'm on the verge of collapse.
So go, go as fast as you can.
Make your old feet run.
RETAINER: King, I'm off.
AGAMEMNON: No sitting down by a shady spring
And taking a nap.
RETAINER: Well, I never!
AGAMEMNON: When you come to that fork in the road
Scan every direction and make sure
No carriage comes rumbling by
And slips past you
With my daughter and her escort
On her way here
Where the Greek fleet waits.
She may have started out,
So if you meet her on the road
Seize the reins and turn her back.
RETAINER: It shall be done.
AGAMEMNON: Go now. Race for Mycenae's walls.
RETAINER: Yes, yes, but why should they believe me?
AGAMEMNON: My seal—see it?—stamped on the letter.
Guard it well . . . Off with you now.
Already the fiery chariot of the sun
Is lighting up the east.
I'm depending on you.

[*The* OLD RETAINER *hurries away in the direction of
Argos.* AGAMEMNON, *shaking his head, rises heavily from
his seat*]

No mortal man comes through life unscathed

Or knows real happiness.
    An unbruised human being has never yet been raised.

[AGAMEMNON *walks wearily into his tent as the young women
of the* CHORUS, *girls and matrons, enter in a slow dance,
chanting. They have come from the nearby town of Chalcis on
the west coast of Euboea, separated from Aulis by the narrow
strait of Eripus. They have come to gawp at the magnificent
display of men and ships mustered at Aulis and are overwhelmed by actually setting eyes on the various famous and
beautiful young warriors. They go on to describe the different
warships with their captains and admirals*]

FIRST CHORAL ODE *

STROPHE I

1: I have come to the sandy shores
    Of Aulis across the race
    Of Euripus' squeezing channel.
2: I have come by boat and left
    My home, the city of Chalcis,
3: Whose river, Arethusa,
    Pours headlong into the sea.
4: I came to see the Achaean
    Army and their fleet
    Of a thousand ships, the heroes
    Manning them; Menelaus
    With his mane of flaming hair,
5: And mighty Agamemnon—
6: Here to get back Helen,
7: So our husbands tell us,
8: Snatched by the shepherd Prince
    Paris from the reedy
    River of Eurotas:
9: Reward from Aphrodite
    Glistening with spray
    When he chose her as the champion
    In that rivalry for beauty

---

*I have divided up the lines of the ode to be chanted severally.

Of three goddesses:
10: Pallas, her, and Hera.

ANTISTROPHE I

1: Hurrying through the grove
Where many a sacrifice
To Artemis is offered,
I blushed at my schoolgirl rush
To gape at the shields and tents,

2: The chariots and horses
Of the warriors of Hellas.

3: I caught a sight of Ajax

4: Sitting with an Ajax
Chatting: one the son
Of Oeleus, and the other

5: Telamon's son, the pride
Of Salamis, oh, and I saw
Protesilaus together
With Palamedes, grandson
Of Poseidon, deep in
A game of checkers, and

6: Diomedes showing off
His muscles at the discus.

7: Near him was Meriones
Of Ares' kin—a marvel.

8: And from the hills of Ithaca,

9: Laertes' son, and Nereus—

10: What a Grecian beauty!

STROPHE II

1: Then I came to the swarm of ships:

2: A vision to thrill the female eye
With the sweetest spasm.

3: The right wing of the fleet was held
By Achilles' Myrmidons from Phthia:
A fast squadron of fifty frigates

4: In battle array;

5: And at their poops engraved in gold
The Nereid goddesses presided—

6: Achilles' coat-of-arms.

ANTISTROPHE II*

1: Next to them keel by keel,
2: Also bristling with oars, stood
   Another fifty ships from Argos
3: Whose admiral was Mecisteus' son
4: (Talaus being his foster father);
5: With him was Sthenelus
   Son of Capaneus.
6: The next post was held by Theseus' son
   Who headed sixty ships from Attica.
7: Pallas riding flying chargers
   Was their ensign.
8: Enough to put heart into any sailor!

STROPHE III

1: Next, the force of Boeotia's naval might
   Riveted my eyes:
2: Fifty galleys flying ensigns
   Depicting Cadmus flaring a golden dragon
   From their hulking sterns.
3: Leitus born of Gaea
   Was this squadron's captain.
4: There were ships too from Phocis
5: And also ships from Locris
   Equal to them in number
   Led by Ajax son of Oeleus,
6: Stemming from the famous town
   Of Thronium.

ANTISTROPHE III

1: From Mycenae's mighty cyclopean walls
   Agamemnon sent
2: A hundred galleys with their men.
3: His comrade, his own brother, stood with him
4: To make sure that Hellas
   Would bring to brook Helen

*This is one of the rare occasions when the number of lines in the antistrophe does not match the strophe. I have followed Euripides in this. Of course, it could mean that the text is uncertain.

5: Who forsook her home
   For an alien's bed.
6: Then my eyes beheld
   Nestor's prows from Gerenon
7: Flying ensigns of Alpheus,
   Neighbor and river god
8: With bulls' feet.

EPODE

1: Then there were twelve Aenian galleys
   Commanded by Goumeus the king,
2: And alongside these
   The lairds of the Elis clan
3: (Called Epeians by everyone)
   With their flotilla:
   Captained by Eurytus,
4: Who commanded too the Taphian battleships
   With their banks of snow-white oars.
5: His master was King Meges son of Phyleus
   From the Echinean Isles:
6: A sailor's nightmare.
1: Ajax of Salamis
   Had his ships lined up from left to right,
2: Twelve of the trimmest galleys,
   Facing the center of the fleet.
3: All this is what I saw and had explained.
4: Woe to any enemy ships
   That have to grapple with these!
5: They'll not get off scot free—
   Not against the armada that I saw there.
6: Everything I heard at home
   Was awesomely confirmed.

[*From the road leading to Argos* MENELAUS *strides into view
with his retinue of soldiers. He is an impressive figure, with
flaming red beard and hair, and clad in all the military
insignia of a general. In his hands he holds* AGAMEMNON's
letter to CLYTEMNESTRA *in which he told her not to send* IPHI-
GENIA *to Aulis. On his heels is the* OLD RETAINER *desperately
trying to snatch the letter from him*]

SECOND EPISODE

RETAINER: This is outrageous, Menelaus, not worthy of you.

MENELAUS: Get out of my way, with your ridiculous loyalty.

RETAINER: I take that as a compliment, not an insult.

MENELAUS: Don't overdo it or you'll be sorry.

RETAINER: You are overdoing it opening the letter I carried.

MENELAUS: A letter that betrays the lot of us.

RETAINER: Convince the world of that, but give the letter back.

MENELAUS: Certainly not.

RETAINER: Then I'll not let go.

MENELAUS: See this stick? D'you want a bloody head?

RETAINER: Go on, kill me . . . make me a martyr to my loyalty.

MENELAUS: Let go. You've too many answers for a slave.

RETAINER: [as AGAMEMNON comes out of his tent]
Sir, this man has snatched your letter
right out of my hands.
He's quite devoid of conscience, Agamemnon.

AGAMEMNON: What's all this rumpus and abuse outside my tent?

MENELAUS: Hear it from me, not from this creature here.

AGAMEMNON: Menelaus, why have you upset him so and used
force?

[The OLD RETAINER steals away, leaving the two leaders to
thrash it out]

MENELAUS: I'll tell you exactly why, right to your face.

AGAMEMNON: Right to my face? Do you think that scares me, a
son of Atreus?

MENELAUS: See this letter? Everything in it is complete betrayal.

AGAMEMNON: I see the letter. First you hand it back.

MENELAUS: Oh no, not till every Greek in the army knows what's
in it.

AGAMEMNON: Do you mean to say you've opened it and read it?

MENELAUS: Unhappily for you, I've opened it and know your
sneaky plot.

AGAMEMNON: How did you get hold of it? . . . Ye gods, what
impudence!

MENELAUS: Waiting for your daughter on her way to the camp
from Argos.

AGAMEMNON: Who gave you the right to meddle? It's unpardonable.

MENELAUS: A canny instinct . . . I am not your slave.

AGAMEMNON: What impudence! Am I not master in my own house?

MENELAUS: No, you are too unreliable—here, there, and everywhere.

AGAMEMNON: How clever you are! I hate a slippery tongue.

MENELAUS: A slippery heart is worse, and a traitorous one.
    Without trying too hard I'll prove it to you,
    and don't go frothing at the mouth.
Do you recall how keen you were to win
    supreme command of the Panhellenic force against Ilium?
You pretended otherwise, but, oh, how you wanted it!
How you crawled to everyone,
    keeping open house to whoever wished to see you,
    being hail-fellow-well-met to all and sundry,
    trying to sell yourself whether anyone wanted it or not.
Then the moment you got command you did a somersault:
    friends were no longer friends,
    locked behind closed doors you were no longer available.
No decent human being when he gets to the top
    ditches everyone he knows.
Once in a position to help
    he is more than ever at the disposal of his friends.
That is the first thing I have against you,
    my first complaint . . . Next comes this.
When you and the entire Panhellenic army arrived in Aulis,
    and the divine dispensation denied us a breeze,
    and the Greeks clamored for the fleet to be disbanded
    and the whole sorry waste of effort at Aulis to be stopped,
    you simply hit rock bottom.
Your jaw dropped when you found you were not to be
    an armada's admiral of a thousand ships
    and would never land a battalion on Priam's plains.
Then you came whimpering to me:
    "Oh, what shall I do? . . . Is there no solution?
    How can I hang on to my command and the glory that goes
                                                        with it?"
When Calchas announced
    you were to offer up your daughter ritually to Artemis,

then the Greeks would sail,
how relieved you were!
How promptly you agreed to kill your child.
And without the slightest pressure from us,
    but of your own free will—you can't deny it—
    you wrote to your wife and told her
    to send her daughter here
    for a trumped-up wedding with Achilles.
Now you've done your somersault,
    are caught sending out a very different message:
    "No no, I can't think of murdering my daughter."
But nothing's changed,
    the selfsame sky records you then and now.

Well, that's the way of it.
Thousands have acted just like you.
They scramble up the ladder to power,
    then come slithering down:
    some because the public is just too dim to understand them,
    but mostly because they themselves haven't a clue about poli-
                                                                tics.

What makes me sad
    is the way poor Greece—all primed for glory—
    is made a laughingstock throughout Barbaria.
    And all because of you and that girl of yours.
I'd never choose a politician or a general for his courage.
Any man who isn't a blockhead can govern a state.
For a general it's brain that's wanted.

CHORUS LEADER: It's a dreadful thing when brothers lose their
                                                            tempers
    and come near to blows.

AGAMEMNON: Now let me tell you where *you've* gone wrong.
    I won't go on and on about it or be unkind,
    but speak like a brother:
    a good man is considerate.
But tell me this:
    why the blustering gestures and the bloodshot face?
Who has wronged you? What are you after?
Is it pining for a virtuous wife?

Such I cannot provide.
The wife you had you stupidly mismanaged.
I'm not to blame for that.
Must *I* smart for your cuckoldry?
Or are you simply jealous of my rank?
No, it's just that you lust for a lovely woman in your arms,
    scandal and decency be damned.
Am I mad because I am trying to right an error?
Not a bit of it! It's you that's mad:
    mad to want that trollop back
    when a kindly heaven rid you of her.
Those suitors who swore the oath to Tyndareus,
    every one of them itched to have her,
    and you won—not because of your manly strength.
    It was wishful thinking, the goddess Hope, that led them on.
Well, you are welcome to them.
    Round them up, be their leader, they are stupid enough.
The gods are not so simpleminded
    as to be taken in by an idiot treaty and forced promises.
I *will* not go murdering my own children.
Do you think it would be fair
    for you to succeed in hunting down a worthless wife
    while I poured out my tears night and day
    for a heinous murdering of my children?
My answer is short, swift, and easy to understand.
Be deranged, if that's your wish,
    but I intend to put my family first.
LEADER: That is not what you said before;
    however, the sparing of a child is welcome news.
MENELAUS: But it puts me in a pitiable position—without
                            support.
AGAMEMNON: You'll have support when you stop trying to
                        destroy your friends.
MENELAUS: And you, can't you show that you and I have the
                        same father?
AGAMEMNON: Common sense in common we can have, but not
                        madness.
MENELAUS: Friendship means sharing the agony of friends.
AGAMEMNON: Then don't add to mine. Show some kindness.

MENELAUS: What about Hellas? Will you share her agony?
AGAMEMNON: Hellas, like you, is mad—has got possessed.
MENELAUS: [*preparing to leave*]
　　Go on, bandy your commander's baton and betray your brother!
　　I shall have recourse to other plans and other friends.

[*A soldier* MESSENGER *hurries in and steps up to* AGAMEMNON]

MESSENGER: King Agamemnon, commander in chief of all the
　　　　　　　　　　　　　　　　　　　　　　　　　　　　　Greeks,
　　I have come here with your daughter, Iphigenia—
　　the name you call her by at home.
Her mother is with her, your noble Clytemnestra,
　　and the baby Orestes too.
She knows how happy that will make you
　　after being away from home so long.
They've had a tedious journey
　　and are now dangling their toes
　　in the cooling waters of a stream,
　　where the horses are as well.
We've turned the horses loose
　　to munch among the meadow grasses.

I've run on ahead to let you know.
The army has already heard
　　(the wildfire way rumor spreads)
　　that your daughter has arrived.
Crowds have come running to get a look and see your child.
Everyone wants to see the rich and famous,
　　the focus of all eyes.
"Is there going to be a wedding, or what?" people are asking,
　　"Or did Agamemnon have his daughter fetched
　　because he misses her so much?"
I also heard people saying:
　　"They are offering a bridal sacrifice to Artemis,* queen of Aulis.

*Artemis was patroness of unmarried girls and of childbirth: the irony here is
painful.

But who is to be the groom?"
Up then, get the sacrificial flower baskets ready,
    and decorate your heads with garlands.
    Today a young girl's happiest day has dawned.
AGAMEMNON: [*to the* MESSENGER, *somberly*]
    Thank you for the news. Now step inside.
    Fate must take its course . . . I daresay for the better.

[*The* MESSENGER, *deflated by the ominous lack of enthusiasm,
goes into one of the tents.* AGAMEMNON *continues his solilo-
quy outside*]

God help me!
    What can I say or do? Where even begin?
I am clamped to a doom I cannot shake off.
Fate has outwitted me at every turn.
I thought I was smart. She was smarter still.
There's something to be said for being of humble birth.
    Such can cry away and pour out everything.
We of the ruling class
    have to keep the stiff upper lip when things go wrong.
We are slaves to popular opinion.
I am not allowed to cry,
    nor allowed not to cry.
What a dilemma, what a pit I've fallen into!
What can I say to my wife? How can I face her?
How can I look her in the eye?
Her bursting in on this crisis
    has upset everything.
Yet I might have known she'd come
    for her darling daughter's wedding, to give her away.
When will she find out the awful thing I've done?
And the unlucky unwed girl? . . . Unwed? Oh no!
    She'll be wed all right, soon enough, to Hades down below.
My heart dissolves
    when I think of how she will plead with me:
"Father, will you kill me?
    Then I hope there is a 'wedding' waiting for you just like
                             mine—
    for you and anyone you love."

Orestes will be there bawling his head off:
    a baby crying meaninglessly with cries so fraught with
                                 meaning.
Damn, damn Paris Priam's son!
With his lust for Helen he has wrecked my life.
He is the cause of all that has been done.
LEADER: I too feel for you,
    if a woman and outsider may weep for the suffering of a king.

    [MENELAUS *approaches with outstretched hand*]

MENELAUS: Brother, let me shake you by the hand.
AGAMEMNON: Here, shake it. You have won, and I am finished.
MENELAUS: Listen, I swear to you by Pelops,
    father of your father and of mine,
    and by Atreus from whom both of us were born,
    that I speak now from the heart,
    simply, with no ulterior motive,
    to say exactly what is in my mind.
When I see your streaming eyes
    I am so moved I can't help crying too.
I cancel everything I said before.
I am not your enemy.
Now I am with you all the way.
I ask you not to kill your child,
    not to put your interests after mine.
    It is wrong to make your life a misery while mine is sweet;
    wrong for a child of yours to die
    while mine still see the light of day.
After all, what am I after?
    If it's a marriage I want,
    why can't I marry again, and better?
What could be more reprehensible
    than to wreck a brother's life
    just to get the likes of Helen back again?
    A choice of evil over good.
I was wrong-headed. I didn't think,
    but when I saw close up what killing children means,
    I was overcome with pity for the poor young woman,
    my own niece—butchered for a failed marriage.

What has your girl got to do with Helen?
Disband the army. Dismiss the lot from Aulis.
And you, my brother, please,
    stop those trickling tears;
    dry your eyes and I'll dry mine.
Give no further thought
    to that seer's prognostication about your daughter,
    and I'll ignore it too.
It interests me no longer—neither you.
What a lightning change, you must be thinking,
    from all his bluster!
Yes, a natural change.
I love my mother's son, my brother,
    and for one who knows what's best—
    no bad turn around either.
LEADER: A generous speech,
    worthy of your forebear Tantalus, Zeus's son.
    Your ancestors would be proud.
AGAMEMNON: Thank you, Menelaus.
    What you say is to the point and does you honor.
When brothers quarrel it's usually over a woman
    or because of sibling rivalry.
It disgusts me—so hurtful to both.
But now we face an unavoidable decision:
    we must go ahead with the bloody murder of my daughter.
MENELAUS: Why? Your own child? . . . Who's compelling you?
AGAMEMNON: The entire Achaean army.
MENELAUS: Not if you send her back to Argos.
AGAMEMNON: *That* I could keep secret. There's something else I
                                                        cannot.
MENELAUS: What? You don't need to fear the mob.
AGAMEMNON: Calchas will tell the whole army of his oracle.
MENELAUS: Not if he dies first. That's not hard.
AGAMEMNON: What a scheming rotten breed these soothsayers
                                                        are!
MENELAUS: Yes indeed, useless and ambitious—*while alive*.
AGAMEMNON: But there's a frightening possibility you have not
                                                        thought of.
MENELAUS: I can't guess what, unless you tell me.

AGAMEMNON: Odysseus, that Sisyphus man, knows everything.
MENELAUS: So what? Odysseus can't hurt you or me.
AGAMEMNON: He's crafty—manipulates the mob.
MENELAUS: Yes, a slave to ambition—a dangerous disease.
AGAMEMNON: Can't you see him, standing up among the Ar-
                                                        gives,
   blurting out the story of the oracle:
   of how I promised Artemis her victim,
   then reneged?
Can't you see him whipping up the mob
   to go and kill you, me, and the girl—the girl as sacrifice?
Even if I escaped to Argos,
   they'd just follow, smash Mycenae to the ground,
   topple the Cyclopean walls.
What an appalling prospect! I'm at a loss,
   cornered by the gods and in despair.
One thing, Menelaus, I must ask you.
   In your perambulations among the troops
   be careful Clytemnestra does not hear of what's afoot
   until I have my child safe in Hades.
Let me do what I have to do
   with the least possible tears.

[*Turning to the* CHORUS]

And you women, you visitors here,
   not a word! Silence must be yours.

[*As* AGAMEMNON *walks to his tent, and* MENELAUS *heads for
the camp, the ladies of the* CHORUS, *shaken by what they have
heard and seen, reflect on the two kinds of love that either
enhance or destroy. Then they attempt to restore their compo-
sure by surveying the age-old principles that keep life steady
and balanced. In an epode they give a thumbnail sketch of
what has caused the outbreak of war: the wrong kind of love*]

SECOND CHORAL ODE

STROPHE

CHORUS: Happy are they whose passion in loving
   Is balanced and Aphrodite's sway
   Lets them go at a gentle pace
   Without the sting of untempered lust.
   When Eros with his golden curls
   Bends his bow for his arrows of love,
   One of the shafts spells lifelong joy,
   The other shaft a life of strife.
   This is the one, I beg you, Queen,
   To keep away from my house and bed.
   Let me enjoy the bliss of love
   But let it be a measured love:
   A tender not a turbid thing.

ANTISTROPHE

Great is the variety of human beings,
   Great the variety of their ways,
   But true goodness is the same
   And virtue is bred by discipline,
   And wisdom lies in reverence
   Which charms right-thinking into bloom
   And gives to life a lasting glow.
   Character is everything.
   Let us as women shelter it
   In love that's chaste. But for a man
   The world is full of different ways
   To show his service to the state.

EPODE

Once, Paris, coming and going in those haunts
   Where you were reared on Mount Ida's slopes
   And lived as a herdsman with your snow-white cows,
Piping away exotic tunes
   That echoed the ancient flute notes of Olympus
   In Phrygian modes . . . One day there came,
   While your fat cattle grazed, three goddesses
For a beauty trial;

And your reward from Aphrodite was
To stir your heart and send you off to Greece,
Where by the ivory palaces you stood
Stunned by the love that darted from the eyes
Of Helen, which your love returned: a passion
That blinded you and was to lead to this
Present strife that drives the whole of Greece
With men and ships against the towers of Troy.

[*Escorted by a retinue of her own guards and attendants,*
CLYTEMNESTRA *in a horse-drawn chariot rattles over the
rough ground into* AGAMEMNON's *compound. In the chariot
are also* IPHIGENIA *and a* NURSE *carrying the infant* ORESTES.
*Behind it trundle a couple of wagons piled high with boxes
and trunks containing the paraphernalia for a wedding. The*
SOLDIERS *of the camp crowd around clapping and cheering,
eager to catch a sight of famous royalty*]

CHORAL DIALOGUE

SOLDIERS: Hurrah! Hurrah! for the rich, famous, and happy.
    Look, there she is, Princess Iphigenia!
    And Clytemnestra, Tyndareus' daughter.
Blest to the heights in a pampered life.
The rich and powerful are like gods
    To us small fry.
CHORUS: We the women of Chalcis standing by
    With gentle hands shall help the queen
    Not to stumble
As she steps to the earth down from her carriage.
    And Agamemnon's daughter need not fear
On her first visit here.
    We too, visitors from Chalcis,
    Shall be careful not to ruffle or dismay
The royal visitors from Argos.

[CLYTEMNESTRA, *smiling indulgently at the enthusiasm of her
welcome, holds up a hand to check the cheering of the* SOLDIERS]

THIRD EPISODE

CLYTEMNESTRA: Thank you for your gracious welcome:
a good beginning for more good to come.
I have every hope of leading the bride
to a joyous wedding.

[*There is more cheering from all sides.* CLYTEMNESTRA *turns to the soldiery*]

Unload the wedding presents from the wagons
and lodge them carefully in the pavilion.
Iphigenia, dear girl,
it is time to leave the carriage,
so step down cautiously on your delicate tender toes.
You young women, give her a hand and help her down.
Someone lend me an arm.
Let me make a decorous descent.
You soldiers there, hold the horses' bridles.
They need steadying. They shy at the slightest thing.

[*Once on the ground,* CLYTEMNESTRA *takes* ORESTES *from the* NURSE *to allow her to dismount and prepares to hand him to one of the women of the* CHORUS]

Here, take him, this wee boy, this mite,
Orestes son of Agamemnon.

[*Caressing him as she hands him over*]

There, there, my baby! Sleepy still?
Was the rocking of the carriage so very lulling?
Wake up now for your sister's wedding.
A hero's little son is going to have a hero uncle:
His mother is a Nereid—related to the gods.

[CLYTEMNESTRA *and* IPHIGENIA *are escorted to seats, while the* NURSE *settles herself on the ground.* SOLDIERS *are busy unloading the wagons. Others stand around still mesmerized by the royal party.* CLYTEMNESTRA *hands* ORESTES *back to the* NURSE]

There, little fellow, sit at my feet.
Iphigenia, stand up—here next to your mother.
   Let these visiting ladies see how happy you make me.
Ah! here your dear father comes.
   Give him a tremendous welcome.

[As AGAMEMNON *emerges from his tent,* IPHIGENIA *runs into his arms*]

IPHIGENIA: [*calling back, laughing*]
   Oh mother, I've beaten you to it! Don't be cross.
   We're going to hug each other breast to breast.

[CLYTEMNESTRA, *conscious of the onlookers, becomes formal*]

CLYTEMNESTRA: Agamemnon, your majesty, my goodly king,
   obedient to your summons, you see we've come.
IPHIGENIA: Oh Father, how I've longed
   to rush into your arms and cuddle you! . . . Mother, forgive me!
CLYTEMNESTRA: Of course, my child!
   Of all my children you love him most.
IPHIGENIA: Father, I haven't seen you for so long. I'm so happy.
AGAMEMNON: So is your father. That makes two of us.
IPHIGENIA: Oh yes yes! It was lovely of you to send for me.
AGAMEMNON: [*shaken*] I . . . I wonder . . . I don't know what to
                                                    say to that.
IPHIGENIA: How come? . . . Glad to see me—with such a worried
                                                          face!
AGAMEMNON: Kings and generals have so much on their minds.
IPHIGENIA: But this moment is mine. Drop all your cares.
AGAMEMNON: You are all mine, then—you and nothing else.
IPHIGENIA: Then smooth away that frown—let love flow in.
AGAMEMNON: [*forcing a smile*] There, you see! I'm all yours,
                                                      darling.
IPHIGENIA: Are you? With those eyes so sad and brimming?
AGAMEMNON: Brimming because . . . because . . . we'll be apart
                                                        so long.
IPHIGENIA: Apart? I don't understand, Father. What do you
                                                         mean?
AGAMEMNON: You're so direct and honest, it makes me want to
                                                         cry.

IPHIGENIA: I'll talk nonsense then, if that will make you happy.

AGAMEMNON: [*to himself*] Dear God! It breaks my heart not to tell her.

[*Aloud*]

. . . and grateful too.

IPHIGENIA: Stay at home, Father—stay with your children.

AGAMEMNON: I wish I could: a wish that tears my heart apart.

IPHIGENIA: Forget this silly war and Menelaus' troubles.

AGAMEMNON: They'll be the end of me, but of others too.

IPHIGENIA: But you've been away too long, bottled up in Aulis.

AGAMEMNON: And we're still waiting for the army to set sail.

IPHIGENIA: Where do they say these Phrygians live, Father?

AGAMEMNON: Where Priam's son Paris comes from . . . I wish he didn't.

IPHIGENIA: So you're going on a long voyage, Father, and leaving me behind?

How I wish you would take me with you!

AGAMEMNON: You are going on a voyage too—then think of me.

IPHIGENIA: Sailing with my mother, or alone?

AGAMEMNON: Alone, without your father or your mother.

IPHIGENIA: Do you mean you've found another home for me?

AGAMEMNON: Don't ask. It's not for a young girl to know.

IPHIGENIA: Come back to me quickly, Father, when you've finished in Phrygia.

AGAMEMNON: First there is a sacrifice I must offer here.

IPHIGENIA: I know, you must do all those holy things.

AGAMEMNON: You shall see it. You'll stand by the sacrificial bowls.

IPHIGENIA: [*excitedly*] Oh Father, shall there be dances round the altar?

AGAMEMNON: How I wish I had your blessed innocence!
Now go inside, where young girls ought to be.
Kiss me. Give me your hand.
You'll be far from your father's home so long.

[*Father and daughter clasp each other in a long embrace, as* AGAMEMNON *murmurs*]

Goodbye, this young bosom, these cheeks, this golden hair.

Overwhelming is the burden Troy and Helen have laid on you.

[*Breaking away*]

Enough! The very touch of you
  fills my eyes with tears.
Now go into the pavilion.
  [*As* IPHIGENIA *leaves,* CLYTEMNESTRA, *who has been silently watching, approaches*]
Forgive me, daughter of Leto, for this show of feeling
  at losing my daughter to Achilles.
No matter how happy the event
  it wrings a father's heart to give a child away
  after all his loving care.
CLYTEMNESTRA: I do not blame you.
  I'm not so dull of soul as not to feel
  the selfsame pang
  as I lead our girl to the wedding songs.
But marriage is a common habit
  and time itself dries tears.

Now the name of the man to whom you are giving your child—
  that I know,
  but nothing about his family or where he comes from.
AGAMEMNON: Well . . . Aegina was the daughter of Asopus.
CLYTEMNESTRA: Married to a man or god?
AGAMEMNON: To Zeus, and he fathered Aeacus, husband of
                                                      Oenone.
CLYTEMNESTRA: Which of Aeacus' children inherited the house?
AGAMEMNON: Peleus. And Peleus married a sea nymph, daughter
                                                      of Nereus.
CLYTEMNESTRA: With the approval of the gods, or regardless of
                                                      them?
AGAMEMNON: Zeus himself promoted it. He gave her away.
CLYTEMNESTRA: Where was the wedding—under the sea?
AGAMEMNON: Under the blessed slopes of Pelion, where Chiron
                                                      dwells.
CLYTEMNESTRA: Isn't that where they say the Centaurs live?
AGAMEMNON: Yes, and where the gods gave a wedding feast for
                                                      Peleus.

CLYTEMNESTRA: Did Achilles' father bring him up or Thetis?

AGAMEMNON: Chiron did, so he wouldn't learn man's evil ways.

CLYTEMNESTRA: Good! A wise teacher and a wiser father.

AGAMEMNON: So that's the man your daughter is to marry.

CLYTEMNESTRA: Seems perfect; but where in Greece is his home?

AGAMEMNON: In Phthia, on the river Epidanus.

CLYTEMNESTRA: Is that where you'll take your girl and mine?

AGAMEMNON: It will be up to *him* when they are married.

CLYTEMNESTRA: I do hope they'll be happy. When is the wedding?

AGAMEMNON: When the moon is at its full . . . That brings good luck.

CLYTEMNESTRA: Have you offered the goddess our child's victim yet?

AGAMEMNON: I am just about to. We have it all in hand.

CLYTEMNESTRA: And the wedding banquet afterwards—that too?

AGAMEMNON: Yes, when the sacrifices have been sacrificed.

CLYTEMNESTRA: Where shall I hold the banquet for the women?

AGAMEMNON: Why here—among our Argive ships' impressive prows.

CLYTEMNESTRA: Well, if that's the decision . . . I hope it's for the best.

AGAMEMNON: My wife, do you know your part in this I want you to play?

CLYTEMNESTRA: Which is what? I have always done what you have asked me.

AGAMEMNON: I shall stay with the bridegroom here, while you . . .

CLYTEMNESTRA: While what? It is a mother's business to be there.

AGAMEMNON: While I give your child away in front of all the Greeks.

CLYTEMNESTRA: And where, pray, shall I be while all this is happening?

AGAMEMNON: Back in Argos looking after the girls.

CLYTEMNESTRA: Deserting my daughter here? Who will light the bridal torches?

AGAMEMNON: I myself shall light the bridal flames.

CLYTEMNESTRA: This is preposterous! Mean-minded too.

AGAMEMNON: It is preposterous for you to be among the troops.

CLYTEMNESTRA: But not for a mother to give her child away.

AGAMEMNON: Leaving young girls at home all on their own.

CLYTEMNESTRA: Safely tucked away in their own domain.

AGAMEMNON: Do what I say.

CLYTEMNESTRA: No, not by our Argive goddess queen!
You go and look after things outside,
    I shall see to things within
    and to all that is needed by the bride.

[CLYTEMNESTRA *leaves with a determined look, and* AGAMEM-
NON *walks dejectedly towards his tent*]

AGAMEMNON: Dammit! A useless move,
    this attempt to get my wife out of sight.
    I work out clever schemes to deal with those I love,
    and at every point my plans are blocked.
Nonetheless,
    I shall go with Calchas the priest to arrange this appeasement
                        to the goddess, this—for me—disaster.
Greece's crisis is mine . . .
If a wise man can't keep at home
    a good compliant wife—he does not marry.

[AGAMEMNON *steps hopelessly into his tent as the women of
the* CHORUS, *anticipating the certainty of* IPHIGENIA's *mar-
tyrdom and the release of the Greek fleet, begin to picture
what the siege of Troy will be like, and the sad aftermath of
the war for the Trojans*]

THIRD CHORAL ODE

STROPHE

CHORUS: Now will come to the silvery stream
    Of Simoïs the panoply
    Of Grecian armament and galleys.
Yes, they will come to Ilium,
Come to the plains of Troy:
    Apollo's Troy where I am told
    Cassandra wreathed in the evergreen leaves
    Of bay tosses her golden tresses

    Whenever she is overpowered
By prophetic ecstasy.

ANTISTROPHE

Around the battlements and walls
    Of Troy the Trojans stand, as over
    The sea the clattering war god comes
With bronze, and bristling oars
As the magnificent galleys
    Enter the shallows of Simoïs. All
    To bring back Helen, the sister
    Of Castor and Pollux who are in heaven;
    Bring her to Greece from the land of Priam
By force of shield and spear.

EPODE

The son of Atreus will tighten the belt
    Round Pergamum, that Phrygian city:
    Girdle the stone of its walls with blood,
    Tumble its silhouette to rubble
    And sever from his neck the head of Paris.
    Then the women of Priam's court
and his wife will mourn
    And Helen daughter of Zeus will sit
In remorse for leaving her man.

    Never let such a shadow of doom
    Fall upon me or my children's children
    As falls on the ladies of Lydia in their gold
    And the wives of Trojans at their loom.
    And they will be asking among themselves:
"What man will it be
    Who clenches his fist on my golden hair
    And plucks me like a weeping flower
Out of my perishing country?"

    All this because of you,
    Helen, child of Leda and
The arch-necked swan,
    If the story they tell is true

That the swan was really Zeus;
Or is this only fable
Culled from poetic annals
Not worth knowing?

[*There is a stir among the women of the* CHORUS *as a strong,
good-looking young man strides into camp:* ACHILLES, *clothed
in all the panache of a Greek officer, and more than pleased
with the impression he is making*]

FOURTH EPISODE

ACHILLES: Where can I find the commander in chief of the
                                    Achaean army?
Will one of you menials go and tell him
    that Achilles son of Peleus is outside and waiting.
This hanging around the straits of Euripus
    doesn't affect everyone the same.
There're us the unwed ones
    who have left empty homes
    and sit here idling by these shores.
But there are others
    who have left wives and children.
What a strange passion for this war
    has smitten Hellas. It's almost demonic.

My own case is this
    (anyone else can speak for himself):
I left my old father Peleus in Pharsalus
    and find myself waiting here for a breath of wind—
    the merest whisper from the Euripus—
    and trying to keep my Myrmidons in order.
They're forever at me, clamoring:
    "Achilles, why are we stuck here?
    How long more do we have to wait for our passage to Ilium?
Do something—anything—
    or just take your army home
    and stop waiting for the shilly-shallying sons of Atreus."

[CLYTEMNESTRA *comes out of the pavilion, eager to introduce herself*]

CLYTEMNESTRA: Son of the goddess Thetis, I've come outside to meet you

as soon as I heard it was you.

ACHILLES: In the name of divine Modesty
who is this lovely lady that I can see?

CLYTEMNESTRA: I am not surprised you don't know me.
We've never met before. But thank you for your graciousness.

ACHILLES: Whoever you are, what made you come to the Greek camp?

A woman in the midst of shields and soldiery!

CLYTEMNESTRA: I am Clytemnestra, daughter of Leda.
King Agamemnon is my husband.

ACHILLES: That was brief and to the point, but my tête-à-tête with a lady

might give the wrong impression.

CLYTEMNESTRA: [*as he begins to leave*]
Wait. Don't run away ... Give me your right hand to hold.

ACHILLES: What are you saying? My hand in yours!
I'd blush for shame if Agamemnon caught me.

CLYTEMNESTRA: It's perfectly proper, son of sea nymph Thetis,
seeing that you are going to marry my daughter.

ACHILLES: Marry? What marriage? ... Madam, I'm completely floored.

Is this a wild delusion?

CLYTEMNESTRA: I know you men are struck with shyness before a wedding

when they have to meet their future in-laws.

ACHILLES: Lady, I've never even met your daughter,
and there's been no whisper of marriage from the Atreus brothers.

CLYTEMNESTRA: I don't understand.
You seem as astonished by my response as I by yours.

ACHILLES: Think back ... We must work this out together.
The two of us may get to the bottom of this.

CLYTEMNESTRA: Have I been made a fool of?
Match-making where there was no match?
I am covered with shame.

ACHILLES: We've both been made a fool of. Don't brood on it.

It's not worth taking seriously.

CLYTEMNESTRA: Goodbye. I'm too mortified to look you in the
face . . .

So humiliated—and made out to be a liar.

ACHILLES: Goodbye then.

I'm going inside to see your husband.

[*As they move away, shamefaced and angry, the* OLD RETAINER
*calls out to them in a conspiratorial whisper from the threshold
of* AGAMEMNON'*s tent*]

RETAINER: Hullo there! Wait, stranger . . . Aeacus' grandson,
and you, my lady, daughter of Leda.

ACHILLES: Who is calling so nervously from a doorway?

RETAINER: A slave, sir, as luck would have it, but no matter.

ACHILLES: Whose? Not one of mine. Agamemnon and I don't
share slaves.

RETAINER: That lady's, over there, sir: given to her by Tyndareus.

ACHILLES: Well, I'm waiting. What was it you called to say?

RETAINER: Are you two alone out there . . . no one within
hearsay?

ACHILLES: We are alone. Come out of the king's tent and speak.

[*The* OLD RETAINER *slips out of* AGAMEMNON'*s tent and stands
before* ACHILLES, *who beckons to* CLYTEMNESTRA]

RETAINER: With a little luck and some smart thinking
I may just save those I want to save.

ACHILLES: Cut the preamble. You can use it another time.

CLYTEMNESTRA: [*as the* RETAINER *tries to kneel*]
No need for that. Get on with what you have to say.

RETAINER: You know me, my lady, loyal to you and to your
children.

CLYTEMNESTRA: Yes, you've long been a servant in my house.

RETAINER: I became Lord Agamemnon's with your dowry.

CLYTEMNESTRA: But you came with me to Argos and have been
mine ever since.

RETAINER: Yes, ma'am, and am less devoted to your husband
than to you.

CLYTEMNESTRA: Very well then, out with the secret information
that you have.

RETAINER: Your child ... her own father ... with his own
hands ... is out to kill her.

CLYTEMNESTRA: What nonsense, old man! You're out of your
mind.

RETAINER: He'll use a sword ... slash through her poor white
neck.

CLYTEMNESTRA: I can't believe it. Has my husband gone off his
head?

RETAINER: Only when it comes to you and your daughter,
ma'am.

CLYTEMNESTRA: For what reason? Is he driven by a fiend?

RETAINER: It's the seer Calchas. Without it he says the army
cannot sail.

CLYTEMNESTRA: Sail where? It's too horrible.
He can't do this to me, to her, kill his daughter.

RETAINER: Sail to Troy ... for Menelaus to drag Helen home.

CLYTEMNESTRA: So Iphigenia has to die for Helen to return?

RETAINER: Exactly that. Her father will sacrifice your child to
Artemis.

CLYTEMNESTRA: So the wedding was just a trick to lure me from
home?

RETAINER: And make you happily bring your daughter to wed
Achilles.

CLYTEMNESTRA: My poor, poor girl! Brought to destruction with
your mother!

RETAINER: A crime, an outrage against you both ... Oh, that
Agamemnon!

CLYTEMNESTRA: I'm overwhelmed, ruined. I can't hold back the
tears.

RETAINER: For an agony like this—to lose a child—let the tears
flow.

CLYTEMNESTRA: But where did you hear all this, old man?

RETAINER: I was sent with a letter to you canceling an earlier
one.

CLYTEMNESTRA: Stopping me or urging me to bring my child
(we know now) for death?

RETAINER: To stop you. Your husband then was sound in mind.

CLYTEMNESTRA: When you had the letter, why didn't you give it
to me?

RETAINER: Menelaus snatched it from me.
He is to blame for all this trouble.

CLYTEMNESTRA: O Achilles, son of Thetis, child of Peleus, do
you hear this?

ACHILLES: I hear it . . . misery for you and an insult to me.

CLYTEMNESTRA: Your wedding used to lure my daughter to her
death.

ACHILLES: This is no trifle. I am as enraged as you are with your
husband.

CLYTEMNESTRA: [*throwing herself before him*]
I am not ashamed to clasp your knees:*
I, only a mortal, you, son of a sea goddess.
Why should I be too proud?
Is there anything I wouldn't do to save my child?
Son of Thetis, be my champion,
rescue me from this disaster:
and her that I brought here—falsely I know—
decked in flowers to be your wife.
You will be a byword of reproach
if you don't stand up for her.
And even though you never married
everybody knew you were to be my poor darling's husband.
And so I implore your help,
by your manly beard, your strong right arm,
by your own mother's name.
It was your fame that led me on,
use it now to save me.
I kneel at the altar of your knees, my only refuge.
I have no friends to turn to,
and as to Agamemnon, you know now
his barbaric cruelty, his immorality.
Here I am, as you see, a woman,
surrounded by a horde of sailors,
lawless sailors itching for a bit of sport.
But even these, if they see you on my side

*Clasping the knee was an accepted gesture of supplication.

and under the cover of your arm, can help.
It's the only way to save us. There is no other hope.

LEADER: The wonderful power of motherhood: a magic all
                                                    mothers have!
   They'll go through fire and water to save their own.

ACHILLES: My chivalrous impulse is to act at once;
   however, I've learnt to temper both my disappointments
   and my enthusiasms.
Men like me, schooled by reason,
   lead a steady self-reliant life.
Of course there are times
   when it pays not to be too cautious,
   and times when simple common sense is best.
Brought up by Chiron, that god-fearing man,
   I learnt to be straightforward in my ways.
Accordingly,
   if the sons of Atreus behave properly, I shall obey them;
   if not, not.
Whether here or in Troy I am my own free spirit
   and shall as far as I am able
   serve the war god with élan.
So you, my lady,
   dreadfully abused by your dearest own,
   I shall champion
   and do everything that a young man can.
My sympathy shall be your shield
   and never shall your girl, my future bride,
   be slaughtered by her father,
   nor I let myself be used in your husband's tricks.
My name, otherwise,
   without my lifting a sword,
   would itself be your daughter's assassin,
   with your husband as accomplice.
If this girl should suffer such intolerable injustice,
   such unheard-of outrage, because of me and our engagement,
   the very temple of my body would be sacrileged.
I would be the lowest man in the Argive camp.
I would be a cipher, and Menelaus a man.
A demon, not Peleus, would be my father—
   yes, if murder were committed by your husband in my name.

I swear by Nereus,
 reared in the swamping waves,
 and by the father of my mother Thetis,
 that King Agamemnon shall never touch your daughter,
 not so much as lay a finger on her dress.
Call barbaric Sipylus a city—where these generals come from—
 call where I come from, Phthia, nothing,
 if this be not so.
That frothy-mouthing Calchas shall be sorry
 for his porridge-mongering offerings,
 his holy-water sprinklings.
What is a soothsayer, anyway?
 a man who utters a truth or two if he is lucky from a legion
               of lies,
 and when he is not, scatters.

I'm not saying all this because I am after a bride,
 not a bit of it:
 thousands of girls would like to bed with me.
No, King Agamemnon has insulted me.
He should have asked my permission
 if he wanted to use my name to trap his child.
It was my name that made Clytemnestra bring her daughter
              to him,
 and I would have lent it to the Greeks too
 if that helped their Trojan expedition.
Now in the eyes of these generals I am nothing:
 of no importance to them whether they treat me well or badly.

[*Stroking his scabbard*]

My sword shall know a thing or two
 before I leave for Troy . . .
 a nice smear of someone's lifeblood
 if he tries to snatch your daughter from me.

So rest assured, dear madam,
 though I may not be a god—if I seem one to you—
 I'm as good as a god, a great one too,
 and shall certainly become one—just for you.

LEADER: A speech worthy of you, son of Peleus.
  Your holy sea-born mother will be proud.
CLYTEMNESTRA: My word!
  How can I ever thank you
  without overdoing it and embarrassing you
  or not enough and appearing insensitive?
Thanks if too effusive
  can make an honest man recoil.
I do apologize for imposing on you
  the story of my private anguish.
My troubles are not yours
  but there's something admirable when a sympathetic man
  holds out a helping hand
  in matters far removed from his.

Pity me, my position is so pitiable.
To begin with, I imagined
  you were to be my son-in-law.
What a forlorn hope!
Not only forlorn but a death's-head
  at any future marriage that you make if my daughter dies.
This is something that you must guard against.
From first to last what you said was so convincing:
  that if you chose to save my child she would be saved.
Well then,
  will you have her come out here as suppliant to hug your
                                                        knee?

Not something that a young girl does
  but if you wish it she shall come:
  come in frank and simple modesty.
But if my entreaty is enough,
  let her keep her shyness to herself at home.
  We should respect it if we can.
ACHILLES: Dear lady, no.
  Don't bring your child out here for me to look at,
  and play into the hands of the gaping crowd.
A rootless army away from home
  feels free to feed on every kind of dirt and gossip.
In any case,
  you'll gain no more by supplication than without.

My main endeavor, my every effort,
   is to get you out of danger.
Keep in mind one simple fact:
I never lie.
   Should I prove a liar or purposely mislead you,
   let me die right here.
Your girl's life is my guarantee.
If I save her, she saves me.

CLYTEMNESTRA: Heaven bless you for helping those in need.

ACHILLES: Now listen carefully, so that we get it right.

CLYTEMNESTRA: Yes, tell me what. I am all ears.

ACHILLES: We must try to make her father change his mind.

CLYTEMNESTRA: Hopeless! He's a coward; cringes before the
                                                        troops.

ACHILLES: Sometimes fear can be overthrown by reason.

CLYTEMNESTRA: Cold comfort that! But tell me what to do.

ACHILLES: First of all,
   go down on your knees and plead with him
   not to kill your child.
If he refuses, come to me.
If you persuade him, there's no need of me!
   you will have won,
   and I shall be on a friendlier footing with a friend.
If through diplomacy not force we gain our ends,
   the army cannot blame me or complain.
So if this succeeds,
   all will be resolved for you and those you love—
   and without my help.

CLYTEMNESTRA: [dubiously]
   It seems sensible, and I'll try to do what you suggest;
   but what if I don't succeed?
Where shall I see you again?
Where shall I ever find you to hurry to my rescue:
   I'll be in despair.

ACHILLES: I shall keep a watchout somewhere for you,
   so don't go raging like a Maenad through the troops
   shaming your family's name.
Tyndareus must not be exposed to scandal.
His esteem is great among the Greeks.

CLYTEMNESTRA: You are right. You must take command,
    I must be your thrall.
If the gods exist, they surely will support your righteous stand.
    Otherwise, why bother with anything at all?

[As CLYTEMNESTRA *leaves for the pavilion tent and* ACHILLES
heads back into camp, the women of the CHORUS *sing a eulogy
of* ACHILLES, *dwelling first on the brilliant celebrations for his
parents' wedding in the land of the Centaurs. They go on to
describe Chiron's prophecy of* ACHILLES' *prowess and glory
at Troy. Finally, they tell of* IPHIGENIA'*s inevitable death and
they decry the collapse of all morality.*]

FOURTH CHORAL ODE

STROPHE

Oh what a joyful wedding song they sang
To the African flute and call to dance of the lute,
    And the piping thrill of the reeds,
    That day the Muses flowing
With their hair of running flame,
Flowed into the swards of Pelion
For Peleus' wedding and the god-blest wedding feast.
    So sweet a music steeped
The glens and woodland dells of Pelion,
    The Centaurs' lair,
    Diffusing celebration
    Of Thetis and her son.
    A prince of Troy,
Zeus's pretty catamite
    Ganymede was there
Ladling out the wine from bowls of gold,
    While on the sun-white sands
The fifty daughters of Nereus circled and wove.

ANTISTROPHE

Greenly crowned with leaves of olive they rode
With their lances of pine, the rout of man-horse Centaurs
    Into the feast where the gods
    Lay in their cups. And they roared:

"O Thetis, daughter of Nereus,
  Chiron the wise seer of Apollo
Tells of a son you will bear who will shine like the sun
    On Thessaly, and he will come
With his army of Myrmidons armed with shield and spear
      To the land of Priam,
        Cuirassed in a suit of mail
      Hephaestus made of gold
        His mother gave him."
  That was the day the gods all blessed
      When sea-born Thetis,
First of the Nereid princesses, came
    To be wedded to Peleus.*

Epode

Meanwhile, the men from Argos, Iphigenia,
Are twisting flowers into the curls of your hair,
  To lead you like a pure white heifer
  Out of a mountain cave for slaughter
  And prick a throat with human blood.
Not to the shepherd's pipe or herdsman's whistle
Were you brought up, but at your mother's side
  To be adorned one day as a bride
    For the son of a king.
  Where can Decency show her face?
  Where has Virtue hidden?
Brute godlessness is all the rage:
    Virtue tossed on the refuse heap.
    Lawlessness now governs law.
    Mankind no longer is concerned
      With not provoking heaven.

[CLYTEMNESTRA, *with a grim look of defiance, issues from the pavilion*]

---

*The antistrophe has only seventeen lines instead of the eighteen of the strophe because line 1062 is missing.

FIFTH EPISODE

CLYTEMNESTRA: I am out here waiting for my husband.
   I can't think why he has been away so long.
My darling child is in tears,
   tears from the very core of her being.
She knows now the death her father plans . . .
Well . . . talk of the devil . . . here he comes.
Here's the man whose criminal secret,
   whose ghastly schemes for his own daughter
   are about to be exposed.
AGAMEMNON: [*enters from the direction of the camp*]
   Ah! daughter of Leda,
   what a blessing to catch you here outside my tent!
   It gives me the chance to talk about the wedding
   with our daughter out of hearing.
For a young girl it is better so.
CLYTEMNESTRA: [*icily*] Gives you the chance? What is this mar-
                    velous opportunity?
AGAMEMNON: [*with a sudden change of tactic*]
   Go and fetch the girl.
Have her come out here to join her father.
The sacrificial waters are all ready;
   so is the barley meal to throw into the purifying flames,
   and of course the nuptial victim to be offered up,
   whose dark blood must spurt and run for Artemis.
CLYTEMNESTRA: Fine words indeed,
   but I have no words for that which you intend.

[*She goes to the pavilion and calls for* IPHIGENIA]

Daughter, come out here,
   though you know it all—your father's plans.
Bring Orestes your baby brother.
Tuck him up inside your mantle.

[IPHIGENIA, *carrying* ORESTES, *enters crying*]

See, she does whatever you tell her!
   I shall speak for her and for myself.
AGAMEMNON: Child, why these tears?

What's happened to those smiles?
Such a downcast face!
And those eyes hiding behind your gown!

CLYTEMNESTRA: [*half to herself*] God help me! Where do I
                                          begin?

The list of the enormities I've suffered
has no beginning, middle, or end.

AGAMEMNON: What *is* this performance?
A concerted plot to face me with a scene
of panic and disaster?

CLYTEMNESTRA: One single question, husband, answer it like a man.

AGAMEMNON: Don't give me orders . . . Of course I'll answer.

CLYTEMNESTRA: This child, your child and mine—are you going
                                          to kill her?

AGAMEMNON: Good God! What a question! What a foul sus-
                                          picion!

CLYTEMNESTRA: Cut the surprise. Just answer me—yes or no?

AGAMEMNON: Ask a reasonable question and you'll get a reason-
                                          able answer.

CLYTEMNESTRA: Just one question, only that: answer it.

AGAMEMNON: Heaven help me! This isn't fair, everything's
                                          against me.

CLYTEMNESTRA: Against you, me, her—all three of us.

AGAMEMNON: Who has wronged you?

CLYTEMNESTRA: You ask me that? Are you brainless? Do you
                                          have any brain at all?

AGAMEMNON: I'm finished. They know everything. My secret's
                                          out.

CLYTEMNESTRA: Yes, I know everything—your whole disgusting
                                          plan.

Even your dumbness gives you away.
You needn't tire yourself with explanations:
    moans and groans will do.

AGAMEMNON: You are right. Not a word. No more evasions.
Why add barefaced bluster to complete disaster!

CLYTEMNESTRA: Now you listen to *me*. I'll speak plain straight.
No more half-hints, no more innuendos.
Firstly, the very first thing I have against you:
    you murdered Tantalus my first husband

and forced me to marry you against my will.
You tore my baby from my breast
   and bashed his head against the floor.
When my twin brothers, sons of Zeus,
   came to my defense on shining steeds
   you went cringing to my ancient father, Tyndareus,
   and he saved you;
   and even got me into your bed as wife.
I was reconciled; became—you must admit it—a model wife,
   for you and for your home:
   considerate in love, a careful housekeeper
   not squandering but adding to your substance
   so that you came and went a happy man.
It's a rare thing for a man to win such a wife;
   worthless hussies are two-a-penny.
I bore this son to you after three girls,
   and now one of them you cruelly mean to rob me of.
If asked why, why do you want to kill her,
   what, pray, will your answer be?
Or must I say it for you?
To get Helen back for Menelaus.
Dear gods, what a price to pay!
One's own child for a prostitute!
Buying back what we hate with what we love!

So you leave me at home and go off to war,
   disappear for years.
What kind of pain, do you think, my heart will feel
   as I wander through the rooms,
   see her empty chair, her empty bedroom in the girls' wing?
I'll sit down in tears, lonely tears, inconsolable, and think:
   "My poor darling baby, he that gave you life, your own father,
   took it from you and killed you with his own hand."
We'd hardly have to hunt for motives, would we,
   my daughters and I, to give you the welcome you deserved
   when you came home.
For the gods' sakes, don't force me
   to take this hard line against you,
   or force yourself to do the same to me.

*   *   *

All right then,
      suppose you do sacrifice your child,
      what will you pray for when you say your prayers?
      What cut will you expect for cutting down a daughter?
      A passage home as hopeless as the passage out?
And what do you think *my* prayers will be?
Blessings on you?
Come, come! Are the gods so cretinous
      they expect kind thoughts for murderers?
And when you do get back to Argos,
      will you have the nerve to embrace your children?
Don't be preposterous! Not one of them will look at you,
      a father who put one of them to death.
Has this thought even entered your head?
      Or is your head too stuffed with playing
      a baton-twirling general?
The right thing would have been to stand up and say:
      "Soldiers of Argos and of Greece,
      do you want to sail to Troy?
      Then cast lots to see whose daughter has to die."
This would have been fair,
      not hitting on your own daughter as the victim.
If Troy must have a victim,
      let Menelaus kill Hermione, his child by Helen.
After all, the quarrel is his,
      and all of it for Helen.

As things stand,
      I who have been utterly faithful to our marriage
      am to lose my child,
      while that whore keeps hers,
      keeps her girl living happily and comfortably in Sparta.
You tell me if this isn't the plain truth,
      and if it is, change your mind,
      don't kill our child, be sensible.
LEADER: Be persuaded, Agamemnon, save your child.
      The whole world would say it's the only thing to do.
IPHIGENIA: [*stepping forward*] Father, had I the tongue of
                                                            Orpheus

to enchant the rocks with song
and make them follow me;
if I could cast a spell with words
on whomsoever I chose,
how I would have used that power,
but now the only resource I have is tears:
tears I offer—*that* I can manage.
Against your knees I'll press myself,
   press this body which this mother here once bore you,
   and I entreat you not to snuff out a life that's just begun.
Sweet is the light of day. Let me see it.
Don't force me to look on the gloom below.
I was the first to call you father
   and you to call me your little girl.
I was the first to clamber on your lap
   to kiss you and be kissed.
"So, my little girl," you used to say,
   "shall I live to see you happily married,
   full of life and busy in your husband's home?
How proud I'll be!"
And I would pull on your beard
   even as I touch it now, and say:
"When you're an old man, Father,
   do you know what I shall do for you?
I'll welcome you into my own house
   and make up for all the trouble you took with me."
I remember it so well, this childish talk,
   but you have forgotten it and are out to kill me.
Do not do that, please no:
   by Pelops, by your own father Atreus,
   by this mother standing here,
   who went through the agonies of childbirth once
   and now must face a second agony.

What have I to do
   with Alexander's* going off with Helen?
Tell me, Father,

Alexander: Paris.

how can it possibly be the end of *me*?

Look at me, Father,
give me one glance, one kiss
    that I can at least treasure at my death
if all my pleas have failed.

   [*Petting* ORESTES]

Little brother, you're too small to help the ones you love
    but you can cry for me:
    cry to your father for your sister's life.

   [*A wail from* ORESTES]

You see, even a baby knows.
Without words, he is begging you, Father:
    have mercy on me, I am so young, pity me.
By your beard your two loving children beg you:
    one a fledgling, one a grown young woman,
In a single appeal I say it all:
    the light of day is passing sweet,
    below is nothingness.
    The worst life is more than worth the best death.
LEADER: Ah! Helen, your shameful love affair
    has overwhelmed in misery the house of Atreus and its chil-
                                                              dren.

AGAMEMNON: I know what is pitiable and what is not.
    I love my children, or I'd be mad.
To do this dreadful thing is torture to me—believe me, wife—
    and torture if I don't. I must.
Cast your eyes over this mass of men, this armada,
    and the warlords of Hellas clanking in their bronze:
    all held back from their passage to Ilium with its towers,
    held back unless, as the seer Calchas says, I spill your blood.
The famous citadel of Troy will not be taken.
The Greek army is possessed by a kind of lust
    to sail at once to this foreign land
    and put an end to the raping of Greek wives.
They will kill my daughters in Argos.
They will kill you and me

if I break my pact with Artemis.
I am not being forced by Menelaus, dear child.
It's not to please him that I came here.
Whether I like it or not, it's all for Greece,
    for Greece I must offer you up.
The pressure of her claim is adamant:
    Greece must be free insofar as you and I can make her.
Greeks we are and we cannot let our women
    be carried off and raped by aliens.

[AGAMEMNON, *heavy-footed, walks off into the camp*]

CHORAL DIALOGUE

CLYTEMNESTRA: You, good strangers, you, my child,
    Your father primes you for death, then runs away.
IPHIGENIA: You dear Mother, you and I
    Must chant the selfsame dirge together.
            No longer the light,
        No longer the rays of the sun
    Belong to me . . . Once long ago
    In a snowy rift on Ida's slopes
In Phrygia, Priam exposed the infant Paris,
Torn from his mother's breast, left him to die,
    And he became the child of Ida.
Paris of Ida he was called when he came home.

    If only he had never been
    Raised as a herdsman among the cows;
    If only he had never found—
    This Paris, Alexander—a home
Among the shining waters and the springs,
    Among the nymphs and flowery meadows
    Where goddesses can gather
        Hyacinths and roses.

    Then one day there came there
        Pallas with her spear,
    Crafty Aphrodite, Hera,
And Hermes too, Zeus's messenger.

Then was enacted the fatal competition,
   The beauty contest and the judgment
   That leads now to my death, dear women,
      And to Greece's glory.
For Artemis accepts my sacrifice for Ilium.
   But he that begot me, my own father
      —Oh Mother! Mother!—
   Has abandoned me and gone . . .
   The bitterness of that bitter day
      I first saw Helen!
   It is the slaughtering of me now,
   My demolition, my undoing
   At the hands of a faithless father.

Why did Aulis ever welcome
      Into her enclave
   The ships with their beaky prows of bronze,
   The armada that will carry the troops to Troy?
    Why did Zeus not spring a breeze
      Along the Euripus
    To end the doldrums that locked us in?
He sends breezes to other men for happy sailings.
    He has a treasury of winds:
      Winds to hoist the sail,
      Winds to haul in the sheets,
      Winds that make one wait.
Poor struggling mortals, how they struggle
    Till the pitiful ending of their day!
And now the house of Tyndarus will spell us
    A tale of toil and agony
      Brought on the sons of Hellas.
LEADER: How I sympathize with you in this dread ordeal:
   A thing so far from your deserts!

[*From the road into camp a disorderly rout of soldiers can be
seen and heard approaching*]

SIXTH EPISODE

IPHIGENIA: Mother darling, I see a crowd of men approaching.
CLYTEMNESTRA: It's him, my girl, Thetis' son Achilles: for
                          whom you came here.
IPHIGENIA: Maids, open the doors . . . I've got to hide.
CLYTEMNESTRA: My child, you mustn't run away.
IPHIGENIA: But I can't face seeing him.
CLYTEMNESTRA: Why ever not?
IPHIGENIA: The phony wedding—I'm just too embarrassed.
CLYTEMNESTRA: You're in no position to be finicky. Stay.
    This is not a time to be coy, we must . . .

[ACHILLES *bursts in upon them. He is no longer the dapper
young officer bubbling with self-confidence. His uniform is
torn and spattered with mud, he has bruises on his handsome
face, and he has lost his swashbuckling plumed helmet. Two
batmen carry his shield and spear. The mob of soldiers halts
some distance away, stones at the ready*]

ACHILLES: [*breathlessly*] Daughter of Leda, you're in for trouble.
CLYTEMNESTRA: Don't I know it!
ACHILLES: There's uproar among the troops.
CLYTEMNESTRA: Uproar, explain.
ACHILLES: It's all centered on your daughter.
CLYTEMNESTRA: Dear gods! I can guess what is coming.
ACHILLES: They insist she be sacrificed.
CLYTEMNESTRA: And does nobody stand up for her?
ACHILLES: I did. And nearly lost my life.
CLYTEMNESTRA: How, my boy?
ACHILLES: By being stoned.
CLYTEMNESTRA: Trying to save my daughter?
ACHILLES: Exactly so.
CLYTEMNESTRA: You? Who would dare to lay a finger on you?
ACHILLES: The whole bloody army.
CLYTEMNESTRA: But weren't your Myrmidons there with you?
ACHILLES: They were the first to set on me.
CLYTEMNESTRA: There's no hope, my child.
ACHILLES: "Marriage-monger!" they jeered.
CLYTEMNESTRA: And what was your response?

ACHILLES: "Kill my bride to be," I said, "you shall not."

CLYTEMNESTRA: Quite rightly too!

ACHILLES: "She was promised to me by her father."

CLYTEMNESTRA: He even sent to Argos for her.

ACHILLES: But I was shouted down.

CLYTEMNESTRA: What a terrible thing mob violence is!

ACHILLES: Even so, I shall protect you.

CLYTEMNESTRA: Take on an army single-handed?

ACHILLES: See my armor-bearers here?

CLYTEMNESTRA: Blessings on your courage, son.

ACHILLES: Yes, I shall be blest.

CLYTEMNESTRA: And the child shall not be slaughtered now?

ACHILLES: No, I will never allow it.

CLYTEMNESTRA: Will they come and lay hold of her?

ACHILLES: Yes, a crowd of them, led by Odysseus.

CLYTEMNESTRA: [*with a grimace*] Nah! The spawn of Sisyphus.

ACHILLES: That's the man.

CLYTEMNESTRA: His own choice? Or appointed by the army?

ACHILLES: His own choice . . . and he needed no encouragement.

CLYTEMNESTRA: An obscene choice . . . to commit murder!

ACHILLES: But I shall stop him.

CLYTEMNESTRA: Will he seize her and drag her away?

ACHILLES: He'll seize her all right—by her golden hair.

CLYTEMNESTRA: Then what must I do?

ACHILLES: Hang on to her for dear life.

CLYTEMNESTRA: No more than that? Then she is safe.

ACHILLES: It may well come to that.

IPHIGENIA: Mother, listen to what I think.
    I see how angry you are with your husband,
    but it does no good.
The odds against us are too great.
So let us thank this young man for his courage,
    but not let his reputation suffer with the troops.
    We should fare no better and he would face disaster.
But the remarkable thing, Mother, as I think it over,
    is that I am willing to die—and die gloriously,
    after putting every petty thing behind me.
On me the sailing of the fleet
    and overthrow of Phrygia,
    on me the remedy against any barbarian

carrying off our women from a happy home—
should such a thing enter his head.
All this my death accomplishes,
and my name shall be blest as the liberator of Greece.
So I must not cling to life.
I was born from you not simply for your sake
but for the common good of Hellas.

Ten thousand men are armed with shields.
Ten thousand men grip the galley oars.
Their country has been hurt
and they are brave enough to be warriors
against the enemy and die for Greece.
Is my life to be the only obstacle?
Would that be fair? How can I defend it?

And another thing.
It is unthinkable that this man*
should pit himself against the whole of Argos
for a woman's sake.
A single man is worthier
to look upon the light than ten thousand women.
If Artemis is determined to have my carcass
shall I a mortal female cheat the goddess?
No, I give my body to Hellas.
So sacrifice me and sack Troy.
That will be my memorial through the ages.
That will be my marriage, my children, and my fame.
For the Greeks to govern barbarians is but natural,
and nowise, mother, for barbarians to govern Greeks.
They are born slaves. Greeks are born free.
LEADER: How courageously, young woman, you play your part!
It is Fate and Artemis that are at fault.
ACHILLES: Child of Agamemnon,
one of the gods intended to make me happy
with you as my wife.
Hellas is blest in you, and you are blest in Hellas.
Your speech is magnanimous,

this man: she means Achilles.

worthy of your fatherland.
You yielded in a battle with the gods
   more powerful than you.
You faced the inevitable and saw your duty.
When I witness the nobility of your soul
   I yearn all the more for your love.
So listen, I long to help you.
I long to win you for my home.
Thetis be my witness, it will be *my* loss
   if I do not check the Greeks and save you.
Remember, death is a terrible thing.
IPHIGENIA: Without misgiving, I must say this:
   Helen the Tyndarid has done enough harm by her beauty
   in whipping up strife and making men shed blood.
Therefore, good stranger prince,
   do not die for me. Kill nobody.
Allow me to save Greece if I can.
ACHILLES: O illustrious one,
   what more can I say if that is your decision?
Your whole attitude is wonderful. That is the truth.
Nonetheless, should you come to change your mind,
   this I want you to know:
   I shall put my weapons at the ready by the altar
   to rescue you from dying.
Perhaps you will take my offer up
   when you see the sword come near your throat.
I shall never let you die for a ridiculous decision.
I'll take these weapons of mine to the temple of Artemis
   and await you there.

   [ACHILLES *departs with his sword, spear, and dagger*]

IPHIGENIA: Mother, why are you crying? Talk to me.
CLYTEMNESTRA: The pang in my heart gives me good reason
                                to cry.
IPHIGENIA: Don't, or you'll turn me into a coward. Please . . .
CLYTEMNESTRA: Whatever you want, my child. I'll do my best.
IPHIGENIA: Don't chop off your glorious hair.
   Don't drape yourself in black.

CLYTEMNESTRA: Daughter, how can you say that, when I have lost you?

IPHIGENIA: Not lost, saved. And through me your fame will be great.

CLYTEMNESTRA: What are you saying? Am I not to mourn for you?

IPHIGENIA: Not in the least. No grave shall be heaped upon me.

CLYTEMNESTRA: How do you mean? Does not death imply a burial?

IPHIGENIA: In my case, the altar of Artemis will be my tomb.

CLYTEMNESTRA: My child, you are right. I shall do what you say.

IPHIGENIA: Because I am blest: the benefactress of Hellas.

CLYTEMNESTRA: What message shall I take your sisters?

IPHIGENIA: Do not dress them, either, in mourning black.

CLYTEMNESTRA: What words of love from you shall I bring to them?

IPHIGENIA: Say goodbye for me.
Make sure baby Orestes grows into a man.

CLYTEMNESTRA: Hug him to you. This is the last time you'll see him.

[*The* NURSE *puts* ORESTES *in* IPHIGENIA's *arms*]

IPHIGENIA: Sweet baby, you did all you could for us.

CLYTEMNESTRA: When I am back in Argos is there anything I can do for you?

IPHIGENIA: Yes, don't hate my father—your own husband.

CLYTEMNESTRA: [*grimly*] Because of you I shall give him a run for his money.

IPHIGENIA: Against his will, he sacrificed me to save Greece.

CLYTEMNESTRA: Treacherously and like a coward: unworthy of Atreus.

[IPHIGENIA *hands* ORESTES *back to the* NURSE]

IPHIGENIA: Will somebody escort me, so I won't be dragged by the hair?

CLYTEMNESTRA: I shall go with you and . . .

IPHIGENIA: No, that wouldn't be right.

CLYTEMNESTRA: . . . cling to your dress.

IPHIGENIA: Listen, Mother, stay.
  It is better for you and for me.
Let one of my father's men escort me
  to the meadow of Artemis where I am to be slain.
CLYTEMNESTRA: O my child, are you going?
IPHIGENIA: Yes, never to return.
CLYTEMNESTRA: Abandoning your mother?
IPHIGENIA: As you see. No easy thing!
CLYTEMNESTRA: Wait! Do not leave me.
IPHIGENIA: No tears, please.

[CLYTEMNESTRA *sinks to the ground, clutching her daughter's dress*]

Young women,
  raise a paean of joy for me to Artemis, child of Zeus,
  and let the Greeks observe a solemn silence.
Let the celebrations begin with the ritual baskets,
  let the pyre blaze
  with the purifying barley meal.
Have my father circle the altar from left to right:
  for I come bringing to Hellas salvation and triumph.

CHORAL DIALOGUE

IPHIGENIA: Conduct me as a sacker of cities,
  Sacker of Troy and Phrygia.
  Load me with garlands, wreathe my head.
  Play the holy fountains on me,
  And in the temple weave and dance
  Around the altar of Artemis:
  Queen Artemis, the blessed one.
  If it must be, let my blood
  Fulfill in sacrifice her bidding.

[IPHIGENIA, *in tears, raises her mother up*]

My lady, my lady, my mother,
  My tears pour down for you,
  We pour them together,
  But I may not weep at the altar.

[*Turning to the* CHORUS, *shouting*]

Holla, my ladies, ho!
   Raise up a chant of praise with me
   For Artemis, worshiped here,
   Facing your Chalcis where
   In the narrow cleft of Aulis
   The irate army itches to fight.
   Holla! my motherland of Argos
   And my home Mycenae.
CHORUS: Are you calling on the city of Perseus
   Which the Cyclops toiled to build?
IPHIGENIA: Which raised me to be the light
   Of Greece. I do not shrink from death.
CHORUS: Your fame shall never leave you.
IPHIGENIA: Holla there! Day, bringer of light!
   Holla there! the radiance of Zeus!
   Another phase of light and life
   Are to be mine . . . Farewell, light,
   Beloved light!

[*Escorts lead* IPHIGENIA *away.* CLYTEMNESTRA, *supported by servants, staggers into the tent. The* CHORUS *chants a congratulation to* IPHIGENIA *for her bravery, then a somewhat sycophantic supplication to Artemis*]

CHORUS: Cheers for the sacker of cities,
   The sacker of Troy and Phrygia,
   As she goes to be garlanded
   And sprinkled with holy water.
   Blood will flow from her throat:
   Her body's lovely throat,
   Upon the altar of Artemis.
   The lustral bowls and droplets
   Await you and your father;
   And of course the army of Hellas
   Impatient to sail for Troy.

Let us praise Zeus's daughter,
   Artemis, huntress queen.

Iphigenia's loss
Is gain, my lady, yes,
Joyer in human blood:
Speed the Greek armada
To Phrygia and dangerous Troy.
Grant that Agamemnon
Will crown the Grecian spears
With wreaths of fame, and his brow
With everlasting glory.

[*The Greek text here becomes more and more suspect. We know that Euripides died before he could finish this play. The conclusion is undoubtedly spurious*]

SEVENTH EPISODE

[*A soldier, the* SECOND MESSENGER, *hurries in from the camp and halts outside* CLYTEMNESTRA's *tent*]

SECOND MESSENGER: Clytemnestra, daughter of Tyndareus, come
                              out and hear my news.
CLYTEMNESTRA: Indeed, I do. Your voice compels me.
   I am shocked and giddy with fear
   in case you have come to tell me
   of another horror piled on the one already.
SECOND MESSENGER: About your child—it was wonderful and
                              awe-inspiring.
CLYTEMNESTRA: Well, get on with it. Do not dally.
SECOND MESSENGER: Of course, dear mistress, you shall hear
                              everything.
I'll tell it all straightforwardly from the start,
   and only hope I don't break down and begin to jabber.

When we had reached the domain of the virgin goddess, Artemis,
   Zeus's child, in her flower-splashed fields,
   and had brought your daughter
   to where the Achaean army mustered,
   the military immediately surrounded us.
When Agamemnon saw the girl
   treading with steady steps towards the place of slaughter,

he heaved a groan, turned his head away, and wept,
  holding his gown before his eyes.
But she came up and stood beside her sire.

"Father, here I am," she said, "as you bid me.
  Of my own free will I bequeath my body
  for my state and for the whole of Hellas.
so lead me to the altar of sacrifice—
  if that is the decision.
May it help you, if that is in my power.
May you be awarded victory
  and return a winner to your native land.
Let no Argive lay his hand on me.
Silent, unflinching, I bare my throat."

Those were her words
  and everyone marveled at the girl's heroism and nobility.

Then Talthybius, whose task it was,
  stepped forward and proclaimed a reverential silence
  and brought the army to a hush.
Calchas the seer, then,
  drew out of its scabbard a dagger, deadly sharp,
  and placed it in a gold-studded basket,
  and put a chaplet on the girl's head.
Then the son of Peleus, Achilles,
  holding the basket and lustral bowl,
  ran round the goddess' altar as he uttered:
"Artemis, daughter of Zeus,
  huntress of wild animals,
  flooder of night with the moon's light,
  accept this sacrifice we offer
  of the pure blood from a virgin's throat,
  grant that our galleys sail unchecked,
  and that our spears topple the towers of Troy."

The sons of Atreus and all the army
  stood at attention with bowed heads.

Gripping the dagger and praying,

the priest took the knife and searched for the spot to strike.
I was in a ferment and
Then suddenly a miracle took place:
    all of us heard the plunge of the stroke
    but none of us knew where on earth the maiden had vanished.
The priest gave a shout
    and the whole army echoed him
    as they beheld a prodigy, an unearthly phenomenon.
A deer in spasms lay panting on the ground:
    a large and handsome hind.
All the altar was speckled with her blood.
Then Calchas spoke—you can imagine with what joy.
"Commanders of the Panhellenic and thwarted host,
    do you see this victim which the goddess
    lays upon her altar, this hind from the hills?
Far more welcome to her is this oblation than a maid,
    that she may not tarnish her altar with noble blood.
She has accepted this sacrifice with joy
    and grants us a favorable passage and attack on Troy.

Wherefore, let every mariner
    march with confidence to his ship;
    for this very day we must set sail
    from the hollow straits of Aulis
    and cross the Aegean surge."
So when the victim was reduced to ashes in the fire god's flame,
    Calchas offered up a prayer
    that the army would in time come safely home.

Agamemnon sent me to tell you this
    and to say how blest by the gods he is,
    and how throughout Hellas his fame is everlasting.
I was there and tell you exactly what I saw.
There is no doubt your child was wafted to the gods,
    so cease from grief and resentment against your consort.
Mysterious to us mortals are the ways of the gods.
Those they love, they save:
    this day has seen your child dead and alive.
LEADER: Happy am I to hear the messenger's news
    that your child lives and abides with the gods.

CLYTEMNESTRA: O my child, what god has stolen you?
How shall I address you? What can I say?
Is this just a story to console me for you
    and heal my broken heart?
LEADER: Here King Agamemnon comes bearing the same report.

[AGAMEMNON *marches in from the direction of the camp*]

AGAMEMNON: My wife, we should be happy for our daughter's
                                                    fate.
    There is no doubt that now she shares the bliss of the gods.
Take this little princeling and go home;
    for the army is ready to set sail.
Farewell till after Troy.
    It will be a long time before I talk to you again.
May you live without chagrin.
CHORUS: Go, son of Atreus, with joy
    To the land of Phrygia,
    And with joy return here
    Loaded with sumptuous spoils,
    I hope, from Troy.

IPHIGENIA
AMONG THE
TAURIANS

ΙΦΙΓΕΝΙΑ Η
ΕΝ ΤΑΥΡΟΙΣ

For Henrietta Sargent

―⊷∾⊷―

"*Iphigenia Among the Taurians* is excellent theater by any standard. Its plot is carefully conceived, its characters are clearly defined and behave plausibly and interestingly in crises that are credible; there is the thrill of danger, the romance of far places and strange ways, the sentimentality of old memories and mixed loyalties and nostalgic yearnings."*

The name Iphigenia means "the strong-born one," and from the story told by Euripides in this play and its predecessor (predecessor in plot, not in composition), *Iphigenia at Aulis*, one sees why. She was the daughter of Agamemnon and Clytemnestra and had been wafted miraculously to Taurus by the goddess Artemis, who made her priestess of the temple there.

The Taurians were a savage race (living in modern Crimea) and required that all strangers happening on their land should be sacrificed to Artemis—a ritual over which Iphigenia as priestess had to preside. Since any stranger would inevitably be a Greek and since the Greeks had sought to kill her, Iphigenia was ready to comply until . . .

CHARACTERS

IPHIGENIA, high priestess of Artemis
ORESTES, brother of Iphigenia
PYLADES, friend of Orestes
CHORUS, captive Greek temple maidens
THOAS, king of Tauria
HERDSMAN, a Taurian peasant
MESSENGER, a soldier of Thoas
PALLAS ATHENA
TEMPLE MINISTERS, attendant on Iphigenia
GUARDS, soldiers of Thoas
CITIZENS, natives of Tauria

Ten Plays by Euripides, trans. Moses Hadas and John McLean (New York: Bantam Books, 1960), p. 241.

TIME AND SETTING

Two young men, Orestes and Pylades, arrive furtively in Taurus
with no less a design than to carry off the famous effigy of
Artemis in the temple. Orestes had been told by Apollo in an
oracle that to expiate the blood-guilt of murdering his mother
(who had murdered his father, Agamemnon), he must secure the
image of Artemis and bring it to Attica. He has no idea that his
sister is still alive but has heard rumors that the Taurians go in
for human sacrifice.

It is morning. Iphigenia, crowned with a chaplet of laurel
and draped in white, comes out of the temple of Artemis in
the seaside town of Taurus and stands at the top of the steps. In
the courtyard below behind a screen can be glimpsed a blood-
splattered altar. Skirting this is a path leading to the bay.

PROLOGUE

IPHIGENIA: With his team of speedy horses
   Pelops son of Tantalus came to Pisa*
   and made a wife of Oenomaus' daughter,
   from whom Atreus was born, and he
   fathered Menelaus and Agamemnon; I, Iphigenia,
   am Agamemnon's child by Clytemnestra, daughter of Tyn-
                                              dareus.

By the banks of the dark blue waters
   of the river Eripus, so often churned by squalls
   into roiling eddies,
   my father Agamemnon immolated me—or so he thought—to
                                              Artemis
   in the well-known dells of Aulis;
   and all because of Helen.
There, Agamemnon, hoping to win for the Achaeans
   a crown of triumph by crushing Ilium,
   had assembled an armada of a thousand ships.
He wanted also, as a favor to Menelaus,
   to avenge his broken marriage and the ravishing of Helen.
A strange dearth of breeze, however,

*Not Pisa in Italy but Pisa in the Peloponnese, famous for its horses.

kept him from sailing and he took to auguries by fire.
Then Calchas the soothsayer spoke.

[IPHIGENIA *slowly descends the steps*]

"O lord and leader of this Greek Armada, Agamemnon,
    you'll not see a vessel leave these shores
    until you sacrifice to Artemis Iphigenia your daughter.
You made a vow that you would immolate
    to this goddess of the flaming torch
    the most precious thing that any year could ever offer.
Well, your wife Clytemnestra in your very palace
    brought forth a daughter: her you must sacrifice . . .
    Not a pretty piece of news for me to bring you!"

[*She halts halfway down the steps*]

Then Odysseus,
    pretending to take me to my wedding with Achilles,
    lured me from my mother and brought me to Aulis:
    a wretched victim held aloft above the altar pyre,
    trussed for the sword thrust.
But Artemis snatched me away
    and leaving the Achaeans a doe as substitute
    wafted me through the clear bright air to the land of Taurus.
And here I've lived ever since:
    here where a savage king reigns over savages.
    His name is Thoas, which means "Swifty,"
    because he is fleet of foot—runs swifter than a bird.
So here I am,
    obedient to a cult and Festival the goddess Artemis delights in,
    though there is nothing festive in it but the name.

[*She breaks off with a shudder*]

For dread of her I'll not say more,
    except that I am slave to a rite that existed long before I came:
    I offer her the lives of every Greek that sets foot in this land.
At least, my part is just to consecrate;
    the butchering is done by others—
    done in the dark depths of this goddess' home.

[*Walking down the rest of the steps*]

Last night I had strange dreams.
Let me vent them on the morning air and perhaps dispel them.
It seemed I was in Argos once again, far from here,
    and lay resting in the bedroom of my girlhood,
    when suddenly the earth shook and I fled outside
    and standing there I saw the cornice of the house collapse,
    the roof and pillars crumble to the floor, all but one:
    one pillar of my father's house seemed to stand up straight
    and from its capitals there sprouted
    a man's golden hair and a voice spoke.
I, in my ministry of sacrificing strangers,
    threw holy water on the pillar
    as if priming it for death. And I was crying.

My interpretation of the dream is this:
    Orestes is dead—I killed him ritually.
    The pillars of the palace are the male offspring of the house,
    and those I sprinkle with holy water die.
They are the only dear ones that the dream could fit.
Strophius*, my uncle, was childless when I "died,"
    so it has to mean my faraway brother.
    To him I must now pour a libation for the dead;
    it is the least that I can do.
Those Greek girls the king has given me can help.

[*She glances impatiently around*]

Why have they not appeared?
I'll go back into my home, this palace,
    the temple of the goddess Artemis.

[IPHIGENIA *remounts the temple steps, and hardly has she disappeared behind the doors when* ORESTES *and* PYLADES *creep stealthily into the courtyard from the path leading to the bay. They are clad in traveling clothes: short kilts, heavy sandals laced up the calf, capes over close-fitting tunics, and caps*]

*Brother-in-law of Agamemnon, father of Pylades, friend of Orestes.

FIRST EPISODE

ORESTES: [*in a whisper*] Look out! Is there any sign of anyone?
PYLADES: I'm looking, scanning in all directions.
ORESTES: [*catching up with him*]
    Oh Pylades, do you think this is the temple of Artemis:
    the very place we've sailed over the seas to find?
PYLADES: I really think so, Orestes . . . Don't you too?
ORESTES: That altar stone there, spattered with blood? . . .
PYLADES: You're right . . . tawny blood-marks along the top.
ORESTES: And up there around the cornice, do you see those
                                human items hanging?
PYLADES: Yes, dead men's remnants from the bodies of the
                                      visitors.

    I'm going off to have a closer look.

[*While* PYLADES *goes off to explore,* ORESTES *throws out his
arms in an attitude of prayer*]

ORESTES: O Phoebus,
    since my mother slew my father and I slew her,
    have you trapped me again in your net of oracles?
I've been pursued by hordes of Furies all over the earth
    far from my native land;
    and when at last I ran to you and begged that you would stop
    this crazy cycle of obsession
    and end the agony, the torture,
    that hurtled me to and fro the length and breadth of Hellas,
    your answer was:
"Go to the land of Taurus
    where my sister Artemis enjoys a shrine,
    and take from there her effigy, which fell, they say, from
                                heaven.
If you are man enough or lucky enough to steal it,
    bring the image when the danger is done
    home to the land of Attica."
You said no more,
    except that when I had accomplished this
    I'd win respite at last from all my labors.
So here I am, obedient to your will,

here in this savage and mysterious land.

[*Turning to* PYLADES, *who has sauntered back*]

Oh Pylades, I ask you, my staunch accomplice,
    what on earth are we to do?
Just look at those walls, their encircling height!
If we are to explore this unknown place,
    are we brazenly to go up to its front door?
    But we'd need a crowbar to break those locks of bronze.
And even if we managed to force an entrance and were caught
    it's certain death.

[*He turns towards the path*]

Come, instead of dying
    let's get back to the good ship that brought us here.
PYLADES: What, turn tail?
    That's unthinkable, not our way.
    And don't go blaming Apollo's oracle.
Let's just leave the temple and go and hide
    in some cavern rinsed by the black surf
    far from our ship in case a native seeing it
    reports the matter to the king
    and we get dragged away.
Then when night with its somber eye begins to shine
    we shall make the attempt, strain every nerve
    to oust the graven image from the shrine.

[*Gazing up at the steep walls*]

Look, between those two triglyphs is a space
    down which a man could slip.

[*Pauses to watch* ORESTES' *reaction*]

Come, lad, a real man ventures everything.
The coward gets nowhere in anything.
ORESTES: No indeed!
    And we haven't sailed all this way
    just to go straight home again.

You are right, so let's do what you say
   and find a place where we can hide.
If the oracle turns out a mere dead end
   at least the fault will not be ours.
Yes, we must do and dare.
Young men should never fear.

[*A gong resounds through the temple precincts, and as*
ORESTES *and* PYLADES *hurry away down the path leading to
the shore the* CHORUS *of* CAPTIVE MAIDENS *issues from the
other side of the temple, chanting*]

FIRST CHORAL LYRIC

FIRST GROUP: Silence, please,
   All who live by the twin rocks,
   That clash in the Black unfriendly Sea.*
SECOND GROUP: Child of Leto, Artemis,
   Maid of the Mountains, we await
   By your gilded shrine, by its colonnades,
   The priestly steps of the high priestess.
THIRD GROUP: We the banished from the towers and walls
   Of Hellas, land of the comely horse;
   Banished from Europe with its gardens
   Luxuriant with trees,† and exiles
   Far from our father's home.

[*The gong sounds again*]

FOURTH GROUP: Here we are, what is the news?
   What anxiety made you summon us,
   You, O daughter of Atreus' son
   Who went to besiege the walls of Troy,
   Went with a fleet of a thousand ships,

---

*Euripides' geography is somewhat awry. He makes the narrow passage of
the Bosphorus known as the Symplegades one with that leading into the
Euxine or Black Sea.
†The maidens are thinking especially of the vine and the olive, supreme symbols of civilization contrasted with the wild forests of Scythia.

An army of ten thousand men?

[IPHIGENIA, *clothed in mourning, accompanied by attendants carrying funeral urns, appears at the top of the temple steps*]

CHORAL DIALOGUE

IPHIGENIA: Listen, my women,
    Hard is the mourning, mournful and hard,
    Dismal the dirges the Muses despise:
    Great is my grief for the death of a brother.
    I saw it in dreams in the dark of last night.
I swoon, I die.
    The house of my fathers is no more.
    Sad, how sad, my vanished race!
    Sad the sufferings of Argos!
    Away with you, away you Powers
    Who have robbed me of my only brother
    And sent him down to Hades' realms.
    For him I sprinkle on the earth
    (That chalice of the dead)
These libations:
    Milk from heifers on the hills,
    Wine, the ruddled drink of Bacchus,
    Honey from the wild bee:
    Consolations for the dead
Perennially.

[*Turning to an attendant*]

Hand me the gilded ewer now,
The offering to Hades.

[*From different vessels, she mixes wine, milk, honey, speaking as she pours them on the ground*]

Under the earth, Agamemnon's son,
To you I send these tokens of demise;
A golden tress of my hair* I cannot

---

*The offering of a lock of hair was typical of the funeral rite.

Nor send a vase of tears.
Far from your country and from mine
I, thought to be dead,
Linger and pine.

CHORUS: Mistress, the antiphon we in response
Utter to you is a primitive chant
Echoing dirges from Asia of old:
The dismal thrill of a dead Paean
Special to Hades.

IPHIGENIA: Alas for the house of Atreus
And the light of a scepter gone!
Alas for the glory of ancestral halls!
Gone the prosperity, gone the power
Of the monarchs of Argos:
Blow upon blow has felled the house.

CHORUS: The winged coursers of the Sun
Have swerved. The holy eye of day
Has swiveled around. The golden lamb*
Has spelt death upon death, sorrow on sorrow.
The duel of the Tantalids long long ago,
Killing and killed, works itself out
To finish this house.
Fate with ferocious zeal has hurled
Itself against you.

IPHIGENIA: From the start sorrow was mine,
On my mother's bridal night—
The sorry night I was conceived.
From the start the goddesses
Of birth have trammeled
The web of my life.
I, first flower of my mother's
Nuptial chamber, Clytemnestra
(Leda's misbegotten daughter),
Was born and nurtured to be murdered
By a lost misguided father:

---

*When Atreus and Thyestes disputed the throne of Argos, a lamb with golden
fleece appeared among the flocks of Atreus, signifying his victory. His wife,
Aerope, however, stole it and gave it to her lover, Thyestes. Atreus retaliated
by throwing Aerope into the sea, killing Thyestes' sons, and serving them up
to him in a banquet.

I a victim vowed for felling
In a joyless sacrifice.
A chariot drawn by horses took me
To the seaside sands of Aulis,
Achilles' bride (the joke of it!),
Achilles, son of Nereus' daughter.

[*She pauses, sighing*]

Here I live plunged in forests,
Hemmed in by a wicked sea:
Husbandless, childless, homeless,
Loveless, banished,
From Hellas for my "honeymoon."
I sing no songs of Argive Hera,
Nor on humming loom embroider
Scenes of Pallas or the Titans.
Instead I render forlorn altars
Gory with the blood of strangers;
Hear them, piteous, cry in pain;
See the piteous tears they shed.

[*She wipes away a tear herself*]

It's not of these I'm thinking now,
It's my brother dead in Argos
Whom I cry for, whom I left
An infant at his mother's breast:
Still a baby, still so tender,
Still a sapling in her arms—
You, Orestes, king of Argos.

[IPHIGENIA *continues to stand sunk in sadness as one of the* CAPTIVE MAIDENS—*the* CHORUS *leader—points towards the path down which a man is seen approaching*]

SECOND EPISODE

LEADER: Look, a herdsman comes with news, approaching from
the shore.

[*The* HERDSMAN *enters breathlessly. He is clad in a smock of homespun belted at the waist, with dungarees of the same, lagged with hessian up the legs, and is barefoot. He makes straight for* IPHIGENIA]

HERDSMAN: O child of Agamemnon and of Clytemnestra,
    just listen to the piece of news I bring.
IPHIGENIA: What? What have you got to say so shattering?
HERDSMAN: Through the dangerous straits of Symplegades
    have sailed intact and landed here, two young men:
    lovely morsels for Artemis our goddess.
Get into your sacrificial gear at once
    and prepare the holy waters.
IPHIGENIA: Where do they come from, these visitors? What country?
HERDSMAN: They're Greeks. That's all I know.
IPHIGENIA: Not even the names of these two men?
HERDSMAN: One is called by the other Pylades.
IPHIGENIA: And what does that one call his friend?
HERDSMAN: I have no idea. We didn't hear his name.
IPHIGENIA: How did you come upon them? How did you catch them?
HERDSMAN: Right on the shoreline of our Wicked Sea we . . .
IPHIGENIA: What are herdsmen doing down by the sea?
HERDSMAN: We'd taken our cattle there to wash them, and . . .
IPHIGENIA: Yes yes, but how did you capture them, by what ruse?
    That's what interests me. That's what I want to know.
    It's been a long time since a flow of Greek blood
    has reddened Artemis' altar.*
HERDSMAN: We had brought our cattle out of the woods down to the sea,
    where it flows out between the Symplegades;
    and there in a rock hollowed by the surf,
    a cavern used by the purple-fishers,†
    a herdsman, one of us, saw two youths.
So he crept away on tiptoe and reported back.

---

*The Greek of lines 258–59 is ambiguous. It has been translated as "After all this time we've never had any Greek blood" etc., but line 347 makes clear that this rendering is incorrect.
†The costly dye of purple, which was confined to royalty, was extracted from a shellfish, the *porphura* (genus *Murex*).

"Can you believe it!" he said.
    "Back in there two gods are sitting. Yes, I've seen them."
One of us, a pious fellow, peeked in.
"Son of the sea goddess Leucothea, saver of ships," he cried,
    lifting up his arms in prayer: "be kind to us.
Are these boys sitting on the shore Castor and Pollux,
    or the handsome sons of Nereus—
    master of the fifty Nereids and their marvelous choir?"
He was interrupted by another fellow,
an irreverent and brazen sinner,
who laughed this prayer to scorn and made out
that the men sitting in the cave were castaway sailors
cringing with fear of what they'd heard,
that strangers here get sacrificed.
    Most of us agreed with him,
so we decided to hunt them for the goddess' altar.

    [*He pauses to wipe the sweat from his brow*]

It was then that one of the strangers ran out of the rock,
    stood outside wagging his head, groaning,
    and trembling to his very fingertips.
In a Fury-pursued frenzy he yelled,
    just like a hallooing hunter:
"Oh, Pylades! Over there! Don't you see her?
Look! Look! Surely you must.
And over there, another—see?—
    coming at me with her nest of vipers,
    a freak from hell—out to kill me.
And up there, another, hovering,
    trailing fire and blood in her clothes.
She's got my mother in her arms—no, a rock—
    She's coming, she's coming, she's going to throw it,
    she's going to smash me.
Oh Pylades, where can I run?"*

---

*It must be remembered that Orestes had yet to be cured of the recurrent mad-
ness that dogged him after the murder of his mother. Reason could suddenly
collapse into frenzy and hallucination, as in schizophrenia.

                    *   *   *

Of course there was nothing: not a form, not a figure.*
His imagination reeled as he staggered towards us.
The mooing of cattle, the bark of dogs,
    became for him the cries of the Furies
    copying the sounds of animals.
We cowered in a heap, not speaking,
    waiting for the worst as he drew his sword
    and bounded like a lion into the midst of our cattle.
He stabbed at their flanks with his steel,
plunging it into their ribs,
convinced that he was fighting the Furies.
    Soon the sea itself was tinged scarlet as a flower.

[*Pausing with horror at the memory*]

At length, every one of us,
    seeing our cattle butchered and falling, began to arm.
    We blew the alarm on our conches,
    calling for help from our neighbors.
    For we knew that we herdsmen were no match
    for a couple of young and athletic men,
    and before long we were a crowd.

Meanwhile, the stranger's spasm had passed
    and he dropped to the ground,
    his chin dripping with foam.
The moment we saw him fall
    every man of us was ready:
    pelting and battering him
    while the other youth wiped away the froth,
    nursed him and warded off our blows
    with the shield of his goodly cape—
    caring for his friend most lovingly.
But he by now had come to his senses and sprung to his feet.
    And when he saw the surge of people round him
    and realized what he and his friend were up against,

*The text of this passage is doubtful and there are several variant readings. It
seems certain that a line or lines are missing.

he gave a groan;
which did not stop us hurling stones at them
and pressing them on every side.
Then we heard his mighty challenge:
"To our death, Pylades," he shouted,
"but we'll die like men. Draw your sword and follow."

At the sight of two hostile naked blades, we fled,
crowding into the copses on the cliffs;
but for every one of us that ran,
another advanced to pelt and attack;
and if these were repulsed the first lot took up stones again.
The extraordinary thing was,
that in spite of the thousands of stones we hurled
not one of them managed to hit these victims of the goddess.

Finally we wore them down, but it wasn't courage.
We'd hemmed them in and when they were off their guard
we knocked the swords out of their hands with stones.
They simply sank to their knees, exhausted.

[*The* HERDSMAN *glances at* IPHIGENIA, *who has been silent all this time and sees on her face only a look of mingled pity, resignation, and disgust. He continues with a forced jauntiness*]

Well, we brought them to this country's king,
who took one look at them and sent them straight to you
to be sprinkled with holy water ready for the blood bowls.
Maiden, may your altar always be blessed
with victims as fine as these.
Give us a few lads like these to butcher
and Hellas will have made amends for your "death":
yes indeed, repay the blood they clamored for at Aulis.
LEADER: What a strange tale you tell of this crazy fellow,
whoever he may be, who has managed to sail
safely here from Greece over a dangerous sea.
IPHIGENIA: [*with a dismissive wave of the hand*]
Enough of that! You'd best go off and bring the young men
here
while I prepare the rites for them.

[*As the* HERDSMAN *leaves,* IPHIGENIA *turns to the* CHORUS
while addressing herself]

Poor wretched heart!
　　You used to be so merciful and tender towards such visitors.
I used to cry when men of my race,
　　shipwrecked Greeks, fell into my hands,
　　but last night's dreams have made me callous.
　　Orestes, I believe, no longer looks upon the light,
　　and because of that, you, whoever you are, will find me
　　　　　　　　　　　　　　　　　　　　　　　　　heartless.
Dear women, how true that proverb is
　　about people down on their luck resenting those more for-
　　　　　　　　　　　　　　　　　　　　　　　　　tunate!

If only Zeus had sent a wind
　　blowing that Helen who has ruined me
　　through the rocky straits of Symplegades,
　　and Menelaus too,
　　wouldn't I just have had my revenge on them!
　　Paid them back for Aulis with an Aulis here!
I'd punish them for the day
　　the Argives hoisted me just like a calf upon the altar,
　　my own father the bloody celebrant.
What a memory! I can never shake it off.
　　Over and over I reached for my father's face,
　　clung to his knees, pleading:
"Father, this wedding party . . .
　　you cannot give me away like this!
　　My mother and the women of Argos,
　　as you get ready to slaughter me,
　　are singing wedding songs;
　　flute notes fill the house while I am being killed—
　　yes, by you.
So Achilles is Death, not Peleus' son
　　whom you tricked me here to marry.
In the war cart you've dragged me here, you traitor,
　　to a wedding full of blood."

[IPHIGENIA *pauses, passes her hand across her eyes as she
recalls the scene*]

Because my face was finely veiled
    I never took my brother in my arms, who is no more,
    nor kissed goodbye my sister.
    I modestly kept my kisses for Achilles, Peleus' son,
    for wasn't I going to live with him and see Argos again,
    when all those kisses could be done?
My poor Orestes, if you are dead,
    what blessings you have lost
    with all the heritage of your father's throne!

[*She pauses as a new thought strikes her*]

I am not impressed with Artemis' subtleties.
    She won't let anyone come near her altar
    who has touched blood or a woman in childbirth or a corpse,
    because they are tainted,
    yet takes delight in human sacrifice.
No, I cannot bring myself to think
    that Leto, Zeus's wife, could generate such absurdity.
Nor do I believe what is said of Tantalus,
    that he gave a banquet to the gods,
    regaling them with children's flesh.
No, I believe that the people of this land
    being murderers themselves
    have foisted their murderous instincts on the goddess.
I refuse to think that any god is evil.

[*As* IPHIGENIA *climbs the temple steps into the temple, the singing*
CHORUS *of* CAPTIVE WOMEN *paints a picture of voyagers coming
from Greece to savage Scythia. Using* ORESTES *and* PYLADES *as
symbols, they question the ambition and greed of men ready to
waste their lives in pursuit of wealth, and they imagine the
scenery of the dangerous passage to the Crimea: a passage they
wish Helen would make so that she could be punished. Finally
they wish that somebody would come and save them*]

SECOND CHORAL LYRIC*

STROPHE I

FIRST GROUP OF MAIDENS: Dark is the blue, dark is the blue
   where one sea meets another
Where over the hazardous passage the gadfly agonized Io
From the lands of Europe to Asia. Who are these men then
   Who have left the lovely river
     Eurotas in Argos
Verdant with rushes, or the rippling holy river
    Of Dirce in Athens . . .
These men who have come to this savage terrain
   Where the daughter of Zeus
Spatters the blood of men on the altars of temples
   With their fine colonnades?

ANTISTROPHE I

SECOND GROUP: With the threshing of double-banked oars and
   billowing sails
   They came in their vessel over the waves, but what were they
                     wanting?
   Wealth on wealth to heap on their houses? What an ambition!
Insatiable greed—oh the pity!
   The damage it does
To mortals. Dear is the cost to the heart of those
   Who over the waves
Come looking for riches, sailing to barbarous shores,
   Chasing the same illusion.
Riches, however, to one man refuse to come
   Though they come to another.

STROPHE II

THIRD GROUP: How ever did anyone pass
   Through the cleft of the Symplegades?
Did they skirt along the fringes
Of the shores of the Phineïdes,
Where the jostling waves never slumber,

*The unusual meters of these choruses are based on Euripides' own, which in
my translations I generally attempt.

Slapping away in the eddies
Of the goddess Amphitrite
Where Nereus' fifty daughters
Sing in the swirl of their dances?
Or did they run with the wind,
The rudder held steady and straining
  As the blasts from the south
    Or the soft breeze of Zephir
Blew them to a country
    Crowded with birds
Towards the White Riviera
    Where Achilles trained
    His stud of horses
On the rim of the dangerous sea.

ANTISTROPHE II

FOURTH GROUP: Oh if only one day the wish
  Of My Lady would bring here Helen
The spoilt daughter of Leda, bring
Her of the city of Troy,* to die
By the hand of our mistress: her beautiful hair
  Bedewed with the blood from her gashed
  Throat, the score would be settled.
But the greatest joy of all
Would be the day that we saw
Sailing here from Hellas
A mariner to deliver
  Us from our sad
And terrible slavery here.
  Oh what a dream
  To be back at home
In our ancestral town,
  To sleep in peace
  And taste the joys
That everyone can share.

[*On the path leading from the shore a group of people are
seen noisily approaching*]

---

*The Captive Maidens probably don't know yet that the Trojan War is over.

LEADER:

[*continuing, with change of meter*]

Look, do you see, here they are bringing
    Both of the men, handcuffed and roped:
    Latest of victims bound for the goddess.
    Silence, my friends! The choicest of Greeks
Now enters the precincts.
    This herdsman certainly told the truth.

[*Turning to the statue of Artemis*]*

Holy Lady, if you are pleased
    With these offerings which your people
Bring you, deign to accept
    A sacrifice which to the Greeks
    Is obscene, but to the public here
In line with tradition.

[*Into the temple courtyard, their hands roped behind their
backs, are brought* ORESTES *and* PYLADES, *escorted by soldiers, the* HERDSMAN, *and a crowd of citizens.* IPHIGENIA
*issues from the portals of the temple and stands with her
hands crossed at the top of the steps*]

THIRD EPISODE

IPHIGENIA: So be it.
    My first concern must be to order everything
    in ritual correctness for the goddess.
Undo their hands.
The consecrated may not be bound.

[*Turning to her attendants*]

Go into the temple and arrange
    everything the rubrics require.

---

*The stone statue of Artemis standing in the courtyard is not to be confused
with the wooden effigy that Orestes has come to get.

[*As the attendants depart,* IPHIGENIA *begins slowly to descend the steps, thinking aloud softly and gazing at* ORESTES *and* PYLADES, *obviously taking them for brothers*]

How sad!
    I wonder who your mother was? And your father?
And did you have a sister?
    What a pair of lovely youths for her to lose!
    Who can predict on whom such misfortune falls?
The will of the gods is a mysterious creeping thing
    and nobody knows what evils lie in store:
    Fate heads us into the dark.

[*Reaching the courtyard,* IPHIGENIA *turns to* ORESTES *and* PYLADES]

Where are you from, you two unfortunate men?
You must have made a lengthy voyage to this place
    and now you go even further from home to a place below.
ORESTES: Lady, who are you to be sad on our account?
    Why grieve about what happens to the two of us?
When Death comes near and hope has fled
    no pity sweetens the horror of extinction.
    It only adds one evil to another.
    One makes a fool of oneself but dies just the same.
Let fate take its course,
    so please don't weep for us.
    We understand, we are well aware of the sacrifices here.
IPHIGENIA: The first thing I want to know is this:
    which of you has the name of Pylades?
ORESTES: He does . . . if that's any satisfaction.
IPHIGENIA: From what town in Hellas does he come?
ORESTES: Lady, what is the good of knowing that?
IPHIGENIA: You have the same mother—you are brothers?
ORESTES: Brothers by love, Lady, not by blood.
IPHIGENIA: And you? What name did your father give you?
ORESTES: Unlucky—or that's the name I should have had.
IPHIGENIA: Which tells me your circumstance. I want your name.
ORESTES: Say I've none, then nobody can gloat.
IPHIGENIA: Does keeping it from me make you more important?

ORESTES: It's my body not my name you are going to sacrifice.

IPHIGENIA: Well, what town are you from? Won't you tell me that?

ORESTES: Does it matter, seeing I'm going to die?

IPHIGENIA: It would be gracious just to tell me that.

ORESTES: From a town in Argos—famous Argos.

IPHIGENIA: [taken aback] Argos? For the gods' sake, man, is this
really true?

ORESTES: Yes, from Mycenae—a place so prosperous once.

IPHIGENIA: Then what made you leave it? Was it banishment?

ORESTES: A kind of banishment . . . willingly unwilling.

IPHIGENIA: Well, to come from Argos is an honor.

ORESTES: It may be for you but not for me.

IPHIGENIA: Now tell me something else I am dying to know.

ORESTES: It's all rather pointless to one in my position.

IPHIGENIA: But what's the news from Troy? It's on everybody's
tongue.*

ORESTES: Troy! I wish I'd never heard or even dreamt of it.

IPHIGENIA: It is no more, they say: toppled by the war.

ORESTES: That is so. You've been told the truth.

IPHIGENIA: And Helen, is she back at home with Menelaus?

ORESTES: Alas, she's back! A threat to somebody I know.†

IPHIGENIA: Back exactly where? I have a score to settle.

ORESTES: She lives in Sparta with her former spouse.

IPHIGENIA: A curse to all the Greeks, not just to me.

ORESTES: I too have suffered from her love affairs.

IPHIGENIA: Did the Achaeans get home all right as is reported?

ORESTES: You're asking me to tell you everything at once.

IPHIGENIA: Of course! I want to know it all before you die.

ORESTES: Ask away, then, if you must, and I shall tell you.

IPHIGENIA: Is Calchas the seer back from Troy?

ORESTES: He is dead, or so the Mycenaeans say.

IPHIGENIA: Thank the gods! I mean goddess!†† . . . And Odysseus?

ORESTES: He's not home yet but is alive—so they say.

IPHIGENIA: I hope he drowns—never reaches home.

---

*It must be remembered that the ten-year war with Troy was only just over.

†Not Iphigenia, who Orestes thinks is dead, but her sister Electra.

††It was Calchas who told Agamemnon that the only way to get a favorable
breeze for his armada to set sail for Troy was to sacrifice his daughter Iphigenia. (See *Iphigenia at Aulis*.)

ORESTES: Don't be so spiteful. His family has suffered enough.

IPHIGENIA: And Achilles, son of Thetis the Nereid?

ORESTES: Dead. His wedding at Aulis was a sham.

IPHIGENIA: A sham indeed! And a disaster for the bride.

ORESTES: Who are you to know so much about the Greeks?

IPHIGENIA: I am from there, but deprived of it since girlhood.

ORESTES: No wonder you want to know everything that's hap-
                                                    pening!

IPHIGENIA: And the commander in chief, said to be so fortunate?

ORESTES: The one you are thinking of was far from fortunate.

IPHIGENIA: Agamemnon the king, said to be the son of Atreus.

ORESTES: He is dead, poor man, and has dragged another down.

IPHIGENIA: Dead? An accident? . . . How terrible!

ORESTES: Why terrible to you? Were you related?

IPHIGENIA: His palmy days . . . they fill me with regrets.

ORESTES: But a horrible death . . . butchered by a woman.

IPHIGENIA: For pity's sake! . . . Poor wretched woman, poor
                                                    murdered man!

ORESTES: [turning away] Please, enough! No more questioning.

IPHIGENIA: One more: is she alive, his wife? The unfortunate man!

ORESTES: She is not: exterminated by her son, so gone.

IPHIGENIA: What an unhappy family! . . . And the motive?

ORESTES: To punish her for murdering his father.

IPHIGENIA: What horror! But justified—his act of vengeance.

ORESTES: Justified, but the gods are hard on him.

IPHIGENIA: Did Agamemnon leave any other children?

ORESTES: Yes, he left a single girl—Electra.

IPHIGENIA: Are you sure? Isn't there talk of one that was sacrificed?

ORESTES: No, except to say that she's dead and gone.

IPHIGENIA: Poor child! What a wretched father—ready to kill!

ORESTES: Wretched and wicked to kill, and for a wicked woman.

IPHIGENIA: Is he alive, in Argos, the son of the murdered father?

ORESTES: He lives a vagabond life—here, there, and everywhere.

IPHIGENIA: Dreams, dreams, goodbye! You were all a lie.

ORESTES: [overhearing]
    And so are the gods—no better than dreams on wings,
    and yet they say so wise!
Confusion reigns among the deities
    just as it does among us mortals.

The only thing one should regret
 is being ruined not by one's own folly
 but by following some crackpot prophecy:
 a ruin that exactly happened to someone
 whom those in the know know.
LEADER: And what of us unhappy creatures?
 Are our parents alive or dead? Who can tell?

[IPHIGENIA *draws* ORESTES *away from* PYLADES, *conspiratorially*]

IPHIGENIA: Listen, I have an idea,
 as suitable to you two as it is to me . . .
 and it always helps if we pull together.
Would you be willing if I spared your life
 to go back to Argos with a letter for my friends?
It was written for me by a prisoner here
 who felt sorry for me because I was no murderess
 and knowing that he died by the fixed law of the goddess,
 who deemed it right.
There's been no one here to take this message before
 to one of my friends in Argos,
 but you are a gentleman and you know Mycenae
 as well as the right people there.
So, save yourself and enjoy the reward.
This piece of writing is a trifle compared to your salvation.
Your friend, I'm afraid, because of the law must stay
 and be offered up to the goddess on his own.
ORESTES: A fine proposal, strange woman,
 all but for a single point:
 the slaughter of my friend here—
 that I don't in the least like.
I am the captain of my ship of troubles;
 he came on board just to help me.
It would be unthinkable for me to escape disaster
 by unloading it on to him.
Let's do it another way:
 Give the letter to *him* to take to Argos,
 just as you desired,
 while I submit to the sacrificial stroke.
For someone to save himself from ruin

by substituting a friend to slay
  is beyond contempt.
This man happens to be my friend.
  I want for him no less than for myself the light of day.
IPHIGENIA: Oh bless your noble heart,
  the clearest proof of a noble seed
  and truest friendship to a friend!
  May my one surviving brother be like you;
  for, yes, I too, you strangers, have a brother,
  though never do I see him.

[*Glancing at* PYLADES, *who has rejoined them*]

Well, as you wish,
  we'll send *him* with the letter,
  and you—you die . . . since you seem so keen on it.
ORESTES: Who will boldly carry out the sacrifice?
IPHIGENIA: I will. On me the goddess has enjoined that office.
ORESTES: An unenviable and doleful office for a girl.
IPHIGENIA: I am forced to do it. I must obey.
ORESTES: A female with a sword cutting down a man?
IPHIGENIA: No no no! I only sprinkle water on your head.
ORESTES: Then who is the butcher—if I may ask?
IPHIGENIA: There are men in the temple to carry that out.
ORESTES: What kind of tomb will my body have?
IPHIGENIA: A rock-hewn tomb glowing with a holy fire.
ORESTES: How I wish a sister's hand would dress my body!
IPHIGENIA: A useless wish, I fear, for whoever you are
  she must live leagues away from this savage land.
However, since you come from Argos too
  you'll get from me all that I can give.
I'll beautify your tomb;
  a golden unguent shall anoint your body,
  and I shall pour on your funeral pyre
  the rich and blossomy honey of the auburn mountain bee.

[*Eyeing him with concern*]

Meanwhile, believe me,
  I am not your enemy.

[*Turning to the guards*]

Guard them well, but no chains.

[*She begins to mount the temple steps, thinking aloud*]

If only my letter to Argos can reach the one I most dearly love
  and let him know that the one he thinks is dead is living—
  oh, what joy he'll have!

[*As* IPHIGENIA *disappears into the temple the maidens of the*
CHORUS, *in lugubrious mood, press around the two young men*]

CHORAL DIALOGUE

FIRST GROUP: [*to* ORESTES] Our hearts are torn for you having to face
  The deadly sprinkling of water then of blood.
ORESTES: No need for distress, good women, but thank you and
                                                          farewell.
SECOND GROUP: [*to* PYLADES] We are happy for you, young man,
                                                who are so lucky
  To be returning to your native land.
PYLADES: There's nothing lucky for a friend in the death of a
                                                            friend.
THIRD GROUP: [*to both*] This is the grimmest of partings:
  One of you dies, one survives.
  Our feelings waver from one to the other:
  Should we be sorry for you or for you?

[*End of Choral Dialogue as the* TEMPLE MAIDENS *file thought-
fully out of the courtyard*]

FOURTH EPISODE

ORESTES: [*clapping his forehead*]
  Good heavens! Pylades, has the same thought not occurred to
                                                            you?
PYLADES: Thought? I don't know what you are talking about.
ORESTES: Well, who is this young woman?
  She must be Greek to be able to ask us all about
the trials of Ilium, the homecoming of the Achaeans,

Calchas the seer, Achilles—even naming him . . .
   Then the way she pitied tragic Agamemnon
and asked about his wife and children.
   She's from Argos undoubtedly,
Otherwise she would not send a letter there
or have questioned me the way she did.
   She has Argos on the brain.
PYLADES: You've taken the words out of my mouth,
   except of course that the calamities of our royal family
   are so well known that anybody could recite them.
But that is not what bothers me.
ORESTES: Then, what? You may as well share it with me.
PYLADES: It's just that to let you die
   I could never show my face again.
I sailed here with you, I'll die here with you,
   or else be thought the most despicable coward in Argos
   and in every Phocian valley.
Cowards abound and people are bound to think
   that I abandoned you to save myself; or worse,
   that, given the sick state of your royal house,
   I murdered you to obtain the throne:
   for as your sister's husband it would come to me.*
I refuse to face the shame of that,
   so there is no way I shall not breathe my last with you:
   knife thrust and flame we must meet together.
I happen to love you and to hate dishonor.
ORESTES: Oh do be quiet!
   I must carry my own load.
   It's heavy enough, I do not want it doubled.
The pain and shame you talk about
   are mine as well if I let you die after sharing in my troubles.
After all, treated as I am by heaven,
   it is no bad thing for me to quit this life.
You are a happy man,
   Your family unbesmirched, not ridden with corruption;
   mine is disreputable and doomed.

---

*With the death of Agamemnon, Orestes is in fact king of Argos. If he died,
the royal heritage would fall to his sister, Electra, and her husband, Pylades,
would become king.

Save yourself. Have my sister's sons.
I bequeathed her to you to be your wife.
My name shall live in them
    and keep my family's name from being erased.
So, off with you, and live.
Dwell in my father's house.
Once back in Greece,
    back in Argos that land of horses,
    I charge you by my own right hand
    to raise a tomb and monument for me.
Let my sister leave a lock of hair there
    and wet it with her tears.
Say that I was slain by an Argive woman's hand
    in a purifying sacrifice.
Oh Pylades, never forsake my sister,
    for you see the weakness and dereliction of my father's house.

   [*Taking his hand*]

And now farewell, you dearest of the dear,
    my boyhood chum, chum at the chase,
    you sharer of my many woes.
Phoebus Apollo though a prophet lied.
He tricked me here all the way from Greece,
    ashamed, no doubt, of his former prophecies.
Foolishly, I gave up everything for him:
    too trusting to his word I killed my mother,
    and now I perish too.
PYLADES: [*embracing him*] My poor Orestes, you shall have your
                                                        tomb,
    and never shall I betray your sister's bed.
    By your death I love you even more than in your life.
And though you are so near to death,
    there's this, there's always this:
    the blackest misery can suddenly turn
    and chance swing back to happiness again.
ORESTES: Oh stop it!
    The oracle of Phoebus is useless to me now,
    for look, the young lady comes.

[IPHIGENIA, *crowned with a filet of laurel and sacrificially dressed as high priestess in a flowing white gown, appears at the top of the temple steps. She beckons to her attendants. The* CHORUS *returns*]

IPHIGENIA: Go into the temple and prepare
all that is needed by those who do the killing.

[*Turning to* ORESTES *and* PYLADES]

Here, strangers, is my letter,
    written on several pages,*
    about which I cannot help but think
    that change from danger can change a man.
I fear that the bearer of my letter to Argos
once he has left these shores
will give scant attention to my message.
ORESTES: Then what do you propose? Should you be concerned?
IPHIGENIA: I want the bearer of these writings to swear
    that he'll put them into the hands of my friends in Argos.
ORESTES: And you in turn must swear an oath to *him*.
IPHIGENIA: Swear what? To do or not to do? Explain.
ORESTES: Not to kill him before he leaves this barbarous place.
IPHIGENIA: How could he then carry out my mission?
ORESTES: There's the king to consider. Will he allow it?
IPHIGENIA: He will when I ask him to,
    and I myself shall go to the ship and see your friend aboard.
ORESTES: [*to* PYLADES] Swear by solemn oath that you will
                                        deliver . . .
IPHIGENIA: . . . this letter to my friends.
PYLADES: I swear that I will deliver this letter to your friends.
IPHIGENIA: And I that I'll let you go scot free through the dark
                                        blue chasm.

---

*Letters could be written on parchment or papyrus, and also on tablets incised with a stylus. Euripides seems to be ambivalent. In lines 641, 727, 756, and 787 he refers to the letter as *deltoi*, or tablets, but in line 727 he calls it *poluthuroi*, which means "many-leaved." Are we to suppose (with Witter Bynner) that the letter is "safe within these folds"? But *poluthuroi* does not mean that, though it can mean "many-doored." In which case Pylades would be carrying a whole casket of wax tablets.

PYLADES: What divinities do you call in witness?

IPHIGENIA: Artemis, whose priestess in this temple I am.

PYLADES: And I, the Lord of Heaven, holy Zeus.

IPHIGENIA: What if you break your oath and let me down?

PYLADES: May I never reach home . . . And you, if I don't
go free?

IPHIGENIA: That I never set foot in Argos again.

PYLADES: Wait! There's something that we have forgotten.

IPHIGENIA: We can always change things if it suits.

PYLADES: A proviso: what if the ship should founder
and the letter with all my belongings goes to the bottom
but I escape? . . . Then I am no longer bound by oath.

IPHIGENIA: Exactly! . . . Then this is what I'll do:
(How chance has an answer for every chance!) . . .
I'll read the letter out aloud to you
and you can recite it to my friends.
That secures it.
If you don't lose the letter, the letter itself speaks,
but if the letter vanishes under the waves and you are saved,
you do the speaking and save me by your speech.

PYLADES: That solves everything, both for you and me.
Now you must tell me to whom the letter has to go in Argos,
then what you want me to say in it.

IPHIGENIA: [*opening the letter*]
The message is to Orestes, son of Agamemnon.
It says:
"I, Iphigenia, supposedly killed in Aulis,
am still alive and speak to one supposedly dead."

ORESTES: Alive, where? Risen from the dead?

IPHIGENIA: [*testily*] You are looking at her—please don't
interrupt—

[*Resumes reading*]

"Dear brother, fetch me back to Argos before I die.
Save me from a savage ritual in a savage land,
where my office is to slaughter visitors . . ."

ORESTES: Pylades, I'm struck dumb. Where are we?

IPHIGENIA: [*continuing to read*] "If you do not, Orestes"—
mark that name, you've heard it twice—

"I become a curse and byword to all your house."
ORESTES: Ye gods!
IPHIGENIA: The gods have nothing to do with it—have they?
ORESTES: Nothing. Go on. My thoughts were straying.

[*To himself*]

One single question might undo this riddle.
IPHIGENIA: [*resumes reading*] Say: "The goddess Artemis de-
                                                    livered me
    and put in my place a hind
    which my father sacrificed
    thinking he plunged the knife in *me*.
Then she brought me here to live." . . .
So here is the letter
    and that is what is written in it.
PYLADES: [*turning to* IPHIGENIA] Oh what an easy oath you had
                                                    me swear!
It won't take a moment to make good.
The letter is to you, Orestes,
    I hand it to you, it's from your sister standing here.
ORESTES: [*taking the letter*] Thank you. I shan't undo it yet;
    sheer happiness has no need of words.
    I am dumbfounded, oh my dearest sister!
    Let these arms of mine fumbling with disbelief and joy
                                                    embrace you.

[*He throws his arms around her*]

LEADER: Sir, this is sacrilege, to touch the priestess of the
                                                    goddess
    and crush her dress in an embrace.
ORESTES: My dearest, fondest sister, child of Agamemnon,
    do not resist me—me the brother that you'd thought you'd
                                                    lost.
IPHIGENIA: [*disengaging herself*] You, my brother? Do not talk
                                                    nonsense.
    It is Argos or Nauplia that his presence fills.
ORESTES: My poor deprived girl, not so, not so!
IPHIGENIA: You'd have to be born of Clytemnestra, then?

ORESTES: Yes, and of the son of the son of Pelops.*
IPHIGENIA: How so? Can you give me any proof?
ORESTES: I can. Question me about our family.
IPHIGENIA: No, you tell *me*. I'll be the judge.
ORESTES: Then I'll tell you first the things Electra told me.
    Do you know how the feud between Atreus and Thyestes
                                  began?
IPHIGENIA: I do. How they quarreled over a golden lamb.†
ORESTES: Do you remember embroidering this in a tapestry?
IPHIGENIA: [*to herself, shaken*]
    He's coming so close to being my beloved brother.
ORESTES: And in the design you put an eclipse of the sun?
IPHIGENIA: Yes, I put that on my canvas too.
ORESTES: And your mother at Aulis preparing your bridal
                                  bath?††
IPHIGENIA: Yes, for the glorious wedding that never happened.
ORESTES: I know. And your giving your mother a lock of hair?
IPHIGENIA: In memory of me should I be dead and buried.
ORESTES: And here is other evidence that I saw with my own
                                  eyes:

    The antique spear of Pelops in my father's palace,
    which he brandished when he slew Oenomaus
    and won the Pisan maiden, Hippodamia—
    the same was in your bedroom, stored away.

[IPHIGENIA, *all doubts removed, throws herself into her brother's arms and breaks into verse. Euripides has* ORESTES *answer in the calmer dialogue meter of the iambic trimiter to* IPHIGENIA'*s excited dactyls and anapests*]

---

*son of the son of Pelops: Agamemnon.
†See note on page 287.
††The nuptial bath was an important feature of the marriage ceremony. The bride bathed on the morning of her wedding in water taken from the sacred spring of her town or birthplace.

CHORAL DIALOGUE

IPHIGENIA: O you beloved, nothing more loved
   Than you, Orestes, now in my arms,
   Coming from Argos . . . O my darling!
ORESTES: And I in my arms are hugging the one thought dead.
   Tears of sorrow wiped away by tears of gladness
   wetting your eyes and mine.
IPHIGENIA: You the little one, you the baby
   I left in the palace, in the arms of your nurse.
   The happiness in my heart is bursting.
   I haven't a word for it; what can I say?
   More than a miracle, beyond all telling.
ORESTES: May we always be as happy as this!
IPHIGENIA: [*turning to the* CHORUS]
   Such unbelievable joy, my friends.
   I fear it will sprout little wings and fly
   Out of my fingers into the sky.
   O you Cyclopean walls of Mycenae!
   O you beloved land of my fathers!
   I thank you for bestowing him life;
   I thank you for bringing him up
   And making him the light of your house.
ORESTES: Destiny gave us a noble birth, my sister,
   but it also gave us a life beset with sorrows.
IPHIGENIA: Do I not know this, when my deranged
   Father threatened my throat with his blade . . .
ORESTES: I was not there but I see the horrible scene.
IPHIGENIA: Tricked to the bed of Achilles, O brother,
   I was led to a fraudulent wedding,
   Wetting an altar with my tears—
   Tears instead of ritual waters.
ORESTES: It makes me groan—my father's sick courage.
IPHIGENIA: Unfatherly father! Some demon has heaped
   Sorrow on sorrow on me without end.
ORESTES: What if you had killed your brother as well!
IPHIGENIA: How I'm ashamed of my terrible daring!
   O brother, I only just missed an act
Unbelievably horrid,

And you a devilish death at my hands.
And now, what is to follow?
    Is there a chance, is there a way
    For me to save you from death in this land,
    Return you to Argos before the sword
Is dipped in your blood?
    This, my soul, this you must find.
    Perhaps an overland route, not sea,
You are fleet of foot.
    But making your way through barbarous clans
On unpassable paths
    You'll be skirting death; and if it's by ship
    Through the dangerous dark blue cliffs—
What a long voyage!
    I'm at a loss, hopelessly lost!
    Is there a deity, is there a mortal,
    Is there a sudden surprise solution
To this impossible pass?
    One that delivers two hard-driven creatures,
The remnants of Atreus,
Out of these dangers?

[*The maidens of the* CHORUS, *consumed with anxiety and sympathy, press around* IPHIGENIA *and* ORESTES]

FIFTH EPISODE

LEADER: There are no words for this unbelievable tale:
    seen with my own eyes and not by report.
PYLADES:

[*waiting for* ORESTES *and* IPHIGENIA *to disengage themselves*]

It is natural enough, Orestes,
    when loved ones welcome again the gaze of loved ones
    for them to take one another in their arms,
    but now sentiment must yield
    to a search for ways of winning our freedom,
    our glorious freedom,
    and escaping from this barbarous land.

The wise don't loiter waiting for a lucky chance,
   they make it happen.
ORESTES: [*releasing* IPHIGENIA] You are right. We may strike luck,
   but heaven helps those that help themselves.
IPHIGENIA: Yes yes, but first, do tell me, I'm bursting to know:
   How is Electra? Everything about her is dear to me.
ORESTES: [*pointing to* PYLADES] Wedded to him her life is bliss.
IPHIGENIA: Where is he from? Who is his father?
ORESTES: Strophius the Phocian is his father.
IPHIGENIA: Agamemnon's sister's son—so a relative?
ORESTES: He is your cousin and my truest friend.
IPHIGENIA: He was not even born when my father tried to kill me.
ORESTES: No. Strophius was for a long time childless.
IPHIGENIA: [*advancing and taking his hand*]
   Greetings to you—husband of my sister.
ORESTES: Not only her husband but my savior.
IPHIGENIA: [*recalling the connection*]
   Yes, the dreadful end of your mother . . . how did you dare?*
ORESTES: Do not bring that up . . . It was to avenge my father.
IPHIGENIA: But what was the reason for her killing her husband?
ORESTES: She is your mother . . . Better not to know.
IPHIGENIA: I'll not ask . . . Does Argos now look to you?
ORESTES: Menelaus reigns and I am a fugitive.
IPHIGENIA: Surely our uncle didn't take advantage of our fall?
ORESTES: No, it was the Furies that drove me abroad.
IPHIGENIA: They told me of your frenzy on the shore.
ORESTES: Not the first time I've made a display of myself.
IPHIGENIA: I understand. They're after you because of your
                                                      mother.
ORESTES: They tried to choke me with my mother's blood.†
IPHIGENIA: Whatever made you come here to this land?
ORESTES: An oracle of Phoebus told me to.
IPHIGENIA: Whatever for? May you not say?

---

*The murder of Clytemnestra was perpetrated by Orestes, Pylades, and
Electra in concert.
†This baffling sentence translates literally "They forced and pushed a bloody
thing into my mouth," which is often rendered as "They forced a bit between
my teeth." Could this then be an idiom meaning "They tried to curb me"? I
like Witter Bynner's guess and have stolen his paraphrase.

ORESTES: I shall.
Let me tell you how my troubles began.
Hardly had I punished my mother for her appalling crime
when the pursuing Furies sent me fleeing in self-banishment,
until Loxias directed me to Athens
to be cross-questioned by the Nameless Ones.*
Zeus long ago had set up a tribunal there
to purge the bloodstained hands of the war god Ares.
So there I went.
But heaven-cursed as I was
I found no sympathetic soul to welcome me
until some through pity took me in.
My meals were set at a separate table
under the same roof as the other guests
but cut off from all converse with them:
I ate and drank apart from them.
Every man had his own cup of wine to enjoy,
each the same amount, but I was alone.
I did not presume to question my hosts
and pretended not to notice
sitting in gloomy silence—
the gloomy silent mother-killer.
Since then I hear that my ordeal
is commemorated in a ritual at Athens:
a Festival of Cups.
Well, I went to stand my trial on the Hill of Ares,
I the defendant on one side
and facing me the senior Fury on another.
My defense for the murder of my mother
ended in acquittal—saved by the testimony of Apollo.
Pallas Athena counted the votes,
sweeping on one side those for me—which were half—
then, by her casting vote,
making me the victor in this murder trial.
Those of the Furies that accepted this
were content to settle in a shrine
not far from the tribunal.

*Nameless Ones: a euphemism for the Furies (Erinyes). Euripides seems not to mind that in fact he has already named them in line 94I.

Those that were against it
  began to hound me so viciously
  that finally I ran back to Apollo's shrine and there collapsed.
I refused to eat,
  vowing that I'd dash my brains out if Apollo
  who had brought me to this pass refused to save me.
At which Apollo's voice from the golden tripod
  reverberated in command.
I was to get hold of the image of Artemis that fell from the sky
  and set it up in Attica.
This was to be my salvation.
So now I need your help.
If only we can secure the goddess' effigy
  I shall be cured of my insanity.
Then I shall carry you away in my ship
  with its powerful bank of oars back to Mycenae.
So my beloved one, my darling sister,
  you must save our father's house, save me.
Unless I get that wooden idol of the goddess
  it is the end of me, the end of the house of Pelops.
LEADER: How extraordinary is the frenzy of these spirits
  harrowing the last of the house of Tantalus!
IPHIGENIA: Even before you came here, brother,
  I yearned to go to Argos and see you there.
So my wish now is the same as yours:
  to cure you of your malady
  and, with forgiveness for my father for trying to kill me,
  to restore our stricken house.
That is my endeavor:
  to save my hands from being tainted with your blood
  and to save our house.
What makes me nervous is how to elude the goddess
  and the king's anger when he finds the empty pedestal.
It is certain death, for what excuses can I plead?
  But if we can succeed in this twin enterprise
  of embarking with you in your noble ship
  and taking the image along with us,
  the risk is worth the taking.
If these two objectives fail, I am lost;

but you can still escape and go straight home.
To save you I am ready to face death.
  A man's death is a family's loss, a woman's is no matter.
ORESTES: I'll not be my mother's murderer then yours.
  Her blood is enough.
I am one with you in wanting to live, or with you die:
  to take you home or stay here with you until death.

[*He pauses in thought*]

You know what I think:
  this undertaking can't be displeasing to the goddess
  if Loxias ordered me to bring the effigy to Athens—
  yes, and to let me see your face.
So, all in all,
  I expect a safe run home.
IPHIGENIA: The question is how to achieve our twin design:
  escaping death and carrying off the prize.
Our home return is full of risks,
  we must think it out.
ORESTES: Is there any way of our killing the king?
IPHIGENIA: What! Guests to destroy their host? No.
ORESTES: It can't be helped if you and I are to be saved.
IPHIGENIA: I couldn't do it, though I admire your thoroughness.
ORESTES: What if you concealed me in the temple?
IPHIGENIA: To creep out at dead of night?
ORESTES: Yes, night's for stealth; daylight for openness.
IPHIGENIA: There are guards inside the temple. We can't evade them.
ORESTES: Then I give up; I see no way.

[*A further pause*]

IPHIGENIA: An idea has just occurred to me.
ORESTES: Spell it out. I am all ears.
IPHIGENIA: It solves our problems.
ORESTES: What clever creatures you women are!
IPHIGENIA: I'll say you came from Argos after murdering your
                                                    mother.
ORESTES: So, putting my criminal record to good use!
IPHIGENIA: And that you cannot be offered to the goddess.

ORESTES: And the reason? Though I think I can guess.

IPHIGENIA: You are unclean. I can only sacrifice the pure.

ORESTES: How does that help us to acquire the idol?

IPHIGENIA: I'll say that I have to cleanse you in the sea.

ORESTES: But the statue we came to get is still inside.

IPHIGENIA: I'll say you fingered it, so it too must be purified.

ORESTES: Whereabouts? In an inlet of the bay?

IPHIGENIA: Yes, where your ship is straining at her hawsers.

ORESTES: Will you or someone else carry the effigy?

IPHIGENIA: It has to be me. I am the only one allowed to touch it.

ORESTES: What part will Pylades play in this?*

IPHIGENIA: His hands, like yours, I'll say are sullied.

ORESTES: And this cleansing, is it to be kept secret from the king?

IPHIGENIA: There's no way of hiding it, so I shall tell him.

ORESTES: Meanwhile my ship is ready, the oarsmen benched.

IPHIGENIA: Yes, it is up to you to look after all the rest.

ORESTES: One thing is essential: the maidens' silence.
Convince them of this; find a way.
  Women are supreme when it comes to feelings.
  As for the rest, I am confident of success.

IPHIGENIA: [*turning to the* CHORUS] My dear dear women, I look
                                        to you.
  The success or ruin of our project is in your hands.
  Am I to lose my country, my dear brother, and my precious sister?
Let me preface my appeal by saying,
  as women we must support our sex
  and defend our own best interests.
So, please, speak not a word.
Assist us in our escape.
A loyal tongue is a beautiful thing.
Consider the three of us: three loving friends,
  all in the same plight: it's home or death.

[*She goes up to individual members of the* CHORUS]

You, once saved, I shall save you.

---

*During all this dialogue there is no word from Pylades. One must suppose that after the impassioned embraces of brother and sister he discreetly withdrew out of hearing.

You I shall take to Hellas and you'll share my happiness.
And you, by your own right hand, I beg you,
   and you, dear, by your sweet cheeks,
   and you whose knees I clasp,
   and all of you by your loved ones at home—
   father, mother, children if you have them . . .
What will your answer be?

[*She waits for their response*]

Who says yes, who says no? Speak.
If my appeal does not move you I am lost,
   I and my harassed brother.
LEADER: Rest assured, dear mistress, and be saved.
   We shall not breathe a word of your design.
   Zeus be our witness for all you ask.
IPHIGENIA: Heaven bless you for that and make you happy.

[*Turning to* ORESTES]

Now it is up to you, [*To* PYLADES] yes, and you,
   when you enter the temple.
This land's ruler will be on his way here
   demanding if the strangers have been sacrificed.

[*As the two young men enter the temple,* IPHIGENIA *walks over
to the stone statue of Artemis—not the same as the wooden
effigy—and lifts up her hands in prayer*]

Great Lady, who in the glens of Aulis
   saved me from my father's murderous hands,
   save me now, and save *them*.
Otherwise, the prophecies of Loxias
   will cease to be believed.

[IPHIGENIA *enters the temple and the* MAIDENS *of the* CHORUS
sing four nostalgic strophes envious of IPHIGENIA'*s return to
Greece. They dwell on the piercing and mournful cry of the
halcyon seagull—the fish swallow—the origin of a myth and a
symbol of sorrow. On board* IPHIGENIA'*s homecoming ship
Pan himself will act as triēraulēs, the flute player at the stern*

of a trireme who gave the time for the oarsmen's stroke. Then the girls recall the dances, weddings, parties they once enjoyed at home]

THIRD CHORAL LYRIC

STROPHE I

O woe-voiced Halcyon Swallow
  Uttering your forlorn past
  Over the rocky ocean cliffs,
  You rend the sorrowing heart
  Crying for your missing mate.
  Your lamentations echo mine:
  I a wingless bird
Pining for Hellas,
Its festivals
  And a mother-loving Artemis*
  Who dwells on the Cynthian Hill
  Near the palm trees' heavy tresses
  By the laurel and the holy
  Branches of the gray-green olive
  Where sad Latona with her sorrows
  Retreated by the rippling circles
Of rounded waters
  Where the swan sang† to the Muses.

ANTISTROPHE I

  O the jet of tears
  Streaming down my cheeks
  As I watched our towers fall††

---

*I.e., a different Artemis from the cruel Artemis of Tauria. Artemis was the goddess both of virginity and of childbirth.

†I wonder who started the ridiculous belief that swans could sing!

††Towers of what town? We are never told who these Captive Maidens are. They sound like Trojans at the fall of Troy but they speak of Hellas as their fatherland. No towers, however, were toppled in Athens, nor prisoners taken. Perhaps these niggling observations are annulled if one thinks of the maidens and the falling towers merely as symbols.

And was dragged off to the ships
In a clang of oars and spears
And sold for the price of gold
In this barbarous land:
Sold as slave
To Agamemnon's girl,
    Priestess of the huntress god
    Whose altars drip with blood
    But, oh, not from sheep!
    Blest is the man who never
    Knew happiness, was nourished
    On sorrow, for he knows
The worst of pain.
    The happy made unhappy
    Feel the leaden weight of living.

STROPHE II

My Lady, a bank of fifty oars
In an Argive ship will row you home.
Pan himself in the poop with his flute
Will pipe the stroke for the rowers' time.
Oracular Phoebus with his lyre
Will pluck the seven strings and chant
Until the shores of Athens shimmer.
Alas, the splash of oars will pull
You away from me as halyards hoist
The billowing canvas to the breeze
And the jib bellies over the spit
And the ship skims.

ANTISTROPHE II

If I could only course with the Sun's
Flaming chariot through an air on fire,
My shoulder blades endowed with wings,
And hover over my own home . . .
If I could only dance and sway
As once at sparkling weddings I,
A virgin still, my mother near,
Shimmied and whirled and laughed away

With the other girls while showing off
A lovely veil, a gorgeous jewel,
My cheek teased by a loose curl
With its flicker of shade.

SIXTH EPISODE

[*King* THOAS *with a train of soldiers marches into the court-yard. He is a rugged, brusque man, heavily bearded and with no other mark of royalty except a purple chlamys (cape)*]

THOAS: Where is the woman from Hellas, the temple warder?
   Has she consecrated the two victims yet?
   Are their bodies by the altar, blazing away?

[IPHIGENIA *appears at the top of the temple steps with the wooden effigy of Artemis in her arms*]

LEADER: Here she is, my lord, and she will tell you.
THOAS: [*advancing*] I see.
   Child of Agamemnon,
   why have you moved the statue from its fixed pedestal
   and are carrying it in your arms?
IPHIGENIA: Stay where you are, King, beyond the threshold.
THOAS: Why, Iphigenia? Has something happened in the temple?
IPHIGENIA: It's disgusting! There's been contamination.
THOAS: I do not understand. Explain.
IPHIGENIA: The victims you gave me, King, they are polluted.
THOAS: What makes you think so? Are you imagining?
IPHIGENIA: [*descending the steps*]
   She turned away, the goddess: turned on her pedestal.
THOAS: What, by herself? There must have been an earth tremor.
IPHIGENIA: By herself. And she shut her eyes.
THOAS: Shocked by the unclean foreigners?
IPHIGENIA: Nothing less. They are sullied criminals.
THOAS: You mean they killed some Taurians on the beach?
IPHIGENIA: No, their hands were bloodied even before they
                                                      came.
THOAS: Whom did they kill? I'm most anxious to know.
IPHIGENIA: Together they put their mother to the sword.

THOAS: Great Apollo, even we barbarians don't do that!

IPHIGENIA: They were pursued and hounded out of Greece.

THOAS: Is that why you've brought the effigy outside?

IPHIGENIA: Yes, to cleanse it in the open air from murder.

THOAS: How did you know the crime of those two men?

IPHIGENIA: I questioned them when the goddess' image turned.

THOAS: Quite right! You're a clever daughter of Hellas.

IPHIGENIA: What's more, they tried to appease me with a bait.

THOAS: With a special piece of news from Argos, no doubt?

IPHIGENIA: News that my only brother Orestes is well and . . .

THOAS: So they thought good news of him would save them?

IPHIGENIA: . . . and that my father was alive and well.

THOAS: But you, of course, were loyal to Artemis?

IPHIGENIA: Yes, I loathed all Hellas. Hellas planned my death.

THOAS: Then what shall we do with these two fellows, tell me?

IPHIGENIA: Scrupulously observe the rules.

THOAS: You mean the lustral waters and the knife?

IPHIGENIA: Yes, but first I must wash away their stain.

THOAS: In spring water or a salt sea bath?

IPHIGENIA: The sea washes away the sins of man.

THOAS: Oh! . . . and make them fit for Artemis.

IPHIGENIA: [on her way with the statue]
    Which is perfect for my purposes.

THOAS: But doesn't the tide reach almost to the temple?

IPHIGENIA: Yes, but I must be alone . . . for other tasks.

THOAS: Go wherever you will. I am not one to pry.

IPHIGENIA: I must bathe the sacred image too.

THOAS: Of course! If the taint of matricide is on it.

IPHIGENIA: Otherwise I would not have moved it from its base.

THOAS: You are so reverent and so thoughtful!

IPHIGENIA: You know what I need now?

THOAS: I will when you tell me.

IPHIGENIA: Have the prisoners fettered.

THOAS: But there's nowhere they could flee to.

IPHIGENIA: All Greeks are treacherous.

THOAS: [turning to his guards] You there—see to the fetters.

IPHIGENIA: And have the prisoners brought out here.

THOAS: It shall be done.

IPHIGENIA: They must be blindfolded.

THOAS: So their sight won't stain the sun?

IPHIGENIA: And send some of your soldiers with me.

THOAS: [*beckoning a group of guards*]
These men shall go with you.

IPHIGENIA: And have it broadcast through the town that . . .

THOAS: Yes?

IPHIGENIA: . . . that everyone must stay at home.

THOAS: So as not to see the murderers?

IPHIGENIA: Yes, that would contaminate.

THOAS: [*to an officer of the guard*] Have this announced to all
the people.

IPHIGENIA: And especially to my friends.

THOAS: And am I also to keep away?

IPHIGENIA: Everyone. Nobody must see.

THOAS: How caring you are of my people!

IPHIGENIA: Rightly so.

THOAS: And rightly are you admired by all the town.

IPHIGENIA: You must stay here near the shrine.

THOAS: What for?

IPHIGENIA: To fumigate the precincts.

THOAS: And make it pure for your return.

IPHIGENIA: When the foreigners exit from the temple . . .

THOAS: What must I do?

IPHIGENIA: . . . shield your eyes with your cape.

THOAS: So as not to risk contagion?

IPHIGENIA: And if I am away too long . . .

THOAS: How long do you think?

IPHIGENIA: . . . do not be alarmed.

THOAS: Take all the time you need to refurbish Artemis.

IPHIGENIA: Wish me well in my purgatorial task.

THOAS: I do, I do.

[*The gates of the temple open and* ORESTES *and* PYLADES, *fettered and blindfolded, are marshaled down the steps into the courtyard. They are followed by servants carrying vessels of water for the purification of the shrine, sprigs of sweet bay to strew upon the floors, and thuribles of smoking incense. Others carry lambs. They wait for* IPHIGENIA *to join them in a procession to the sea. She turns to the bystanders, with the wooden effigy of Artemis still in her arms*]

IPHIGENIA: Here come the two aliens from the temple,
    and all the train of Artemis with newborn lambs
    to wash away blood with blood.
They come with the dazzle of torches
    and all that I prescribed to purge the goddess of these men.

Citizens, I warn you to be careful of this plague.
    Ministers of the temple who need clean hands to approach
                                    the gods,

    couples to be wed,
    and above all, women with child—oh, I tell you, flee:
    keep far from this pollution.

[*She steps towards the stone statue of Artemis*]

O Virgin and Queen, daughter of Zeus and Leto,
    once I have washed away the blood guilt of these men
    and sacrificed at the appointed place,
    you shall dwell in a pure home
    and we shall be content.

[IPHIGENIA *takes her place in the rear of the procession as it
moves off.* THOAS *obediently secludes himself in the temple,
and the courtyard is now deserted except for the* CHORUS *of
Temple* MAIDENS. *They sing an ode to Apollo and his sister
Artemis, extolling Apollo as the slayer of the python that
haunted the Oracle at Delphi. They expatiate on the marvels
of the Oracle and tell of the struggle between Earth and
Apollo to possess it*]

FOURTH CHORAL LYRIC

STROPHE

Beauteous the offspring of Leto
Born in the fruit-bearing valley of Delos:
A boy with gold-glinting hair;
A girl with her bow and proud of her prowess.
Apollo she took from her seaside cliff
Where she had gloriously borne him,
To Parnassus the Mother of Waters:

High point of Bacchus' revels
Where the wine-blotched python
With his speckled mail of a back
(An Earth-spawned freak) slid through the laurel-deep shadows
Haunting the underworld Oracle.
And you still a baby, yes, still frisking
In the arms of your mother—
You, O Phoebus,
Slaughtered that snake and entered
The Oracle holy of holies,
Where at the golden tripod
You preside on a throne of the truth,
Dispensing to mortals the future
From the depths of that innermost shrine.
You, by the springs of Castalia,
Dwell in your temple near the navel of earth.

ANTISTROPHE

Ah! but his entry unseated
Themis the daughter of Gaia, the Earth,
From the oracular shrine of Pytho,
Where Gaia had engendered
Nocturnal visions and dreams of the future
For mortals asleep on their beds in the dark
Of that which had happened, was happening,
And that which was still to be.
Zealous for her daughter,
So did Earth dispossess
Phoebus of the Oracle.
But the sibling Apollo immediately ran to Olympus
And with his infantile arms
Hugging the throne of Zeus, he begged him
To wrest his Pythian home from Earth.
Zeus had to smile
Seeing how quickly the child
Had rushed to possess
A sanctuary larded with gold.
With a toss of his head he agreed
To stop the visions at night;
So revelations at night were abolished

And Loxias' honors restored.
Once again pilgrims believed and flocked to the shrine.*

SEVENTH EPISODE

[*A distraught* MESSENGER, *bruised and begrimed, comes running from the coastal road into the courtyard*]

MESSENGER: Hey there! you keepers of the temple and altar
                                                    ministers,
    where is the king of this country?
Unbolt the gates, fling them open,
    summon from the palace the ruler of this land.
LEADER: What on earth . . . if I may ask?
MESSENGER: The two young men have got clean away
    in collusion with Agamemnon's daughter.
They've vanished with the holy effigy
    and loaded it into the Greek ship's hold.
LEADER: [*delighted*] You don't say!
    Anyway, the king, whom you wanted,
    has just left the premises.
MESSENGER: Which way? My news is most important.
LEADER: [*coolly*] We don't know.
    You'll simply have to find out and hurry after him.
MESSENGER: You're a treacherous lot, you women . . .
    You are all part of the plot.
LEADER: Are you crazy? What do we care about the aliens'
                                                    flight! . . .
    Well, aren't you going to knock at the king's door and find
                                                    out?
MESSENGER: Not if I know he isn't in.

[*He waits for help from the* MAIDENS, *gets none, and runs up to the heavy doors of the palace—next to the temple—and begins thumping*]

---

*The significance in this ode of the antistrophe is that Apollo's oracle was proved right (that Orestes was alive) and Iphigenia's dream wrong (that he was dead), so that henceforward the ancient clairvoyance by dreams was to be abolished in favor of that by the Oracle at Delphi.

Hullo, you in there! Unlock the door, open up.
Tell your master I'm outside with bad news for him.

[*The doors open and* THOAS *walks out*]

THOAS: Who is this making such a din outside the goddess' home,
  banging the door and bawling away?
MESSENGER: Sire, these creatures here tried to get rid of me
                                                    and lied,
  saying you'd gone out when you were still at home.
THOAS: Why should they lie? What did they hope to gain by it?
MESSENGER: Sire, I'll come to that, but first I have to tell you
  that the young woman who served the altars, Iphigenia,
  has decamped with the two foreigners
  and taken the holy image with her.
All that show of purification was just a cover.
THOAS: Is that so? Was that the way her breeze was blowing?
MESSENGER: Yes, to liberate Orestes . . . Is that a shock?
THOAS: Not Orestes? Not the son of Clytemnestra?
MESSENGER: The very same. Destined for the altar of the god-
                                                         dess.
THOAS: It's fantastic! There is no other word for it.
MESSENGER: I daresay, sir, but hear me out and mark my words:
  you must decide how you are going to hunt these fellows
                                                         down.
THOAS: Indeed! But there's no way these foreigners can sail
                                      beyond my power.
  Speak on.
MESSENGER: When we had reached the shoreline,
  at the inlet where Orestes' galley was secretly moored,
  Iphigenia, whom you had sent with those two men,
  waved at us to keep away,
  because she was about to light the purifying fire
  and carry out the cleansing for which she'd come.
Taking the fetters of the two men in her hands
  she walked along with them upon the strand.
I began to be suspicious,
  though your servants, sire, seemed satisfied.
Time passed,
  and to convince us that she was busy with solemn rites

she broke into a wild barbaric chant
    as if she were purging away the guilt of blood.
After we'd been sitting there some time
    it occurred to us that the strangers might break loose,
    kill her, and get away.
However, we didn't want to think of this
    and went on sitting there in silence
    until, in spite of her injunction,
    we all decided to see where they had gone.
And there we saw the hull of a Greek galley
    with its fringe of oars raised like a bird's wing
    and fifty oarsmen ready to take off.
The crew were steadying the prow with poles:
    some hauling the anchor up,
    others feverishly playing out the ropes,
    while a ladder was dropped to the sea for the two boys.
When we saw that we'd been tricked,
    we did not hesitate a moment more.
We grabbed the woman, seized the hawsers,
    and tried to wrench the rudder from its socket.
A shouting match ensued:
    "By what right do you go stealing
    images and priestesses from our land?
    Whose son are you to kidnap her?"
He shouted back:
    "I am Orestes, son of Agamemnon,
    I am her brother, I'll have you know.
    It is my sister lost to me so long ago that I am taking home."

Meanwhile we did not loosen our grip upon this foreign wench
    and would have dragged her into your presence,
    but that was when I got these bruises on my face;
    for though they had no weapons, only their fists, like us,
    they rained such blows on us
    and kicked us in the stomach and ribs so lustily
    they knocked us limp and left their marks all over us,
    until we bolted to the cliff—
    with black eyes and bloody heads.

           *   *   *

From the cliff we renewed the fight more cautiously,
    pelting rocks at them,
    but they had drawn up archers on the poop
    who let fly at us and drove us farther and farther back.
Then came a mighty wave that heaved the ship towards the
                                                    shore.

The girl was petrified of stepping into the surf
    so Orestes hoisted her onto his left shoulder,
    waded into the sea, sprang up the ladder,
    and put her down safely in the kindly ship
    together with the statue of Artemis—
    the statue that fell once from the sky.
From midship a great shout rang out:
    "Sailors of Hellas, grasp your oars
    and churn the sea white with foam.
    We have what we came to get—
    came through the dangerous straits of Symplegades."
They with a roar of triumph
    battered the sea with their strokes,
    and the ship was making way in the harbor
    and was clearing the mouth of the bay
    when she ran into a swell and began to judder.
    Then a squall hit her and swung her around.
The sailors desperately struggled against the billows
    but the surge drove the ship towards the rocks,
    till Iphigenia, standing up erect, cried out in prayer:
"Artemis daughter of Leto,
    save me your priestess, save me for Greece
    and forgive me for my theft.
    You too, goddess, love your brother,
    so indulge me in my loving mine."

The mariners echoed her prayer in a shout
    and stripped to the waist pulled hard with their bare arms.
But nearer and nearer the rocks the ship was driven.
Some of us breasted the waves,
    others tried to make cables fast.
As for me, I hurried here to you
    to tell you, sire, what was going on.
Quickly go to the scene with chains and ropes.

If the sea does not subside, these aliens do not stand a chance.
The lord of the oceans, Poseidon,
  is showing himself Ilium's* friend
  and Argos' enemy.
I expect him soon to deliver into your hands
  and your people's the son of Agamemnon and his sister,
  who has so brazenly betrayed the goddess,
  forgetting her generosity at Aulis.

LEADER: O Iphigenia, you poor devastated lady
  once again in the tyrant's grip:
  you and your brother will surely die.

THOAS: Onwards, citizens of my wild untamed land,
  harness your horses and gallop to the shore.
  Seize the Greek ship and its stranded occupants
  and with the help of the goddess hunt them down—
  every cursed man of them . . . but hurry.
And you others,
  haul my fastest vessels into the ocean
  so that by land and sea, by horse and ship,
  we capture them and hurl them from the highest cliffs
  or plunge them onto sharpened stakes.

[*Turning to the* CAPTIVE MAIDENS]

As for you women,
  who were privy to the plot,
  I shall punish you later at my leisure;
  I'll not waste time now for a more urgent matter.

[PALLAS ATHENA *appears, looming imperiously over the scene.
As a goddess her presence and voice are ubiquitous, reaching
both the shore and the courtyard*]

ATHENA: Where, King Thoas, where are you directing this pur-
                                                            suit?
Listen to what I, Athena, have to say.
Curb your streaming forces from the chase.

*This reference to Ilium seems to me a strong indication that Tauria was an
ally of Troy, and perhaps even that the captive Greek maidens came into its
possession during the war.

It was by Apollo's oracle that Orestes came here
  to escape the avenging Furies and to fetch
  his sister back to Argos.
And he came to put an end to all his troubles
  by bringing the holy effigy to my land.
Now listen carefully.
  Orestes, stranded by the surf, whom you planned to kill,
  even now Poseidon at a word from me
  has prodded forward on a waveless sea.

And you, Orestes,
  attend to what I tell you:
  my words though distant are divine.
Go with the image and your sister
  and when you come to Athens my godly city,
  make for a place called Halae,
  a holy place of mine
  on the borders of Attica near the Carystian Rock.
Build a temple there and set the image up.
Name the spot after Tauria
  to remind you of your sufferings here
  and your Fury-driven rovings all through Greece.
In days to come
  pilgrims will sing hymns to Artemis of Tauropolis.
Establish there this rite:
  on the feast days that celebrate your escape from slaughter,
  bring a sword to a human throat and prick it,
  spilling a little blood:
  just as a past reminder to Artemis of the past.

  [*Turning to* IPHIGENIA]

You, Iphigenia,
  shall be keeper of the keys to the shrine of Artemis
  on the holy terraces of Brauron.
There you shall be buried when you die
  and be offered the fabulous attire, weaved at home,
  for women who died in childbirth.
As to these Greek captive maidens, Thoas,
  they have been loyal and you must let them go.

[*After line 1468 there is a gap in the ms. It probably detailed instructions to the* MAIDENS *of the* CHORUS *for when they reached Greece. The text resumes with injunctions to* ORESTES]

I saved you once before on Ares' Hill
  with my casting vote.
So let it be tradition that
  he who wins an even count of votes prevails.
Now, son of Agamemnon, take your sister and be off.
And you, Thoas, be not grieved.
THOAS: Sovereign Athena,
  whoever hears the words of heaven and does not heed
  has lost his wits.
I shall not be angry with Orestes or his sister
  for carrying off the goddess' image;
  to fight the power of gods is futile.
So I let these people go, as you enjoined,
  home to your country with the holy image
  to set it up with prosperous auguries.
These young women, too,
  I send back to happy Hellas;
  and I curb my spear against the two young men,
  and call in my fleet, Goddess, as you required.
ATHENA: I commend you.
Necessity rules us all—even the gods.
Come, kindly breezes,
  waft the son of Agamemnon home.
I shall go with them to guard my sister's image.

[PALLAS ATHENA *fades from view as the* MAIDENS *of the* CHORUS *muster for the exodus march*]

CHORUS: Go, be happy you are saved,
  Blest by destiny. And you,
Pallas Athena,
  Whom mortals and immortals cherish,
  We shall do everything you say,
  Glad beyond our dreams by what we've heard.
  May Victory, mighty deity, possess
  My life and crown it always with success.

MEDEA

—∞—

ΜΗΔΕΙΑ

For Pandora and Rowland Smith

Euripides was only eighteen when he produced his first plays, and about twenty-five when his *The Daughters of Pelias* won third prize at the Great Dionysia in 455 B.C.—the year of the death of Aeschylus. Twenty-four years later, in 431, he mounted his *Medea*, in competition with Sophocles, who won second prize, and Euphorion, who took the first. *Medea* did not score at all, and one can't help wondering what were the two plays that were considered superior.

To us the person of Medea, if one strips away the accidentals of her as princess and sorceress, represents in a masterly way womanhood at its most tender and most fierce. Here is a passionate character, lucid in mind, courageous in spirit, prompt in action, who is transported from the wild regions east of the Black Sea to balanced and cultured Greece—*médenagan*, "nothing too much"—and brings with her a barbaric and ruthless intensity. She sees clearly where her single-mindedness will take her, but the importunity in her blood (spilt blood demands more spilling) smashes through all restraint.

The quality of Euripides' language throughout is not only brisk, mobile, elastic, and beautiful but a seismograph of sound, triggering the very nerve of the character speaking. Listen to Medea, for instance, in line 476, hissing out her fury like an adder about to strike:*

esōsa se esōsa hōs iasi hosoi [*Hellēnōn*]
I saved your life; yes, saved it—as every son of Greece
[who stepped on board the *Argo* knows] . . .

Jason too becomes vivid in the sound of every syllable he utters. His language has all the plodding huff-and-puff self-righteousness of the cornered male—like a man belligerently trying to explain away an affair with his secretary. Line 530:

. . . *hōs Erōs s'ēnagkase*
tuksois aphuktois toumon eksōsai demas.

*I am indebted to the late Professor Moses Hadas for this observation.

> . . . how it was infatuation, sheer shooting passion,
> that drove you to save me.

Listen to those wooden recalcitrant K's in the Greek, the succession of blustering T's, and enough sibilants to echo Medea's.

As to the curious preternatural ending of a play so consistently natural—Medea's appearing in a chariot drawn by dragons—it seems to me that Euripides is saying: "Yes, you are right to be disconcerted by the fantasy of a dragon-chariot to whisk Medea away to safety. This woman needs no divine help, only human."

CHARACTERS

NURSE
TUTOR to Medea's sons
MEDEA, foreign princess
CHORUS of Corinthian women, including LEADER
CREON, king of Corinth
JASON, husband of Medea
AEGEUS, king of Athens
MESSENGER
TWO SONS of Jason and Medea
HANDMAIDS of Medea
ATTENDANTS AND GUARDS of Creon and Aegeus

TIME AND SETTING

It is midmorning outside the house of Jason and Medea. Ten years have passed since the Argonauts sailed home after capturing the Golden Fleece. During that time Jason and Medea have been living modestly in Corinth, models of an unassailable married life and devoted to their two boys. But news has just broken that Jason intends to marry the daughter of the king of Corinth. The nurse enters from the house, distraught.

PROLOGUE

NURSE: Oh why did the winged oars of the Argo
   ever weave between those gnashing blue fjords
   towards the land of Colchis?

Why did the pines in the dells of Pelion
  ever fall to the ax and fill
  the rowing hands of heroes sent by Pelias
  to fetch the Golden Fleece?
My mistress Medea
  never would have sailed to Iolcus with its towers
  or been struck to the heart with love of Jason.
She never would have baited Pelias' daughters
  to the murder of their father
  or be living here in Corinth
  with her husband and her children . . .
How she has merited this city's good opinion,
  exile though she came,
  and been in everything Jason's perfect foil—
  in marriage that saving thing:
  a woman who does not go against her man.

  [*With a despairing glance towards the house*]

Now everything has turned to hate,
  her passion to a plague.
Jason has betrayed his sons and her,
  takes to bed a royal bride,
  Creon's daughter—the king of Corinth's.
Medea, spurned and desolate,
  breaks out in oaths,
  invokes the solemnest vows,
  calls the gods to witness
  how Jason has rewarded her.
She does not eat,
  lies prostrate slumped in anguish,
  wastes away in day-long tears.
Ever since she heard of Jason's perfidy
  she has not raised her eyes
  or looked up from the floor.
She might be a rock or wave of the sea,
  for aught she heeds of sympathy from friends.
At times she tilts her pale head away
  and moans to herself about her father—
  whom she loved—

and her country and the house she sacrificed
to journey here with a man . . .
oh, who so disdains her now.
Yes, now she knows
at a terrible first hand
what it is to miss one's native land.

[*She pauses, almost whispering the next words*]

She hates her sons.
Takes no pleasure in their sight.
I dread to think
of what is hatching in her mind.
She is a fierce spirit:
takes no insult lying down.
I know her well. She frightens me:
a dangerous woman,*
and anyone who crosses her
will not easily sing a song of triumph.
But here come the boys after their run,
suspecting nothing of their mother's tragedy.
Oh, it is true,
unhappy thoughts and youth never go together.

[*The* TUTOR *enters with the* TWO BOYS, *aged about seven
and nine. They wear a kind of short kilt and their heads
are covered in woolen caps. The* TUTOR *is an old man,
dressed loosely in an ocher-colored cloak. The* BOYS *hang
about in the background, laughing and talking, while the old
man advances*]

TUTOR: [*with half-teasing familiarity*]
Ah, Nurse, you old retainer of my lady's home!
What are you doing here all forlorn
standing moaning to yourself outside the gates?
Does Medea really want to be left alone?
NURSE: You dogged old pedagogue of Jason's sons,
like a good slave my heart is stricken too

---

*Lines 40–43 in the Greek are bracketed by many editors as doubtful, and I
have not included them.

when the fortunes of a mistress are struck down.
I am plunged in such a depth of grief
  I came out here to tell the earth and sky
  Medea's catastrophe.
TUTOR: What! Has the poor woman not stopped weeping yet?
NURSE: Stopped! You amaze me.
  Her ordeal far from halfway done,
  hardly has begun.
TUTOR: The silly innocent! . . . To be quite frank about our
                                                    mistress—
  she knows little of the latest blow.
NURSE: Latest? What's that, old man? Don't keep it from me.
TUTOR: Nothing, nothing . . . I'm sorry I even spoke.
NURSE: Come now, we're both slaves here, are we not?
  By your own gray beard, don't hold it back.
I can keep a secret if I must.
TUTOR: Well, I'd gone to where the old dice players sit,
  near Pirene's sacred spring,
  and there I overheard—pretending not to listen—
  someone say: "Creon, this country's king,
  is making plans to drive those boys from Corinth,
  their mother too."
I don't know if the story's true.
NURSE: No, surely no?
  Jason would never let his sons be treated so,
  however far he'd parted from their mother.
TUTOR: [*grimly*] Old loves have half the strength of new.
  That man is not this house's friend.
NURSE: We're finished, then—
  if we ship this second wave before we've bailed the first.
TUTOR: Now listen:
  this is not the time to let our mistress know.
Keep quiet about it. Not a word.
NURSE: [*with an anguished glance over her shoulder*]
  Poor little boys—
  do you hear how much your father loves you?
I wish he were . . . no, not dead—he is my master still—
  but, oh, what an enemy he's proven
  to those he should have loved!

TUTOR: What human being is not?
    Is this news to you,
        that every person's dearest neighbor is himself:
        some rightly so, some out of greed and selfishness.
This father does not love his sons;
    he loves his new wedding bed.
NURSE: Come along, boys, into the house.
    Everything is going to be all right.

    [*Dropping her voice*]

Keep them away as much as you can.
Do not let them near their mother—
    so long as she is in this deadly mood.
Already I have caught her eyes on them:
    the eyes of a mad bull.
There's something she is plotting
    and her fury won't abate—this I know—
        until the lightning strikes and someone's felled.
Let us hope it's enemies, not friends.

    [*A long-drawn-out sob from* MEDEA *inside the house*]

L Y R I C   D I A L O G U E

MEDEA: I am so unhappy—oh!
    The misery of it! I wish I were dead.
NURSE: [*hustling the children towards the door*]
    Listen there . . . poor children—your mother
    Raking her heart up, raking her rage.
    Quick, into the house at once.
    Don't come anywhere near her sight.
    Don't approach. Beware. Watch out
    For her savage mood, destructive spleen;
    Yes, and her implacable will.
    Off with you now. Hurry inside.
    Soon, I know, her cloud of misery
    Will gather and burst in a storm of rage.
    What will she perpetrate then—that proud,
    Importunate, heart-stung soul?

[*The* TWO BOYS *and the* TUTOR *leave. There's another long cry from* MEDEA *inside the house*]

MEDEA: What misery! Oh what pain!
　　Cursed sons, and a hateful mother!
　　Death take you all—you and your father.
　　Let the house rot.
NURSE: [*sobbing*] Oh, how it grieves me! Why make the sons
　　Share in their father's guilt? Oh why
　　Should *they* be hated? Poor little boys?
　　Your danger appals me. How ruthless is
　　The temper of royalty: often commanding,
　　Seldom commanded. Terribly slow
　　To forgive and forget . . . How much better
　　To live among equals! I want no part
　　Of greatness and glory. Let me decline
　　In a safe old age. The very name
　　Of the "middle way" has health in it,
　　Is best for human beings. Good never comes
　　From overreaching, never to mortals,
　　And when it provokes the gods it destroys
The house to its portals.

PARADOS OR ENTRY SONG

[*The* CHORUS *of women of Corinth enters, full of apprehension and concern for* MEDEA]

CHORUS: I heard a voice, I heard a shout,
　　It was the most unhappy
　　Woman from Colchis, raving still.
　　But tell us, old woman, for I
　　In the porch outside have heard
　　Her moans within . . . Oh, women,
　　I cannot delight in the pain of Jason's house,
　　A house I have loved very well.
NURSE: House there is none; life of it gone.
　　The master is had—by a princess' bed.
　　The mistress in her boudoir pines.
　　There are no words her friends can find

To touch her inconsolate heart.

MEDEA: [*in another spasm from within*] Ahhh!
Cleave my brain with a flash from the sky.
What good is left for me in living?
Alas! Alas! Come, Death, unloose
My life from a life I loathe.

STROPHE

CHORUS: Listen, O Zeus and Earth and Light
To the stricken tune of this plangent wife.
And you, loveless lady,
What yearning for love on a bed of delight
Could make you hurry to death—the night?
Pray not for that.
If your husband has gone to adore
A new bride in his bed, why, this
Has often happened before.
Do not harrow your heart; for Zeus
Will succor your soul. What use
To consume your life with grieving
For a lost lord?

MEDEA: [*from within*] O mighty Themis, and Artemis, Queen,
For all the fine vows I bound him with,
See what my hated husband has done.
Grant me to see him at last with his bride,
Palace and all, crumble in ruin.
How dare they do to me what they have done!
O my father, my country, the land I abandoned,
Flagrantly killing my brother!*

NURSE: Hear what she says with her cry from the heart
To Zeus and Themis—goddess of rights—
And him whom mankind makes keeper of vows.
My mistress' rage will stop at nothing
Before it plays itself out.

ANTISTROPHE

CHORUS: If she would come out and face to face

my brother: Medea slew her brother Absyrtus when she escaped with Jason,
and tossed him in pieces over the side of the ship, knowing that their pursuers
would stop to pick the pieces up.

Listen to what we have to say,
She might let go this rampant wrath,
This spite of soul.
I hope I never fail my friends,
So go, Nurse, entice her to come.
Say we are with her. We are her friends.
Hurry, before she does any harm
To those inside.
Sorrow can swell to enormity.

NURSE: [*walking to the door*] I'll do my best but am afraid
I won't be able to sway my lady.
And yet I'm glad to shoulder the burden
Though she glares like a lioness with whelps
If anyone dares to approach and speak.

[*She turns at the door*]

What incompetent fools they were,
Those composers of old:
making music for life and joy,
for grand celebrations and groaning boards,
but, oh, nothing for sorrow and pain:
No music or song on hand-plucked lyre
For the world's travail
And the death and destruction of many a home.
Oh, what solace is missed
By having no music for this!
What a waste of it, then, by singing in vain,
When fullness at feasts is its own joy and gain.

[*She goes into the house*]

CHORUS: Deep is her sobbing from depths of pain.
Shrill is the answer her suffering gives
To the news of a marriage betrayed,
A love gone wrong.
Outraged, importunate, she prays
To Themis the daughter of Zeus
And keeper of vows,
Who steered her through

Those dangerous straits at night to Hellas
Across the salt of the sea.

FIRST EPISODE

[MEDEA *comes out of the house. She is wan and her eyes are red with weeping, but she is surprisingly in control*]

MEDEA: Women of Corinth, be indulgent, please.
   I have obeyed you and come out.
The charge of aloofness, as I know too well,
   is something often leveled
   at both the retiring and the busy person.
One who chooses a quiet life
   has this alleged against him too:
   laziness and lack of spirit.
Public opinion has most shallow eyes.
People hate at sight a harmless human being,
   knowing nothing of the real man.
I agree, of course, that a foreigner should conform
   and adapt to his society.
Besides, a citizen is censurable no less
   when too self-centered or uncouth
   to avoid offending his companions.
Nevertheless, I . . .
   I . . . out of a clear sky
   have been struck a blow that breaks my heart.
My friends, it is over.
I want to die.
Life has lost all point.
The man who was my life
   —and he knows it too—
   has become for me beneath contempt.

[*She surveys the women*]

Of all creatures that can feel and think,
   we women are the worst-treated things alive.
To begin with,
   we bid the highest price in dowries
   just to buy some man

to be dictator of our bodies.
How that compounds the wrong!
Then there is the terrifying risk:
    shall we get a good man or a bad?
Divorce is a disgrace
    (at least for women),
    to repudiate a man, not possible.
So, plunged into habits new to her,
    conventions she has never known at home,
    she has to guess like some clairvoyant
    how to handle the one who shares her bed.
And if we learn our lesson well
    in this exacting role,
    and our husband does not kick against the marriage yoke,
    oh, ours is an enviable life!
Otherwise we are better dead.
When a man gets bored with wife and home,
    he simply roams abroad to relieve the tedium of his spirit,
    turns to a friend or finds his cronies.
We women, on the other hand,
    turn only to a single man.
We live safe at home, they say.
They do battle with the spear.
How shallow!
I had rather stand my ground three times in battle
    than face a childbirth once.
Your case, however, and mine are not the same.
You have your city.
You have your father's home.
Life offers you the sweet fellowship of friends.
I am alone,
    without a city, wronged by a husband,
    uprooted from a foreign land.
I have no mother, brother, cousin;
    am without a haven in this storm.
So, please, I ask you this:
    if I can find a way to pay my husband back—
    your silence.
Woman, on the whole, is a timid thing:

the din of war, the flash of steel, unnerves her;
　but wronged in love, there is no heart more murderous.
LEADER: As you wish, Medea.
　You have a score to settle with your lord
　and I do not wonder that you smart . . .
But, look, I see Creon coming, this country's king:
　bristling, I dare say, with new decisions.

[CREON *enters with attendants. He is a bearded man of about
sixty, royally but modestly dressed. His face wears a troubled
look of resolution*]

CREON: Go, Medea. Remove yourself.
　Get packing from this land.
I order you—you with your black-faced fury
　lowering against your lord.
And take your brace of offspring with you;
　no dallying either.
I am here to see this order done,
　and until I've pushed you out and over the border,
　I'll not go home.
MEDEA: So,
　I am lost, crushed utterly.
My enemies let out the sail,
　while I have no place to disembark from doom.
Nonetheless,
　hard pressed as I am, I ask you this:
　for what reason, Creon, do you drive me out?
CREON: Fear.
　No need to camouflage the fact.
I am afraid you'll deal my child some lethal blow.
Many things conspire to make me fear.
You are a woman of some knowledge:
　versed in many unsavory arts.
Your husband's gone.
Your soul is raw with loss of love,
　and now it is reported that you threaten me:
　mean to hurt the father of the bride,
　and of course the bride and groom.
That is what I want to guard against—

an accident.
Madam, better to be hated by you now
   than soften and pay for it later on.
MEDEA: Heaven help me!
   My reputation is a curse.
This is not the first time, Creon,
   it has done me lasting harm . . .
Oh, let the perspicacious man
   keep his children from enlightenment
   above the general run.
It will earn them only the sneer of uselessness,
   and the spiteful jealousy of fellow men.
Bring education to the dolt
   and far from being accounted wise
   you will yourself be cast as dolt.
Outshine a pundit of established fame
   and you become a byword of distaste.
This precisely is what I have to face.
Because I have a little knowledge,
   some are filled with envy,
   others think me secretive and crazy.
In point of fact, my knowledge
   does not amount to very much.

[*She turns to* CREON, *her eyes pathetic with innocence*]

And yet it frightens you:
   you think I'll strike some death knell on your house.
No, I'm not like that.
Creon, forget your fear.
I have no criminal intent against a king.
For how have *you* wronged *me*?
You simply gave your virgin daughter
   to a suitor of your bent.
No, it is my husband that I hate.
You, I think, have acted prudently
   and even now I don't begrudge your enterprise success.
Marry them both and blessings on you,
   only let me go on living in this land.
Ill used though I am I shall keep quiet and submit.

CREON: This is reassuring talk
   but it chills me to the marrow.
What are you really hatching in your mind?
I trust you, madam, even less than I did before.
The impassioned woman, like the impassioned man,
   is easier to guard against than the crafty and the quiet.
So, I say, leave at once,
   and no speeches, please. My mind's made up.
You are dangerous and all your cleverness
   shall not keep you here.
MEDEA: Please, I beg you—on my knees—
   by your fresh young daughter-bride.
CREON: You waste your words. I am adamant.
MEDEA: Will you expel me—heedless of my prayers?
CREON: I will. For I love you less than I love my home.
MEDEA: Ah, home! My beloved country,
   what memories crowd upon me now!
CREON: Next to my children, that is my dearest love as well.
MEDEA: Love? It is mankind's greatest curse.
CREON: In my opinion . . . that depends.
MEDEA: O Zeus, remember the author of this crime.
CREON: Go away, you poor deluded thing. Rid me of my troubles.
MEDEA: The troubles are all mine. I have a glut of them.
CREON: [turning on his heel]
   I'll have my servants put you out by force.
MEDEA: [clinging to his knees]
   No, not that, Creon . . . I'm beseeching you.
CREON: You seem determined, madam,
   to make a nuisance of yourself.
MEDEA: No, no, I'll go into banishment.
   That is not what I beg for now.
CREON: Then why not go, and let this land be rid of you?
MEDEA: Just let me stay this single day to . . .
   to arrange my exodus from here
   and make provision for my children;
   whose father cannot bring himself to care.
Be kind to them. You are a father too,
   and know what kindly feelings are.

As for me,
    it means nothing to me whether I stay or go.
It's them I shed my tears for,
    their lot is hard.
CREON: [*after a tussle with himself*]
    My soul is not tyrannical enough.
My heart has often let me down . . .
So now, Medea,
    though I know I take a false step:
    have it your own way.
But let me warn you solemnly,
    if the divine light of tomorrow's sun
    sees you and your offspring
    still within the borders of this realm, you die.
Every word of this I mean.
So, stay if you must, but one day only—
    not long enough for you to perpetrate anything I dread.

    [*Exit* CREON *and his suite*]

LEADER: Ill-starred woman, oh what a nightmare
Of anguish is on you!
Whom will you turn to? Where will you turn?
What country, what stranger,
What home for a haven?
A god has certainly steered you
—Oh, my poor Medea!—
Into a sea-race of sorrows.
MEDEA: [*turning on them with a gleam of resolution*]
    In the center of disasters, yes,
    but all is far from lost—make no mistake.
An ordeal awaits the newlyweds—
    no little test for the happy pair.

    [*With a laugh of derision*]

Do you think I would have toadied to this man
    if nothing could be got from it, no gain, no tool?
No, not one syllable,
    not a touch with my little finger.

The fool!
He could have scotched me with one stroke,
    flung me out.
Instead he lets me stay one extra day:
    one day to make three enemies three corpses;
    Yes indeed, father, daughter, husband.

[*She leans towards the* CHORUS *conspiratorially*]

Friends,
    I can think of several ways to bring their death about.
Which one shall I choose?
Shall I set their house of honeymoon alight,
    or creep into the nuptial bower
    and plunge a sharp knife through their innards?
One thing makes me pause:
    if I am caught entering the palace
    or red-handed in the act—I die,
    and give my enemies the last laugh.
No, there is a surer way,
    one more direct;
    for which I have a natural bent:
    death by poison.
Yes, that is it.

[*She walks, thinking*]

Well, suppose they are dead . . .
Will any city take me in?
Will any man afford me home and haven in his country
    and shield me from reprisals?
No, there is none.
I must wait a little therefore
    till some tower of strength appears for me
    and I can proceed to the murder with trickery and stealth.
If none of this works out, however,
    I'll simply seize a sword,
    face certain death,
    and with my own hands run them through.
I shan't shrink from such a step,

by Hecate, no, the goddess who resides
in the shrine of my own inner hearth:
she whom I reverence most of all the gods,
she whom I have chosen to abet me.
Nobody breaks my heart with impunity.
Their wedding I'll reduce to agony and grief:
agony for the match they've made,
and grief for having banished me.
Good, Medea!
Use your magic to the hilt.
Conspire and plot:
advance to the deadly act that tests your courage.
See how you are being treated,
laughed at by the seed of Sisyphus and Jason:
you, the daughter of a king
and scion of the Sun.
Be aware of that.
Besides, you are a woman:
feeble when it comes to the sublime,
marvelously inventive over crime.

FIRST CHORAL ODE

[*The* CHORUS *sings about the topsy-turvy changing standards
of the world. Out of the turmoil will come a new importance
for women, and a new reverence. Meanwhile,* MEDEA *is the
harbinger of female independence and vitality*]

STROPHE I

Back to their fountains the sacred rivers are falling,
The cosmos and all morality turning to chaos.
The mind of man is nothing but fraud
And his faith in the gods a delusion.
But a day will come when the story changes.
Then shall the glory of women resound,
And reverence come to the gender of woman,
Reversing at last the sad reputation of ladies.

ANTISTROPHE I

The ballads of ages gone by that harped on the falseness
Of women will cease to be sung. If only Apollo
Prince of the lyre had put in *our* hearts the invention
Of music and songs for the lyre, wouldn't I then
Have raised a paean, a feminine paean, to answer
The epic of men? Time in the roll of the ages
Has much to unfold of the fortunes of women
No less than the fortunes of men.

STROPHE II

So you, Medea, sailing away
   from your father's house,
Threading a passage with heart on fire
   through the jowls of the Euxine*
Cliffs to inhabit a strange land
   where your bed is now empty of man
(The lover you lost, O heartbroken lady)
   are chased from the realm, shamed and banned.

ANTISTROPHE II

The joy of a bond is gone, gone,
   and wide of the world of Hellas
All shame has flown—high in the sky
   and away. And you bereft
Of a fatherly home have no harbor
   to sail to, away from the storm.
Unfortunate woman! And your bed is usurped
   by another queen in your home.

SECOND EPISODE

[JASON, *a young-looking man dressed in a swashbuckling
cloak and plumed helmet, hurries in from the road that leads
to the palace. He wears a look of exasperation*]

JASON: So . . . this is not the first time.
   I have seen irrevocable damage done by a recalcitrant tongue.

*Euxine: The Black Sea (between northern Turkey and the Crimea).

You could have stayed here,
  in this land, in this house,
  had you only submitted quietly to your ruler's plans.
Instead, you ranted like a barbarian.
So now you are banished.
To me your tirades do not mean a thing.
Go on declaiming what a monster Jason is;
  but when it comes to royalty—the princess and the king—
  count yourself lucky only to be banished.
I have tried continuously to smooth things down
  —for I should like you to remain here—
  but you, madam, obstinate in your folly,
  continuously revile our royalty.
So you are banished.
Yet in spite of everything,
  and patient to the last with someone I am fond of,
  I come, Medea, to do what I can to help.
You and the children
  need not leave the country penniless and unprovided . . .
  exile drags with it a chain of troubles.
Hate me though you may,
  I cannot bring myself to wish you harm.
MEDEA: Monster—
  an epithet too good for you . . .
  so you come to me, do you,
  you byword of aversion both in heaven and on earth,
  to me your own worst enemy?
This is not courage.
This is not being brave:
  to look a victim in the eyes whom you've betrayed
  —somebody you loved—
  this is a disease and the foulest that a man can have.
You are shameless.
But you have done well to come.
I can unload some venom from my heart
  and you can smart to hear it.
To begin at the beginning,
  yes, first things first,
  I saved your life—

as every son of Greece who stepped on board the *Argo* knows.
Your mission was to yoke the fire-breathing bulls
   and sow the death-bearing plot of dragons' teeth.
I came to your rescue,
   lit up life for you,
   slew the guardian of the Golden Fleece—
   that giant snake that hugged it sleepless coil on coil.
I deserted my father and my home
   to come away with you to Iolcos by Mount Pelion,
   full of zeal and very little sense.
I killed King Pelias
   —a horrid death, perpetrated through his daughters—
   and overturned their home.
All this for you.
I bore your sons, you reprobate man,
   just to be discarded for a new bride.
Had you been childless,
   this craving for another bedmate
   might have been forgiven.
But no: faith in vows was simply shattered.
I am baffled.
Do you suppose the gods of old no longer rule?
Or is it that mankind
   now has different principles?
Because your every vow to me, you surely know,
is null and void.
Curse this right hand of mine
   so often held in yours,
   and these knees of mine sullied to no purpose
   by the grasp of a rotten man.
You have turned my hopes to lies.
Come now, tell me frankly,
   as if we were two friends,
   as if you really were prepared to help
   (I hope the question makes you wince):
   where do I go from here?

   [*With a bitter laugh*]

Home to my father, perhaps, and my native land,

both of whom I sacrificed for you?
Or to the poor deprived daughters of Pelias?
They would be overjoyed to entertain
     their father's murderer.
So this is how things stand.
Among my loved ones at home I am an execrated woman.
There was no call for me to hurt *them*
     but now I have a death feud on my hands—
     and all for you.
What a reward!
What a heroine you have made me
     among the daughters of Hellas!
Lucky Medea, having *you*!
Such a wonderful husband and so loyal!
I leave this land displaced, expelled,
     deprived of friends,
          only my children with me and alone.
What a charming record for our new bridegroom this:
     "His own sons and the wife who saved him
     are wayside beggars."

[*She breaks off and looks upward*]

O Zeus, what made you give us clear signs for telling
     mere glitter from true gold,
     but when we need to know the base metal of a man
     no stamp upon his flesh for telling counterfeit?
LEADER: How frightening is resentment, how difficult to cure,
     when lovers hurl past love at one another's hate!
JASON: I'll have to choose my words with no uncommon skill,
     it seems, if like a good sailor riding out a storm
     I am to sail close-sheeted, madam,
     through your lashing, dangerous tongue.
You pile up what you did for me
     into pinnacles of grace.
Well, as far as I'm concerned,
     it was Aphrodite and no one else in heaven or earth
     who saved me on my voyage.
Your cleverness played a part, of course,
     but I could stress, if I wanted to be ungenerous,

how it was infatuation, sheer shooting passion,
    that drove you to save my life.
I shall not emphasize the point.
Your service, after all, did no harm.
But this I do maintain:
    that what you gained by saving me
    was far more than you gave.

[*He holds up a hand to stop* MEDEA *from interrupting*]

In the first place, you have a home in Hellas
    instead of some barbarian land.
You have known justice:
    the benefit of laws that never yield to might.
You have had your talents recognized all over Greece
    and won renown.
For were you living at the world's ends,
    your name would not be known.
To me houses crammed with gold,
    or a sweeter song than Orpheus sang,
    are nothing with no name.
But enough discussion of my perilous voyage,
    an argument that you provoked.
Now to your vindictive challenge of my royal marriage.
I'll show you first it was an act of common sense,
    secondly, unselfish,
    and finally a mark of my devotion
    to you and all the family.

[MEDEA *gives a gasp of incredulity*]

No, be still.
When I came here from the land of Iolcos,
    frustrations crowding on my trail,
    could I, a wretched fugitive,
    have hit on a greater stroke of future luck
    than marriage to the daughter of a king?
It was not—which cuts you to the quick—
    that I was tired of your attractions
    and smitten with a longing for a new wife;

still less that I was out to multiply my offspring.
I am quite satisfied with the sons I have.
No, it was simply that I wanted above all
   to let us live in comfort and not be poor.
I know too well how the pauper is avoided by his friends.
I wanted our children to be reared
   in a manner worthy of my ancestry;
   and begetting others, brothers for your sons,
   to knit them all together in one close happy family.
What point was there for you to have more children?
   My intention was—and it seemed real gain—
   to help the ones I have through those I hope to have.
Was this such a wicked plan?
You would not say so,
   except through jealousy—that stinging jealousy of bed.
You women are all the same.
If your love life goes all right
   everything is fine;
   but once crossed in bed,
   the liveliest and best that life can offer
   might as well be wormwood.
What we poor males really need
   is a way of having babies on our own—no females, please.
Then the world would be
   completely trouble-free.

LEADER: [*sternly*] Jason, this speech of yours is plausible,
   but say what you like, it is not right
   to sacrifice your wife.

MEDEA: [*as if to herself*] Yes, I suppose my outlook
   is very different from most.
To my mind, the glib hypocrite
   is the lowest scoundrel of them all.
The more he glozes falsehood with his tongue,
   the more brash he grows in villainy,
   but ends up by not being very clever.

   [*Turning to Jason*]

So you with me.
You'd best stop your special pleading;

one simple observation lays the whole thing flat:
were you not a coward you would have consulted *me*
about this new alliance,
not gone sneaking off to marry.

JASON: And you, of course, would have welcomed the suggestion.
Why, even now, you can't contain your blazing rage.

MEDEA: *That* was not what governed you:
you felt your glory tarnished by an aging wife.

JASON: Please, please believe me:
it was nothing to do with women
that I made this princely match
but, as I have already said,
to safeguard you and rear young princes
to be brothers to my sons—so make our family solid.

MEDEA: [*with a bitter laugh*]
Not for me, not ever—a solidity that hurts,
a happiness that stings me to the core.

JASON: Could you possibly change your prayer to this,
and make more sense:
"May success not seem to me sad failure.
Nor good fortune ever a disaster."

MEDEA: Don't joke with me.
You have roof and shelter.
I am deserted, flying for my life, alone.

JASON: You chose it. Blame no one else.

MEDEA: Did I? Was I the one who wed and then betrayed?

JASON: No. You just swore a heap of filthy curses on the king.

MEDEA: Curses, ha! You'll find them coming home to roost.

JASON: [*preparing to go*]
There's no point in talking any more with you.
Anything that you or the children want in exile,
let me know; I'll gladly furnish it,
or send letters of introduction for you
to friends abroad who will be kind.
To turn this offer down, Medea,
is nothing short of madness.
Forget your feelings of resentment,
let yourself be helped.

MEDEA: [*spitting out the words*]
 Not your friends, not your things;
 I would not touch anything of yours—
 how dare you offer it.
The offerings of a bad man are worse than worthless.
JASON: [*flinging his cloak about him*]
 In that case, heaven be my witness:
 all my design to help you and your sons
 is thwarted by your preference for evil.
Your self-will cuts you off.
Suffer then accordingly.
MEDEA: Go.
 Don't waste your passion here.
Go to the fresh young virgin you can't wait for.
Have her.

 [*As JASON leaves, furious and embarrassed*]

God grant the match you make
 you'll long to have unmade.

SECOND CHORAL ODE

[*The women of the* CHORUS, *appalled by what has happened
to* MEDEA, *speak of the dangers of love and the sufferings of
banishment*]

STROPHE I
Love is a dangerous thing,
Loving without any limit.
Discredit and loss it can bring.
But, oh, if the goddess should visit
A love that is modest and right,
No god is so exquisite.
Great lady, aim not at me
Your gold and infallibly
Passion-tipped poisoned delight.

ANTISTROPHE I
Ease me with innocent living:
Most beautiful gift of the gods.

Never let Cypris* the fierce
Queen of desire propel
My heart to a dissolute lust
From old to a new and another
Bed with a dissonant longing,
But test with a sweet eye for peace
The love-bonds of reverent women.

STROPHE II

O my country, my home, never let
Me lose my state and my city,
To live that desperate loss:
So helpless and hard, without pity.
Death, I would bargain with death
And die such a day to a finish.
For nothing is like the sorrow
Or supersedes the sadness
Of losing your native land.

ANTISTROPHE II

The thing is before my eyes,
Learned from no rumor or lies:
Medea without city or friends
And nowhere where pity extends—
Oh, how you must suffer!
Let a man rot in an odious lot
If he never unshutters his heart
To the cleansing esteem of another.
He'll not be my friend—no never.

THIRD EPISODE

[AEGEUS *enters from the country. He is a man in his early middle years and dressed in traveling clothes. His kindly open features wear a look of preoccupation. He is attended by a few noblemen and servants*]

---

*Cypris: another name for Aphrodite, born out of the foam near the island of Cyprus.

AEGEUS:

[*stretching out his hands*]

Medea, all health and happiness!
And can one say a fairer thing when greeting friends?
MEDEA: [*wanly*] Health and happiness to you, good Aegeus,
  wise Pandion's son.
But where do you stem from?
AEGEUS: I have just left Apollo's ancient oracle at Delphi.
MEDEA: What, a pilgrim there—the nub of the world of prophecy?

AEGEUS: I went to ask how I can beget children.
MEDEA: [*suddenly interested*]
  In the name of heaven, have you been childless
  all this time?
AEGEUS: Yes, childless . . . by some design of heaven.
MEDEA: But with a wife? Or have you never married?
AEGEUS: I am married, yes. I have a wife that shares my bed.
MEDEA: And what did Apollo say about your begetting children?
AEGEUS: Something too deep for me a mere mortal to unravel.
MEDEA: Am I allowed to know the god's reply?
AEGEUS: Certainly. It would take a mind like yours to fathom.
MEDEA: Tell me . . . what did he say . . . since you are allowed?
AEGEUS: Why, just this:
  "Do not uncock the foot of the wineskin* till . . ."
MEDEA: Till you have done what? Been where?
AEGEUS: [*baffled*] Until I'm back home again.
MEDEA: Then what made you sail your vessel here?
AEGEUS: There is a man called Pittheus, king of Troezen . . .
MEDEA: Yes, son of Pelops: a very pious man, they say.
AEGEUS: He's the one I want to ask about the god's prediction.
MEDEA: Yes, a clever man and an expert in such matters.
AEGEUS: And of all my old battle pals, my favorite.
MEDEA: Well, I hope that all your dreams come true.
AEGEUS: [*with a searching glance*]
Medea, you look so pale, so sad. What is it?

---

*A *wineskin* was the complete skin of a goat, one of whose feet was used for the spigot. The meaning is: Do not have sexual intercourse until . . .

MEDEA: My husband, Aegeus: he is the world's most evil man.
AEGEUS: You don't say? Come, tell me all about your troubles.
MEDEA: Jason has hurt me deeply. I never did him harm.
AEGEUS: What exactly has he done? Tell me clearly.
MEDEA: He's set up a mistress to queen it in my home.
AEGEUS: No? Would he really do a thing like that?
MEDEA: Yes, yes . . . And I am despised—the one he loved.
AEGEUS: Did he fall in love . . . or is he just tired of you?
MEDEA: In love—ha!—head over heels . . . flinging all fidelity to
                                                    the winds.
AEGEUS: Let him go, then, since he's as wicked as you say.
MEDEA: It was with royalty that he fell in love: a king's daughter.
AEGEUS: Who gave her away? Please go on.
MEDEA: Creon, who rules over this land of Corinth.
AEGEUS: In that case, madam, I can understand your bitterness.
MEDEA: My life is in ruins, and besides, I am being expelled.
AEGEUS: Expelled? That indeed is a crowning blow. But by
                                                    whom?
MEDEA: Creon. He wants to banish me from Corinth.
AEGEUS: And Jason agrees? I find that monstrous.
MEDEA: [*with fierce irony*] Oh, he says he doesn't—but he'll bear
                                                    it bravely.

[*Suddenly on her knees*]

Aegeus, I beg you,
    by your beard, by these knees of yours I clasp,
    pity me, pity my unhappiness.
Do not see me banished and alone.
Let me come to Athens. Shelter me. Accept me in your home.
The gods will pay you back,
    give you the children you long to have:
    who will surround your death with comfort.
You cannot guess how Providence has blessed you,
    meeting me.
I mean to end your childlessness
    and make your seed bear sons.
I promise it. I know the drugs.
AEGEUS: [*impressed*] Medea, many reasons make me ready
    to acquiesce in your request,

not least of all the gods.
Then because you've given me a promise:
   my heart's desire—promise of children.

  [*Raising her up*]

My proposition, then, is this:
   get yourself to Athens,
   and there as is incumbent on me
   I shall do my utmost to protect you.
However, I must tell you clearly,
   I cannot take you with me out of Corinth;
   but if you reach my palace on your own,
   there you shall have sanctuary
   and to no one shall I give you up.
So by your own means you must leave this land;
   I cannot risk offending the Corinthians
   who are also friends of mine.
MEDEA: Just as you say . . . however . . .
   if only you could promise it on oath,
   it would make it all so . . . settled between us.
AEGEUS: Don't you trust me? What is the matter now?
MEDEA: [*glancing nervously over her shoulders*]
   I do trust you but . . . I have my enemies.
It isn't only Creon,
   there is the house of Pelias too:
   they'll want to prise me from your territories.
If you are bound by an oath
   you will not give me up.
But if you have only made a promise
   —not sworn it to the gods—
   there is always the chance that sheer diplomacy
   will win you to their wishes.
I have no weapons on my side.
On theirs is wealth and all the weight of royalty.
AEGEUS: You are very provident, Medea,
   however, if that is what you wish
   I shall not gainsay it.
In point of fact, to swear an oath protects me too:
   I can counter those who wish you ill with a clear excuse.

You of course are well secured.
So name your deities.

MEDEA: [*in crystal-cold syllables*] Swear by the Earth on which
you tread
Swear by the Sun, my father's father dread
Swear by every god and godhead.

AEGEUS: Yes, but what to do or not to do? Please say.

MEDEA: Never yourself to drive me from your land,
and never while you live to let
any enemy of mine snatch me away.

AEGEUS: I swear by the Earth and sacred light of the Sun
to abide by the words you have just pronounced.

MEDEA: [*relentlessly*] Good . . . But if you break your word, what
penalty?

AEGEUS: The penalty for sacrilege.

[*They clasp hands in silence*]

MEDEA: Go now and be glad. All is well.
I shall come to Athens as quickly as I can,
but first I have some work to do to carry out a plan.

LEADER: [*as* AEGEUS *is leaving*] May Hermes, master of journeys
Hasten you home safely to Athens:
Home to the hope of your heart's desire.
For, Aegeus, you are
A most magnanimous man.

[*As* AEGEUS *disappears,* MEDEA *wheels around and faces the*
CHORUS]

MEDEA: O Zeus, and lady daughter, Justice,
O resplendent Sun and you my friends,
at last we are on the road to vengeance
and to our song of triumph.
At last there is hope.
We shall see my enemies put down.
At the very point my plot could founder,
this man opens up a port, an anchorage.
So to Athens I shall go
and moor myself to the citadel of Pallas.

[*Beckoning the women closer*]

Now I can unfold to you my whole design.
There is nothing sweet in it, as you will see.
I send a servant of my house to Jason
    asking him to come to me.
He comes.
I tell him in the softest accents how I now agree:
    how it is all for the best—his royal marriage,
    his sacrifice of me—everything he has planned
    is for the best.
But I ask him to let my children stay . . .
    with no intention, you understand,
    of leaving any child of mine in a hostile place
    for those who hate me to maltreat.
No, this is just a device
    for murdering the daughter of the king.
I send them there with presents in their hands,
    presents for the bride—as a kind of plea
    against their banishment—
    yes, a gown of gossamer and a diadem of beaten gold.
If she takes this finery and puts it on,
    the girl will die in agony and anyone who touches her:
    so deadly are the poisons I shall steep the presents in.
But now my whole tone changes:
    a sob of pain for the next thing I must do.
I kill my sons—my own—
    no one shall snatch them from me.
And when I have desolated Jason's house beyond recall,
    I shall escape from here,
    fly from the murder of my little ones,
    my mission done.
No, my friends, I *won't* be laughed at by my enemies.
Well, so be it. What good is life to me?
I have no father, home, defense against misfortune.
The mistake I made was when I left my father's house,
    trusting the word of a man from Greece . . .
    and he shall pay the price.
Never again shall he see alive the sons he had by me,
    nor any child by this new bride of his—

poor girl, who has to die a wretched death, poisoned by me.
Let nobody think me insignificant or weak.
I am no meek martyr. Quite the contrary:
   relentless to enemies, generous to friends.
That is the peculiar genius of souls like mine.
LEADER: [*imploringly*] Though you have shared all this in confi-
                           dence with us, Medea,
   and though I long to help,
   we must uphold the laws of life,
   and so I say to you: You must not do it.
MEDEA: There is no other way,
   and though I understand your sentiments
   you have not been through agony like mine.
LEADER: But, my lady, to kill your own two sons . . . ?
MEDEA: It is the supreme way to hurt my husband.
LEADER: And it makes you the most desolate of women.
MEDEA: Be that as it may.
   Argument is now superfluous.

[*Turning to the* NURSE, *who has entered during the previous dialogue*]

Nurse, when I need your loyalty
   you are the one I always turn to.
Go now and fetch Jason here;
   but as you are a woman
   and faithful servant of your mistress,
   whisper no syllable of what I plan.

[*Exit* NURSE, *dragging her feet*]

THIRD CHORAL ODE

[*The* WOMEN OF CORINTH *desperately try to move* MEDEA *from her purpose. Does she imagine Athens, that blessed land, will welcome a murderess? Surely she herself will flinch from the cold-blooded killing of her sons?*]

STROPHE I

The people of Athens are blessed through the ages,
   Seeds of the all-hallowed gods,

Born on a soil unravaged and holy,
   They feed on the wide
   Bright pastures of knowledge.
Lightly they walk through the crystal air
   In a land where Harmonia
     Goldenly fair,
Once gave birth, they say, to the nine
     Muses, the pure
     Maids of Pieria.

ANTISTROPHE I

And out of the sweetly flowing currents
   Of Cephisus, they declare,
Aphrodite sprinkles the land
   And fragrantly breathes
   Delicate breezes.
Forever she sheds from the stream of her hair,
   Plaited with roses,
   Scented petals,
And sends the Erotes—the Loves—to preside
   With Wisdom, over the heart,
     For the glories of art.

STROPHE II

How then shall a glorious city,
   City of sacred streams,
   Host of the salutary guest,
Kindly take to the killer of children,
Harbor among them a murderess?
Think of how you are stabbing your sons.
Think too of the blood you assume.
Do not, please, we beg by your knees,
By everything and all we know,
   Murder your children.

ANTISTROPHE II

Where, when, will you find the mind
   The hand or the callous heart
   Hardened enough to strike

These, yours—oh, heartless enough!
How will you see, then, through your gaze
Swollen with tears as you sight your aim?
No, no, when your little ones kneel
Crying for mercy, you will not
Find the nerve, ever be able   .
    To bloody your hands.

                FOURTH EPISODE

    [JASON *enters with the* NURSE *behind him. On his face is
    written apprehension mixed with hope; on hers, despair*]

JASON: I have come, Medea, because you asked me.
    I put myself at your disposal,
    even though you are against me.
What, madam, can I do for you?
MEDEA: [*in a small, contrite voice*]
    Jason, please forgive me for all the things I said.
Bear lightly with my outbursts, will you,
    if only in remembrance of our great love together.
I have been arguing with myself,
    have taxed myself severely.
"You raving fool," I said,
    "to antagonize those who want to do you good,
    setting yourself against your rulers and your husband.
His royal marriage
    and his design to bring up brothers for your sons
    does you the greatest service that he could.
Why not calm yourself?
Are you suffering because the gods are good?
Have you no children of your own?
And are you not aware
    you came as fugitive with not too many friends?"
    Such reflections made me realize
    I have been out of my mind, hysterical.
Now I thank you.
Now I am convinced
    that in securing us this benefit
    you are the wise one, *I* the fool:

I that should have been your ally
  and encouraged you.
Yes, I should have been at hand to help,
  decked the bed, dressed the bride—
  and been glad to do it.
But we women . . .
  well, we are what we are. Let's leave it at that.
Do not copy us in our perverseness
  or try to get your own back, giving tit for tat.
I ask your pardon
I admit to being wrong.
I've thought better of it now.

[*With an upsurge of sham joy*]

Children, children, come out here out of the house.

[*The*.TWO BOYS *appear with their* TUTOR]

Come, greet your father, hug him, join with me
  in loving, not resenting him.
Your mother's rancor is over.
There's peace between us: the fighting's done.
Come, take his hand.

[*As the children run into their father's arms*]

O God, what a presentiment!
What an image looming in the dark!
JASON: My sons, my sons,
  if only you could go on living, go on loving,
  with your arms stretched out like that forever.
MEDEA: [*choking*] It breaks my heart.
  I am far too prone to tears, too full of tears . . .
  it is the sudden ending of my quarrel with your father
  which makes them flow.
A sight too touching . . . it overflows.
LEADER: My eyes, too, are stinging.
If this could only be the worst that is to come.
JASON: [*gently releasing the* BOYS] I praise you now, Medea,
  and I did not blame you even then.

It is natural for a woman to be enraged
    when her husband goes off making second marriages.
But now
    you are in a better frame of mind—
    even if it took a little time.
You realize the good points of this plan.
The decision is a level-headed woman's.

    [*Turning to the children*]

As for you, my boys,
    your father has been far from idle
    and, heaven willing, has made good settlements for *you*.
In time I shouldn't wonder
    if you were not first citizens in Corinth,
    along with your newborn brothers.

    [*Laying his hands on their shoulders*]

Grow up now fine fellows.
Your father and a kindly providence
    have the rest in hand.
How I look towards the time
    when you will be two strapping grown young men,
    trampling down my enemies.

    [MEDEA *has averted her head and is sobbing. Her emotion,
    though genuine, is being used to further the next move*]

But, Medea, what is this:
    these dewy eyes, these tears;
    your white face turned away
    as if my words struck pain not joy?
MEDEA: It is nothing.
    I was just thinking of our sons.
JASON: Well, be of good heart now:
    I shall see them through.
MEDEA: I shall do my best.
    It isn't that I don't believe you . . .
    but you know how women weep.
JASON: I know, but don't be sad for them . . . Why should you?

MEDEA: [*watching the tender look on* JASON's *face*]
    I am their mother and when you prayed just now
    for a fulfilled life for them, your sons,
    a sudden sadness whispered: "Will this be?"

    [MEDEA *breaks off and shifts into a businesslike mode*]

But to get back to what I want to ask you:
    one part has been said and I want to talk to you
    about the rest.
Since the king has set his mind
    on sending me away from Corinth,
    and since I've come to recognize that this is best
    (for I'd only be an obstacle to you
    living with the royal family here,
    who think I'm a menace to their house),
    I shall take myself away, go into exile;
    but the children, please, I should like *them*
    to grow up under your own hand.
Persuade Creon to let them stay.
JASON: [*taken off his guard, but flattered*]
    I—I am not certain that I can:
    it'll take a little doing.
MEDEA: But you could ask your wife to beg her father
    to let the two boys stay.
JASON: [*reflecting*] Why not? I think I can get her to agree.
MEDEA: Of course you can . . .
    if she's the least bit like any woman.
And here *I* can play a useful part.
I shall send her a present
    more ravishingly beautiful, believe me,
    than anything this age has seen:
    a gown of gossamer and a diadem of beaten gold.
These the boys shall carry to her.
Let one of my maids go and fetch them.

    [*She claps her hands and a* MAID *appears*]

Go quickly and bring the gorgeous presents here.

    [*The* MAID *hurries into the house.* MEDEA *turns to* JASON]

What a double delight!
What a shower of happiness for her
    to have you for a hero husband
    and now these treasures that were handed down
    by my father's father—Helios, the glorious Sun.

[*The* MAID *comes back with a casket.* MEDEA *turns to the* BOYS]

Boys, take hold of this wedding gift.
Carry it to the happy princess-bride.
Place it in her hands.
It's not the kind of present she'll despise.
JASON: [*as the* BOYS *step forward*]
    You foolish woman—why empty your hands?
Do you think a royal wardrobe is in want,
    or a palace short of gold?
Keep these things. Don't give them up.
If my wife values me at all,
    my mere wish will have more weight than *things*,
    I'm sure of that.
MEDEA: [*with desperate insistence*] Do not deny me.
Even the gods, they say, succumb to gifts.
Gold is stronger than ten thousand words.
She is lucky, *she* is blessed, *she* increases.
This banishment I would barter for my babies
    not just with gold but with my life.

[*Forcing the casket into the* BOYS' *hands*]

Go, my sons, into the halls of wealth:
    down on your knees and beg her
    —this new wife of your father's and my mistress—
    to let you stay in Corinth.
Most important of all,
    see that she takes the precious things into her own hands.

[*Packing them off*]

Quick now, go. Success be yours.
Come and tell me the good news.
Your mother waits to hear it with her own ears.

[*The* BOYS *leave with their* TUTOR, *followed by* JASON]

FOURTH CHORAL ODE

[*The women of the* CHORUS *see the multimurders as imminent.
Woe to the victims! Woe to the murderess!*]

STROPHE I

Now has the last hope gone of the children living:
Gone and forever, they walk already to murder.
The bride is taking the golden diadem,
   Is taking the poison and doom.
Over her yellow hair her hands are fitting
   The decorated dying.

ANTISTROPHE I

The gorgeousness of the gossamer gown will win,
And the beaten gold of the diadem embrace her.
The bride is decked and ready to meet the dead.
   The trap is lethally set.
Doomed miserable woman, doomed to fall in,
   Ineluctably caught by Fate.

STROPHE II

And you who are groomed for a murder,
   Son-in-law of a king,
   Jason unsuspecting,
Are to bring on your sons a demise, and a death
   On your bride of a hideous kind.
   Unhappy man, how far
     You have fallen.

ANTISTROPHE II

And you the unenviable mother,
   How I weep for your pain,
   You killer of children for
A vengeance of love that is gone, betrayed
   By your man for another
   Bride whom he sleeps beside
     In his wrong.

FIFTH EPISODE

[*The* TUTOR *hurries in from the palace with the two* BOYS,
breathless with excitement]

TUTOR: My lady, your boys—they won't be banished.
  And the princess, the bride, with her own hands,
  she took your presents, oh, so gladly.
Now the children's danger is done.

  [*Baffled by* MEDEA*'s grim response*]

Well I never! Isn't this good news?
What transfixes you?

  [*From* MEDEA *a muffled cry of pain*]

What I hear is out of tune with what I say.
I thought I brought good news.
What kind of news, I wonder, have I brought?
MEDEA: What you have brought you have brought.
  The fault is not with you.
TUTOR: Why, my lady, these shuttered eyes,
  these tears falling?
MEDEA: I am pressed, old man, hard pressed . . .
  the gods and my own evil counsels.
TUTOR: Courage! One day your sons will bring you home.
MEDEA: [*in a kind of trance*]
  Home? First I must send others there—miserable woman!
TUTOR: You are not the only mother to be severed from her sons.
We have to bear our own humanity—humanely.
MEDEA: [*pressing his hand*] I shall try . . . Now go inside
  and see to what the children need today.

  [*Exit* TUTOR, *worried*]

MEDEA: [*throwing out her arms towards the two* BOYS]
  My sons, my sons,
  you will have a city and a home
  far from me.
I shall be left lonely,
  and you will live without your mother always,

for I must go in exile to another land,
never to have my joy in you
or see your bright young progress;
never deck your brides, your marriage beds,
or light you radiant to your wedding day.

[*The* BOYS *are now in her arms*]

Oh what a blight my ruthlessness has been!
How pointless, my little ones,
    my nursing all your growing up!
How pointless all the cares endured:
    the wearying solicitudes,
    the sharp agony of giving you your lives.
And now how miserably have dwindled
    my dreams for you:
    the comfort of your love when I am old,
    your dear hands dressing me when I am dead:
    a passing every person might desire.
Such sweet fancy vanishes.
Wrenched from you I shall drag out my life alone.

[*She cups their faces in her hands in turn*]

Your sweet eyes shall miss forever
    your poor mother's face—
    your life and hers utterly apart.
Oh my children,
    do your eyes now stare their fill,
and your last smiles linger to the last?

[*She turns to the* CHORUS, *panting*]

O-h! What shall I do?
My heart dissolves
    when I gaze into their bright irises . . .
No, I cannot do it.
Goodbye to my determination.
I shall take my boys away with me.
Why hurt *them* in trying to hurt their father?
I'll only hurt myself twice over.

No, I cannot. Goodbye to my decisions.

[*She pauses, then breaks away from the* BOYS]

What! What undermines me now?
Do I really mean to let my enemies go?
To laugh at me?
Steel yourself, Medea:
  away with this cowardice, these arguments that melt.

[*Almost pushing the* BOYS]

Go, boys, into the house.

[*She turns to the* CHORUS *grimly*]

Those whose conscience will not let them stay
  must look to it and avoid my sacrifice.
This hand of mine shall never falter.

[*Another spasm of emotion grips her and she runs to the* BOYS
as they reach the door]

No, no! Stop me my heart.
We must not do this thing.
Let them go, you stricken woman. Spare your sons.
Let them live with you in Athens: they will be your joy.

[*Throwing her arms around them*]

Ah! Not by all the haunting spirits of the underworld
  shall I leave my children to the mercy of my enemies.

[*With a stab of realization*]

But . . . they have to . . . die.*
The whole thing is settled anyway.
Yes, the diadem is on her head . . .
  the royal bride at this moment rots,

---

*With many editors, I omit lines 1062 and 1063 as a melodramatic interpola-
tion: ". . . and since they must, let it be by the hands of her who gave them life."
Line numbers refer to the Greek text in the Loeb Classical edition.

dying in the gown—I know it.

[*She turns to the* CHORUS *as if to explain her second impulsive embrace*]

You see, the path I have to tread
    is unutterably sad,
    but the one I set these children on is sadder still.
Now to say . . . goodbye to them.

[*She seizes their hands*]

Give me your right hands to kiss,
    each of you, my little ones—
    give them to your mother.

[*Covering their hands, their faces, their bodies, in kisses*]

How adorable—this hand—and this . . .
These lips—how very much adored!
And this face and form of childhood's ingenuous nobility.
How I bless you both . . . not here . . . beyond.
Every blessing here your father has despoiled.
So sweet . . . the mere touch of you . . .
    the bloom of children's skin so soft . . .
    their breath—a perfect balm.

[*Gently releasing them, then almost savagely pushing them towards the house and turning her back*]

Go, go . . . I cannot look at you.
I am in agony and lost.

[*The two* BOYS, *weeping, hurry into the house*]

The evil that I do, I understand full well.
    But a passion drives me greater than my will.
    Passion is the curse of man: it wreaks the greatest ill.

FIFTH CHORAL ODE

[*If there can be a feminist philosophy of parenthood, is its
honest judgment likely to be that children are worth it after
all?*]

So often before
    Have I gone towards concepts far too tenuous
    And come upon questions far too deep
    For the race of woman to try to unravel.
    Nevertheless even we women
    Have a muse of our own (though alas not all)
    That ushers us into the world of wisdom.
    Perhaps you might find it one in a thousand:
    Women with insight in tune with the Muses.
    This makes me able now to proclaim:
    That mortals without the mission of parent
    Are happier than begetters of offspring.
    The childless have no way of telling
    Whether they miss a curse or a blessing.
    Nonetheless, the childless person
    Certainly misses many a burden.
    But those with children sweetly growing
    In their homes are worn with worrying:
    How to make sure they are properly nourished,
    How to leave them a livelihood.
    And then after all to be in the dark—
    Were all the worries worth it or not?
    Were they a worthy or worthless lot?
But now let me tell
    Of the worst and saddest sorrow of all
    —For all mankind. Suppose they've grown,
    Reached their teenhood honest and fine;
    Then what if a fate like Death the cruel
    Carries them downward body and soul?
    What is the use of it after all
    (On top of all those other ones)
    That the gods let loose this grief as well . . .
    Just for the joy of having sons?

SIXTH EPISODE

[MEDEA *leaps up from her seat as she sees a man approaching.
He staggers breathlessly before them*]

MEDEA: Somebody with news at last, my friends:
  news I've been waiting for from the palace.
Now I can make him out: one of Jason's men,
  panting with haste, and surely with desperate news.

[*The* MESSENGER, *an official of the bride's house, bursts in,
hardly able to get his words out*]

MESSENGER: Run, Medea, run!
  What you have done . . . is . . . too unthinkable . . .
  too awful . . . Seize whatever means you can . . .
  pinnacle or chariot . . . Escape!
MEDEA: Run? Escape? Is it then so vital?
MESSENGER: Dead . . . They are this minute dead . . .
  the princess royal with her father—
  and through your poisons.
MEDEA: [*with a whoop of glee*] Oh what a pretty word you bring!
  My benefactor and my friend forever!
MESSENGER: [*recoiling*] What are you saying, madam?
  Are you in your right mind, not unhinged?
A king's home a charnel house—and you rejoice?
Are you not afraid?
MEDEA: I have my answers too,
  so take your time, my friend, and tell me how they died.
An appalling death would give me double joy.
MESSENGER: [*supporting himself against a pillar*]
  We were so pleased to see your brace of boys
  come hand in hand to the bride's house with their father:
  for your ordeal had upset us servants greatly.
The rumor went racing through the house
  that all was well again between your husband and yourself.
Some of us kissed the children's hands,
  kissed their golden tops;
  and I in my enthusiasm even followed them to the women's
                                                        wing.

There the mistress
   —I mean the one we have to honor now—
   had eyes so taken up with Jason
   she did not at first even see the two boys hand in hand.
But when she did,
   a veil of scorn dropped over her eyes,
   she turned her lovely face away,
   bristling at your sons' intrusion.
Your husband then began to woo her
   from her petulance and girlish tantrums, saying:
"You must not hate your friends.
Stop being hurt and turn your head around.
Consider yours your husband's loved ones.
Come, won't you take their gifts
   and beseech your father
   to let these boys off banishment—just for me?"

   [*Pauses and sits down hopelessly on a step*]

When she saw how exquisite the presents were,
   far from holding out on him
   there was nothing she withheld,
   but gave in completely to her groom.
Hardly had your husband and your children left the house
   when she took the gorgeous robe and put it on,
   and placed the golden circlet on her curls,
   arranging the ringlets in the brightness of a mirror
   and smiling at her own dead image there.
Then rising from her stool
   she minced off through the halls
   on dainty milk-white toes,
   wildly pleased with what she had received;
   over and over again running her eyes
   down the clear sweep to the heels.
But all at once
   a hideous spectacle took place.
Her color changed. She tottered back;
   shuddered in every limb; was able just in time
   to fall into a chair and not upon the floor.
An old woman there, attending her,

thinking that the fierce possession of Pan
or some other power was on her,
broke into a chant of wonder,
then saw the white froth spuming at her lips,
her eyeballs bulging all askew,
her skin quite leached of blood,
and changed her chanting to a yelp,
a wail of horror.
A maid went dashing to her father's halls,
another went to tell the fresh-wed groom
what was happening to his bride.
The whole place rang with footsteps running.
It took no longer than a sprinter takes
to go the hundred yards
before the poor girl lay unconscious with her eyelids shut.
Then suddenly she rallied
and gave a curdling shriek,
fighting off a double nightmare.
The golden diadem that clasped her temples
burst into a voracious and uncanny flow of fire,
while the robe of gossamer your children gave her
began to eat her tender flesh away.
Streaming with flame,
she leapt up from her seat and fled,
tossing her mane of hair from side to side
in a frantic bid to shake the diadem off.
But its grip was adamant: the golden circlet held.
The more she tossed, the more the fire flowed,
till overwhelmed with pain she sank down to the floor:
unrecognizable to all except her father—
her calm regard all twisted,
her sweet symmetry all shattered;
and from the crown of her head in molten clots
fire and blood dripped down together.
The flesh curdled off her bones
like the teardrops congealing out of pines,
inexplicably dissolved by those ravening venoms.
It was curious and horrible to see.
No one dared to touch her body:

the warning was too obvious.
But her father, unaware, poor man,
   rushed headlong through the room,
   flung himself lamenting on the body,
   hugged and kissed it, sobbing out:
"My stricken darling, what evil power
   has done this to you;
   has so brutally destroyed you
   and left me like some ancient tombstone, derelict?
O you gods! . . . let me die with you, my daughter."
But . . . but when he ceased from these outpourings,
   these melancholy sobs, and tried to lift
   his aged carcass up, he found himself stuck fast,
   clamped to the flimsy robe
   like ivy to a laurel bole.
A ghastly wrestling match then ensued.
He would try to raise a knee.
She would drag it back;
   and when he took to force, his own decrepit flesh
   pulled off from the bone.
At last, exhausted,
   pathetically unable to lift himself above the shambles,
   he gave his spirit up.
There they lie, corpse by corpse,
   father and young daughter . . .
   fit objects for our tears.

[*He rises, swaying*]

To you, Medea . . . from me . . .
   there are no words to say.
Retribution? You yourself will know the best escape . . .
   though in my esteem—and not just from today—
   the whole of life is shadow and I would even say:
   the people who know best or seem to know
   —the subtlest professors—
   are the very ones that pay the dearest price.

[*Flinging his cloak about him*]

A happy human being? Ha, there's no such thing.
More prosperity, more success in one maybe,
    but happier? Never.

[MESSENGER *leaves*]

LEADER: Justice personified this day
    has brought on Jason's head—oh, we have seen it!—
    the richest retribution.
But it is you we weep for,
    poor blighted child of Creon:
    walking through the gates of death
    because you married Jason.
MEDEA: [*in clear cold tones*]
    Now, friends, to complete this mission with dispatch:
    to slay my children and hurry from this land.
I must not dawdle and betray my sons
    to much more savage hands than mine to kill.
There's no way out. They have to die;
    and since they must, let me be the one to cut them down,
    who gave them life.

[*She walks to the door, almost like a sleepwalker, talking to herself*]

Yes, heart, be steel. Why vacillate?
The act is . . . necessary . . . as it is cruel and hard.
Come, reluctant hand,
    grip the sword—grip it, Medea:
    cross your borderline of lifelong pain.
Away this flinching!
Away this longing!
Consign to oblivion the love you have for them,
    the children of your flesh.
Even when you kill them they are dear . . .
Oh, my sons! . . . I am in despair, despair.

[MEDEA, *with the* NURSE *mutely following and in tears, passes into the house*]

SIXTH CHORAL ODE

[*The women of the* CHORUS *pray desperately for something to stop the imminent murders*]

STROPHE

Come, Earth, come sunshafts of the Sun,
Behold this woman and withhold her
From her laying scarlet fingers
On the children of her blood.
Gold of your gold are they begotten.
Heinous it is to spill the holy
Ichor in the blood of mortals.
Curb her, stop her, godborn Light, oh
Keep this house from murder! Keep it
Never haunted by the Furies.

ANTISTROPHE

Were those birthpangs wasted bearing?
Children's birthpangs wasted birth?
You, my lady, after sailing
Safe between the dark blue clashing
Gorges, will you clutch a rankling
Hatred to your heart, a loathsome
Rage for murder and revenge?
Those who spill the blood of family
Stain themselves with heaven's anger,
Haunt their homes with doom forever.

SEVENTH EPISODE AND DENOUEMENT

[*Cries are heard from inside the house*]

FIRST WOMAN: A shout—listen—a shout from the boys.
FIRST BOY: O-oh! What can we do? . . . Our mother is on us.
SECOND BOY: Brother, brother! . . . We're going to be killed.
SECOND WOMAN: That murderous relentless woman!
THIRD WOMAN: Shall we break in? Snatch them from death?
FIRST BOY: Yes, by heaven! . . . Save us . . . Help!

SECOND BOY: We're trapped, cornered . . . now . . . by her sword.

[*As the women of the* CHORUS *beat on the barred doors, behind which they hear groans and cries, they severally address* MEDEA. *Then they see the trickle of blood oozing from under the doors*]

FIRST WOMAN: Woman of stone, heart of iron,
　　Disconsolate woman, ready to kill
　　Your seed with your hands, the hands that tilled.
SECOND WOMAN: One other only, one have I known
　　Murderously handle the fruit of her womb:
　　Ino the maniac, god-driven one.
THIRD WOMAN: Whom the wife of Zeus drove out to roam—
　　Desperate woman goaded to slaughter
　　the sons of her flesh, clean against nature.
FOURTH WOMAN: She pitched from the precipice into the sea,
　　Fell where her foot fell into the ocean,
　　Dashing two infants to death with her own.
　　What deadlier thing is left to be known?
FIRST WOMAN: Women, O women, in love and in pangs,
　　What ruin you have brought on human beings!

[JASON, *breathless, his face twisted with hatred, bursts in with a troop of servants*]

JASON: You women standing here outside this house,
　　is that she-ravager still at home
　　or has she got away?

[*He waits for a reply, but the women cower before the door*]

In the bowels of the earth that woman will have to hide,
　　or wing into the highest alcoves of the sky,
　　if ever she escapes the vengeance of this royal house.
Does she imagine she can kill
　　a princess and a country's king
　　and vanish with impunity?

[*He strides towards the door*]

But it is my sons, not her, I fear for.
She, she shall have done to her what she has done.
I have come to save my children's lives
    from some enormous retribution by the family of the dead
    to answer the enormities their mother did.
LEADER: Jason, you poor hopeful man,
    you still don't know the full supplement to your sorrows,
    or you would not say what you have said.
JASON: What? Does she mean to kill me too?
LEADER: Your sons are dead, and by their mother's hand.
JASON: [*reeling*] What—did—you—say?
    Oh, woman, you've just killed me.

[*As the women of the* CHORUS *form an avenue to the door,*
JASON *sees the blood trickling down the steps*]

LEADER: Yes, your children . . .
    you cannot think of them as living.
JASON: [*limply*] Where did she kill them—
    here outside or in the house?
LEADER: Force the doors
    and you will see your children in their blood.
JASON: [*drawing his sword in a frenzy*] Servants, on the double,
    break these bolts, force the hinges.
Let me look on the double horror:
    the dead and the victim soon to die.

[*As* JASON *and his attendants batter the door, a rumbling
sound is heard and out of a cloud above the house* MEDEA
*appears in a chariot drawn by winged dragons. By her side
are the two dead* BOYS]

MEDEA: [*in triumphant disdain*] Why this battering, this beating
                                              at doors?
Are you looking for their bodies
    and for me that did this thing?
Save yourself the trouble.
If there's anything you want, then ask.
But me you shall not lay a hand upon.
This chariot my father's father the Sun

gave me to save me from my enemies.
JASON: Miserable, mephitic woman,
   beyond abhorrence,
   by me, the gods, the rest of men—
   you could put your own sons to the sword,
   the sons you bore,
   and kill me too with childlessness . . .
   yet still look upon the sun and earth
   after such enormity . . . may you be damned!
At last I understand
   what I never understood before
   when I took you from your barbarian home to live in Greece:
   the sheer wickedness of you—
   the treachery to your father and the land that reared you.
You are possessed
   and the gods have released the fiend in you on *me*;
   on your own brother too, cut down in his home*
   before you came aboard the good ship *Argo*.
Your evil work already had begun
   when you married me, bore my sons,
   whom now you've butchered through jealousy of love.
No woman in the whole of Hellas
   would have dared so much; yet you were the one I married
   instead of a girl from Greece.
Oh, I married a lioness all right—not a woman.
I yoked myself to a hater and destroyer,
   to a viciousness more fierce than any Tuscan Scylla.

[*Turning away from the door in a gesture of hopelessness*]

But why go on?
Ten thousand accusations would not make you wince.
You are shameless to the core—you, you
   bloodstained ogress, child-killer . . . Hell take you.
Leave me to mourn my destiny of pain:
   my fresh young wedding without joy,
   my sons begot and reared and lost—

---

*Euripides here follows the alternative story about her brother Absyrtus, who in the other version she kills on board the *Argo*.

never to be seen again.

MEDEA: [*with acid imperiousness from her chariot*]
How tediously I could rebut you point by point!
Zeus the Father knows
exactly what you got from me and how you then behaved.
I refused to let you or your royal princess
set our wedded life aside and make me cheap
so that you could live in bliss;
or let that match-arranger, Creon,
dismiss me from the land without a fight.
So call me a lioness, if you like,
or a Scylla haunting the Tyrrhenian shore,
I have done what I ought:
wounded you to the very core.

JASON: [*wheeling around to face her*]
You are in agony too.
You share my broken life.

MEDEA: It is worth the suffering since you cannot sneer.

JASON: Poor children, what a monster fate gave you for a
mother!

MEDEA: Poor sons, what a disaster your selfish father was!

JASON: It was not *his* right hand that struck them down.

MEDEA: No, it was his pride and lust for his new mate.

JASON: You think it right to murder just for a thwarted bed?

MEDEA: And do you think that a thwarted bed is trifling to a
woman?

JASON: To a modest woman, yes, but you are sunk in vice.

MEDEA: [*pointing to the two dead* BOYS]
See, they are no more. I've stung you to the heart.

JASON: They'll live, I think, in your tormented brain.

MEDEA: The gods know well who began this whole calamity.

JASON: Yes, the gods know well your pernicious soul.

MEDEA: Hate away! I scorn the wormwood from your lips.

JASON: As I do yours; so let us be rid of one another.

MEDEA: Rid, indeed, but how? That's also what I crave.

JASON: Let me have the boys—to mourn and bury them.

MEDEA: Never!
My own hands shall bury them, they shall be carried
to the shrine of Hera on the Cape,

where no enemy shall ever do them harm
or violate their sepulcher.
Here in Corinth, the land of Sisyphus,
I shall inaugurate a solemn festival
with rites in perpetuity to exorcise this murder.
As to me, I shall go to Athens, land of Erechtheus,
to live with Aegeus, Pandion's son;
you to a paltry death that fits you well:
your skull smashed by a fragment of the *Argo*'s hull—
ironic ending to the saga of your new young love.

THE EXODOS

[*As the women of the* CHORUS *begin to form for the Exodos march, the meter changes from the iambs of the dialogue to anapests and dactyls.* JASON *strides into the center of the arena*]

JASON: Murder is punished and you'll be destroyed
By the avenging phantoms of your children.
MEDEA: What power or divine one is ready to hear you:
perjurer, liar, traitorous guest.
JASON: Vile, vile murderess of little ones!
MEDEA: Go to the palace and bury your bride.
JASON: Indeed I go—bereft of two sons.
MEDEA: Your tears come too soon, wait till you're old.
JASON: Oh my children—sweetest, beloved!
MEDEA: Yes, to their mother—not to you.
JASON: And so she slew them.
MEDEA: To strike at your heart.
JASON: You did! You did! . . . How I long to kiss
The lips of my little ones—I the accursed.
MEDEA: Now you are longing, now you call;
You utterly turned from them before.
JASON: For the love of the gods, allow me this
To stroke my children's tender skin.
MEDEA: No, you shall not. You waste your words.

[MEDEA*'s chariot moves out of sight, and* JASON *flings out his arms in a gesture of despair*]

JASON: Zeus, do you see how I'm at bay,
  Brought down to ruin by this horrible woman:
  Lioness and slayer of children.
  So I mourn and call on the gods as I may.
  I call on the powers above to attest
  How she slew my children and then wouldn't let
  Me fondle their bodies with my hands
  And give them burial. Oh, that they'd never
  Been born to me that I should ever
  Have lived to see them destroyed by her.

[JASON *walks slowly out of the arena as the* CHORUS *moves
towards the exit*]

E N V O I

CHORUS: Wide is the range of Zeus on Olympus.
  Wide the surprise the gods can bring:
  What was expected is never effected,
  What was not, finds a way opened up.
So ended this terrible thing.

THE BACCHAE

⤞⤝

BAKXAI

For Pat Gilbert-Read

The Bacchae or *Bacchants* is one of the last plays Euripides wrote. He wrote it with two others away from Athens at the court of King Archelaus of Macedon, where he was an honored guest from 408 B.C. till his death in 406.

In the wild terrain of Macedonia new to him, and away from his nagging critics in Athens, Euripides seems to have recaptured the artistic zest of his younger days, evincing a renewal of inspiration and his sense of tragedy. It is significant that in this renascence of vigor the experienced playwright, now almost seventy-four years of age (with some eighty-six plays behind him), should have cast *The Bacchae* in the primitive form of the choral lyric, in which the whole opening of the play is carried by the chorus.

Like all Greek drama, *The Bacchae* is a richly layered construction in which almost every aspect of the human condition is addressed. Most Greek plays take well-known myths as their starting point—myth always having some foundation in reality. *The Bacchae*, on that level, is about the bringing of the grape to Europe from the East. Curiously, Europe has no wild, no indigenous grape; unlike North America, where the wild vine festoons the woods and forests.

On that level one might say the play is a celebration, but there is much more to it than that. *The Bacchae* asks the question: is there an equation between faith and reason, religion and fact, freedom of spirit and law-and-order?

Euripides' conclusion seems to be that too much law-and-order leads to a social tyranny which we would call fascism, too much freedom of spirit to chaos, too much religion to fanaticism.

In the play, the young King Pentheus, who is the same age as Dionysus (Bacchus), believes that law-and-order is the sole end of the state. For him freedom of spirit is tantamount to anarchy. So he goes out to suppress the new cult coming from the Orient promoting Dionysus. In the process he becomes a fanatic, and as fanaticism does with life, so it does with him—tears him to pieces.

Dionysus tries to save him: make him see that there are many levels to life and that law-and-order is only one of them—Dionysus himself being both a constructive and destructive force, like a law of nature, against which it is perilous to hurl oneself.

The psychology of the two young protagonists is brilliantly contrasted and could not be more tellingly manifested by any psychiatrist of today.

Every line of this horror story of disconcerting beauty is both exquisite and sinister and leads inexorably, if not to fulfillment, then to death and worse: to death through mutilation—mutilation by one's nearest and dearest.

The Bacchae was probably first presented at the court of King Archelaus. It was certainly produced in Athens in 405, the year after Euripides' death, and directed by his son. On that occasion it was awarded first prize.

CHARACTERS

DIONYSUS, the god of nature, wine, mysticism, ecstasy, also called Bacchus, Evius, Bromius

CHORUS of women from Asia who have followed Dionysus as his devotees

TIRESIAS, the old blind seer of Thebes

CADMUS, founder and former king of Thebes

PENTHEUS, grandson of Cadmus and king of Thebes

SOLDIER, palace guard of Pentheus

HERDSMAN from Mount Cithaeron

AGAVE, mother of Pentheus and daughter of Cadmus

MESSENGER, palace official

GUARDS of Pentheus

WOMEN, attendants of Agave

SMALL CROWD of Thebans

TIME AND SETTING

The past: It is the Heroic Age, many hundreds of years before the time of Euripides. Semele, the daughter of Cadmus, during a love affair with Zeus had exacted from him the promise to grant her whatever she wished and was persuaded by the jealous Hera (disguised as Semele's nurse) to ask her lover to come to her as he came to Hera, in all his glory. Reluctantly, Zeus complied. The mortal frame of Semele could not support so much power and she was consumed by lightning, giving birth in her death throe to a six-months child by Zeus, who to save him from Hera stitched the infant into his thigh and let him be born in due time as the god Dionysus.

The present: It is some twenty years later. The action takes place on the Acropolis of Thebes, outside the palace of Pentheus. Nearby, fenced off by a trellis of luxuriant grapevines, is the tomb of Semele, from which a wisp of smoke still curls. The young king, Pentheus, new in his reign and apparently full of righteous intentions (though raw in self-knowledge), is determined to stamp out the worship of the young god Dionysus (his cousin), who has just returned to Greece from the East, bringing with him the cult of the vine.

Dionysus, disguised as a man and incognito even to his troupe of women from Asia, walks on. He wears a panther skin loosely hanging from one shoulder, and a fillet binds his long fair ringlets. In his hands he holds the sacred thyrsus (an ivy-entwined staff sometimes surrounded with a pine cone and carried by Bacchanalian revelers). He steps lightly and firmly. On his lips plays an enigmatic and slightly ironic smile.

PROLOGUE

DIONYSUS: So, the son of Zeus is back in Thebes:
   I, Dionysus, son of Semele—daughter of Cadmus—
   who was struck from my mother in a lightning stroke.
I am changed, of course, a god made man,
   and now I approach the rivulets of Dirce,
   the waters of Ismenus.
There by the palace is my mother's monument,
   my poor mother blasted in a bolt of light.
Look, those ruins, her house, smoking still,
   alive with a most unnatural flame,
   Hera's present to my mother:

it curls with undying insolence.
But praised be Cadmus,
   who made this untrodden ground
   a sanctuary to his daughter.
And I, I festooned it with green,
   clustered it with vine.

[*He steps forward majestically, making a grand sweep*]

I come from Lydia,
   its territories teeming with gold;
   and from rich Phrygia.
I am all-conqueror
   in the sun-beaten steppes of Persia,
   the walled cities of Bactria,
   the wintry land of Media,
   and in Arabia Felix—land of the blest.

All Asia is mine,
   and along the fringes of the sea,
   the pinnacled glory of all those mingled cities
   of Greeks and many races.
But in the land of Hellas
   this city Thebes is the first place I have visited.
Elsewhere, everywhere, I have established
   my sacraments and dances,
   to make my godhead manifest to mortals.

Yes, here in Hellas, Thebes
   is the first city that I fill
   with the transports of ecstatic women.
I've put their bodies into fawn skins,
   thrust the aggressive thyrsus in their hands—
   my ivy-entwined wand.

You see, they should have known—known better—
   they at least, my mother's sisters,
   who said that I, Dionysus, was no son of Zeus;
   that Semele simply loved a mortal
   and then palmed off on the Almighty

(the idea was Cadmus')
her unwed motherhood.
"Don't we know," they cried,
    "she lied about her lover and that is why
    great Zeus has struck her down."

Aha! these sisters, the very same,
    I've driven from their wits and from their homes:
    out to the mountains and out of their minds.
I've dressed them up as bacchanals
    in my own orgiastic uniform;
    and all the women of Thebes,
    every female in this city,
    I've started on a wild stampede from home
    to join the Cadmus daughters.
There they sit among the rocks,
    under the silvery pines—
    a congregation in the open.

[*Grimly*]

Like it or not, this city has to learn
    what it is to go through true conversion
    to the rites of Bacchus.
So do I defend my mother's cause,
    making mortal man endorse the fact I *am* a god
    and born to her of Zeus.
You know that Cadmus makes his grandson Pentheus king,
    with all the kingly perquisites;
    that Pentheus opens war on deity in me,
    wards me off his sacrifice,
    cuts me from his prayers.
Very well,
    I'll show myself to him and all of Thebes
    a god indeed.
And when everything has happened as I wish,
    I'll remove myself to another land
    and there reveal myself.
If the town of Thebes becomes inflamed
    and tries to oust my Maenads from the mountains,

I shall go out there myself
and lead my Bacchants in the battle.
That is why I'm in this mortal form,
changed into the semblance of a human being.

[*At the sound of flute and timbrels and women chanting,*
DIONYSUS, *without revealing himself, exclaims in an enthusi-*
astic aside]

Onwards! My women of Tmolus, you bulwark of Lydia,
you, my sisterhood of worshipers
whom I led out from foreign lands to be my company
in rest and march . . .
Raise up the native music of your home,
the timbrels great mother Rhea and I invented.
Surround the palace of Pentheus, the king.
Clash out the sound,
and turn this city out to see.

[*Looking towards the mountains*]

I must hasten to the dells of Cithaeron
where the Bacchants are and join them in their dances there.

[DIONYSUS *slips away as the* CHORUS *of women from Asia*
moves into sight, chanting. They are led by a flute player.
Some of them have timbrels, some castanets]

PARADOS OR ENTRY SONG

[*In a vehement dithyrambic hymn to* DIONYSUS, *the* CHORUS
celebrates his birth, his orgiastic rituals of music and dance
on the mountains, and the enthusiasm of his devotees]

CHORUS: *1st voice:* From the purlieus of Asia I come
Deserting Tmolus the holy.
For the roaring god I toil
In an easy exquisite task:
A paean in praise of the god
Great Dionysus.

2nd voice: Is anyone in the street?
   Is anyone at home?
   Let him go into holy retreat:
   Silence on every lip
   While I sing in the old, old way
   Glory to Bacchus.
3rd voice: Happy the man whom the gods
   Love, and whose secrets he knows:
   Their rubrics, his life is designed
   For sacred dances and joy . . .
   In the mountains the wild delight
   Of Bacchus in his soul.
   His ritual he undergoes:
   Cybele's orgies, great Mother's,
   He shakes the thyrsus on high,
   With ivy he crowns his brow
   For great Dionysus.
4th voice: On, Bacchanalians, on!
   Bring Bromius home, the god
   Dionysus—son of the god—
   From foreign Phrygian hills.
   Bring Bacchus to the squares,
   The open squares of Hellas
   Spacious for the dance.
5th voice: Him whom his mother when gravid
   In bitter travail brought forth;
   Him whom his mother miscarried
   In a blast of light from Zeus,
   He in that very chamber
   Wherein her life was shattered
   Was taken by Zeus and sheltered
   Deep within his thigh:
   Stitched with golden brackets,
   Secreted from Hera.
6th voice: He when the Fates had shaped him
   A perfect baby there
   His father then unfolded:
   An ox-horned crescent god
   Swaddled in the twisting
   Serpents. That is why

The Maenads catch wild snakes and
Twist them in their hair.

STROPHE

O Thebes, Semele's nurse
Put ivies round your turrets,
Break forth in green, oh break
With bryony—its brilliant
Berries. Deck yourself
A Bacchant with the branches
Of oak and fir. Put on
Skins of kid. Entassel
Your hems with silver fleece
Of goat; and with the fennel*
Join reverence to riot.
Soon the land will dance;
For whoso leads the revel
He is always Bacchus . . .
Will dance out to the mountains—
Mountains where the women
Waiting in their concourse
Have raged from loom and shuttle
To rave with Bacchus.

ANTISTROPHE

O Chamber of Curetes,
You holy haunts of Crete,
Who saw great Zeus's birthday,
In your caves the triple-
Crested Corybantes
Made the rounded timbrel
Tight with hide and beat its
Tense ecstatic jangle
Into the sweetened airs
Breathed by Phrygian flutes.
They gave it in the hand of
Mother Rhea to drum-beat

---

*_fennel:_ the thyrsus. Actually the thyrsus was undoubtedly a stalk not of fennel
but of the stronger hogweed or cow parsnip.

For shouting Bacchants raving.
The run-mad satyrs snatched it,
Joined it to the dances
Triennially when Bacchus
In his feasts rejoices.

EPODE

Full chorus: My love is in the mountains:
   Limp upon the ground he
   Sinks. The revel races.
   Vested in his fawn skin, he
   Hunts the goat and kills it . . .
   Ecstasy the raw
   Flesh . . . And to the mountains
   Of Phrygia, of Lydia
   He rushes. He is Bromius,
Evoë!*
   Leader of our dance.
   The ground there flows with milk and
   Flows with wine and flows with
   Honey from the bees.
   Fragrant as the Syrian
   Frankincense, the pine fumes
   From the torch our spellbound leader
   Holds high. Its ruby flames
   Flaring as he runs,
   Shooting as he dances.
   And while he cheers
   His checkered followers forward
   And shouts them to their feet,
His supple hair
   Is rampant on the breezes.
"Evoë!" he cries
   Loud among the Maenads . . .
   "On my Bacchantes! On!
   Chant to the glittering Tmolus
With its golden streams;

Evoë: a cry used by worshipers in either exultation or supplication.

Chant to Dionysus
    Through the clash reverberant of tambourines.
    Cry down glory with your Phrygian cries
    Upon the god of joy
While the holy
    Honey-throated flute
    Holily invents
    Its piping gaiety
    For my roaring troubadours
    Raving to the mountains—
    Oh, to the mountains!"

    Then the Bacchanalian girl
    Is full of happiness and gambols
    Lightfooted as a filly
    Round its mother in the pastures.

FIRST EPISODE

[*Enter* TIRESIAS, *the blind seer. He is dressed in a goatskin and his head is crowned with ivy. In spite of his age his manner is brisk, even excited. He knocks at the palace doors with his ivy-crested staff*]

TIRESIAS: Where is the porter?

[*A servant answers from within*]

Go call Cadmus from the house—
    that son of Agenor who came from Sidon
    and raised the pinnacles of this Theban town.
Will someone go and tell him Tiresias waits him.
He knows already what we plan to do, he and I . . .
    a man even older than me, and yet
    we dress the thyrsus up,
    put our fawn skins on—he he!—
    wind trailing ivies round our heads.

[CADMUS *comes out of the house. He too is ancient, garlanded*

*with ivy, and wearing a goatskin. He supports himself on a
luxuriantly crested thyrsus, and is spry but impatient*]

CADMUS: Good, my intelligent old friend,
   I knew it was you, even from the house—
   your wise old voice.

[*They embrace*]

I'm all ready, see,
   complete in Dionysiac trappings.
And why not?
He's my own daughter's child,
   and he's proved his divinity to mortals;
   so of course we've got to work to build him up.

[*Snapping his fingers and looking around*]

Well, where do we dance?
Where do we let our footsteps fall
   and waggle our decrepit grizzly heads?
Be my monitor, Tiresias,
   one antique to another, but you the expert . . .
I'll never tire night or day
   drumming my thyrsus on the ground.

[*Thumping his thyrsus on the ground*]

Oh how lovely to forget just how old we are!
TIRESIAS: [*taking his arm*] My feelings too. I'm young again.
   I too shall try to dance.

[*They execute a rickety jig together, but* CADMUS *soon tires,
panting*]

CADMUS: You don't think we should get a carriage
   to take us to the mountains?
TIRESIAS: No, no: that wouldn't show the same respect towards
                                          the god.
CADMUS: Well, shall one old man be nursemaid to another?

TIRESIAS: The god will show the way. We'll have no trouble.
CADMUS: Are we the only ones in town to dance to Bacchus?
TIRESIAS: The only ones, all right. The rest all wrong.
CADMUS: Then we're wasting time. Here, take my hand.
TIRESIAS: Fine! Hand in hand . . . Yours in mine.

[*They totter forward for a few steps, then* CADMUS *stops*]

CADMUS: I'm only a man, I don't belittle the divine.
TIRESIAS: No, *we* don't play at theologians with the gods.
    We stay close to the hallowed tenets of our fathers,
    old as time. Nothing can undo them ever.
I don't care how brilliant or abstruse the reasons are.

[*Fiddling with his fawn skin*]

No doubt people will say I've got no self-respect,
    dancing, binding up my head with ivy—at *my* age . . .
Well then, let them.
Where does the god assert that only the young must dance,
    or only the old?
He wishes to be worshiped by one and all,
    no discrimination.

CADMUS: [*watching the approach of a resolute young man*]
    Tiresias, you can't see,
    so let me be your see-er,* ha!
Pentheus is striding towards the palace,
    you know, Echion's son,
    to whom I've given over the ruling of this land.

[*Clicking his tongue*]

My, my, how upset he is!
What is he going to tell us now?

    [PENTHEUS *strides in, with guards behind him. Shod in jack-
    boots, wearing a short riding tunic, and carrying a hunting*

---

see-er: a play on words in the Greek. Cadmus jests that on this occasion he,
not Tiresias, is the seer.

*crop, he stalks into their presence with a downright no-
nonsense manner*]

PENTHEUS: I've come straight back from abroad,
    hurried home by rumors.
Something very strange is happening in this town.
They tell me our womenfolk have left their homes
    —in ecstasy if you please—
    and gone gadding to the mountains, the shady mountains,
    dancing honor on this brash new god:
    this—this Dionysus they've got hold of.
In the middle of each coterie of god-possessed
    . stands a bowl of wine—brimming.
Afterwards, they go sneaking off one by one
    to various nooks
    to lie down—with *men,*
    giving out they're priestesses—inspired, of course!
I warrant their devotion
    is more to Aphrodite than to Bacchus.
The ones I've rounded up, my police have handcuffed
    and safely clapped in jail.
The rest I mean to harry off the hills,
    including Ino and Agave, my own mother,
    and Autonoë, mother of Actaeon:
I'll snap them up in iron traps;
    put a stop to this immoral rollicking.

[*He begins to stride back and forth, not having even noticed*
CADMUS *and* TIRESIAS]

They say we have a visitor,
    a mysterious wizard-conjurer from Lydia:
    a fellow sporting scented goldilocks,
    with rosy wine-flushed cheeks
    and the spells of Aphrodite brimming in his eyes.
He passes nights and days with girls,
    dangling in front of them his mysteries of joy.
Let me once have him here inside my house,
    I'll soon stop him drumming with his thyrsus,
    tossing his mane of curls.

I'll separate his head from carcass,
    this character who claims
    that Bacchus is a god . . . Oh yes, he does . . .
    stitched up once upon a time in Zeus's thigh.
Well, we know what happened to that little shoot:
    sizzled by a thunderbolt along with mother and her lie.
She'd had the nerve to name Zeus the Father
    as her lover . . . What gall! What effrontery!
Enough to put a man in danger of the gallows—
    mysterious visitor indeed!

[*He is suddenly aware of* TIRESIAS *and* CADMUS *in their incongruous costumes*]

Ye gods! What is this?
Tiresias the prophet decked out like a spotted goat!
And my grandfather—it's preposterous—
    playing the Bacchant with a fennel wand?

[*He steps up to them*]

Sir, sir, this is not my mother's father—
    so ancient and so idiotic!
Please, throw away that ivy.
That thyrsus—get rid of it, let it go.

[*Rounding on* TIRESIAS]

This is your idea, Tiresias:
    another trick of yours to squeeze some profit
    out of bird-watching* and burnt offerings.
A new god, eh?
Introducing novelties to men?
Your gray hairs and nothing else
    save you now from sitting down in chains
    among these mad Bacchants.
Ha! Bringing in such squalid rites . . .
    when it's wine that has to sparkle female celebrations,

---

bird-watching: Prophets and seers interpreted anguries from the movement
of birds.

there's something very unhealthy going on,
oh, I'm telling you.
LEADER: What blasphemy, strange man!
Have you no reverence for the gods?
No reverence for Cadmus,
who sowed the crop of dragon's teeth?
Is Echion's son to bring his family to disgrace?

TIRESIAS: [*turning to* PENTHEUS]
A clever man with an honest brief
finds it easy to be fluent,
but in your case, sir, your tongue runs on
as if you really made some sense
when in fact you're talking nonsense.
A brash bold man
who lets himself depend entirely on his tongue
is a dangerous citizen and a foolish one.

This new god you think so fatuous,
words cannot encompass
the greatness of his coming power in Hellas.
I tell you, young sir,
mankind has two blessings:
the goddess Demeter is the one—
Earth, that is, call her what you will—
who keeps us alive with solid food;
the other is Semele's son,
who came afterwards and matched her food with wine.
He it was who turned the grape into a flowing draft
and proffered it to mortals;
so when they fill themselves with liquid vine
they put an end to grief.
Besides, it gives them sleep
which drowns the sadness of each day;
there is no other anodyne for sorrow.
So when we pour libations out
it is the god himself we pour out to the gods,
and by this bring blessings on mankind.

*   *   *

You ridicule the myth
   of his being stitched inside the thigh of Zeus.
Let me teach you how you should interpret that.
When Zeus had snatched the baby god
   from the searing fork of light
   and sheltered him on Mount Olympus,
   Hera wanted him expelled from heaven;
   but Zeus thought up a scheme to counter this—
   as one might imagine from a god.
He chipped off a piece of sky that domes the earth
   and presented it to nagging Hera
   as a disembodied dummy Dionysus.
In time, however, men confused the word
   and said the child had been *embodied** into Zeus
   instead of being just a substitute to humor Hera—
   a god's sop to a goddess.
And so the story was invented
   of his being sewn up inside a godhead's thigh.

He is a god of prophecies.
Those whom his spirit fills become possessed
   and have clairvoyant powers;
   and when he enters someone absolutely,
   he mouths the future through that person's mouth.
He also has assumed some of Ares' duties.
A regiment in arms, for instance,
   actually in line of battle,
   has been known to bolt in all directions
   without a spear being raised.
This hysteria too is something sent by Bacchus.
A day will come when you shall see him
   on the very rocks of Delphi,
   plunging over the pronged peaks of Parnassus,
   his pinewood torches flaring

---

*embodied: It is possible only to paraphrase lines 293–95. A crucial line (or
lines) is missing, and there is, moreover, no equivalent English for the play on
words on which the exegesis turns.

as he shakes his Bacchic thyrsus,
   tossing it in the air.
All through Greece his name shall be extolled.
So, listen to me, Pentheus:
   do not imagine men are molded by sheer force,
   or mistake your sick conceits for insights.
Welcome this god to Thebes.
Pour out libations; yes,
   wreathe your head and revel in his mysteries.

It's not for Dionysus to make women modest.
Foolproof chastity depends on character,
   and in the Corybantic celebrations
   no decent woman is seduced.

[*He points to a small crowd that has gathered*]

Look, even you are gratified
   when a crowd stands at your gates
   and the name of Pentheus is exalted in the city.
It is not improbable, I think,
   that he also would like to be acclaimed.
I therefore, sire, and Cadmus, whom you ridicule,
   shall wreathe ourselves with ivy and shall dance:
   an ancient grizzly couple, it is true,
   but dance we must;
   and no argument of yours
   shall ever make me spar with gods.

[*Turning to go*]

You are a fanatic, sir, a sick fanatic.
There is no cure for madness
   when the cure itself is mad.
LEADER: Your argument, old man,
   does no dishonor to Apollo*
   and yet shrewdly treats Bromius as a mighty god.
CADMUS: My boy, Tiresias has advised you well.

*Tiresias implies that the mystical gifts of Dionysus are worthy of Apollo,
god of clairvoyance and prophecy.

Stay with us.
Don't break with our old ways.
You are all in the air just now.
Your reasons are unreasonable.
Even if this god were no god, as you insist,
    tell yourself he *is*;
    act out a very advantageous lie,
    which makes our Semele—just think of it—
    the mother of a gòd.
The whole family can take credit.
You know the miserable mistake Actaeon made:
    how those meat-eating dogs of his—
    which he had reared himself—
    tore him piecemeal in these very dells,
    and all because he bragged he was a better huntsman
    than the goddess Artemis.
Do not risk the same.

[*He places an arm on* PENTHEUS' *shoulder*]

Come, let me put some ivy round your head.
Be one with us in honoring the god.
PENTHEUS: Keep your hands off.
    Go and play at bacchanals.
I don't want your foolishness wiped off on me.
Your feeble-minded preacher will reap what he deserves.

[*He turns to the crowd*]

Go someone on the double,
    get to this man's lair,
    where he scrutinizes birds,
    and heave it up with crowbars.
Turn it upside down;
    make a shambles of the place.
Throw his holy ribbons to the winds,
    yes, to the whirlwinds:
    that'll touch him on the raw more than anything.

[*Striding about*]

Others of you go and scour the realm.
Track this foreign effeminate down
    who infects our women with a new disease,
    befouls our beds.
If you catch him, bring him here in irons.
I'll have him stoned:
    the death that he deserves.
He'll find his fun in Thebes not so very funny.

[*Exits, sweeping into the palace, while* TIRESIAS *gazes after him and shakes his head*]

TIRESIAS: Poor fool, you don't know what you say!
    You were out of your mind before.
Now you rave.

[*To* CADMUS *in a voice from which all enthusiasm has been drained*]

Cadmus, let us go, you and I,
    to beg the god in spite of this man's boorishness
    to be merciful to him and merciful to Thebes.

[*Extending a hand*]

Come with me and bring your ivy staff.
You'll help to hold me up, as I will you.
It would be embarrassing for two old men to fall.
So be it. The god Dionysus must be served.
Oh, Cadmus, yes, you must make sure
    that Pentheus, that sorry man,*
    does not swamp your house with sorrows.
This is not a prophecy but sober fact.
Foolhardy says as Foolhardy does.

[*The two old men hobble away together*]

---

*The name Pentheus is from *penthos*, meaning grief or sorrow.

FIRST CHORAL LYRIC

[*The* CHORUS, *echoing the fears of* TIRESIAS *and surveying scenes of beauty all over Greece, sings an ode to the Spirit of Holiness, which does not turn its back on the sacraments of* BACCHUS *and the simple acceptance of the things that bring love, peace, and happiness to mankind*]

STROPHE I

Holiness, angel of heaven,
Holiness, gliding on golden
Wings over earth, do you hear
    This man's unholy
Impudent mocking of Bacchus,
Semele's son, the primal
God of gladness and garlands
Among the blessed immortals.
Whose reign is the trance, is the dance,
    With flute and with laughter—
Is cessation from cares at the feasts of the gods
When the bloom of the grape and the crater of wine
    Throw sleep in the shadows
    Round ivy-crowned men.

ANTISTROPHE I

The braggart's unbridled tongue,
The anarchical folly of fools
Leads to untimely demise,
    But unshaken abides
The life of the quietly wise,
Holding the home together.
For the gods in the faraway skies
Still look upon men.
Mere cleverness is not wise.
    Given immortal airs
Life quickens and dies. A man in pursuit
Of mere grand desires misses his time.
Oh that is the way of fanatically
    Willful men, I surmise.

STROPHE II

Oh to set foot on Cyprus,
Island of Aphrodite
Where the Spirits of Love, the Erotes,
Stroke us with love—poor mortals;
Or the strange and myriad-mouthed
    Deltas of Pharos
Rainlessly feeding the river;
Or where, flush in its beauty, Pieria,
    Is seat of the Muses;
    Or the holy hill of Olympus . . .
There, Bromius, lead me, Bromius,
      To romp in reverence.
      For there dwell the Graces,
      There is Desire
      And there it is blessed
      To revel with Bacchus.

[PENTHEUS *has entered from the palace and stands listening*]

ANTISTROPHE II

The divine son of Zeus, who rejoices
In blossomy feasts and abundance
Is lover of Peace, great Irene,
Who cherishes young men and bliss.
He gives to the rich and he gives
    To the poor his wine:
Sweet spell against sorrow;
Despiser of him who despises living
    His days and loving
His nights, content to the end
Or wise in keeping mind and heart
    From passing beyond
    The horizons of man.
    Whatever the many,
    The simple allow,
    That will I follow.

SECOND EPISODE

[*A group of* SOLDIERS *enters, bringing in* DIONYSUS *as the Mysterious Stranger. He is manacled and pinned by the arm*]

SOLDIER: [*laconically*]
  King Pentheus, all present and correct, sir.
We've made the catch you sent us to make.
The operation was successful.

  [*Prods the prisoner forward*]

The animal we found was tame, sir:
    put himself without resistance in our hands;
    didn't even blanch
    or lose that wine-rose glow of his;
    actually smiled and said we'd got to handcuff him;
    even waited for me to make my job the easier.
I felt quite awkward and I said:
  "Sorry, I have no wish to take you in,
    but that's king's orders, sir."
Meanwhile, if you please,
    those raving women that you rounded up and manacled
    and clapped into the public jail—
    they're free, they've vanished,
    gone gamboling off to the mountain glens,
    shouting out the name of Bromius, their god.
The fetters on their feet just fell apart,
    the prison doors slid back their bolts—
    and not a human touch.
He's chockful of miracles, sir, this man,
    this stranger visiting our Thebes . . .
    the rest is up to you.
PENTHEUS: Take his handcuffs off.
  He's in my trap.
No agility will set him free.

  [*The* SOLDIER *unfastens his hands.* PENTHEUS *looks him up and down with distaste*]

Hm, my man—not a bad figure, eh?

At least for the ladies;
   which is why you came to Thebes.
Nice ringlets, too . . .
   no good for wrestling, though;
   very fetching, all the same—
   the way they ripple round your cheeks.

[*Walking around* DIONYSUS *as if he were buying a slave*]

And such clear skin!
You take good care of it—
   keep it out of the sun, what! . . .
   hunt Aphrodite and beauty in the shade?
Well, who are you?
Where do you come from, first?
DIONYSUS: [*smiling*] Without boasting I can easily tell you that.
   Have you heard of Tmolus, the mountain of flowers?
PENTHEUS: Certainly. It ranges in a ring round Sardis city.
DIONYSUS: I am from there. Lydia is my country.
PENTHEUS: What makes you bring these rituals here to
                               Greece?
DIONYSUS: Dionysus sent me, the son of Zeus.
PENTHEUS: Some Zeus! Does he breed new gods there?
DIONYSUS: [*still smiling*]
   No, the same Zeus there wedded your own Semele here.
PENTHEUS: Was it in a dream or with your eyes wide open
   that he gave you this commission?
DIONYSUS: Face to face . . . he gave the rituals of possession.
PENTHEUS: Rituals of possession? Of what peculiar form?
DIONYSUS: That may not be divulged to the incommunicate.
PENTHEUS: Well, what do the holy communicants gain by it?
DIONYSUS: Something well worth knowing, but I may not tell
                                 you.
PENTHEUS: Clever of you, what! You make me want to hear.
DIONYSUS: The god's sacred rites are kept from the profane.
PENTHEUS: You say you clearly saw the god. What's he like?
DIONYSUS: Whatever he wants. That's not up to me.
PENTHEUS: Another neat evasion! It tells me nothing.
DIONYSUS: To the foolish ear the wise speak foolishly.
PENTHEUS: Is this the first place, then, you've brought your god?

DIONYSUS: By no means: every land in Asia celebrates his dance.

PENTHEUS: Naturally! Foreigners have much less sense than
Greeks.

DIONYSUS: In this they have much more—a different tradition.

PENTHEUS: And these rites of yours, are they at night or day?

DIONYSUS: Mostly at night. There's mystery in the dark.

PENTHEUS: Of course! Perfect for seduction and undermining
women.

DIONYSUS: Some can dig out dirt even in broad day.

PENTHEUS: What sophistry! You should be chastened.

DIONYSUS: And you too, for your crude impieties against the god.

PENTHEUS: What ho! Our mystery priest gets bold: an acrobat
with words.

DIONYSUS: [*sarcastically*]

So what's my punishment, tell me? Something dreadful!

PENTHEUS: First I'll—I'll chop your dainty lovelocks off.

DIONYSUS: My hair is holy. I grow it for the god.

PENTHEUS: Next, let go that—that thyrsus in your hands.

DIONYSUS: Just try to take it. I carry it for Bacchus.

PENTHEUS: We'll lock up your carcass in a nice safe jail.

DIONYSUS: And whenever I want, the god will set me free.

PENTHEUS: [*sneering*]

. Of course! You'll just beckon him from among your Bacchants.

DIONYSUS: He's beside me now and sees my trials.

PENTHEUS: Really? Where? My eyes don't see a thing.

DIONYSUS: Where I am . . . But you, blasphemer, cannot see.

PENTHEUS: [*to his guards*]

Seize him. The fellow is jeering at me and all Thebes.

[*The* GUARDS *advance but stop dead*]

DIONYSUS: I dare you to. You'll be fools acting like fools.

PENTHEUS: I say bind him. I am in command.

DIONYSUS: You—you have no idea what you say, what you do,
what you are.

PENTHEUS: [*shaken*] I—I am Pentheus, Agave's son, Echion is
my father.

DIONYSUS: Pentheus, indeed: the name spells sorrow.

PENTHEUS: Away with him. Lock him in the stables near.

Give him all his darkness and his murk.
Dance away there.
And these women that you brought with you,
     these associates in your evil work,
     I'll either have them sold as slaves
     or give their fingers something else to do
     besides just thumping drums and beating tympanums:
     I'll keep them slaving at my looms.
DIONYSUS: Very well, I'll go along with this wrongful
     undestined destiny, but remember this:
     Dionysus, who you say does not exist,
     will wreak revenge on you for this.
When it is me that you arrest
     it is him that you molest.

[PENTHEUS *stalks out, followed by* DIONYSUS *under guard.*
SOLDIERS *close in upon the women of the* CHORUS]

SECOND CHORAL LYRIC

[*In a desperate appeal to Thebes, the* CHORUS *members de-
nounce their persecutor and call on their god*]

STROPHE
O daughter of Achelous,
O Dirce, holy maiden,
Once in the well of your waters
You welcomed the baby of Zeus,
Who sired him and snatched him
Out of the living embers
And into his thigh ensconced him,
Shouting: "Dithyrambus,
In this male womb of mine
Be buried and be famous
With his name in Thebes."
     Yes, O Bacchus!
Then why, beatific Dirce,*

Dirce: here a synonym for Thebes.

When I come to you in garlands
Do you spurn my spellbound dances
And thrust me from your kingdom?
Why do you scorn and flee me?
The grapes of Bacchus one day,
Full of grace—believe me—
    Will make you love him.

ANTISTROPHE

Infamous Pentheus proves his
Earth-bound line, his birthday
From dragon and from snake-man.
A freak and a monster he,
No normal human being:
A butchering earth-born giant
In war with the divine.
He'll manacle me soon
Dionysiac though I am.
He holds in his house already
Deep in the gloom of a prison
My leader in the dance-spell.
Do you see these things, O son of
Zeus, O Dionysus?
Your devotees on trial
Grappling with oppression.
Descend, lord, from Olympus,
Shake your golden thyrsus,
Quell this man of blood's
    Brash obsession.

EPODE

Where on Nysa nurse of fauna
Are you, Dionysus, leading
Wild processions with your thyrsus?
Up among Corycia's crags?
On Olympus deep in green
Bowers where the harp of Orpheus
Making music marched the trees
Towards him once, and marched the savage
Beasts . . . Oh, blessed are you, valley

·Of Pieria! Bacchus loves you.
He will come and set you dancing.
With the rubrics of possession.
He will cross the racing river
Axius, lead his Maenads whirling
Through the stream of Lydias—father
Of all currents, fathering
· Wealth and well-being for the world,
Letting loose his lovely waters
Through a land made rich for horses.

[*The* SOLDIERS, *who have been listening, now break ranks and begin to hustle the women of the* CHORUS *away. Suddenly there is a crack of thunder, the earth quakes, buildings rock, and lightning plays over the tomb of Semele. The* SOLDIERS *scatter, the women run about shrieking, and the voice of* DIONYSUS *rings out from the heart of the palace*]

CHORAL DIALOGUE

DIONYSUS: Ho hullo! Do you hear me calling—
Hear my voice? Hullo Bacchanalians!
Ho Bacchantes!
CHORUS: What is it? What is it? Where is the voice
Coming from, calling me straight from Bacchus?
DIONYSUS: [*louder*] Hullo, hullo! Hear me again:
Son of Semele, son of Zeus.
CHORUS: Master, our master! Ho hullo!
Come to our company, come to dance
Holily, Bromius. Bromius, ho!
DIONYSUS: Terrible Ennosis, Spirit of earthquake,
Shake the earth.

[*More tremors and a clap of thunder. The architrave of the palace cracks*]

CHORUS: Ah, aah!
The castle of Pentheus shivers and soon
Shall be shaken to ruin.
FIRST VOICE: Great Dionysus is in the palace.

Bow down before him.

SECOND VOICE: Bow we do.
Look at the capitals crack from the pillars.
Bromius is chanting within the walls.

DIONYSUS: Touch off the thunderbolt's sizzle of light.
Burn down, oh burn down the palace of Pentheus.

[*Lightning sears through the buildings and a new flame from
Semele's ever-smoldering tomb*]

CHORUS: Aaah! Aaah!
Look, do you see the fire leaping
Round Semele's holy tomb?
The very flames the god of thunder
Left there once: the bolt of Zeus.

[*Crashing masonry makes the* CHORUS *women throw themselves on their faces*]

LEADER: Down on the ground, fling yourselves bodily,
Terrified Maenads . . . See, our master
Is turning the palace upside down:
The son of Zeus.

[*The doors of the palace burst open and* DIONYSUS, *still in disguise but wreathed in smoke and smiling, stands brandishing
his thyrsus. He begins to tease them for having thrown themselves to the ground*]

DIONYSUS: Come, my oriental ladies,*
Have I frightened you so thoroughly
You have fallen to the floor?
Seems that you were pleased when Bacchus
Shook and shivered Pentheus' palace.
Come, get up and stop your trembling.

---

*Euripides renders lines 604 to 640 in trochaic tetrameter (-u-u-u-/-u-u-u-u),
in which I follow suit. The only other instance I can think of where Euripides
casts dialogue and narrative in trochees are lines 444 to 461 in *The Trojan
Women*, when Cassandra makes her great speech prophesying her own death
and the murder of Agamemnon. It is a meter that draws attention to liveliness
of feeling. Line numbers refer to the Greek text in the Loeb Classics edition.

[*The women of the* CHORUS *pick themselves up and gaze with relief and admiration at their leader, who they don't know is* BACCHUS]

LEADER: O brightest light of Bacchic dancing
     Sweet it is to see you! We were
     Quite alone and abandoned.
DIONYSUS: Did you lose all hope when Pentheus
     Plunged me into the gloom of prison?
LEADER: Indeed we did, for who would guard us
     When you yourself had come to grief?
     How ever did you flee the clutches
     Of that man who has no conscience?
DIONYSUS: Easily! I freed myself.
LEADER: Weren't your hands in handcuffs? Weren't they
     Locked by him in manacles?

[DIONYSUS *steps among the women of the* CHORUS *smiling. They form a ring around him*]

DIONYSUS: There I made him look so foolish.
     When he thought that he was binding
     Me, he did not even touch me:
     He was glutted with delusion.
     In the stables where he shut me,
     There he came across a bull;
     Began to throw his slipknots round it,
     Bind it by the hooves and knees,
     Panting with emotion, dripping
     Sweat from off his body, digging
     His teeth into his lips—oh yes!—
     While I sat and quietly watched him.
     Then Bacchus came and shook the building,
     Fired the tomb of Semele.
     Pentheus saw it, thought the palace
     Was on fire, ran about
     Ordering slaves to carry water.
     Every slave was put to work.
     All for nothing. When he thought
     That I'd escaped, he stopped his labors,

Charged into the palace lunging
With his dark and gloom-drawn sword.
Meanwhile Bromius (or I thought so,
I can only give a guess),
Made a phantom Pentheus flew at
In the courtyard, stabbing only
Thin bright air but fondly thinking
He was really butchering *me*.
Bacchus had much worse in store:
Flattened out the stable buildings,
Turned the whole place into rubble . . .
Pentheus must regret his putting
Me in prison. Sheer exhaustion
Now has made him drop his sword.
He is prostrate: not surprising
Seeing a man has challenged a god.
As for me, I calmly sauntered
Out of the house here to you,
Without a second thought for Pentheus.

[DIONYSUS *turns his head at the sound of* PENTHEUS'
approach]

Ha! it sounds as if his jackboots
Stamp along the hall. Milord will
Show himself. What will he say
After this? . . . Let him come
Snorting tempests, I shall be
The soul of peace: a cool detachment
Is the thing a man of wisdom
Ought to bring.

[PENTHEUS *bursts out of the palace, his face distorted with
frustration and rage*]

THIRD EPISODE

PENTHEUS: It's a disgrace: the stranger's got away,
bound up as he was just now in chains.

[*He sees* DIONYSUS *and gasps*]

Awh! . . . the man is here . . . what?
How ever did you manage to get out
and materialize outside my door?
DIONYSUS: Keep your feet and keep your fury quiet.
PENTHEUS: But how did you shed your chains and get out here?
DIONYSUS: Did I not say—or did you not listen—
that somebody would set me free.
PENTHEUS: Who? . . . With you it's one queer enigma on
another.
DIONYSUS: He who grows the clustering grape for mortals.
PENTHEUS: Dionysus? Ha, a pretty gift indeed!
DIONYSUS: What you sneer at does Dionysus honor.
PENTHEUS: [*turning to his guards*]
Ring the city around. Seal off every outlet. That's an order.
DIONYSUS: Whatever for? Can gods not somersault your walls?
PENTHEUS: Clever, very clever, but not quite clever enough!
DIONYSUS: Supremely clever—in what is necessary.

[DIONYSUS *breaks off with an expectant look towards the
country, from which a* HERDSMAN *is now seen approaching*]

However, listen first to what this man from the mountains
has come to tell you.
We shall wait for you. We shall not run away.

[*The* HERDSMAN *hurries in. He is clad in goatskin and wears a
tasseled cap. A satchel hangs from his shoulders, and he carries a staff*]

HERDSMAN: [*breathless*] O Pentheus, ruler of this realm,
I come here straight from Cithaeron,
where the dazzling snowdrifts never leave the ground.
PENTHEUS: [*testily*] Yes yes, you've come here to tell me what?
HERDSMAN: Oh sir, I've seen the raving ladies—
those who streamed out from their homes stung mad,
their white limbs flashing.
I am bursting to tell you, King, and tell the town
the fantastic things they do, past all wondering.
But first, sir, may I know

if you are really ready to hear what's going on,
  or must I trim my tongue?
Your quick temper frightens me . . .
  your hot temper, sir—too much like a king.
PENTHEUS: Speak on.
  From me you do not have a thing to fear.
  It is never right to fume at honest men.
But the worse you tell me of these intoxicated worshipers,
  the worse shall be my punishment of that crooked man
  who undermined these women.
HERDSMAN: Our pasturing herds had just begun to climb
  the uplands at the hour the sun's first rays
  break their warmth upon the ground,
  when I see three bands of women who have danced:
  Autonoë at the head of one,
  Agave, your own mother, of the second,
  and Ino, so, the third:
  all stretched out in sleep,
  collapsed at random wherever they had tossed;
  Some lying on their backs upon the piney needles,
  others pillowed on the oak-leaved floor . . .
  All modestly, not as you suggested, sir,*
  Not in their cups, or in a flute-inducèd trance,
  or any wildwood chase of love.

Then your mother, at the lowing of the horny cattle,
  stood up in the middle of the Bacchic ones
  and called upon them loudly to bestir their limbs from sleep.
And they shook the rank slumber from their eyes
  and straightened up:
  a sight strangely orderly and beautiful—
  women young and old, and maidens still unmarried.
First they let their hair fall down their shoulders,
  then fastened up the fawn skins that were loose
  around their dappled hides.
Some fondled young gazelles
  or untamed wolf cubs in their arms

---

*This line makes clear that the herdsman was present during Pentheus' earlier
intransigent speech and took note of what he said (lines 220–25).

and fed them with their own white milk:
  those, that is, who were young mothers
  with babies left at home
  and breasts that burgeoned.
Then they wreathed their heads
  with ivy, oak, and bryony in flower.
One of them took up her thyrsus, struck the rock,
  and water gushed from it as fresh as dew.
Another hit her rod of fennel on the ground,
  and the god for her burst forth a fount of wine.
Anyone who fancied liquid white to drink
  just scratched the soil with fingertips
  and got herself a jet of milk;
  while from their ivy-crested rods
  sweet streams of honey dropped.

Oh, if you had been there, sire, and had seen,
  you would have come with prayers
  towards the god whom now you execrate.
We cowherds and shepherds came together,
  talked among ourselves, debated
  these marvelous goings-on.
Then a fellow who was fond of gadding up to town,
  very glib of speech,
  held forth to all of us and said:
"Hey, you people here
  who live upon these holy mountain terraces,
  what d'you say we go and hunt Agave out,
  Pentheus' mother,
  and chase her from her mad ecstatic rapture,
  so do a service to the king?"
He spoke convincingly, we thought,
  and we laid an ambush in the copses and hid ourselves.
At a certain hour,
  the Maenads shook the thyrsus for the Bacchic dance
  and with a common throat called out:
"Iacchus, son of Zeus, great Bromius!"
Then the whole mountainside became convulsed
  and god-possessed; even the animals:
  nothing but it moved with the mystic run.

Agave, as it happened, came sprinting past me
    and I leapt out to grab her
    from the ambush where we hid.
But she at the top of her lungs cried out:
"Come, my flying hounds,
    we are being hunted by these men.
Wield your thyrsus in defense,
    and follow, follow after."
Well, we fled:
    escaped being torn to pieces by these god-struck maniacs,
    who with their naked unarmed hands fell upon our heifers
    grazing on the grass.
You could see a woman with a bellowing calf
    actually in her grip, tearing it apart.
Others ripped young cows in little pieces.
You could see their ribs and cloven hooves
    being tossed up high and low;
    and blood-smeared members dangling from the pines;
    great lordly bulls,
    one minute glaring in all the pride of their horns,
    the next dragged to the ground like carcasses
    by the swarming hands of girls,
    and the meat flensed from their flanks
    quicker than you could wink a royal eye.
They burst like a wave of birds over the ground,
    skimming across the delta flats of the river Asopus
    (so fertile for Thebes).
They tore like an invading army
    through the villages of Hysiac and Erythrae
    which nestle on the lower spurs of Cithaeron
    and turned them upside down.
They snatched up babies out of homes.
The loot they loaded on their shoulders
    stayed put without being tied.
Nothing tumbled to the ground, not even brass or iron.*

*There is probably a sentence missing here. E. R. Dodds suggests: "Nothing
resisted their assault, not bolted doors, not bronze, not iron." It is not likely
that the Maenads would have wanted to carry away pots and pans. *The Bacchae*, ed. E. R. Dodds (Oxford: Clarendon Press, 1966).

They carried fire on their flowing heads
    and it did not burn them.
The villagers, of course, enraged at being plundered,
    took arms against these manic ones.
Then what a spectacle, my king, how sinister!
Their spear points drew no blood,
    while the women, hurling thyrsi from their hands,
    oh, the women wounded men, set men to flight . . .
    that was not without some unknown power.
They went back then to the place where they began:
    to the fountains which the god had sprung for them.
They washed their hands of blood
    and from their faces the serpents licked the clotted gore.

After all this, my lord,
    whoever this spirit be you must receive him in our city.
He is powerful in many things.
He even—so I am told—gave wine,
    that sorrow-curing cup, to human beings.
Sire, if the god of wine does not exist,
    then neither does the goddess of love:
    no pleasures left for man.
LEADER: I hesitate to speak my mind before the king
    but cannot keep from saying
    there is no greater god than Dionysus.
PENTHEUS: So,
    like a wildfire it already hurries here,
    outrageously, this mass hysteria,
    disgracing us before the whole of Thebes.

[*Turns to the captain of the* GUARDS]

There's not a moment to be lost.
Go to the Electran Gate,*
    call out the heavy infantry,
    and mobilize the cavalry in full . . .
    all—all who can bear a shield or spring a bow.
We must march against the mad Bacchants.

Electran Gate: one of the seven gates of Thebes.

It is not to be endured.
It goes too far—
   if we let these women get away with this.
DIONYSUS: So you are not moved, Pentheus, by any words of mine!
   Nonetheless, in spite of all you've done to me,
   I cannot help but tell you:
   you must not take up arms against a god.
Rather, be still.
Bromius will never let you hustle his possessed
   from their ecstatic hills.
PENTHEUS: No sermons, if you please.
You have broken out of jail, savor that;
   or I shall have the law on you again.
DIONYSUS: Would you so?
   If I were you I'd offer offerings up to him and not offense.
   Don't kick against the goad—a man against a god.
PENTHEUS: Offerings? Yes indeed,
   a most appropriate sacrifice:
   women's blood and massacre in the glens of Cithaeron.
DIONYSUS: You will be routed—all.
   And what a disgrace:
   the Bacchanalian thyrsus beating back your shields of bronze.
PENTHEUS: [*strutting towards his* GUARDS]
   Can't get the better of our stranger—can we?
Passive or active, he has the answer.
DIONYSUS: Friend, it is still possible to mend these things.
PENTHEUS: By doing what?
   Making myself a slave of my own slaves?
DIONYSUS: Without the wielding of weapons I can bring the
                          women here.
PENTHEUS: Exactly—another trick of yours.
DIONYSUS: Trick? It is my sole device to save you.
PENTHEUS: No, it is a conspiracy with them
   to make your Bacchic debauches permanent.
DIONYSUS: Conspiracy, if you like—that much is true!—
   but with a god.
PENTHEUS: [*turning to leave*] Servants, bring my armor here,
   and *you*—keep quiet.

DIONYSUS: Wait!*

How would you like to see their mountain seances?

PENTHEUS: [*taken off his guard*] Very much. I'd pay a fortune in gold for that.

DIONYSUS: Why? What gives you such a strong desire?

PENTHEUS: [*hedging*] Well . . . of course . . .

I should be sorry to see them drunk, but . . .

DIONYSUS: But you would like to see them—sorrow and all?

PENTHEUS: To be sure, if I could crouch quietly under the pines.

DIONYSUS: They would discover you, though you came unseen.

PENTHEUS: Then, openly . . . I take your point.

DIONYSUS: [*smiling*] Well, shall we go? You'll undertake the journey.

PENTHEUS: [*the words slipping out*]

Yes yes, take me there . . . I can hardly wait.

DIONYSUS: Then you must put on a linen shift.

PENTHEUS: What! I a man be taken for a woman?

DIONYSUS: They'll kill you if they see you as a man.

PENTHEUS: You've made your point again. Always a wise one, what!

DIONYSUS: It's Dionysus who advises me.

PENTHEUS: But how shall I carry out your excellent advice?

DIONYSUS: We'll go inside and I'll dress you up myself.

PENTHEUS: What kind of dress? A female's? I shall look a fool.

DIONYSUS: [*pretending to turn away*]

So you're no longer anxious to watch the raving Maenads?

PENTHEUS: All right, tell me the dress you say I have to wear.

DIONYSUS: I'll fit you with a wig of spreading locks.

PENTHEUS: [*gulping*] And . . . and the next item in my outfit?

DIONYSUS: A robe down to your ankles, and for your head a snood.

PENTHEUS: And besides all this, what will you load me with?

DIONYSUS: A thyrsus in your hand, and a spotted fawn skin on.

PENTHEUS: No no, I can't—cannot bring myself to dress up as a woman.

DIONYSUS: Then blood will flow if you battle with the Bacchants.

*This is the turning point of the play. Up till now Dionysus has genuinely wanted to save Pentheus. Now he sees that he refuses to grow and must be destroyed.

PENTHEUS: All right then. Let us go and reconnoiter first.

DIONYSUS: That's more sensible than hunting viciousness
with vice.

PENTHEUS: But how shall I pass through the Cadmean capital?

DIONYSUS: We shall go an unfrequented way and I shall lead.

PENTHEUS: Anything is better than being jeered at by the Bacchants.

Come, let us go inside. There I must make provision.

DIONYSUS: As you please. I am ready to assist you in every way.

PENTHEUS: So I shall go in and make my decision:

either to head my army and attack, or fall in with your advice.

[PENTHEUS *walks into the palace, followed by* DIONYSUS, *who turns at the doors with a sinister smile as he addresses the* CHORUS]

DIONYSUS: The fish, my women, heads now for the net.

He will reach the Bacchants and his becoming death.

So, Dionysus, to your work. You are not far away.

Make his mind unsteady first.

Imbue him with a dizzy fantasy.

Sane, he never will consent

to put a woman's clothing on,

but once deranged he will.

After all his threats and arrogance

I want all Thebes to laugh

as he walks, a woman, through the town.

[*He moves towards the doors*]

Now to go and groom him in the gown

he shall wear to Hades and his death:

Pentheus murdered in his mother's grasp

will come to know full well at last

Dionysus, son of Zeus, a god indeed:

to man most gentle—and most dangerous.

[DIONYSUS *walks quickly into the palace*]

THIRD CHORAL LYRIC

[*The* CHORUS, *using the image of a doe rapturously escaping the hunters, sings a song of hope. They go on to repudiate the arrogance of those who think they are a law unto themselves and can dispense with the simple wisdom of the ordinary mortal. In an ominous refrain they anticipate a grim reckoning for* PENTHEUS]

STROPHE

Oh shall I ever again
Dance in a spell through the night
   With the flash of my white
Feet and my head thrown back in the clean
Dewy air, like a fawn at play in the green
Joy of a meadow, escaped from the flight
   Of the chase when she leapt
Clear of the mesh of the net from the eyes
Of the hallooing huntsman and his racing hounds,
As over the water-flat fields she flies
Tense as the breeze to solitudes empty of men—
Oh to the sweet shooting green
Beneath the shadowy hair of the trees.

REFRAIN

What is wisdom? What is beauty?
Heaven blest in sight of man
But to hold a hated rival's
Head beneath one's hand.
Beauty is a joy forever.*

ANTISTROPHE

Slowly but surely divine
Power moves to annul
   The brutally minded man
Who in his wild delusions refuses
To reverence the gods. But the gods creep up
By stealth in the creeping of time to trap

*John Keats knew his Euripides!

The unscrupulous man.
Trying to know or meddle beyond
The divinely established norm is wrong.
Slight is the price of an act of faith
In the mysterious and numinous strength
Of the gods and what is grounded in being,
Believed in as long as time.

REFRAIN

What is wisdom? What is beauty?
Heaven blest in sight of man
But to hold a hated rival's
Head beneath one's hand.
Beauty is a joy forever.

EPODE

Lucky the sailor who flees
    From storm into port.
Lucky the man who rides
    Above all his cares.
In one way one or another
Surpasses in riches and power.
There are always a thousand hopes
For a thousand mortals, and some
Hopes are crowned with success,
Others run into the sand.
To me the one who is lucky
Is he who day by day lives happy.

FOURTH EPISODE

[DIONYSUS *enters from the palace. His demeanor has changed. The latent power that underlay his smiling meekness has broken surface and shows him in a new and ruthless light. He no longer tempts but commands. He summons* PENTHEUS *from the palace in a voice that rings with cruel authority*]

DIONYSUS: Come on out, you perverted man,
    so passionate for what is not for sight
    and acts that are not right . . .

Out, Pentheus, I say, before the palace.
　　Show me what you look like dressed up as a woman,
　　a mad woman and a Maenad—
　　prying on your mother and her mob.

[PENTHEUS *shuffles in from the palace. In terms of breakdown techniques we should say that he shows every symptom of having been brainwashed. "What follows Dionysus on the stage is less than man: it is a giggling, leering creature, more helpless than a child, nastier than an idiot, yet a creature filled with the Dionysiac sense of power and capable of perceiving the god in his true shape, because the god has entered into his victim."* *PENTHEUS is now dressed with a wig of long flowing hair, a filet round his head, a linen shift like a priest's alb reaching down to his ankles, and in his hands the ivy-crowned thyrsus*]

DIONYSUS: My word! You do look like one of the Cadmus daughters.
PENTHEUS: [*peering at him*] Yes yes, I'd say I see two suns
　　and a double city Thebes,
　　twin sets of seven gates,
　　and a bull seems to beckon me: he walks before me.

[*Leaning towards* DIONYSUS *with his mouth open*]

Now I'd say your head was horned . . .
　　or were you an animal all the while?†
For certainly you've changed—oh, into a bull.
DIONYSUS: [*as if talking to a child*]
　　The god is walking with us; before unfriendly,
　　but he's come to terms with us and now
　　you see things as you ought.
PENTHEUS: [*preening himself*] Well, how do I look?

---

*The Bacchae, ed. E. R. Dodds, p. 192.
†Euripides' words are *ai e pot ēstha thēr? Tetaurōsai gar oun.* Professor Dodds comments: "The dragging rhythm . . . due to the strong pause of the third foot, suggests the King's slow bewildered utterance" (p. 193, note 920–22). I make a similar pause after the word "changed." It is possible that Pentheus sees another figure behind the Stranger: his double but with horns— Dionysus in his beast incarnation. A sinister effect could be had by the use of two actors, one bull-headed and one speaking the more ominous lines.

Don't I have Aunt Ino's air,
  and Agave my mother's carriage?
DIONYSUS: Seeing you I'd say my eyes saw them.

[*Walks around surveying him*]*

Tut tut! A curl is out of place—
  not as I fixed it underneath your bonnet.
PENTHEUS: [*guiltily*] It must have shaken loose inside the house
  when I was tossing my head being a Bacchant.
DIONYSUS: Let me put it into place again. I'm your lady's maid . . .
  Now hold your head up.
PENTHEUS: There, *you* dress it. I'm all yours now.
DIONYSUS: [*scolding*] Tch! Tch! Your girdle's loose,
  And your skirt's all uneven at the ankles.

[PENTHEUS *looks down at his toes, then twists around to see
the back*]

PENTHEUS: Yeah, I think so too—especially on the right foot.
  On the left heel, however, it's hanging well.
DIONYSUS: [*fiddling with the clothing*]
  You're going to call me your best friend, I think,
  when you see the Bacchants stone sober, not as you expected.
PENTHEUS: [*not listening*] Do I hold the thyrsus in the right hand
                            or the left
  to make myself a better Bacchant?
DIONYSUS: Hold it in the right: lift it in strict time to the right
                               foot . . .
  I'm so pleased your mind is changed.
PENTHEUS: [*with an upsurge of manic strength*]
  Do you think I could lift the whole of Cithaeron,
  Bacchants and all, high upon my shoulders?
DIONYSUS: You could indeed, if you wished . . . You were not
                          healthy in mind before;
  Now you are—exactly right.
PENTHEUS: Shall we carry crowbars?
  Or should I put an arm and shoulder to the crags

---

*Lines 925–70 are a reversal of the ridicule that Pentheus attempted to heap
on Dionysus earlier in lines 453–506.

and tear the peaks up with bare hands?

DIONYSUS: Now now! No destroying the purlieus of the nymphs,
the places where our Pan sits piping.

PENTHEUS: You are right.
Women are not impressed by brute force . . .
I'll hide myself among the pines.

DIONYSUS: [*with secret and ominous irony*]
Yes, you'll be wonderfully hidden
when you go to do your spying on the Bacchants.

PENTHEUS: [*leering*] I fancy I can see them now, in the bushes,
crouched like little birds in the sweet traps of love.

DIONYSUS: That's exactly what you're going to watch.
Perhaps you'll take them by surprise . . .
if *you* are not taken first.

PENTHEUS: [*thrusting out his chest*]
Conduct me through the public heart of Thebes.

DIONYSUS: [*with a sly look at the* CHORUS]
Yes, you are the only man that lets himself be—vulnerable
for this city, the only one.
And so the struggles that await you are uniquely yours.
Come then, I shall take you safely there . . .
another bring you home.

PENTHEUS: Oh yes, my mother.

DIONYSUS: A sight for all to see.

PENTHEUS: That's what I've come for.

DIONYSUS: You'll be carried home . . .

PENTHEUS: [*giggling*] What luxury!

DIONYSUS: . . . in your mother's arms.

PENTHEUS: [*coyly*] You're trying to spoil me.

DIONYSUS: In a very special way.

PENTHEUS: Yet I deserve it.

[*He begins to walk*]

DIONYSUS: [*laughing behind his back*]
Oh, you are formidable,
and what you walk towards is formidable indeed!
You will find a fame that hoists you to the skies.

[*As* PENTHEUS *moves out of hearing*]

Open your arms, Agave, and you her sisters:
   you daughters of Cadmus, to this young man
   whom I lead out to a mighty challenge
   wherein I and Bromius shall triumph.
The rest shall soon be seen.

[DIONYSUS *follows* PENTHEUS *into the streets of Thebes*]

FOURTH CHORAL LYRIC

[*The women of the* CHORUS *sing a hymn of vengeance, covering the interval during which the events unfolded later are actually taking place and are seen clairvoyantly by the* CHORUS. *Knowledge is not more real than mystery, nor the unconscious mind less than the conscious. Those who try to control everything by brute force are punished by death*]

STROPHE
Hurry you hounds of hell to the mountains where
The daughters of Cadmus hold their wild seance.
   Worry them into a frantic trance
Against the man disguised in the dress of a woman:
A roaring one who comes to spy on the Maenads.
Oh as he peers from the rump of a rock or top of a tree trunk,
         His mother will see him first.
      Then she will call to her spellbound band: "Hulloo!
   Who is this peeker who comes—has come—to the mountains
         And pries on us Cadmean daughters:
We who run to the hills, the hills, to revel, O Bacchus?
      Who was it that bore him?
      He's not of the blood of a woman
      But whelped from a she-lion
      Or some Libyan Gorgon.

REFRAIN
   Let Justice walk,
   Let Justice sworded walk
   To strike through the throat and kill
This godless ruthless lawless man—

This earth-sported scion
  Spawned from Echíon.

ANTISTROPHE

See how he lawlessly ruthlessly raving advances
On you and your mother's god-possessed worship, O Bacchus!
    Expecting his lunatic cunning
  And cheating courage to master by force
What cannot be conquered. For such aberrations death
Is the discipline—yea yea—divine dispensation requires
    The homage of man, for a life
To be lived without sorrow. Oh, cleverness never was mine.
    I am ready to hunt it down.
  As to the rest, the sublime is simple and leads
To a beautiful life, yes pure and pious as long as the day
    And into the night.
    It sheds from it everything wrong
      In pursuit of the right
      And homage to heaven.

REFRAIN

    Let Justice visible walk,
    Let Justice sworded walk
    To strike through the throat and kill
This godless ruthless lawless man—
    This earth-sported scion
    Spawned from Echíon.

EPODE

    Appear as a bull or be seen as
      a many-headed dragon.
    Or come as a fire-breathing
      vision of a lion.
    Yes, Bacchus, come and snare him,
      this hunter of the Bacchants.
    With a smile on your face enmesh him
      under the deadly netting
    Of Maenads' mad stampeding.

FIFTH EPISODE

[*A* MESSENGER, *the personal attendant of* PENTHEUS, *staggers
in from the country, breathless and disheveled*]

MESSENGER: Ah! House so blessed once all through Hellas.
House of that old man of Sidon
who harvested the dragon's seed in the reptile's land . . .
how I weep for you—slave though I am.
LEADER: Why, what is it?
Have you news of the Bacchic ones?
MESSENGER: Pentheus is no more—Echíon's son.
LEADER: [*in a cry of triumph*]
Lord Bromius, your godhead is made manifest.
MESSENGER: What was that?
Woman, do you mean to say my master's end can give you
joy?
LEADER: Oh, let me shout my song in foreign tunes:
a foreigner who need no longer tremble in fear of fetters.
MESSENGER: But do you reckon the men of Thebes such cowards
that . . .
LEADER: It is not Thebes but Dionysus, son of Zeus, who rules
me.
MESSENGER: That I understand, but is it seemly, ladies,
to crow upon disaster?
LEADER: Tell it all. Explain exactly how he died—
this perverse man, this purveyor of perversion.
MESSENGER: [*moving into the center*]
When we had left behind
the homesteads of our Theban countryside
and crossed the waters of the Asopus,
we struck into the foothills of Mount Cithaeron,
Pentheus and I (for I attended on my master)
together with that stranger who was acting as our guide.
After we had settled on a grassy clearing,
our feet and tongues as quiet as we could
so as to see without being seen . . .
There in a glen, cliff-bound and full of streams,
we saw them, the Maenads,
sitting in the crowded shadows of the pines,

their hands all busy with their happy tasks.
Some were making thyrsi thick again with crests of ivy;
    some, frolicsome as fillies loosed from festal yokes,
    chanted back and forth in Dionysiac antiphons.

Pentheus, unhappy man,
    could not well see the throng of women.
"Stranger, from where we stand I cannot quite make out
    these lewd maniacs," he said,
        "but if I climbed a tall pine on the precipice
        I should have a perfect view of them and their debaucheries."
Then I saw the stranger do a marvelous thing:
    seizing a sky-soaring sapling pine
    he began to tug it downward—down and down
    towards the dark earth till it arched there like a bow
    or like a peg-line compass
    curving the circumference of a wheel.
So did the stranger take that mountain pine,
    take it in his hands and tug it to the ground:
    a feat beyond a mortal human being.
Then lodging Pentheus on this tip of pine
    he slowly let the pine trunk spring up straight,
    carefully slipping it along his grip
    so as not to throw him off again.
Sheer into the sheer sky it went,
    my master sitting straddled on the top:
    more conspicuous to the Maenads now than they to him.

Hardly had he settled into sight
    high up on his perch,
    when the stranger was nowhere to be seen,
    but a voice came out of the void,
    the voice, I think, of Bacchus, calling:
"My maidens, look, I bring you
    the man who made a mock of you and me
    and our rituals of possession.
See you punish him."
And while the voice yet spoke
    there streaked from heaven to earth a flame,
    an uncanny flare of light.

The very air stood still
   and in the glens the woods themselves
   held stillness in their leaves,
   and from the beasts no cry was heard.

The Bacchants had not caught the voice distinctly
   and leaping to their feet they gazed around.
Then the voice exhorted them a second time,
   and when the daughters of Cadmus recognized
   the clear behest of Bacchus
   they shot forth like ringdoves on the wing—
   such was their speed of stride:
   Agave—his own mother—and her sisters
   and all the bacchanals.
Up the valleys, through the torrents,
   over boulders, there they leapt
   breathing out the very spirit of the god.
And when they saw my master perched up on the pine,
   first they tried to climb up near him on a pinnacle
   and using all their might to pelt him down with stones.
Some threw shafts of pine branch at him,
   others sent their thyrsis flying through the air
   in a miserable attempt to reach him;
   but still their aim fell short of the wretched victim:
   trapped and sitting there past all escape;
   the distance far outdid even their fanaticism.
Finally, as if lightning had struck,
   they stripped an oak tree of its branches
   and using these as levers
   tried to pry the tree up from its roots.
When all these efforts were of no avail,
   Agave said: "Come, my Maenads,
   make a circle round the bole and grip it fast.
We must take this climbing animal
   or he will spread abroad the mysteries of our god-struck dance."

A rage of hands then swarmed around the pine
   and loosened it from earth.
Then down, down

from his high perch towards the ground,
    plunged Pentheus with one continuous yell,
    aware of what was going to come.
His mother
    as priestess of the bloodbath
    was the first to fall upon him.
He snatched the headdress from his hair
    to let Agave, wretched woman, see
    who it was and so not murder him.
He touched her on the cheek and cried:
    "Mother, it is I, your child, your Pentheus
    born to you in Echion's house.
Have mercy on me, Mother,
    and because of my mistakes do not kill your son—your son."

She was foaming at the mouth.
Her dilated eyeballs rolled.
Her mind was gone—possessed by Bacchus—
    she could not hear her son.
Gripping his left hand and forearm
    and purchasing her foot against the doomed man's ribs,
    she dragged his arm off at the shoulder . . .
It was not her strength that did it
    but the god's power seething in her hands.
Ino, active on the other side,
    was ripping at his flesh,
    while Autonoë now and the whole rabid pack were on him.
There was a single universal howl:
    the moans of Pentheus—so long as he had breath—
    mixed with their impassioned yells.
One woman carried off an arm,
    another a foot, boot and all.
They shredded his limbs—clawed them clean.
Not a finger but it dripped with crimson
    as they tossed the flesh of Pentheus like a ball.

His body lies in pieces:
    some of it under the gaunt rocks,
    some of it in the deep green thickets of the woods—

by no means easy to recover
except for his poor head,
which his mother, clasping in her hands,
has planted on her thyrsus point.
She fancies it the head of a mountain lion
and carries it through the heart of Cithaeron,
leaving her sisters still capering with the maddened ones.
She is on her way here inside these walls,
exulting in her most pathetic quarry;
raising up her voice to Bacchus
as her "master of the hounds," her "master of the hunt."

[MESSENGER *begins to move away*]

Oh what a prize champion!
What a tear-drenched triumph!
But I am going. I mean to get away
from this most grisly happening
before Agave reaches home.

[*He turns to the* CHORUS *with a dead stare answering their previous question in a passionless voice*]

That is beauty which is humble
Obeisance to heaven.
That is also wisest wisdom.
So I think, if men could follow.

[*The* MESSENGER *hurries away*]

FIFTH CHORAL LYRIC

[*The women of the* CHORUS *sing of triumph, but as their thoughts turn from* PENTHEUS *to* AGAVE, *the song becomes tinged with pity and horrific irony*]

Dance away now for great Dionysus.
Sing away, sing for the doom that befell
The dragon's descendant, Pen-the-us.
Who dressed himself up in the dress of a woman,
And blest with the fennel

Wand—for his dying—
　　Was led by a bull to his wild demise.
O Cadmean Bacchants,
　　What infamous paean have you fashioned
Of sorrow and crying!
How pretty a triumph
to plunge red hands
　　Into the life of one's child!
LEADER: Look, I see surging towards the palace
　　the rolling-eyed Agave, Pentheus' mother.

[*A swell of chanting and cries from the rest of the* CHORUS]

Welcome to you, revelers of the Bacchic god!

[*Enter* AGAVE *with her troupe of Maenads. The lyric dialogue that follows marks a climax of horror.* AGAVE *in a grisly pas seul, with her bloodied clothes, her voice and eyes wild, and the head of* PENTHEUS *mounted on her thyrsus, dances with the* CHORUS *while the rest of the Maenads form a ring around them, clapping and miming*]

LYRIC DIALOGUE

STROPHE

AGAVE:

[*thrusting the head towards the* CHORUS]

Bacchants from Asia, look!
CHORUS: You are asking me to . . . ? Oh, no!
AGAVE:

[*She points to the top of her thyrsus, where the hair of a human head takes the place of ivy*]

See what we bring you down
　　From the mountains here to these halls:
　　A freshly cut cutting of ivy . . .
　　Oh, what a wonderful hunt!
CHORUS: [*recoiling but humoring her*]
　　I see it . . . Come join in our revels.

AGAVE: [*stroking the matted hair*]
    Without a trap I trapped him:
    This tenderest whelp of a terrible lion.
Look, don't you see it?
CHORUS: From where in the wilderness, where?
AGAVE: Cithaeron.
CHORUS: Cithaeron?
AGAVE: Cithaeron butchered him.
CHORUS: Which of you smote him?
AGAVE: I was the first to. I won the prize.
    Lucky Agave, they call me
In our Bacchic seance.
CHORUS: Nobody else?
AGAVE: Yes, Cadmus' . . .
CHORUS: Cadmus?
AGAVE: Cadmus' daughters
    Handled this creature after
    I did. But only after.
    Oh, what beautiful hunting!
CHORUS: But what will you do now, poor woman?*

ANTISTROPHE

AGAVE: Now for the feast. Come join in the feast.
CHORUS: [*drawing back in horror*]
    The feast? . . . Ah! . . . deluded woman!
AGAVE: [*gently pulling her fingers through* PENTHEUS' *beard*]
    How lovely and young, little bull!
    Your cheek is just growing down
    Under your delicate crown.
CHORUS: [*still humoring her*]
He looks like a beast of the wild with his hair.
AGAVE: Yes, Bacchus, that cleverest huntsman,
    Mustered the Maenads against him
    In such a clever deploy.
CHORUS: Of course! Our king is a hunter.
AGAVE: Do you praise me?
CHORUS: We praise you.
AGAVE: And soon

*This line is missing in the Greek. I have conjectured it for the sake of coherence.

The sons of Thebes . . .
CHORUS: Together with *your* son
    Pentheus . . .
AGAVE: Will praise his mother for catching
    this cub of a lion.
CHORUS: Extraordinary quarry!
AGAVE: Extraordinarily caught!
CHORUS: Are you happy?
AGAVE: In raptures for the killing, the glory
    Of this most glorious hunt.

[*End of Lyric Dialogue*]

FIFTH EPISODE

LEADER: Then hold up, you poor unhappy woman,
    this hunting trophy that you've carried home
    for the whole of Thebes to see.
AGAVE:

[*proudly mounting the palace steps and holding out* PEN-
THEUS' *head*]

Come all of you who dwell in this high-towered town
    and realm of Thebes;
    come and see our catch:
    the animal we Cadmus daughters caught and killed . . .
    and not with nets or thonged Thessalian spears
    but our own strong white hands.
Oh, why must huntsmen brag,
    who go and get their useless tools from armorers,
    when we with our own bare hands took *him*
    and ripped apart our animal joint by joint?

[*Turning to a servant*]

Where is that old man my father?
Let him come out here.
And Pentheus, my son, where is he?
Let him fetch a ladder, set it up against the house
    and nail this lion's head high on the facade:

this lion I went hunting, I, and have brought home.

[*The* SERVANT *returns leading* CADMUS *from the palace.
Behind them, other servants carry a bier on which are the
remains of* PENTHEUS *covered with a sheet.* CADMUS, *still in
his Bacchanalian gear—an exhausted, hopeless old man—
turns to the bier-carriers*]

CADMUS: Come, follow me with your forlorn load,
    follow me, servants, carry him home:
    poor Pentheus whose dead remains
    in a dismal search I found
    scattered in a thousand pieces through the glens of Cithaeron,
    deep in the woods, undetectable,
    not one fragment together with another.

[*He pauses to control himself*]

I had left the Bacchants and come home
    and was already in the city walls, with old Tiresias,
    when someone told me of my daughter's perpetrations.
I turned back at once, back to the mountain,
    to redeem this son left lying by the Maenads.
There I saw Autonoë
    (she who once bore Aristaeus his Actaeon),
    and Ino also,
    both among the oak woods still,
    still flushed with their ghastly frenzy.
But Agave, with frenetic pace, someone told me,
    was on her way here.

[*Suddenly sees her and shudders*]

So it is true—I see her:
    a far from blessed sight.

[AGAVE *advances, parading and preening*]

AGAVE: Father, you can make the grandest boast:
    you've sired the finest daughters in the world—
    oh, by far—all three of us, I say, but especially me.

I've deserted loom and shuttle
and gone on to greater things,
to wild beast hunting with bare hands.

[*She takes the head from the thyrsus, cradles it in her arms,
and offers it to* CADMUS]

In my arms, as you can see, I carry the prize I won.
Hang it in your halls.

[CADMUS *steps back*]

Receive it, Father, in your hands.
Celebrate my hunting prowess.
Call on your friends and feast.
You are a lucky man—lucky,
because of me and what I've done.
CADMUS: [*with averted head*] Oh, immeasurable distress!
Vision beyond all seeing!
Murder is what your tragic hands have done.
Beautiful the victim cut down by the gods:
the sacrificial feast you call me to and Thebes.
I weep for your disaster, yours and then for mine.
How just but overwhelming, the god who brings us down!
Bromius, our master, though begotten of our line.

AGAVE: [*turning to bystanders*]
How disagreeable old age is . . . in men!
How crabbèd of eye!
I wish my son took after me, were a great hunter,
went hunting wild animals with the other youths of Thebes.
Hm, he is only good, that fellow,
for picking quarrels with the gods.
He ought to be corrected, Father,
and you're the one to do it.
Well, is no one going to call him here before my eyes
to witness my triumph?
CADMUS: [*with a groan from the depths*]
Oh, if you ever come to understand what it is you've done,
you'll suffer with a suffering past belief.
But if until the end

you stay forever in the state you are,
    this misery will be some miserable relief.
AGAVE: Ha! What is there amiss in this? What call for sorrow?
CADMUS: [*gently taking her arm*]
    Turn your eyes first, please, to the skies up there.
AGAVE: I am looking. What am I supposed to see?
CADMUS: Is it still the same? Or do you see some change?
AGAVE: [*dreamily*] It is lighter than before: more luminous.
CADMUS: And do you feel the same . . . the same unrest inside
                                                    your soul?
AGAVE: I do not understand your meaning.

    [*With a slight twinge*]

I seem to be becoming . . . somehow . . . aware.
    Something in my mind is changing.
CADMUS: Can you hear me? Can you answer me distinctly?
AGAVE: [*from a long way off*] Yes . . . but I've forgotten . . .
    What were we talking of, my father?
CADMUS: Whose house did you marry into, child?
AGAVE: You gave me to Echion: sprung from the dragon's teeth,
                                                    they say.
CADMUS: And in your house—the son you gave your husband,
                                                    who was he?
AGAVE: Why, Pentheus—the son we had together.
CADMUS: Then . . . whose face is this . . . you are holding in your
                                                    hands?
AGAVE: [*uneasily*] A lion's . . . or they that hunted it said so.
CADMUS: Now look straight at it. It does not cost you much
                                                    to look.
AGAVE: [*with a gasp*]
    Aah! What am I seeing? What am I cradling in my arms?
CADMUS: Gaze at it. Study it more clearly.
AGAVE: Oh! I see a giant grief—myself in agony.
CADMUS: Does it look to you just like a lion?
AGAVE: No . . . No . . . It's Pentheus' head I hold . . . most
                                                    wretched woman!
CADMUS: Before you ever realized, I was mourning him.
AGAVE: But who murdered him? Who put him in my hands?
CADMUS: Ah, ruthless truth, how unseasonable you are!

AGAVE: Tell it. Break my heart with horror of what's to come.

CADMUS: You killed him, you; and those sisters that you have.

AGAVE: Where did he perish? At home? . . . What possible
place?

CADMUS: Where once before, dogs tore Actaeon apart.

AGAVE: Cithaeron? What evil genius possessed him to go there?

CADMUS: He went to mock the gods and you at your Bacchic rites.

AGAVE: But we, how did *we* get there?

CADMUS: Out of your minds. The whole city was possessed by
Bacchus.

AGAVE: Destroyed . . . by Dionysus . . . Now I understand.

CADMUS: You bristled with rank hubris. You denied his deity.

AGAVE: My son's dear body, Father? Where is that?

CADMUS: Here. We carry it—so arduously retrieved.

AGAVE: And the limbs all put together—decently composed?

CADMUS: As best we could—after what you and your sisters did.*

AGAVE: Maddened, yes, but how did Pentheus share in this?

CADMUS: He proved himself to be like you,
    a blasphemer of the god, and so the god
    has brought us down together all in a single crash:
    you, your sisters, Pentheus, and me—
    to obliterate my house, for now I have no heir:
    no, none, the stripling from your womb—you stricken woman—
    is most hideously and horribly cut down:

[*He turns his gaze to the bier*]

Light of this house's eyes, son, my grandson,
    pillar of my palace beams!
This city held you in its awe,
    and as for this old man,
    no one while you were near ever dared to slight me,
    for you would make him pay for it in full.
But now, now I shall be harried from my home in shame,
    I, Cadmus the great, who sowed the Theban race
    and harvested a crop so beautiful.
Oh, most beloved of men—

---

*This line does not appear in the Greek. I have conjectured it to supply the connection of some three missing lines of Agave's.

for even dead I count you with the most beloved, my child—
     never more will you touch my chin, calling me Grandfather,
     hug me, my son, and say:
"Is anyone annoying you, old man?
Is anyone a nuisance, rude, upsetting you?
Tell me, Grandfather.
I'll punish anyone who does you wrong."
But now I am bereft and you are lost,
     your mother racked, our family broken.
Does anyone dismiss the powers above?
Look on this poor creature's end, and then believe.
LEADER: Cadmus, I feel your agony;
     for though your grandson reaps no less than he deserves,
     the agony is yours.
AGAVE: [*falling to her knees*]
     Father, you see how everything for me is overturned.*
Everything is deserted, dark,
     and who but myself put out the light?
You brutal hands, smoking with gore,
     once you washed and sped this baby to his bed.
Wicked hands that should have decked a young man for his bride,
     now you dress a corpse to speed him to the world below.

     [*Turning to* CADMUS]

See, Father, these polluted fingers,
     already pale and rinsed with tears—
     they beg to make amends.
Grant me this, at least,
     to kiss each limb and bid farewell to the body of my son.

---

*After this line there follows a gap of about fifty lines in the extant manu-
scripts. They include Agave's lament and the farewell to her son; also, the
first part of Dionysus' speech. From various sources and some twenty-one
papyrus fragments recently discovered, we can form a general picture of the
contents of the lacuna. I have translated these fragments and fitted them into
the framework of the reconstructed scene. Agave, flung in a moment from
ecstasy to despair, and conscious of being a polluted creature, begs permission
to lay out the body for burial and to bid it a last farewell. Cadmus consents,
warning her of the conditions. Over the body she accuses herself and moves
the audience to pity, kissing each limb in turn and lamenting over it.

CADMUS: So be it, daughter.
    Prepare his poor remains to fit his journey to the dead;
    but with dispatch: a filicidal killer
    may not linger on the harm she did.
AGAVE:

    [*kneels by the bier, which has been lowered to the ground*]

My son, my son,
    whom these blind fingers tore apart
    and these callous eyes attacked,
    we know not what we do, when we pride ourselves we know.

    [*She is about to raise the body but recoils with horror*]

How can I, wretch that I am,
    place on my lap this mangled body that I dare not touch?
What lament can I intone?
I would kiss every part of you, my son,
    yes, kiss the flesh that once I fed.
This head of matted curls
    once nestled on my breast.
O much loved face!
O young and tender visage!

    [*Turning to the* CHORUS]

Pity me, you women,
    I who must compose from ruins this noble edifice
    she so lately has demolished.

    [*She signals to a* SERVANT]

Fetch some princely shroud
    that we may caparison for burial
    the body of a king.
Come, my father,
    we must order head and body of this stricken one.
Let us, as far as we may,
    restore the beauty of his robust frame.

[*The* SERVANT *returns bearing a costly fabric, which she hands to* AGAVE]

Look, I shall cover your dear head and all your limbs
    with this shroud—these limbs besmirched with gore,
    this body which these nails of mine have raked with furrows.

SIXTH CHORAL ODE*

[*The women of the* CHORUS *celebrate* DIONYSUS *as the cherisher and champion of true, uncluttered humanity*]

STROPHE
Great Dionysus, breaker of barriers
    Son of the Father imperial;
Vine-clad god and priest of the natural,
    Sodden with light in purpureal
Cypress glooms and mystical pines:
    Now we adore and address you.
Capture the nights and ambush the days
    Of the impiously stupidly clever:

ANTISTROPHE
Those that put faith in prowess of brain
    And the force of a master plan
To change the world, and think they know better
    Than the age-old wisdom of man.
But us, O Bacchus, bind us with bryony,
    Crown us with ivy, and
Let every peak of Cithaeron ring
    With the triumph of animal holiness.

*This chorus is not in any of the extant manuscripts, but there must have been a chorus at the end of the Fifth Episode. For the sake of balance and completion and relying on my sense of context, I have presumed to compose one.

SIXTH EPISODE

[DIONYSUS, *no longer in disguise, appears above the palace and addresses the people of Thebes and then turns to* CADMUS *and* AGAVE]*

DIONYSUS: The sins of jealousy and anger
  made this Pentheus deal unjustly with one bringing blessings,
  whom he disgracefully imprisoned and insulted;
  and so he met his end at the hands of his own kin—
  an unnatural end and yet a just one.
I shall not curb the flail
  under which these culprits have to smart.
They shall be exiled from the city
  to expiate the guilt this murder cries for.
Not one of them shall ever see their fatherland again,
  nor shall murderers live beside the tomb.
As to you, Cadmus,
  you shall be changed into a snake,†
  and your wife, Ares' daughter,
  whom you married though you were a mortal,
  shall take reptilian shape as well.
You shall drive a chariot drawn by bullocks
  with your consort at your side
  —so says Zeus's oracle—
  leading a barbarian tribe.

---

*The first thirteen lines of Dionysus' speech are among the papyrus fragments recently recovered. With this line we are back with the extant text.

  If I were directing this play I would be tempted to end the performance at this line, Agave's "Father, you see how everything for me is overturned." The *ex machina* appearance of Dionysus and the whole of the Denouement is something of an anticlimax. I think Euripides is saying: "The play is over, but I know you people won't be content without your dose of mythology and bad theology—so here it is."

†"This bizarre prediction has puzzled mythologists no less than it startles the common reader. The story bears traces of having been put together at a relatively late date out of heterogeneous older elements." Thus E. R. Dodds, who gives a detailed exegesis of its original character in his notes to line 1330, p. 235. I see no point in distracting a modern audience with a fairy-tale story that has nothing to do with the essence of this masterful play.

Their uncountable battalions
   shall ransack many cities;
   but when they loot Apollo's shrine
   they shall receive short shrift on their return.
You, however, and your wife,
   Ares will preserve,
   translating you to the land of the blessed ones
   and everlasting life.
This I speak to you as no mortal man but Zeus-begotten.
If only you had been willing to be wise
   instead of otherwise
   you would be happy now and your friend the son of Zeus.
CADMUS: Have mercy, Dionysus, we have sinned.
DIONYSUS: Too late to know me now; you did not when you
                              should.
AGAVE: Ah! . . . we understand, but you are merciless.
DIONYSUS: Yes, because you flouted my born divinity.
AGAVE: But gods should not repeat the passions of mere men.
DIONYSUS: My father sanctioned this in ages past, great Zeus.
AGAVE: Old man, it is decreed—the sadness of banishment.

[DIONYSUS *disappears, but his voice echoes around the hills*]

DIONYSUS: Then why do you delay when your destiny is plain?
CADMUS: [*taking* AGAVE's *hand*]
   My daughter, what an evil we have come to!
All of us: you, your poor sisters, and my unhappy self:
   an old man as an alien, his home in alien lands.
Then the sad prediction
   that he must lead barbarian mongrel hordes against our Hellas,
   he a vicious serpent, my wife a serpent too—
   Ares' child, Harmonia.
I am to head an army, armed to raze the altars
   and sepulchers of Hellas.
Cadmus full of sorrows
   shall find no respite ever, even after crossing
   the dungeon river of Acheron.
AGAVE: [*clasping his knees*]
   Oh, Father, torn from *you* I go into banishment.
CADMUS: What help is it to throw your arms around me,

my unhappy child, like a little bird:
you a white-downed cygnet and I a decrepit swan.*
AGAVE: Where then shall I turn, cast out from home?
CADMUS: I do not know, my daughter. Your father is no help.

LYRIC DIALOGUE AND DENOUEMENT

[*The women of the* CHORUS *and the women of the Maenadic group from the mountains begin to get into their formations for the exodus march, to the accompaniment of flute, tambourine, castanets, and drum.* CADMUS *and* AGAVE *in a slow melancholy walk move towards the gates of the city. The meter changes from the iambic trimeter of the ordinary dialogue to the traditional envoi of anapests and dactyls*]

AGAVE: Goodbye to my house, goodbye to my city.
I leave you for exile and flee from my bridal home.
I leave you for misery.
CADMUS: Go to Aristaeus, my child, your sister's husband.
AGAVE: I weep for you, Father.
CADMUS: And I weep for you:
Tears for yourself and tears for your sisters.
AGAVE: Hard is the brutally ruthless fate
Lord Dionysus has visited on you:
On you and your house.
CADMUS: Ruthless, yes, because of the way
You dishonored his name in Thebes.

[*They halt and embrace*]

AGAVE: Father, farewell.
CADMUS: Sad daughter, farewell . . . .
A "well" for a way that will never fare well.

[AGAVE, *joined by a group of Maenads, walks slowly towards the open country as* CADMUS *too moves off in a different direction*]

AGAVE: Escort me, my friends, to where I shall find

*A lot of ink has needlessly been spilt over this image by scholars. The whole point is that Agave is not offering protection but seeking it.

My pitiful sisters—comrades in exile.
I want to go far from the horrible eyes
And my own vision of butchering Cithaeron
To a place no memory of thyrsus haunts.
Let others meddle with Bacchants.

[*Exit* AGAVE *into the distance*]

CHORUS:

[*in a rhythmic march from the arena*]

Many the forms of divine intervention.
  Many surprises are wrought by the gods:
  What was expected was never effected,
  What was ignored, God found a way to.
Such was this story today.

THE TROJAN WOMEN

~⚬~

ΤΡΩΙΑΔΕΣ

For Christian and Florence Ficat

There is little doubt that Euripides wrote this nightmare lamentation in a state of despair, and that he wrote it to shock. The islands of the Aegean, indeed the whole Greek world from the Peloponnese to the shores of Asia Minor, bristled with alarms, threats, recriminations, and reports of atrocity. Athens, though locked in a sixteen-year stalemate with Sparta, was nevertheless equipping a grandiose expedition against Sicily, ostensibly to help an ally but with all the trappings of an imperial conquest. A fleet of over a hundred ships stood ready to sail, carrying a muster of several thousand men.

Euripides, with that foresight which would make Shelley call poets "the unacknowledged legislators of the world," wrote *The Trojan Women* as a prophecy of tragedy to shock Athens to her senses. Perhaps he nearly succeeded, for there was discussion and hesitation among the councillors of the *boulē*, the Athenian senate. The Sicilian campaign, however, went ahead, and it proved the greatest disaster ever to befall Athens, one from which she never really recovered. Her entire fleet was either captured or sunk, and some fifteen thousand young men—the flower of her manhood—were turned into slaves and spent the rest of their lives brutally toiling in the salt mines of Sicily.

In *The Trojan Women*, Euripides, the master of pathos, spells out the misery and stupidity of war. His language, as always, is brittlely modern, but the contrast between the verbal prettiness of the choruses and the lugubrious horror strokes of the stichomythia—dialogue in which two characters deliver alternate lines—has all the bitterness of a twisted smile.

The play was presented at the city Dionysia in Athens in 415 B.C., it being the third part of a lost trilogy which ended with a satyr play called *Sisyphus*. It took only second prize—which is not to be wondered at. Indeed, it speaks well for the broad-mindedness of the Athenians that, given its message of foreboding and doom, it was presented at all.

Euripides was then in his sixty-fifth year or so and writing at the top of his form.

CHARACTERS

POSEIDON, god of the sea
PALLAS ATHENA, protectress of Athens
HECUBA, widow of Priam, king of Troy
CHORUS, of captured Trojan women
TALTHYBIUS, Greek officer and herald
CASSANDRA, daughter of Hecuba and Priam, a prophetess
ANDROMACHE, widow of Hector son of Priam
MENELAUS, king of Sparta and husband of Helen
HELEN, wife of Menelaus and cause of the Trojan War
ASTYANAX, a small boy, the son of Hector and Andromache
GREEK SOLDIERS
ATTENDANTS

TIME AND SETTING

It is midmorning in the Greek camp on the plains of Troy. In the
distance smoke still rises from the fallen city. A huddle of
women awaiting their sentence of slavery and prostitution are
grouped around the prostrate figure of Hecuba near a few
disheveled tents. Poseidon strides into view. He is cloaked in a
greenish mantle and his swarthy bearded face is turned towards
Troy. He holds in his hands a trident.

PROLOGUE

POSEIDON: From the salt sea depths of the Aegean
   where the lacy feet of the Nereids weave and dance,
   I, Poseidon, come.
Never have I lost my fondness
   for this Phrygian city of Troy.
No, not since the day that Phoebus and I
   with line and plummet threw up around her
   a stone girdle of towers.
But look at her now,
   smoldering and wrecked by the Argive spear.

It was Epeius the Phocian from Parnassus
   who with the help of Pallas built the wooden horse,

crammed it with men, and thrust this load of ruin
   into the walled city.
It will be known hereafter
   as the Wooden Horse—pregnant with spears.

The groves are now a desert,
   the sanctuaries of the gods spattered with blood.
On the altar steps of Zeus the Protector
   Priam lies dead—dead where he fell.
The opulence of Phrygia,
   all its gold and all its plunder,
   are being loaded on to the Achaean ships
   as they lie in wait for a favorable breeze
   to carry home those Greeks who yearn to see their wives and
                          children
   after a decade of useless seasons
   since they brought an army here to sack this city.

As for me,
   I too have been overwhelmed:
   overruled by those two goddesses in harness:
   Hera, patroness of Argos, and Athena,
   who together have set out to break this Phrygian town.
So I must say farewell to famous Ilium,
   farewell to all my shrines there . . .
   for when grim doom lays its clutches on a city,
   all piety sickens too and devotion to the gods.

Loud are the wailings on the banks of the Scamander
   of the many captive women being allotted to their masters.
Some go to the men of Arcady, some to men of Thessaly,
   others to the scions of Theseus, the Athenian princes.
Inside the tents here are the rest of the Trojan women
   who have not yet been assigned: they are waiting
   to be picked by the chief men of the army.
Among them is the daughter of Tyndareus,
   rightly deemed a prisoner: Helen of Sparta.

[POSEIDON *turns his gaze towards the prostrate* HECUBA]

If you want to see misery at its worst,
   look at the creature lying there, poor Hecuba,
   weeping a plethora of tears for a plethora of disasters.
Her daughter Polyxena was murdered secretly
   and died bravely on Achilles' tomb, unhappy child.
Priam is no more; her children gone:
   all except Cassandra, still a virgin and discarded by Apollo
   to rave her prophecies.
Agamemnon means to flout all decency and the god's decision
   and drag her in the dark to bed.

   [*Turning again towards the ruins of Troy*]

And now goodbye to my once so blessed city
   pinnacled in stone.
You would be standing yet
   if Zeus's daughter Pallas had not marked you out for ruin.

   [*The goddess* PALLAS ATHENA *appears. Dressed like a soldier and wearing the famous aegis—a breastplate with a Gorgon's head entwined with snakes—she holds a shield and spear, looming over the landscape*]

FIRST EPISODE

ATHENA: [*approaching* POSEIDON]
   Will you permit me to address you
   and call a halt to our ancient quarrel:
   you my father's closest kin and a mighty deity,
   so awed among the gods?
POSEIDON: I will. Ties of kinship, my lady Athena,
   work no small magic on the heart.
ATHENA: Thank you for your graciousness ... And now, my lord,
   there is something that you and I must plan together.
POSEIDON: About some message from the gods—
   Zeus perhaps, or some other deity?
ATHENA: No, about Troy—where we are standing now.
   I need your help in a matter that affects us both.
POSEIDON: What! are you jettisoning your former hate,

moved to pity now that Troy is flames and ash?

ATHENA: First things first. Will you join with me
and help me carry out a plan?

POSEIDON: Of course! Once I'm told what it is.
Are you helping the Achaeans or the Phrygians?

ATHENA: I want to make the Trojans whom I hated happy,
and the homecoming of the Achaeans a disaster.

POSEIDON: How you shift from mood to mood,
plunging from hatred to excess of love!

ATHENA: So you haven't heard how my temples and I have been
dishonored?

POSEIDON: I have. How Ajax hauled Cassandra from your
sanctuary.

ATHENA: And the Achaeans have not done or said a thing.

POSEIDON: Although it was through your power that they took
Ilium.

ATHENA: That is why I want to punish them.

POSEIDON: I am ready and willing. What do you propose?

ATHENA: I want you to wreck their passage home.

POSEIDON: What, before they start, on land, or out on the salt
sea main?

ATHENA: After they've embarked from Troy for home.
Zeus will pelt them with rain and hail.
Black tearing winds will blot out the sky,
and to me he said he would give his thunderbolts and lightning
to smash the Achaeans and set their ships on fire.
You for your part
must make the Aegean roar with mountainous surf and swirl-
ing currents.
Choke the inlets of Euboea with bodies.
Let the Achaeans in future learn
to respect my shrines and reverence the other gods.

POSEIDON: It shall be done. This favor needs few words.
I'll whip up the Aegean to a spume.
The shores of Myconus,
the reefs of Delos, Scyros, Lemnos,
the capes of Caphareus
shall be strewn with the washed-up bodies of the drowned.

*   *   *

Go now to Olympus,
   get from your father's hands the thunderbolts
   and watch for the moment when the Argive fleet casts off.

[ATHENA *takes her leave*]

He is a fool that man who does not stop at sacking cities
   but lays temples waste and tombs—
   those sanctuaries of the dead.

[POSEIDON *retires as* HECUBA *stirs. Half rising from where she
is lying, she leans on one elbow. She is dressed in the pathetic
rags of a once regal gown*]

LYRIC MONOLOGUE

STROPHE I

HECUBA: Lift up your head from the ground, you stricken one:
   This is not Troy nor Troy's royal family.
   Change with the spirit of change, the changeable.
   Sail with the current, drift with the tide.
   Do not point your prow straight into the billows.
   Aiai! Aiai!
   Why should I not lament in my misery,
   With country and spouse and children gone?
   How all the pomp of ancestry dwindles!
   How little did it ever amount to!

ANTISTROPHE I

To be still or not to be still is the question:
   Whether or not to cry out in regret—
   Stretched as I am on a rack of calamity,
   My limbs and my back heavy with weariness?
   Oh my head, my temples, oh my sides!
   Oh to toss and give rest to my spine!
   To rock in a rhythm to the song of my tears!
   Such is the music of sorrowful souls.
   Such is the chant and the jangled tune
   Of ruin and doom, where there is no dance.

[HECUBA *struggles to her feet*]

STROPHE II

You prows of ships so neatly forging
With flaying oars across the purple
Seas from the sheltering harbors of Hellas
With piping challenge of flute and fife,
You made fast your Egyptian hawsers
In the bay of Troy—how sad! sad!—
When you came here to retrieve
That cursed woman, Menelaus' bride:
That disgrace to her brother Castor,
Shame to the whole of Sparta, that
Murderess of Priam—father
Of fifty sons—who leaves me here,
The wretched Hecuba, collapsed
In utter dereliction . . . Oh!

[*She moves to a rock and sits*]

ANTISTROPHE II

What a sorry place to sit
Throned near Agamemnon's tents!
I who am to be transported:
Slave, old woman, gray head cropped
By sorrow . . . Come then, woebegone widows
Of Trojan heroes armed in bronze
And you husbandless virgins, weep
For smoldering Ilium. I, screeching
Like a mother bird for her young,
Intone for you a song most different
From the song I used to sing, when beating
Time with my foot as I leant on Priam's
Scepter and led the choir in worship
And dance to the strains of Phrygian music.

[*Out of the tents there emerges a band of women—unkempt, haggard, in rags—who are some of the older captive Trojans and form* CHORUS *1. They press around* HECUBA, *concerned and lost*]

CHORAL DIALOGUE

STROPHE I

LEADER: Hecuba, why this bawling? why this baying?
    What is the news? These hovels are ringing
    With your howls of anguish, and here inside
    The Trojan women about to be slaves
    Tremble in terror.
HECUBA: My poor child, down by the ships
    The oarsmen are already preparing to row.
LEADER: Don't tell me! . . . Oh . . . then does it mean
    It's time to say goodbye to my native land?
HECUBA: I am not sure, but suspect the worst.
LEADER: The worst? Ah, the worst!
    Come out of the tents, you women of Troy.
    Come and hear your horrible future:
    The men of Argos are setting sail.
HECUBA: No, no! do not bring out
    My wandering, possessed Cassandra—
    To be the butt of Argive jeers.
    Do not heap grief upon grief.
    Troy, my stricken Troy, is over:
    All are lost—living and dead.

[*A second group of women, younger, straggles from the tents,
as pathetic in garb and demeanor as the first. They are*
CHORUS 2]

ANTISTROPHE I

LEADER: Trembling I've crept from these tents, Agamemnon's,
    To attend you, my queen. Is it death that they plan
    For miserable me, or are the mariners
    Manning their ships, getting ready to row?
HECUBA: My child, since dawn I've been waiting and watching,
    My sleepless heart numb with foreboding.
LEADER: Has any message come from the Greeks
    Turning me into a miserable slave?
HECUBA: No, but the lots are about to be drawn.
LEADER: Oh no! . . . Who will it be that gets me?
    Shall I be taken to Argos or Phthia,

Or to some islet far from Troy
Where I shall be desolate?
HECUBA: I know! I know! . . . And as for me,
Whose miserable slave am I to be?
And where? Where shall this old woman
Be a drudge, a futile drone, the image
Of a corpse and a ghastly uselessness . . .
Perhaps as porter at a gate,
Or a children's nurse—I who once
Was the honored queen of Troy.

[*At this point the two* CHORUSES *unite. The members speaking severally survey with apprehension, curiosity, and sometimes almost with enthusiasm the possible places they may be taken to*]

STROPHE II

CHORUS I AND 2

  1: Aiai! Aiai! Heartbreaking
     Are your lamentations . . .
  2: Never again shall I work my shuttle
     Nimbly on a Trojan loom.
  3: For the last time I look on the graves
     Of my parents . . . Oh, for the last time!
  4: There's worse for me, much worse:
     Forced to lie in the bed of a Greek—
     The greatest nightmare of them all.
  5: Or a female slave fetching water
     From Pirene's sacred spring in Corinth.
  6: For me, I hope it's glorious Athens . . .
     Never never Sparta, Helen's
     Damnable home, where I'd have to
     Look on Menelaus as master—
  7: That pillager of Troy!

ANTISTROPHE II

  8: There's lovely Thessaly, land of Peneus
     At the foot of Mount Olympus, rich
     Beyond all dreams—or so I've heard—
     Fertile and fruitful in abundance.
  9: Let me go there, my second choice

'After glorious, holy Athens.
10: What about Etna, the domain
   Of Hephaestus, and Sicily
   The mother of mountains, which looks across
   To Phoenicia: famous I am told
   For its faraway crown of challenging peaks.
11: And opposite, if you sail away
   Over the Sea of Ionia, a place
   The pretty river Crathis waters,
12: Which turns your hair a flaming gold
   And nourishes a land of vigorous men.
LEADER: But here comes an officer of the Greek army.
   He must have news: he's in such a hurry.
   What will it be? What will he tell us?
   We're slaves already of the Dorian Greeks.

[TALTHYBIUS *marches briskly towards* HECUBA. *He is a man in the prime of life and wears the dashing uniform of the Greek army: short kilt, body-hugging tunic, heavy sandals laced up the bare calves, a flowing crimson cloak, and plumed helmet. In spite of his downright manner it becomes obvious that he is embarrassed by his mission and would like to get it over as quickly as possible.*]

SECOND EPISODE

TALTHYBIUS: Hecuba, madam, you are aware that . . .
   I've made . . . have made . . . several . . . er, trips before
   as a staff officer of the, er, Achaean army.
So I'm known to you already, my lady . . .
I'm Talthybius and I've come with official news.
HECUBA: [*dropping, trancelike, into verse*]
   Here it comes, dear women of Troy,
   What I have so long been dreading.
TALTHYBIUS: You've all been allotted. Was that your dread?
HECUBA: So, to a town in Thessaly?
   Phthia perhaps, or is it to Thebes?
TALTHYBIUS: You are all personally assigned, each to a man.
HECUBA: [*with bitter sarcasm*] Personally assigned!
   To whom? Who are the lucky ones

Among us ladies of Troy?

TALTHYBIUS: I can tell you. But ask one at a time, not all at once.

HECUBA: Very well. My poor Cassandra,
Tell me who got *her*.

TALTHYBIUS: Very specially chosen ... King Agamemnon got
her.

HECUBA: What? A slave for his Spartan wife?
No no no!

TALTHYBIUS: Not that, but concubine: secret concubine.

HECUBA: N ... o? A consecrated virgin
of Apollo, who won the right
From the god with hair of gold
To remain unwed forever.

TALTHYBIUS: He's shot through with lust for the maiden prophetess.

HECUBA: O my daughter, throw away
Those temple keys, cast off
Those chaplets and those vestiges
Of your sanctified profession.

TALTHYBIUS: So it goes for nothing to share the bed of a king?

HECUBA: [*after a long pause*] And my youngest child
You wrenched from me—
Where is she?

TALTHYBIUS: You mean Polyxena ... who else?

HECUBA: Yes, her. Who drew *her*?

TALTHYBIUS: [*hedging*] She's been assigned to serve at the tomb
of Achilles.

HECUBA: Great heavens! Have I borne a child
To be lackey at a tomb? What curious
New law or ritual, my friend,
Among the Greeks is this?

TALTHYBIUS: Her life has reached completion. She is free from
cares.

HECUBA: [*reluctant to probe further*]
And unfortunate Andromache, my stalwart Hector's wife—
what fate has she?

TALTHYBIUS: She? The son of Achilles got her. A real prize.

HECUBA: And me? Whose servant am I—this ancient carcass
who has to use the third leg of a stick to walk?

TALTHYBIUS: Odysseus king of Ithaca drew you as his slave.
HECUBA: [*lapsing into verse again*] Ee . . . h!
    Batter that cropped pate of mine,
    Claw my nails through my cheeks . . .
    O . . . h!
    The lot I've drawn makes me slave
    To that loathsome perfidious beast,
    That enemy of every right,
    A monster who knows no law:
    A twister with a double tongue
    Who lies and breaks his promises
    And turns all friendship into hate.
    Cry for me, you daughters of Troy.
    This finishes me; it's total ruin:
    The worst, unluckiest lot of all.
LEADER: Your fate, my queen, now you know; but what of mine?
    Who is to be my master? . . . In what part of Greece?
TALTHYBIUS: [*turning to the women of the* CHORUS]
    Enough!
Go at once and bring Cassandra out.
I must hand her over to the commander in chief,
    then conduct the other captive women
    to the men to whom they've been allotted.

[*He stops short, seeing one of the tents all lit up*]

Hey, hey! What's going on in there?
All that blazing light!
Are the Trojan females burning down their nest
    with them inside just to avoid the trip to Argos?
My word! free spirits like these
    don't easily adjust to their misfortunes.
Open up in there! Open up!
Dying may be all right for you but not for the Greeks,
    and I'd be blamed.
HECUBA: No, it's not what you think, there is no fire:
    only my manic child Cassandra.
    Here she comes on the double.

[CASSANDRA *comes tumbling out of a tent in a kind of dance,
holding aloft a flaming torch. She is dressed like a priestess in*

*a flowing white alb, but it is crumpled and dirty. Her face is
smudged and her hair wild. Her head is crammed with wilted
sprigs of laurel and streamers of white wool. She imagines
she is about to be married to Agamemnon and that Hymen
himself, the god of marriage, is in the temple ready to celebrate the wedding]*

LYRIC APOSTROPHE

*[In the following two strophes, Euripides lays the ground for a
stunning irony. That which in the confused mists of impassioned euphoria on the part of* CASSANDRA *looks like an
excited anticipation of her union with* AGAMEMNON *is contra-
dicted in the ensuing dialogue by a most sinister threat:
nothing less than the murder of* AGAMEMNON *and the destruction of the house of Atreus]*

STROPHE

CASSANDRA: Lift it up, let me parade this holy light.
　Look at it! Look at it
　Flooding this wedding shrine!
　O Lord Hymeneus
　Bridegroom blest!
　And blessed am I about to be matched
　With a king in Argos, yes, Hymen, you nuptial god,
　While you my mother do nothing but moan and weep
　For my dead father and dearest fatherland.
　So I must for myself for my own wedding
　Lift up aloft the flaming torch
　Flashing and flaring
　In your honor O Hymen,
　In your honor O Hecate,
　With all the rubrics of light for a virgin's wedding.

ANTISTROPHE

Lift up your foot in the air and on with the dance.
　Hurray! Hurrah!
　Just like the glorious times
　Of my father. The choir
　Is blessed. O Phoebus,

Inside the temple festooned with laurel
You yourself lead it to honor your priestess. Yes Hymen,
Hymen hymeneal! . . . O mother take part in the singing,
Take part in the dance: swing out, swing in.
To please me measure your footsteps with mine
And shout out the nuptial song for the bride.
Shout out her joy
With relays of hymns.
Sing, you maidens of Troy
For the spouse that destiny brings to my bed.

THIRD EPISODE

[*While* CASSANDRA, *flourishing her torch, continues to fling
herself around in her manic dance, the* CHORUS LEADER
approaches HECUBA *with concern*]

LEADER: Queen, can you not restrain your wild daughter
    before she prances her way into the Argive camp?

[HECUBA, *at a loss, throws up her arms in a bitter appeal to
Hephaestus, god of fire*]

HECUBA: Hephaestus, you who light up the nuptials of mortals
                                                    with torches,
    how cruel of you to parody with flame
    all the hopes I had so long ago!

[*Advancing on* CASSANDRA]

O my poor child,
    never did I think you'd celebrate your marriage
    amid the spears and lances of the Argives.
Give me that light.
    In your hectic gyrations you cannot hold it straight.
Our sufferings have not made you sensible:
    you are the same as you always were.

[HECUBA *gently takes the torch from* CASSANDRA *and hands it
to one of the Trojan women*]

Take these torches,* dear women,
   and let your response to these bridal overtures be tears.
CASSANDRA: Mother, crown me in triumph,
   Congratulate me in my royal match.
Escort me to it,
   and if you detect a lack of zeal, give me a push.
For by Loxias I swear
   I shall be a far more lethal bride
   than famous Agamemnon king of the Greeks
   ever bargained for.
I shall kill him
   and in my turn devastate his house
   and so avenge my brothers and my father.
But let me not dwell on atrocities,†
   or chant of the ax that will sever my neck
   and the necks of others;
   nor of the matricidal struggles
   that my marriage will engender;
   nor of the annihilation of the house of Atreus.

Let me talk instead
   of how our city is more fortunate than the Greeks'.
Possessed I may be
   but I shall rise above my frenzy.
For the sake of a single woman and a single passion
   the Greeks have thrown away thousands of lives.
Their oh-so-intelligent commander in chief
   lost what he loved most
   for something he loved least.
Yes, he gave up for his brother

---

*No one knows why Euripides uses the plural here, when we have been led to believe that Cassandra was brandishing a single torch. Perhaps some of the women surrounding Cassandra also carried torches and Hecuba would like to get rid of the lot.
†The chain of atrocities that Cassandra will only hint at comprises Clytemnestra's adultery with Aegisthus, leading to her murder of her husband, Agamemnon, and of Cassandra; the murder of Clytemnestra by her son Orestes; and the subsequent madness of Orestes.

the jewel of his hearth, his own daughter,*
all for a woman who was nowise dragged away
but went of her own free will.
By the banks of the Scamander their armies died
in battles for which neither their own borders
nor their towering cities were at stake.
And those the war god Ares took
never saw their children, never were enfolded
in their shrouds by wifely hands.
There they lie in an alien soil;
while back at home were more miseries still:
wives dying as widows,
lonely old men in houses without sons—
sons they'd reared for nothing—
over whose graves no one will come to sprinkle a little earth
and the blood of sacrifice.
What a lovely panegyric for their whole campaign!
And best leave unsaid the ignominies at home:
I'm not one to chant and celebrate obscenities.†

The Trojans on the other hand
reaped the richest reward of all,
to die for their native land.
And those that fell to the spear
were carried home by loving hands,
cradled in the caressing earth of their fathers
and tended in their obsequies by pious hands.
Moreover, those Trojans who did not die in battle
lived at home with their wives and children:
a happiness denied the Greeks.
As to the loss of Hector, listen and remember:
he died the greatest of men;
a thing made possible only by the coming of the Greeks.
Had they stayed at home,

*Iphigenia, whom Agamemnon sacrificed at Aulis to solicit favorable winds for the Greek armada to sail to Troy.
†Cassandra is thinking of the sexual scandals taking place in Argos, headed by the queen herself. During the ten years of war, wives and daughters would be an easy prey to crops of unenlisted young men growing up since the war began.

all that glory would be hidden.
And Paris:
    had he not wedded the daughter of Zeus,*

Of course, any man of sense shrinks from war,
    but should war come, a brave man's death
    is a country's crowning pride—
    as a coward is its shame.
So, Mother, there is no need
    to feel sorry either for your country or my match,
    for by this mating of mine
    those that you and I hate most
    I shall dispatch.
LEADER: It is all very well to laugh off your family's miseries,
    but everything you blithely chant you'll see is fiction.†
TALTHYBIUS:

[*who has been listening amazed and with considerable irritation*]

Were it not for the fact that Apollo has frenzied away your
                                      reason,
    you'd not get off scot free for sending off my generals
    with such a blast of nonsense.

[*After a pause*]

It amazes me how the great and supposedly intelligent
    are not one whit superior to nonentities.
Look at the way this monarch of united Greece,
    the precious son of Atreus,
    has fallen for this crazy girl!
Plain man that I am,
    I'd never let her near my bed.

[*Turning back to* CASSANDRA]

---

daughter of Zeus: Helen.
†Cassandra, for having refused the sexual overtures of Apollo, was fated by
 him always to prophesy the truth but never to be believed.

As for you,
    because you are mentally deranged
    I'll consign to the breeze your insults to us Greeks
    and your overblown eulogy of Troy.
Come on, then, follow me to the ships—
    you, oh, so lovely bride of our commander.

[*Turning to* HECUBA]

And you,
    as soon as Odysseus, Laertes' son, summons you,
    be ready to follow.
At least you'll be a good woman's* slave,
    as say all who went to Troy.

CASSANDRA:

[*With a dismissive and derisive glance at* TALTHYBIUS]

What a lackey!
How do such creatures manage to usurp
    all the kudos of staff officers,
    universally hated as they are
    and mere pawns of kings and states?
So, you tell me that my mother
    will reach Odysseus' home?
What then becomes of Apollo's prophecy,
    made clear to me, which flatly says she dies right here?
    Of which the circumstances are too monstrous to mention.

And Odysseus, miserable man,
    he has no idea of the trials in store for him.
All my sufferings and all of Troy's
    are golden in comparison.
Heap ten years on these past ten
    before ever he reaches his native land—alone.
He will see the rock haunts and the clamping gorge
    of the terrible Charybdis,
    and the mountain-lowering Cyclops who devours human flesh,

good woman's: i.e., Penelope's, she being Odysseus' wife.

and Circe on the Ligurian shores
who turns men into swine.
He will suffer shipwreck on the briny deep,
and the craving for the lotus flower;
see the sun god's sacred cattle
whose butchered carcasses cry out in words
that send Odysseus into panic.
To cut the saga short:
he shall go down into Hades
and survive the marshes of the dead
only to find at home a thousand sorrows.

But why should I go on about Odysseus' afflictions?
Let me be brief.*
Hades is where I hurry, to join my groom.
Black will be the darkest night not day when he is buried.
Yes, you so seeming great commander of the Greeks.
Me? My naked body shall be tossed
down the gullies where the winter torrents gush,
near to where my buried bridegroom lies,
there to be food for beasts of the wild—
I priestess of Apollo.

[CASSANDRA *begins to tear at her clothes and the various insignia of her office*]

Off with you, wreaths of my beloved god,†
talismans of ecstasy, farewell:
I turn my back on the festivals at which I shone.
Yes, off with you, I flense you from my skin,
I a virgin still;
let the breezes waft them to you—you my prophet king.††

---

*Euripides heightens the dramatic emotion of Cassandra's next seventeen lines in the Greek by adopting a trochaic line of eight beats. I follow with a looser trochaic meter of four to six beats (allowing for the faster pace of the Greek).
†*my beloved god:* Apollo.
††*my prophet king:* also Apollo.

[*Turning to* TALTHYBIUS]

Where is the commander's ship? Where do I embark?
Watch for the wind, don't wait to swell the sails
    bearing me away, me one of the three
    Furies . . . Mother, goodbye—you must not cry.
Darling land of my birth, farewell, and you my brothers
    under the earth, and you my father who gave us life,
    you'll not be waiting long for me.
Down to the dead I go victorious,
    ruining the house of Atreus that ruined us.

[*At a sign from* TALTHYBIUS, *two guards roughly take hold of*
CASSANDRA *and march her away.* HECUBA *faints. There is a
stunned silence. At length the* CHORUS LEADER *turns to the rest
of the women*]

LEADER: You ladies-in-waiting to old Hecuba,
    do you not see how your queen has fallen to the ground—
Speechless, are you not going to raise her up?
Or will you just leave her lying there?
HECUBA: [*lifting her head*] No, let me lie where I have fallen.
    Such kindness, dear girls, would not be kind.
Let me be submerged
    beneath all I have suffered and have still to suffer.
And you gods,
    how useless to expect any help from you!
And yet, and yet, to call upon the gods is salutary
    when any of us runs headlong into trouble.

Let me simply tell myself how happy once I was,
    though the contrast will be pitiable.

[*She raises herself on one arm*]

I was a queen and married a king;
    became mother of princely sons:
    no mere ciphers but Phrygians most magnificent.
No woman of Troy or Greece or any foreign part
    could boast of mothering such sons as these;

yet these I saw laid low by Grecian spears,
and at my dead sons' graves I sheared my hair.
And Priam the sire of these, I witnessed—
with my own eyes and not from some report—
being butchered on his own hearth, and Troy sacked.
I saw my virgin daughters,
bred for bridegrooms of the highest rank,
torn from my arms and all their breeding thrown to foreigners.

Last and worst of all my woes
is being removed to Greece—an old slave woman.
What chores will they put me to,
an old crone like me?
Portress and keeper of keys? I who gave birth to Hector!
Baker of bread? The bare ground the prop
for this old bony back that lay once in a royal bed?
And the clothes of this scarecrow? . . .
Tattered rags to match a tattered frame—
fit symbols of my fall from bliss.

Yes, wretched me!
For one sex-driven drive of one single woman
what have I not suffered and have still to suffer?
Then Cassandra, my poor child,
ecstatic medium of the gods,
what a sorry end to your sacred virginhood!
And you, Polyxena, unhappy girl, where are you now?
Of all the children that I bore,
not a son, not a daughter is left to help me—
me this most wretched woman.
So why bother to lift me up?
What good is there?
Just guide my footsteps that once proudly trod in Troy
to some mattress of straw and pillow of stone.
There let me flop with my face to the floor
and waste away in tears.
Of all those seeming to succeed
count no one happy till he is dead.

[*Two of the* TROJAN WOMEN—*former ladies-in-waiting to the queen—take* HECUBA *by the hand and escort her to a straw palliasse among the tents, where she lies down. The* CHORUS *chants ironically of the joy manifested in Troy when the citizens dragged the fatal Wooden Horse, its belly pregnant with armed Greeks, into the center of the city*]

FIRST CHORAL ODE

STROPHE

Utter this song, O Muse of Troy,
A new song, a dirge of tears
To dedicate to Ilium:
Telling of how that four-footed thing-
On-wheels of the Greeks ushered in
Our ruin and turned
Us into slaves when the Achaeans
Left that horse outside our gates
Caparisoned in gold without,
Clattering with spears within;
And all the citizens of Troy
Gathering on the rocks outside
Shouted: "Wheel the wooden idol in:
A sacred gift to Zeus's daughter.
It spells the end of all our woes."
What girls or ancients did not stream
Out of their houses? All of them
Singing with joy as they welcomed in
    This deadly ambushed gin.
All the populace of Troy
Ran to the gates to gaze upon
This ingenious Grecian thing
Cut from mountain pine wherein
Lurked the dread Dardanian doom:
A gift to her,
The immortal maid . . . With ropes they hauled
It like a black vessel launched
To the temple home of Pallas where
The very pavement soon would run
With Trojan blood. The happy task

Was hardly done when night came down
And all was dark. The air thrilled
With Libyan flute and Trojan song,
And the fluttering feet of dancing girls
Singing their joy; whilst everywhere
Torches blazed, and the houses too
Were all lit up—till blackness came
    And the fires died down.

EPODE

LEADER: And on the very same night I
    Myself was singing among the choirs
    In front of the temple of Artemis
    (Maid of the mountains, Zeus's daughter)
    When suddenly the citadel
    And all the city rang with shrieks.
    Fragile infants clung with terror
    To their mothers' skirts as the god of war
    Ares burst from his ambushed lair;
    And Pallas thus achieved her end.
    Around the altars then began
    The butchering of Phrygians.
    And on their solitary beds the girls
    Cut off their hair: a fillip for
    The Greek young men but mourning for
The land of Troy.

[*A four-wheeled cart drawn by a mule and conducted by Greek soldiers rattles into view over the stony ground. In the cart, sitting on top of a heap of captured Trojan spoil, is* ANDROMACHE, *clutching her son* ASTYANAX. *Prominent in the pile is Hector's enormous shield.* HECUBA *slowly rises*]

LEADER: Hecuba, look, here comes Andromache
    Carried in a strange-looking wagon.
    Clutched to her apprehensive heart
    Is Astyanax Hector's son—
    Dear little fellow . . . Where will they take you,
    Bereft wife sitting on top
    Of a wagonload of Hector's armor

And plunder from Troy, which Achilles' son
Will hang up in the temples of Phthia
When he returns from Ilium?

LYRIC DIALOGUE

STROPHE I

ANDROMACHE: Our Greek masters are taking me away.
HECUBA: Aiai! Aiai!
ANDROMACHE: What good is weeping for me . . .
HECUBA: Aiai! Aiai!
ANDROMACHE: . . . and this stark ordeal?
HECUBA: O Zeus!
ANDROMACHE: And all my crushing sorrow!
HECUBA: My poor children!
ANDROMACHE: Once so long ago.

ANTISTROPHE I

HECUBA: Troy is gone.
    All joy is gone from me . . .
ANDROMACHE: Tragedy.
HECUBA: All gone my noble brood.
ANDROMACHE: Cruel, so cruel.
HECUBA: For me terribly cruel.
ANDROMACHE: Horrible.
HECUBA: I know, it is the end . . .
ANDROMACHE: . . . of my city.
HECUBA: . . . in smoke and burning.

STROPHE II

ANDROMACHE: Husband of mine, oh could you come to me.
HECUBA: You summon my son from Hades, stricken girl.
ANDROMACHE: Come to the help of your wife.

ANTISTROPHE II

HECUBA: And you, martyr of the Achaeans . . .
ANDROMACHE: Father
    Of my lord: venerable old Priam.
HECUBA: In Hades let me slumber.

STROPHE III

ANDROMACHE: An infinite desire.

HECUBA: Deep as my agony.

ANDROMACHE: A city sacked.

HECUBA: Pain lying on pain in layers.

ANDROMACHE: All caused by the gods' antipathy when your son
    Was snatched from death.* And lusting after an odious wom-
                                          an
    He crumbled the towers of Troy . . . Blood all over the floors
    Of Pallas' temple; bodies strewn for vultures' picking.
    So did he bend Troy under slavery's yoke.

ANTISTROPHE III

HECUBA: My sad beloved land!

ANDROMACHE: I weep on leaving you.

HECUBA: You see the pitiful end.

ANDROMACHE: The home where I gave birth.

HECUBA: Children, you have left your mother in a derelict city
    Resounding with dirges, lamentations and tears.
    What a surfeit of wailing! Surfeit of suffering!
    Cry, cry and cry again for our lost homes.
    Death at least lets go of tears, cancels sorrows.

[*End of Lyric Dialogue*]

FOURTH EPISODE

LEADER: Mother of Hector, who with his spear
    slew so many Argives once, do you see what is happening?

HECUBA: I see the scheme of the gods: to raise to the skies the
                                        worthless
    and dash to the ground the exalted.

ANDROMACHE: Yes, I with my son are captive stock:
    highbirth to slave—what a reversal!

HECUBA: Fate is remorseless. Just moments ago
    Cassandra was torn from me and is gone.

ANDROMACHE: Terrible! Terrible!

---

*Paris as a baby was exposed on Mount Ida but saved by shepherds.

Like a second Ajax a second time
   assaulting your child; but there is more.
HECUBA: I know. Without stint and measureless
   one disaster hurries on another.
ANDROMACHE: Your daughter Polyxena is dead:
   butchered on Achilles' tomb to appease his corpse.
HECUBA: No! No!
   So that is what Talthybius meant.
   His riddle now is deadly clear.
ANDROMACHE: I myself saw her and I left this cart
   to cover her corpse and to bewail her.
HECUBA: I cry for you, my child, and your heinous slaughter.
   Yes I cry for your appalling death.
ANDROMACHE: She is dead, she is gone,
   but her death is happier than is life for me.
HECUBA: No, my child: sight and daylight are not death.
   One is a nothingness, the other has hope.
ANDROMACHE: Mother, mother, listen, there is a greater truth—
   if I can only touch your heart with it.
Never to have been born I count as death,
   a death superior to a life of bitterness.
In death there is no pain, no awareness of struggle;
   but one who falls from happiness to tragedy
   is riven with regret and memories of blessedness.
In death it is as if Polyxena had never known the light
   and nothing of her trials.
But I who aimed at happiness
   hardly had attained it when it went.
All that a woman can contrive through a balanced life
   I worked at under Hector's roof.
Even if a woman has no other mark against her,
   one single flaw will bring her to notoriety,
   which is, not keeping to the house.
So that was my priority:
   to put such urges from me and stay at home.
I never allowed the frilly gossip of women
   to infiltrate my house,
   and kept to the steady counsels of my heart,
   with quiet tongue and eyes serene before my spouse.

I knew when to rule my husband
   and when to let him win:
   a virtue the Achaeans came to know of
   and it proved my downfall,
   for when I was captured the son of Achilles* claimed me for
                               his own,
   so I shall be a slave in the house of my husband's murderers.

And now if I put away the image of my darling Hector
   and open my heart to a new man
   it will seem like disloyalty to the dead,
   but if I turn from this new lord
   I'll only earn his hate.
Yet they say that a single night in bed
   suffices to end a woman's aversion to a man.
I, however, feel nothing but disgust
   for the woman who forgets her former man
   and beds down with a second.
Why, even a dray-mare
   separated from the horse she pulls with
   shows repugnance for another partner in the yoke,
   and this in a mere animal of a lower order
   without speech or reason,
   whereas you, my dearest Hector, were my perfect mate:
   noble, intelligent, rich, brave—a man great in every way.
You took me chaste from my father's house
   and you were the first to enter my bed.
But now you are no more
   and I am about to board a ship for Greece,
   a prisoner of war and a subservient slave.

   [*Turning to* HECUBA]

So I ask you:
   isn't your loss of Polyxena, whom you mourn,
   less harrowing than mine?
For me, not even those vestiges of hope common to mankind
   are left, and I do not deceive myself

son of Achilles: Neoptolemus.

with the delusion, sweet though it be,
of anything being right again.

LEADER: You face the same pain that I must face
and your lament gives lessons to my own.

HECUBA: Never have I been on board a ship
but from all accounts and pictures that I've seen
I know what it is like.

If a merely moderate storm is looming
the sailors bestir themselves in all directions.

One is at the helm, another grappling with sails,
another bailing water.

But if the full fury of the ocean is unleashed
they resign themselves to fate and run with the sea.

So with me:
I am dumb before the surge of all my sorrows
and without a word succumb,
powerless to withstand
the tide of misery the gods sweep over me.

And so, my dearest daughter,
let us commit Hector to his destiny.
No tears from you will bring him back.

To your new master show respect,
with that winning way of yours that charms a man.

If you do this you'll spread joy among your friends
and render Troy a mighty service
by bringing up this son of my son
whose issue may one day rebuild Ilium
and make our city rise again.

[*Glancing across the barren plain*]

But now we'll have to talk of something else,
for whom do I see approaching but the Achaean errand boy,
coming with a set of new injunctions.

[TALTHYBIUS *with an escort of guards marches in. His features register embarrassment and reluctance as he walks across to* ANDROMACHE, *who has left the cart and stands near* HECUBA, *holding* ASTYANAX *by the hand*]

TALTHYBIUS: Lady wife of Hector, once hero of the Phrygians,
   I beg you not to hate me. I'm no willing messenger
   of the decision the Achaeans and the Argives have made.
ANDROMACHE: What is this? What prelude to a new disaster?
TALTHYBIUS: The boy here . . . they have decreed . . . Oh how am
                                          I to say it? . . .
ANDROMACHE: Not, I hope, that he and I will be given to
                                          different masters?
TALTHYBIUS: No . . . No Greek will ever be his master.
ANDROMACHE: You mean he is to be left in Phrygia?
TALTHYBIUS: How do I break this to you? . . . It is awful.
ANDROMACHE: Thank you for demurring . . . unless you have
                                          good news.
TALTHYBIUS: Your son's to be killed. Now you know.
ANDROMACHE: No no no! This is worse than making me a whore.
TALTHYBIUS: The vote went with Odysseus in the Panhellenic
                                          council to . . .
ANDROMACHE: Aiai, aiai . . . this outmeasures every outrage.
TALTHYBIUS: . . . to not let grow up the son of such a famous
                                          father.
ANDROMACHE: Oh, would that his own children could suffer this
                                          decree!
TALTHYBIUS: He must be flung from the battlements of Troy.

   [ANDROMACHE *throws her arms around* ASTYANAX *as if to
   protect him*]

Come, let it happen.
   You'll find that wiser in the end.
Let go of him.
Bear this agony with dignity.

You are powerless. Do not imagine that you're strong.
There's no help anywhere.
Consider: your husband and your city are no more,
   you yourself are held in bondage.
   We are quite capable of dealing with a single woman.
Do not go looking for a fight.
Do not make a raving spectacle of yourself.
I do not want you upsetting the Achaeans.

That would anger the military
   and the boy may not get a burial or proper obsequies.*
Keep quiet. Let things take their course,
   then at least you will not leave your boy unburied
   and you'll find the Greeks will treat you better.
ANDROMACHE: [*gathering* ASTYANAX *to her*]
   My most precious, my most beloved boy,
   you must say goodbye to your desolate mother:
   our enemies want you dead;
   your gallant father is your ruin,
   as he was for others the salvation.
Yes, your father's valor spells your death knell now.
My own marriage, my night of honeymoon,
   my very coming into Hector's home,
   were not for this: not for bringing into the world
   a babe for Greeks to butcher but to conceive a king—
   a king for Asia and prosperity.

Poor child, are you crying?
   What good to cling to me, to clutch my skirts
   like a little bird cowering under its mother's wings?
There is no Hector
   to rise up from the earth with his glorious spear
   and deliver you;
   no kinsman of your father, no strong men of Troy.
You must plunge from the heights in a piteous leap
   and most hideously dash your breath away.

   [*Folding him to her*]

My tender seedling, your mother's dearest baby,
   the sweet smell of your skin swaddled at my breast,
   and all for nothing.
The labor pains, the enduring care—all for nothing.
Kiss your mother now for the last time.
Smother yourself in her.

*One must bear in mind how essential the Greeks regarded burial. The mere
ritual of sprinkling earth on a corpse was a kind of sacrament ensuring the
deceased a better life in the next world.

Put your arms round me and hug me tight.
Press your lips to mine.

[*She turns fiercely towards* TALTHYBIUS *and his escort of soldiers*]

You barbarians! what un-Greek cruelties can you invent?
Must you kill a child—wholly innocent?
And you, Helen, daughter of Tyndareus,
    Zeus was never your father.
Let me tell you who your many fathers were:
    Destruction first, then Hate, Bloody Murder, Death,
    and whatever refuse spawns itself on earth.
Zeus your father? Don't tell me that!
    You born curse to uncountable Achaeans
    and to all the world besides.
Death take your lovely eyes
    that have ransacked the famous plains of Troy.

[*She prises* ASTYANAX *from her and pushes him towards* TALTHYBIUS, *turning away her gaze*]

Go on, take him. Carry him away.
Hurl him to his death if that's what you want.
Feast on his broken flesh . . .
    the gods are out to destroy us
    and I cannot shield from death one little child.

Now make a parcel of my wretched carcass and toss it in the
                                                            hold.
    Today's my wedding day—the day I lost my child.
LEADER: Troy, unhappy Troy, where so many thousands of
                                                young men were lost
    all for one woman's sake, one wanton lust!
TALTHYBIUS:

[*Advancing on* ASTYANAX]

Come, boy, now that you've left your sad mother's arms,
    you must climb the battlements that ring your ancestral
                                                            towers.

There it has been voted that you end your life.

[ASTYANAX *turns and rushing back to his mother clings to her.*
TALTHYBIUS, *his face grim with reluctance, strides forward
and drags the screaming boy from his mother, then hands the
struggling boy to a soldier*]

Take hold of him.
This kind of order needs a brute, someone merciless,
much more heartless than I can be.

[*As the screams of* ASTYANAX *recede in the distance,* ANDRO-
MACHE *is dragged back to the cart and* TALTHYBIUS, *rounding
up his escort, marches away with the cart.* HECUBA, *swaying
on her feet, stares in the direction of* ASTYANAX]

HECUBA: Goodbye my child, son of my pitiable son,
So cruelly torn from your mother and me.
How can I bear it not to be able
To do a thing for you. All I can offer
Is tearing my hair, beating my breasts.
That is all I can do . . . Farewell
My child. Farewell my city. Nothing,
No agony for us is missing.
Could anything make it more complete.

[HECUBA *collapses*]

SECOND CHORAL ODE

[*Beginning with a brief eulogy of Athens, the women of the*
CHORUS *survey in a litany of contrasts legendary history and
chant of a mythological attack on Troy in the past, setting it
against the present sack of the city. Then, in an ironic reversal
of what the power of love has done to Ilium, they cite the
example of two beautiful Trojan boys who were abducted:
Ganymede, the cupbearer, whom—suggests Euripides—Zeus
wafted on high for highly dubious purposes, and Tithonus,
with whom Aurora fell in love and whom she carried away in
a four-horse chariot*]

STROPHE I

CHORUS: Telamon, monarch of Salamis,
   island buzzing with bees,
You set up your home on that sea-fingered
   isle that faces the hills
Where Athena first planted the glaucous
   cuttings of olive—the crowning
Glory of shimmering Athens.
   Then you coupled your valor
With Heracles, son of Alcmena,
   the archer. So you departed,
Alas, you departed to sack
   our city of Ilium: Ilium
Even then our beloved
   country such ages ago,
When you came to these shores from Hellas.

ANTISTROPHE I

In a rage for the loss of his horses*
   Heracles came with Greece's
Flower of manhood over
   the ocean and anchored their ships
In the lovely bay of Simoïs
   and fastened their sterns with hawsers.
With his infallible bow then
   he went to kill Laomedon.
With rubicund fire he tumbled
   the walls that Apollo with chisel
And plumb had erected so straightly.
   The land of Troy he demolished.
So this is the second occasion
   that Troy has been stricken. Yes, twice
That its blood-spattered walls have fallen.

---

*In return for saving Hesione, daughter of Laomedon, king of Troy, from a
monster, Heracles was to be given a team of horses. However, after Heracles
had rescued Hesione, Laomedon reneged on his promise. Hence Heracles'
rage against Troy.

STROPHE II

In vain, in vain with your golden
   cups do you prettily amble,
You Ganymede, to fill the
   goblets of Zeus—such an honor—
While the country that gave you birth
   is eaten up by fire,
And the shores of the sea are raucous
   with cries like the screams of a seagull
Over her fledglings in danger.
   Oh the howling and wailing for children,
For husbands, for elderly mothers.
   No more are the baths that refreshed you,
No more the gymnasiums and racetracks;
   yet you by the throne of Zeus
Serenely pose with the beauty
   of your young face while the javelins
Of Hellas are crumbling
   the empire of Priam.

ANTISTROPHE II

Love, O Love, long ago
   you came to Dardanus' palace
Having inflamed with passion
   the gods themselves in heaven.
Those were the days when you lifted
   Troy to the skies with divine
Bondings (I shall not refer
   to Zeus's disgraceful intentions).
Yet today is the day that Dawn,
   white-wingèd solace of mortals,
Saw Pergamum in shambles;
   yet a son of this very soil,
Tithonus, was her husband,
   bred children in her bed,
Till a four-starred golden chariot
   carried him to heaven.
He was the hope of Troy,
   which the gods no longer love.

[MENELAUS, *with a detachment of soldiers behind him, strides into camp. He is a man in his middle forties, complete in military uniform—sword, cape, plumed helmet, heavily strapped sandals—and is obviously pleased with his appearance*]

FIFTH EPISODE

MENELAUS: What a lovely sunny day
  to get my hands on my wife again—that Helen!
Yes, after so many trials
  I Menelaus am here at last with the Greek army behind me.
My coming to Troy was not as you might think
  because of a woman but because of a man:
  that treacherous creature who was a guest in my house
  and snatched my wife away.
Well, thanks to the gods,
  that man has had his punishment:
  he with his country has collapsed under the Grecian spear.
As to that Spartan slut, my former wife
  (and I cannot bring myself to speak her name),*
  I am here to drag her back.
She's with the rest of the prisoners in the barracks,
  lumped together with them as a Trojan woman.
My brave allies, who have gone through hell to get her back,
  have given her to me to kill,
  or if I do not kill her to bring her home to Argos.
I have decided not to settle the fate of Helen here in Troy,
  so our mariners will take her with me across the main to Greece.
There I'll give her over to be killed
  by those who are crying to avenge their loved ones at Troy.

[*Summoning two of his soldiers*]

Go men, probe the barracks and fetch her here.
Drag her by the hair, the whore,
  and when the right wind blows
  we'll carry her to Greece.

---

*He has already spoken her name once (line 861) and is to do so again (line 877 in the Greek). This is no slip on the part of Euripides the master ironist but a subtle hint of Menelaus' peculiar "thickness." Line numbers refer to the Greek text in the Loeb Classics edition.

[*As the soldiers depart,* HECUBA, *who has been listening, rises from her couch. She spreads out her hands in prayer*]

HECUBA: O thou, the fundament of our universe
with your throne on earth—
thou whoever thou art, beyond our comprehension, Zeus,
be thou a law of nature or invention of mankind—
thee I invoke.

MENELAUS: Meaning precisely what? . . . That's an odd prayer
to make!

HECUBA: [*ignoring his obtuseness*]
I approve, Menelaus, of your killing your wife,
but don't let her near you or she'll entangle you again.
She rivets men's eyes, she topples cities, she burns down houses,
she casts such spells.
We know her well,
you and I and all her other victims.

[*The two soldiers reappear, pulling* HELEN *along with a rope. Despite the fact that she has suffered the same herding together and indignities as the other captive women, she has contrived to make the most of her appearance and is still stunningly beautiful*]

HELEN: Menelaus, if you want to frighten me, this is a good
beginning.
I've been dragged from the tents by your minions here.
Of course I'm not surprised you probably hate me,
all the same, I'd like to ask:
what decision have you come to, you and the Greeks,
about my life?

MENELAUS: Nothing is settled,
except that the entire army has given you to me to kill
because of all the trouble you have caused.

HELEN: Am I not at least to have the chance of showing
that if I die I die unjustly?

MENELAUS: I came here to kill you, not to argue.

HECUBA: Give her a hearing, Menelaus:

at least *that* before she dies.
But allow me to state the case against her.
    You have no idea of the havoc she has caused in Troy.
My indictment, every item in it,
    without the slightest room for doubt,
    will call for her death.
MENELAUS: A waste of breath!
    But if she must, let her speak.
It's for your sake, Hecuba, not hers—
    I hope she knows—that I grant this favor.
HELEN: [*turning to face* MENELAUS]
    Whether my arguments seem good or bad to you,
    your response undoubtedly will be antagonistic.
Nonetheless,
    knowing the kind of charges you will level at me
    I shall rebut them point by point as if we were debating.
In the first place,

[*throwing an icy glance at* HECUBA]

    this woman here who gave birth to Paris
    is the one who gave birth to all our troubles.
The second cause of the ruin of Troy,
    and my ruin too,
    was old Priam, who failed to kill the newborn brat,
    even though he had been warned in dreams
    that a firebrand, the future Alexander,*
    would burn down Troy.

Listen to what happened next.
    Alexander becomes the judge in the beauty contest of three
                                                        goddesses.
Pallas Athena promised him conquest of Greece
    at the head of a Phrygian army.
Hera promised that if Paris made her win
    she would give him the whole kingdom of Asia

Alexander: Paris.

and the farthest frontiers of Europe.
But Aphrodite,
   expatiating on the marvels of my body
   promised him exactly that
   if *she* came out on top in the contest of goddesses.

Now consider the results:
   the blessings heaped on Greece are incalculable;*
   you are not slaves of a foreign power,
   you have not been ousted in battle
   nor crushed beneath some imperial tyranny.
But I, I benefactor of Greece, have been ruined,
   sold for my beauty,
   and am being punished instead of being crowned with
                garlands

That is not the point, you'll counter.
Why did you elope from home?
Why? Because of *him*—
   call him Paris or Alexander or what you will—
   the spellbinding son of this Hecuba.
He came here with no mean goddess in his wake,
   while you, Menelaus, my husband you
   criminally left him in your palace,
   took off from home and sailed away to Crete.

Well, I won't ask what prompted you
   but I'll ask myself: was I quite mad
   to abandon fatherland and home
   and go chasing after this foreign man?
Ask Aphrodite. Punish her.
   Be mightier than Zeus, who may be master of the gods
   but not of her.
So I should be let off untouched.

All right, you'll say,

---

*Helen means that if Pallas Athena had won the contest, Paris would have
been given Greece, which would have been conquered by Troy. If Hera had
won, Greece would have come under the suzerainty of a European empire.

but what about when Alexander died and passed to Hades
and divine interference in my life had stopped?
Shouldn't I have fled from his house to the Argive ships?
That is exactly what I tried to do.
I have witnesses: the sentries at the gates,
    the watchtower patrols.
Ask them how many times they caught me
    trying to slither down the battlements on ropes.
But my new husband, the lately deceased Deïphobus,*
    kept me prisoner as his wife despite the Trojans.

So, my husband,
    by what right can you with any justice kill me
    when I was impelled to marry Paris
    and when I've brought such benefits to Greece?
Instead of crowning me in triumph,
    you plunge me into the cruelest slavery. Why?
If your aim is to outdo the gods
    it is the silliest of pretensions.
LEADER: Queen, stand by your children and your country,
    explode the specious pleading from this harlot's lips . . .
    Oh, she is formidable!
HECUBA: First let me defend the goddesses
    and undo the lies of her slanderous tongue.
Never would Hera have been so completely brainless
    as to sell Argos to foreigners,
    or Pallas the Virgin to let Athens become a slave of Troy.
When they had their beauty contest on Mount Ida,
    they went in a flirtatious spirit, a spirit of play.
Why should the goddess Hera set her heart on a beauty prize?
To win a husband preferable to Zeus?
    And was Athena simply panting for a spouse among the gods,
    she who'd wheedled from her father the promise
    of perpetual virginity—
    So great was her horror of getting married?
Do not try to camouflage your flagrancy
    by imputing such idiocy to gods.
Nobody with sense believes you.

*Deïphobus: Son of Priam and Hecuba, who married Helen after raping her.

*   *   *

As to Aphrodite,
   you tell us that she came to Menelaus' palace with my son.
Don't make us laugh! . . .
   as if she couldn't transport you and your whole town of
   Amyclae to Ilium while remaining blissfully in heaven.
My son enjoyed good looks beyond compare.
It was your itch for him that you revamped into "Aphrodite."
When men make fools of themselves it's always "Aphrodite":
   the very name of the goddess spells mindless slavering.
So when you saw my son in his exotic garb,
   dripping in gold,
   you were stunned and lost your head.
There was nothing like it in dull old Argos.
Quitting Sparta for our Phrygian town
   you imagined rivers of gold that you would wallow in.
The palace of Menelaus could not contain
   your impudent drive for luxury;
   yet my son, you say, had to drag you away by force . . . Really!
Who in Sparta saw this happening?
How loud did you cry out?
The young man Castor was there, his twin brother too,
   not yet caught up among the stars.

And so you arrive at Troy,
   the Argives hot on your tracks,
   and the murderous clash of arms begins.
Each time there was news of a win for Menelaus,
   you'd praise him to the skies to annoy my son
   and prove how superior Menelaus was—in bed.
Each time the Trojans gained the upper hand,
   what was Menelaus? Nothing!
In this way, however fortune veered
   and with no regard to morals,
   you were always on the winning side.

Now you talk of ropes around your body
   and slithering down the walls,
   altogether loath to stay in Troy.
Did anyone ever find you putting a noose around your neck

or sharpening a dagger—
as any decent woman would have done, pining for her husband?
How many times did I not remonstrate with you and say:
    "Listen, my girl—just go!
    My sons can always find other women.
    I'll help you to slip away to where their navy is
    and so stop this senseless war between Greece and us."

But no, this wasn't to your taste.
You luxuriated in Alexander's palace.
You basked in the obsequiousness of us Orientals.
It was a big thing for you;
    and all the time you had the gall to deck yourself out
    and parade in broad day by your husband's side—
    you, you disreputable trollop!
Not insolence but humility should have been your mood.
You should have come cringing with shaven head,
    dressed in rags and trembling with compunction
    for all your shameless past.

[*Turning to* MENELAUS]

The crux of my indictment, Menelaus, is:
    cap Greece's triumph with a crown of glory.
Set a precedent by law:
    death to every wife unfaithful to her spouse.
LEADER: Menelaus, be worthy of your ancestors and your house:
    punish your wife. Do not let Greece label you as soft
    when you've shown yourself so gallant in the field.
MENELAUS: I agree wholeheartedly with you
    that of her own free will she left my house for the bed of a
                                                    foreign man
    and that blaming Aphrodite is a ruse.

[*Turning to* HELEN]

Go, get ready to be stoned.
In a single instant expiate the years of Achaean suffering.
Let death be your lesson for disgracing me.
HELEN: [*throwing herself at his feet*]
    I clasp your knees and beg you:

don't stamp me with a crime that came from heaven.
Forgive me, do not kill me.
HECUBA: [*with a sharp glance at* MENELAUS]
    Do not betray your allies whom she's slaughtered.
Do not, I beg you, for them and their children's sake.
MENELAUS: That's enough, old woman . . . She means nothing
                                                    to me.

[*Turning to his guards*]

Men, take her to the galleys. This is a command.
Prepare her for the crossing.

[*The guards seize* HELEN *to lead her away*]

HECUBA: Make sure her galley is not the same as yours.
MENELAUS: Why? Has she put on weight? Ha ha!
HECUBA: Once a lover, forever vulnerable.
MENELAUS: That depends on the loved one's depth of love.
    However, you have a point. Let it be as you wish.
She shall not board the same ship as I.
Once in Argos this disgraceful woman
    shall come to the disgraceful end she merits
    and give a lesson to all wives in chastity . . .
No easy matter, certainly,
    but her death will go some way
    to strike a little fear into wanton hearts
    be they even more depraved than hers.

[*As* HELEN, *led by the guards, passes* MENELAUS, *she meets his gaze and notes the sweat breaking out on his forehead. She throws him a smile that seems to say:* "Wait till we get to the ships and the long passage home. Oh yes, you are vulnerable still!" MENELAUS *turns on his heel, followed by his guards.* HECUBA, *overcome with grief, apprehension and exhaustion, sinks back on her palliasse. The women of the* CHORUS *chant a lament to Zeus for having forsaken Ilium, listing the various sacred rituals that will never again take place in Troy. They then think of their dead husbands lying somewhere still unburied, and of their children destined to live as orphans in unknown Greek cities. Finally, they express*]

a wish that a storm will strike MENELAUS' *ship and that the
still dangerous* HELEN *will never reach Argos*]

THIRD CHORAL ODE

STROPHE I

CHORUS: Gone, done, never again
  Will wafted fragrance arise
  From the altars of Ilium.
  Zeus, you've given them away
  To the Greeks: the savory flames,
  The rising fumes of myrrh,
  Pergamum the holy,
  And Ida—oh, the glens
  Of Ida with their ivy
  Trickling beside the icy
  Torrents, and the peaks
  Catching the early sun:
  Bright purlieus of the divine.

ANTISTROPHE I

  Gone too, beholden to you,
  The sacrifices, choirs, psalms,
  Hymns of praise. And now no more
  The celebrations in the dark
  Of feasts at night for the gods.
  Gone are the gilded effigies
  In wood, the twelve-mooned cakes
  Offered under the Phrygian moon.
  I wonder, my lord, I wonder
  If you give a single thought
  From your celestial throne
  To the leaping flames and the lights
  Of my city burning still.

STROPHE II

  Dearest, my husband, now dead,
  Unwashed, unburied, you roam
  In the realms of Hades while I

On the wings of a fast-moving ship must fly
Over the waves to the plain
Of Argos where horses graze
And the people live behind walls
Which the hefty Cyclops raised
Soaring into the sky . . .
Children throng the gates,
They wail and cry.
A young girl is shouting:
"Mother, I'm alone and the Greeks are taking me
Far from the sight of you:
Away in a melancholy ship
Thrashing the waves with its oars
Towards Salamis the sacred
Or to Corinth on its isthmus
Standing between two seas:
The strong portals of Pelops.

ANTISTROPHE II

When the galley of Menelaus
Is half across the main
May Zeus's Aegean lightniñg
Zigzagging from his holy hands blaze down
Onto the bridge of his ship
As he carries me away
From Ilium in tears
For slavery in Greece:
Right at the hour when girls
Hold up their golden mirrors
Like Helen daughter of Zeus.
Never let him see
The land of his fathers, Laconia, not
Even his hearth, his bedroom, the streets
Of Pitana, nor the bronze
Gates of Athena's temple
For he has forgiven
The marriage that brought such shame
On noble Greece; such sorrows
To the banks of Simoïs—Troy.

LEADER: Horrible! Horrible! Blow upon blow

On a blighted land . . . and now what's coming
To the desolate wives of the heroes of Troy?
I see Astyanax, whom the Greeks have thrown
From the heights of the battlements and have slain.

[TALTHYBIUS *and his men arrive carrying the torn body of*
ASTYANAX *on Hector's enormous shield.* HECUBA *rises as they*
approach her. TALTHYBIUS, *crestfallen and dejected, tries to*
distract HECUBA *from the horror of the scene by babbling*
about preparations to depart]

SIXTH EPISODE

TALTHYBIUS: Hecuba, one ship remains, its oars at the ready
    to ply for the shores of Phthia
    with the rest of the booty of Achilles' son.*
Neoptolemus himself has put to sea already,
    having heard a dismal report
    that his grandfather, Peleus,
    has been driven from the land by Acastus son of Pelias.
For which reason he has left at once,
    taking with him Andromache, torn from her country in tears
    as she bade farewell to Hector's tomb . . . I too broke down.
She begged Neoptolemus to give this poor son of Hector
    hurled from the walls, a grave and have him laid out
    on Hector's enormous shield—
    the shield of bronze that protected his flanks
    and filled the Achaeans with terror.
She asked him not to take the body to the house of Pelius†
    nor to her own—the dead boy's mother's—
    new forced bridal abode in Argos:
    it would be too much for her to see her mangled son.
Instead of a stone or cedar coffin
    she wants her child buried here beneath this shield.
He is to be laid in your arms
    for you to enshroud his body as best you can with what you
                                                          have left,

Achilles' son: Neoptolemus.
†*house of Pelius:* in Sparta.

and covered in flowers.
Her master was in such a hurry.
   she could not herself bury her boy.
The rest of us,
   as soon as you have dressed the corpse,
   shall heap a mound for him and crown it with a spear.*
Please perform this task as quickly as you can.
One labor I have spared you:
   when I passed the banks of Scamander River
   I bathed the body and washed the wounds.
Now I shall go and dig his grave,
   so when your work and mine is quickly done
   we can make all speed for home.

[*At a sign from* HECUBA *two of her women advance and take
the shield from* TALTHYBIUS. *On it lies the pathetic little frame
of* ASTYANAX, *curled up as if asleep. Although hideously
bruised, his body has been washed clean and the golden curls
of the young princeling lie around his ashen face. As* TALTHY-
BIUS *turns gently away and joins his escort of soldiers,*
HECUBA *beckons the two women*]

HECUBA: Set the shield down on the ground—Hector's shield:
   the great arc of it a heartrending sight,
   no joy for me to see.

[*She turns fiercely on the groups of Greek soldiers who are
never far away*]

Oh, you spear-mongering Greeks,
   if only your intelligence could match your prowess!
This was mindless murder—murder unmentionable.
What did you fear in this little child?
That he would raise up fallen Troy? . . .

*This phrase in the Greek is capable of two readings: *aroumen doru* means
either raise a spear or (possibly) raise a mast. I prefer the first, for I know no
other instance when *doru,* which *can* mean a plank of timber, is used for the
mast of a ship. Moreover, the masts of galleys and triremes were fixed—
already raised. If we adopt the second reading (which most translators have
done) it makes the last line of Talthybius' speech redundant.

So all your bravery of old was sham.
Our city taken, Phrygia in rubbles,
    all Hector's triumphs and thousands of strong arms
    powerless to avert our ruin,
    and you are terrified of one little boy.
What blind panic! I despise you.

[*Glancing down at the dead body*]

My sweet baby,
    how untimely death has taken you!
Had you only fallen in blooming manhood
    fighting for your city,
    or tasted the joys of wedlock and that royalty that makes
                                                    us gods,
        that at least would have been some blessing—
        if indeed there can be any blessing here.
The pleasures that you caught a glimpse of,
    enough to know their worth, are snatched from you,
    and your happiness of home is lost, forgotten.

[*Cradling his head*]

My stricken child,
    how ironically your own ancestral walls,
    Apollo's handiwork, have carded out your curls:
    those curls your mother used to stroke and kiss,
    which now are pierced by splintered blood-leached bone.
Nothing can describe the horror of it.
And your hands, so like your father's,
    out of joint and limp!
Your dear lips,
    that sent forth so many childish sallies—silent now.
Bounding on to my bed you used to cry:
    "Grandmother, I'll chop off a big curl for you
    and bring a crowd of my pals to your burial
    to send you my love and last farewell."
It has not happened so.
It is not you but I, your grandmother,
    an old cityless, childless crone

that has to bury your torn body.
Wasted, lost forever,
   all those cuddles, all that care,
   all that watching while you slept.
What frame of words is possible for your tomb?
Here lies a guileless babe
Killed by the Greeks who were afraid.
An epitaph to disgrace all Greece.
And now you possess nothing of your father's heritage
   except this shield of bronze—and for your tomb.

[*Running her hands along the rim*]

Sweet shield that guarded Hector's brawny arm,
   you have lost your valiant keeper.
Lovely the imprint of his flesh
   on the sling of your handle still.
Lovely the sweat marks on the sweep of your rim:
   the sweat that in the heat of battle ran from his face
   and dripped from his leaning chin.

[*Clapping her hands to summon her women*]

Come, my women,
   fetch whatever trappings you can find from what remains to us
   to enshroud this most tragic dead.
Fate has shorn us of all finery
   but you shall have from me all I have.

[*After a pause*]

What a fool that mortal is
   who rests complacent in prosperity!
Fortune is the prey of whims
   and like a maniac turns somersaults.
   No man for long escapes her jolts.
LEADER: Madam, from the Phrygian remnants left to us
   your women are bringing you some trappings for the dead.

[*The women come dragging a heavy basket from one of the tents. In it are disclosed a hodgepodge of items flung there in their last minutes of freedom: clothes, baubles, jewelry. As* HECUBA *and her handmaids sort through these, the dressing of* ASTYANAX'*s body begins*]

HECUBA: Dear child, among your fellows,
   no victory in horsemanship or archery was yours
   (pursuits admired in Phrygia, but modestly),
And yet, I, the mother of your father,
   wrap you in this finery:
   all that is left of your inheritance:
   ripped from you by that she-devil Helen,
   as she has ripped from you your life
   and from top to bottom wrecked your home.
LEADER: These words break my heart, yes, break it,
   for this child born to be a city's mighty king.

[HECUBA, *reaching down into the basket, pulls out a magnificent tunic*]

HECUBA: This is the raiment you would have worn on your
                                 wedding day,
   with the noblest princess of Asia as your bride.
It is of Phrygian workmanship the most gorgeous.
And you, beloved shield of Hector,
   victorious mother of a thousand trophies,
   here is a wreath for you.

[HECUBA *festoons the shield with a garland of wildflowers which her women found growing on the plain*]

Without being dead you died with this dead body.
Much more honored should you be
   than the armor of Odysseus*—that corrupt and devious man.
LEADER: Aiai, aiai! . . . a bitter hole . . . ready to receive you, child.
   Mother, cry.

---

*Odysseus, for his services, was awarded the arms of Achilles by the Greeks. These he hung up for display in the temple of Athena in Phthia, the town in Thessaly (northern Greece) where Achilles was born. Euripides' allusion, however, in the mouth of Hecuba is something of an anachronism. It would be many years before Odysseus was anywhere near Phthia.

HECUBA: Aiai! Aiai!
LEADER: Let us chant a dirge for the dead.
HECUBA: For tragedy.
LEADER: Overwhelming tragedy for you.
HECUBA:

[*stooping over the body of* ASTYANAX]

Let me be the one to bandage up your wounds . . .
    a useless doctor, one who cannot cure.
Your father among the dead must do the rest.
LEADER: Batter your heads, oh, batter them.
    Clench your fists into clubs . . . O . . . h!
HECUBA: Listen, dear daughters . . . .

[HECUBA *breaks off and gazes into the distance as if having a revelation*]

LEADER: What is it, Hecuba? . . . Open your heart
    to us your ever faithful friends.
HECUBA: Just that it is clear now
    the gods have singled me out for suffering
    and Troy for hate—above all other cities.
In vain have we slaughtered our hecatombs, and the divine reply
    is to bury us under the earth, heap it on us, pack it down.
It is as if we were to be smothered from view:
    unsung by the Muses, unchanted, unrecorded
    in ages to come.

[*She beckons to two of the women to take* ASTYANAX *from her and lay him on Hector's shield*]

Come, lift the dead onto his sad tomb.
Whatever is necessary has been done.
Not that the rituals of funerals, in my opinion,
    have any interest for the dead.
They are performed to satisfy the living.

[*At a sign from* TALTHYBIUS *two soldiers come forward and take up the shield with the limp body of* ASTYANAX *upon it and*

carry it to the grave which TALTHYBIUS *has had dug.* HECUBA
stares after them with a look of blankness and hopelessness]

LEADER:

[*calling out after the cortege*]

An agonized mother having to watch
　Her brightest hopes of life put out.
　Once it was thought how grand to be
　Engendered from a noble race,
　But a horrible death has ended that.

[*In the distance along the battlements of Troy, soldiers are
seen scurrying about with lighted torches*]

　On the heights of Ilium what do I see?
　A waving of arms and firebrands:
　Some new disaster threatens Troy.

[TALTHYBIUS *hurries in leading a detachment of soldiers, all
carrying firebrands.*]

TALTHYBIUS: Orders are for the officers in charge of firing the
                                                city of Priam
　to proceed at once with the incendiary flares
　and burn down Ilium, down to the ground.
Then at last with hearts at ease we can sail for home.
Meanwhile—to accomplish two commands in one—
　you daughters of Troy, as soon as you hear
　from the officers' camp the trumpets blare,
　get yourselves to the ships. It is the signal to leave.
And you, old woman, laden with sorrows, follow these men.
They come from Odysseus to fetch you:
　your lot is to be his slave, far from your fatherland.
HECUBA: Yes, laden with sorrows!
　And now to cap it all as I say goodbye,
　my city is given up to flames.
Very well then, start walking, you poor old feet,
　make one last effort to salute your broken town.

[*She takes a few steps and then stands with her arms open as if embracing the last of burning Troy*]

O Troy, great city,
  once breath of grandeur on the barbarian scene,
  how fast your glory is extinct!
They burn you down, and we,
  we are being herded off as slaves.
O you gods . . .
  but why bother to invoke the gods?
  In the past they never heard my prayers.
So, hurry, hurry into the flames.
Let my glory be
  to die in the bonfire of my home.

[*As* HECUBA *begins to totter towards the flames,* TALTHYBIUS *signals to a group of guards*]

TALTHYBIUS: The poor creature is possessed, crazed by sorrow.
  Go, retrieve her. Don't hesitate.
  She is Odysseus' prize.
  We must put her in his hands.

[*The soldiers approach her, but she halts. Then she utters a long, ritual animal howl*]

LYRIC DIALOGUE

HECUBA: Ottototototoi.
  Cronos' son, lord of Phrygia,*
  Father of our race, do you see
  The perpetrations they have done,
  Done to the seed of Dardanus?
FULL CHORUS: He sees, but our glorious city
  Is a city no longer. There is no Troy.
HECUBA: Ottototototoi.
  The roofs of the citadel and the town,
  The crests of the ramparts—all aflame.

Cronos' son, lord of Phrygia: Zeus.

CHORUS: Up like smoke into the sky
   Our country vanishes in fire,
   Obliterated by the war.
   The lance has raged through all the halls.

[HECUBA *throws herself on her knees and beats the ground with her fists—a ritual gesture whereby one summoned the dead from the bowels of the earth*]

HECUBA: Earth that has fed my children!
CHORUS: Eee . . . h! Eee . . . h!
HECUBA: Hearken, my children, answer the call of a mother.
CHORUS: Your cries are summoning the dead.
HECUBA: They are—my withered limbs stretched on the ground.
   My two fists batter the earth.

[*The women of the* CHORUS *throw themselves down and imitate the behavior of* HECUBA]

CHORUS: We as well kneel on the earth
   And call on our husbands who are dead.
HECUBA: We are driven off, herded away . . .
CHORUS: How your cries rend the heart!
HECUBA: . . . away to become household slaves.
CHORUS: Far far away!
HECUBA: Priam, my Priam, without a tomb,
   Dying too without a friend
   You do not see my misery.
CHORUS: Black was the veil that shadowed his eyes:
   Unholy the murder of a holy man.

[HECUBA *and the rest of the women rise from the ground and with their arms flung wide address the burning city*]

HECUBA: Farewell you courts of the gods, my beloved town!
CHORUS: A . . h!
HECUBA: Demolished by deadly spear and flame.
CHORUS: Soon to be rubble and a nameless land.
HECUBA: Smoke and ash rise in the air.
   The place of my palace is blotted out.
CHORUS: Yes, a land without a name.

Little by little all is gone.
Troy doomed does not exist.

[*They hear a tremendous crash*]

HECUBA: Listen, did you hear—realize . . .
CHORUS: It is the collapse of the citadel.
HECUBA: Gone. Everything is gone.
CHORUS: A wave of ruin spreads through the ruins.

[*Several long blasts on the trumpet echo over the plain*]

HECUBA: [*gathering herself together*]
Shake your silly shaking legs,
Hecuba, begin your walk
Towards your new life as slave.
CHORUS: Sad, stricken Troy, farewell.
We too must walk away
To the Greek armada and set sail.

[*As Troy continues to burn,* TALTHYBIUS *and his guards marshal the* WOMEN OF TROY *and lead them off.* HECUBA *stands for a moment with bent head and her back to the city. Then she slowly begins to follow, but her footsteps get slower and slower till at last she sinks to the ground with her eyes riveted on the burning city. Several of the* WOMEN *run back to help her, but when they reach her she is dead. Euripides does not include this scenario, but with Cassandra's prophecy in line 430 (and she is never wrong)* HECUBA'*s death at Troy is foretold*]

THE CYCLOPS

~~~

ΚΥΚΛΩΨ

For Martin, Lucy and Maximilian Roche

In *The Cyclops*, Euripides gives us the only satyr play that has come down to us—except for extended fragments of *The Trackers* by Sophocles. The date of its composition is uncertain. The satyr play was the fourth piece offered by each playwright after his three tragedies at the dramatic festivals, and as with the tragedies its subject matter was taken from the stories of Greek mythology derived from Homer and elsewhere. In the satyr play, however, these were given a comic, even a grotesque, twist. The form was in fact more ancient than that of tragedy (which by the middle of the fifth century B.C. had lost a sense of its Dionysiac origins) and harked back to its links with Bacchus.

We do not know what three tragedies or trilogy Euripides presented with *The Cyclops*, nor have we any way of comparing his comedy with all the lost satyr plays of Aeschylus and Sophocles.

There were two types of satyr: the Silenus satyr, stemming from Anatolia in Asia Minor and the offspring of Silenus, who was born on the island of Lesbos; and the Arcadian satyr, stemming from Arcadia in the Peloponnese and the offspring of Pan, the woodland god.

The Silenus satyr sported a horse's tail and ears, and sometimes a horse's hooves. The Arcadian satyr (favored by the Romans, who called it a faun), was a goat from the waist down, sprouted two horns and the ears of a goat, and, unlike the Silenus satyr, which was snubnosed, had a rather long shaggy face. Both types of satyr were well known for their lechery and liked nothing better than pursuing nymphs.

The two most famous satyrs, apart from Pan, were Marsyas and Silenus. Marsyas was of the goat variety and was so proficient at the flute that he challenged Apollo, god of music. Apollo defeated him in the contest, then strung him up to a tree and flayed him alive.

As to Silenus, who was the foster father of Bacchus, there are two traditions regarding him: one that he was the wisest of the satyrs and something of a philosopher—it is interesting that the

bust of Socrates wears the squashed-nosed face of a Silenus—
and the other that he was a fat old rollicking buffoon.

The Cyclopes were one-eyed giants spawned by Poseidon,
inhabiting Sicily. They were shepherds and cannibals.

CHARACTERS

SILENUS, an old satyr, once tutor to Bacchus
CHORUS of satyrs, the sons of Silenus
ODYSSEUS, king of Ithaca and sacker of Troy
THE CYCLOPS, named Polyphemus
CREW of Odysseus' ship
SERFS of the Cyclops

TIME AND SETTING

It is the heroic age in Sicily, not long after the Trojan War.
Silenus and his satyr sons, having gone off to rescue Bacchus,
who had been captured by pirates, fall into the hands of
Polyphemus the Cyclops on their return journey and are made
into his slaves.

The time is early afternoon. Silenus, old and fat, comes out of
a cave (the den of the Cyclops) dragging a rake. In the fore-
ground a small stream threads through a meadow. Mount Etna
lowers in the distance.

PROLOGUE

SILENUS: Dear me, Bacchus,
   what chores you've saddled me with
   ever since I was young and strong!
And I'm still at it.
First, remember that time that Hera drove you crazy
   and you bolted from your nurses the mountain nymphs.
Then there was that battle with the Giants
   when I stood stalwart at your side
   and put a sword clean through the shield of the ogre Ence-
                                                              ladus.
I killed him, of course . . . Or did I dream this up?

Couldn't have. No, by Zeus!
   for I actually presented you with the monster's spoils.

But all this is nothing to the troubles I'm enduring now.
Good gracious, no!
The moment I learnt that Hera
   had set those Lydian pirates on you
   to sell you as a slave in foreign parts,
   I hoisted sail with my sons to look for you.
Oh yes, I took the helm,
   stood up there in the stern
   with the tiller in my hands,
   while my boys thrashed the ocean with their oars
   making the green sea white . . .
All in search of you, my king.
But just as Malea* hove in sight
   an east wind smote us and pummeled us here
   to this rocky shore of Etna,
where the Cyclopes,
   those one-eyed man-devouring brutes spawned by the sea god,
   haunt their forlorn caverns.
One of them,
   whose name is Polyphemus, pounced on us
   and turned us into his personal denhold slaves.

Goodbye, Bacchanalian song and dance!
We're shepherds now:
   shepherds of this noxious Cyclops' flocks.
My poor lads (mere boys)
   are out there tending his beasts beneath the mountain,
while I stay behind,
   filling the troughs, sweeping the den,
   cooking the stinking dinners of this stinking Cyclops.

   [*Shaking the rake in his hands*]

And now my orders are

---

*Malea, on the island of Lesbos, was where Silenus was born.

to rake up the mess in this cave
and welcome home my one-eyed master with his animals.

[*He cocks an ear as a general rumpus of shouting and singing
breaks on the air*]

Ah, here they come, my lads,
    driving their flocks before them!
But . . . but . . . dancing? How come?

[*He shouts*]

Hey hey! D'you think you're at a Bacchanal
    having fun and games?
Strains of the lyre too,
    dancing your way to Althaea's* palace!

[*The* CHORUS *of* SATYRS, *led by a flute player and driving their
beasts before them, bounds on to the scene—laughing,
shouting, miming. Like their father they sport a horse's tail
and have horses' feet and ears. They are clad in goatskins but
are naked from the waist down, and long exaggerated phal-
luses dangle between their legs*]

PARADOS OR ENTRY SONG

STROPHE

CHORUS:

[*a single voice as a* SATYR *chases after a he-goat†*]

See here, billy goat, even if both
    Sides of your pedigree prove you a prince,

---

*Althaea, the mother of Meleager, became the patroness of goats. Silenus is
referring sarcastically to the Cyclops' cave, where the goats are penned.
†Louis Meridier in the scholarly French edition of the play insists, on insuffi-
cient evidence it seems to me, that lines 41–54 refer to sheep, not goats. In the
Odyssey they are definitely goats. Perhaps we should assume that there are
both sheep and goats. (When line numbers are given in the notes, they refer to
the Greek text in the Loeb Classics edition.)

Must you go prancing off to the rocks?
Here there's a lovely breeze blowing;
There's pasturing grass green for grazing.
Water from the stream sluices through
Your troughs by the cave
Where the little kids bleat . . .

[*He chases after another goat*]

You there, hey!
Off to enjoy the dew on the slopes?
Shoo! Shoo! or you'll get a stone.

[*Grappling with another goat*]

On with you, on with you, into the cave,
You horny old thing, into the corral,
Our Cyclopean master's stable.

[*Another* SATYR *grabs an ewe*]

ANTISTROPHE*
You there, Honeybunch, ease the pressure
Of those bursting tits. Your kids are waiting
Ever since you left them in their pens
Dozing the day away, now they want you:
Yes, they're bleating their poor hearts out.
So get along now and into the fold.
Forget your cropping in the pastures,
Go into the rocky depths of Etna.

[*Another* SATYR, *pulling a long face in mock mourning*]

EPODE
There ain't no Bacchus, ain't no dancing,
There ain't no Maenads a-thyrsus-shaking
Or tambourines like splashing water.
There ain't no golden-greeny fountains

---

*This is a rare example of an antistrophe not following the full pattern of the strophe.

Gushing wine, and not a sign
Of the nymphs of Nysa shouting "Bacchus!
Bacchus!" as I chase the girls of
Aphrodite, flying after
Their milky feet . . . O lovely, O lonely
Bacchus tossing your mane of curls,
Where are you off to, forfeiting me
Your servant to the one-eyed Cyclops
As his lackey, where in my filthy
Garb of goatskin I potter about
Shorn of your friendship?

[SILENUS, *who has been half watching the antics of his children with an indulgent eye and half scanning the horizon, suddenly holds a finger to his lips*]

FIRST EPISODE

SILENUS: Shush, boys! Hurry!
Tell the serfs to get the flocks into the cave.
LEADER: [*running up to him*]
On the double, Dad, but what's the hurry?
SILENUS: I see down by the shore a Greek ship.
A body of oarsmen led by a captain
are climbing towards this cave.
They've got empty baskets slung from the neck.
They'll be wanting food,
and of course kegs of water.
Poor wretched wanderers, who could they be?
Little do they know what kind of welcome
they can expect from their host, Polyphemus—
tramping blithely into the jaws
of his man-eating maws.

[*A hubbub of speculation swells among the* CHORUS *of* SATYRS.
SILENUS *holds up his hand for silence*]

Quiet now!
We need to discover where they come from

and why they are here in Sicily at the foot of Etna.

[*As the* SATYRS *and the* SERFS *bustle the flocks into the cave, a weary body of men trudge into view: they are* ODYSSEUS *and members of his* CREW. *Some carry empty pitchers slung from the shoulder, and some wineskins full of wine. They are obviously hoping to barter wine for water*]

ODYSSEUS: Friends, can you tell me where to find
  fresh water to slake our thirst?
And perhaps—if you can be so kind—
  sell some food to us hungry tars.

  [*Gazing around in amazement*]

Great Zeus!
We seem to have struck a Bacchic city.
I see satyrs—a mob of them—outside the cave.
Let me salute this ancient one, their senior.
SILENUS: [*stepping up to him*]
  Good afternoon, good stranger,
  who are you and where are you from?
ODYSSEUS: I am Odysseus of Ithaca. That island's king.
SILENUS: Why of course, son of Sisyphus—that clever bastard.
ODYSSEUS: That's me, and I'll thank you to be polite.
SILENUS: Well, what port did you sail from to this land of Sicily?
ODYSSEUS: From Troy, and the terrible war that's been raging there.
SILENUS: Do you mean to say you couldn't find your way back
home?
ODYSSEUS: A great storm caught us and tossed us here.
SILENUS: What bad luck! The same thing happened to me.
ODYSSEUS: You don't say! You were tossed here too?
SILENUS: We were chasing the pirates who had kidnapped
Bacchus.
ODYSSEUS: But what's this place? Who are living here?
SILENUS: Over there's Mount Etna, the highest peak in Sicily.
ODYSSEUS: But where are the walls? Where are your city's
towers?
SILENUS: There ain't no such things. No humans live here,
stranger.

ODYSSEUS: But who does the place belong to? Wild animals?

SILENUS: Cyclopes. They live in caves, not houses.

ODYSSEUS: Ruled by whom? Or is it a democracy?

SILENUS: Hillbillies—ruled by no one no how.

ODYSSEUS: Do they till and sow? How do they live?

SILENUS: Milk, cheese—and the eternal mutton chop.

ODYSSEUS: And vineyards, surely? They must make wine?

SILENUS: [*throwing up his hands in disgust*]

Not a chance. This is a grim land. No frolics, dancing.

ODYSSEUS: Hospitable? Are they nice to strangers?

SILENUS: [*with a grimace*]

Charming. Strangers make the best eating of all, they say.

ODYSSEUS: Don't tell me they gorge on human flesh?

SILENUS: Every guest that comes here gets devoured.

ODYSSEUS: [*shuddering*]

Where's this Cyclops at the moment? . . . Not at home?

SILENUS: He's out hunting on Mount Etna with his dogs.

ODYSSEUS: D'you know what you can do for us before we make
                                                    our getaway?

SILENUS: No, I do not, Odysseus. But for you I'd do anything.

ODYSSEUS: Sell us some bread. We're completely out of it.

SILENUS: As I told you, the only thing here is meat.

ODYSSEUS: Meat'll do. Not a bad cure for famine.

SILENUS: And we've got curds and cheese—as well as cow's milk.

ODYSSEUS: Bring them out. A buyer should buy in light of day.

SILENUS: Show your money first and say what you'll pay.

ODYSSEUS: No money, but . . . what I've got is—wine.

SILENUS: [*clapping his hands*]

Wine? Oh, blessed word! I haven't heard that for ages.

ODYSSEUS: Given me by no less than Maron,* your wine god's
                                                    son.

SILENUS: But the wine? Still on board? D'you have to go and
                                                    get it?

[ODYSSEUS *craftily uncovers a corner of a wineskin*]

ODYSSEUS: It's all in here, old man, right before your eyes.

SILENUS: [*in disgust*] That? Why it wouldn't make a single swig.

*Odysseus met Maron in North Africa when he touched upon the coast.

ODYSSEUS: [*whipping off the whole covering*]
   There's twice as much in there as you could ever hold.
SILENUS: Oh, beautiful! Oh, fountain of light!
ODYSSEUS: Like a little sip? It's neat.
SILENUS: Well . . . I suppose a buyer ought to know what he's
                                                        buying.
ODYSSEUS: I'll draw you off a cup. One's hanging from the skin.
SILENUS: [*trembling with anticipation*]
   Out with it quick. I can't wait to remember.
ODYSSEUS: [*pouring*] There, see?
SILENUS: [*bending down and sniffing*] Ye gods, what a bouquet!
ODYSSEUS: [*teasingly*] Is it something you can actually see?
SILENUS: See be damned! I can smell it.
ODYSSEUS: Go on, take a swig. Clinch the word with the deed.
SILENUS: [*gulping a mouthful*]
   Mmmmm . . . O Bacchus! . . . I've simply got to dance.

   [SILENUS *executes a pirouette*]

ODYSSEUS: How's that for slipping down your gullet?
SILENUS: My gullet, man? Right down to my toenails.
ODYSSEUS: And we'll add some cash for it as well.
SILENUS: To hell with cash! Just keep pouring.
ODYSSEUS: Fine! But now bring out the cheese and mutton.
SILENUS: [*beginning to feel merry*] Consider it done.
   I don't care a fig for my boss.
I'd go crazy for just one cup of that wine.
I'd sell the entire flocks of all the Cyclopes.
I'd leap into the briny sea from the Leucadian* rock,
   for just one little tipple to smooth my frown.
A man who isn't merry in his cups
   is a solemn fool.
Besides,

   [*pointing between his legs*]

   it makes you stand up straight
   while you get your two hands around

---

*Leucadia was an island in the Ionian Sea (northern Greece) whose rocky
promontory was a famous site for suicides.

some lovely little soft boobs—and elsewhere.
That's when you can really dance
and put paid to all your worries.
So why shouldn't I blow a kiss to a drink like that
and tell that mindless Cyclops
to go and cry his one big eye out?

[SILENUS *goes into the cave and a young* SATYR *from the* CHORUS *steps forward*]

SATYR: Look here, Odysseus,
there's a matter we'd like to discuss with you.
ODYSSEUS: Go ahead . . . Friend to friend. Nothing nicer.
SATYR: Well, when you laid waste Troy, did you also lay Helen?
ODYSSEUS: [*rather shocked*] We laid waste the whole house of
Priam.

SATYR: Yes, but,
when you got hold of that little piece of fluff,
did you all line up to run her through
in a gang-bang fuck—
give her for once her fill of a man?
The slut!
Bowled over by the sight of men
with embroidered pants and pretty legs,
and a gold chain dangling from his neck,
deserting the best of men all forlorn . . .
Poor Menelaus!
I just wish there were no women at all in the world,
except one or two—for *me*.

[SILENUS *and a troupe of* SATYRS *come out of the cave car- rying bowls and wicker panniers of cheese, and dragging along several bleating lambs*]

SILENUS: King Odysseus,
here are some fatted firstfruits of the flock for you,
these bleating lambs;
also curds and cheese galore.
Take them and be off from this cave as fast as you can . . .
but not before you've handed over that divine wine.

[*The trudge of heavy feet can be heard and the sound of deep breathing—getting nearer*]

ODYSSEUS: The fat's in the fire, old man, where can we fly to?
SILENUS: Into the cave. There are hiding places there.
ODYSSEUS: Sheer madness! Right into the trap.
SILENUS: Nonsense! The rocks are riddled with hiding holes.
ODYSSEUS: [*striking a pose*] I think not.
    Great Troy itself would groan
    if we scattered before one solitary human being.
Why, many a time have I stood
    blocking a horde of a thousand Trojans with my bare shield.
If die we must, then let's die gloriously,
    or gloriously live with untarnished name.

[SILENUS *in a panic stampedes into the cave.* SATYRS *from the* CHORUS *bolt helter-skelter in all directions. Some follow* SILENUS, *some huddle around* ODYSSEUS. *Some snatch up pan-pipes and begin to dance innocently. The* CYCLOPS, *a bearded giant, followed by dogs, tramps into sight. He lowers his club*]

CYCLOPS: Ho ho! What's this? This idle celebration?
    You won't find any Bacchus here,
    no, nor rattle of castanets or beating of drums.
How are my little lambkins doing in the cave?
Are they nuzzling away under their mothers?
Is there lots of fresh cheese
    pressed into the wicker crates?

[*He waits for a reply, then wheels on the leading* SATYR]

No speak, eh? Nothing to say?
Look up, damn you, not down,
    or I'll have you blubbering with a good clubbering.
SATYR: [*gazing up at the sky*] Right away, sir.
    We're focusing on Zeus himself
    and I can see Orion and all the stars.
CYCLOPS: Got a good dinner ready for me?
SATYR: Absolutely. You can guzzle all you want.
CYCLOPS: And the milk? Are the basins brimming?
SATYR: Whole barrelfuls ready to swill if you're in the mood.

CYCLOPS: D'you mean cow's milk or sheep's milk or a mix?
SATYR: Whichever, so long as you don't swallow *me*.
CYCLOPS: Not likely!
 I wouldn't last long with you dancing sikinnis* in my belly.

[*He sees* ODYSSEUS *and his men, as well as all the provender they are about to carry away*]

Ho ho! What's this rabble I see beside my house?
Have pirates and robbers taken over the land?
And what's this I espy:
 my own lambs from my own cave,
 all trussed up with plaited withies?
 And panniers of packed cheeses and . . . and . . .

[*He catches sight of* SILENUS *stumbling from the cave, having made himself up with eye patches, head patches, and plenty of rouge to look like someone who has put up a good fight*]

 . . . the old satyr,
 his whole bald pate puffed up with bruises?
SILENUS: Ooooh! They've blasted me into a red-hot fever.
CYCLOPS: Who have? Who's been bashing at your skull, old
 thing?
SILENUS: [*waving his hands*]
 O Cyclops, *they* have. Because I tried to stop them robbing
 you.
CYCLOPS: Didn't they know I am a god and son of a god?
SILENUS: I kept telling them
 but they just went on hauling the stuff away.
 And I couldn't stop them gobbling up the cheeses
 or carrying off the lambs.
They said they'd strap you into a dog collar three feet thick
 and squelch out your innards through your one big eye,
 and flay your backsides with a whip,
 and toss you on board their ship
 and hire you out to someone heaving rocks
 or work you in a treadmill.
CYCLOPS: They did, did they?

sikinnis: the characteristic dance of the satyr play.

Well, you just go and strop my razors up
and throw a big bundle of kindling on the hearth to start a fire.
I'll butcher them on the spot,
    grill them over the red-hot cinders,
    and stuff them into my paunch without even bothering to
                                                carve.
I'm sick of overboiled meat from the cauldron
    and all that mountain fare.
Enough of gorging on lions and stags.
It's time for some juicy human steaks.
SILENUS: Aye, master,
    it's always pleasant to make a change;
    and it's been quite a while
    since we've had any guests coming to your cave.

[ODYSSEUS, *who has been listening dumbfounded, strides forward*]

ODYSSEUS: Cyclops,
    you'd better wait and hear what these guests have to say.

We needed food:
    we got off our ship to come to your cave and do some bar-
                                                tering.
This creature here
    offered to exchange some lambs for a flagon of wine—
    after taking a swig.
It was agreed on both sides. No force was invoked.
There's not a single sound syllable in what the fellow says.
He's been caught peddling your animals, that's all.
SILENUS: What, me? . . . Go damn your eyes!
ODYSSEUS: If I'm lying . . .
SILENUS: Cyclops, sir, I swear
    by great Poseidon, your own sire,
    by mighty Triton and Nereus himself,
    by every blessed wave and every kind of fish . . .
    I adjure you, my handsome, my imperial,
    my dear little Cyclopsy—
    never, never did I sell
    any of your goods to these strangers here:

or you can strike dead these naughty boys of mine.
SATYR (leader): Strike you dead, too, Dad!
   I saw you with my own eyes trading all that stuff,
   yes, trading with these visitors.

[*Turning to the* CYCLOPS]

If I'm lying
   you can annihilate my father,
   but you mustn't hurt these strangers.
CYCLOPS: Liars all!
   I'd rather believe Silenus,
   he's the more reliable of the two—
   even if Rhadamanthus were to judge.
But I have questions to ask.
Strangers, where did you sail from?
What country and what city raised you?
ODYSSEUS: We're Ithacans by race.
   We've come from Ilium after sacking it.
Oh, Cyclops,
   we were driven by wind and sea
   and cast up on your shores.
CYCLOPS: So you're the ones that went off to Troy—
   Troy by the Scamander River—
   to lay hold of that worthless Helen?
ODYSSEUS: The very ones. And what a painful job it was!
CYCLOPS: Well, you ought to be ashamed of yourselves:
   sailing off to Troy and all that fuss
   just for one single female.
ODYSSEUS: It was the act of a god.
   Mortals are not to blame.
   Therefore we implore you,

[*Going down on his knees*]

O noble son of the sea god,
   we beseech you as free men,
   do not be so ruthless as to slay
   those who come as guests to your cave.
Do not chew them between cannibal jaws:

not us, lord king,
   who have saved your father's shrines in every corner of Hellas.
The holy harbor of Taenarum,
   as well as Malea's sacred summit, remain intact.
   And the divine Athena's silver-veined cliffs of Sunium,
   and the sanctuary of Geraestus . . .
No, we never shamed Greece
   by giving in to intolerable Troy.
In all this you have a share,
   for you dwell on the edges of Greece
   under the rocks and fiery roots of Etna.

[CYCLOPS *yawns; some of the* SATYRS *are giggling, others making rude gestures.* ODYSSEUS *continues*]

And even if you don't agree with me,
   you surely must respect the universal practice of mankind
   to clothe and husband shipwrecked mariners,
   and not cram them down your gullet
   like chunks of spitted ox
   and stuff them into your belly.
Enough is enough!
The land of Priam has bankrupted Hellas,
   drunk the blood of thousands felled in battle,
   left wives widows,
   graying mothers without sons,
   and bereft fathers gone snow-white.
If you now roast us remnants for a crapulent feast,
   where can anyone turn?
Listen to me, Cyclops,
   restrain your drooling jaws;
   choose righteousness, not wrong.
Many have sinned through greed
   and paid for the damage it has wrung.
SILENUS: Take my advice, Cyclops:
   eat him up. Don't leave a scrap.
And if you want the gift of the gab,
   munch on his tongue.
CYCLOPS: [*turning to* ODYSSEUS]
   Money, my little mannikin,

is the god of those who have any sense.
Everything else is pumped-up talk, mere cosmetics.
As to my father's farflung establishments along the coast,
stuff them! Why do you even mention them?
And I'm not one to shudder at Zeus's thunder either.
I even doubt that Zeus is a greater god than I.
Anyway, I don't give a damn.
And why don't I give a damn?
Because when he showers anything down from above,
I'm all snug in my rocky shack,
and after a good dinner of roast lamb or game,
washed down with a tank of milk,
I'm flat on my back.
So when Zeus claps out his thunder,
I from my blankets blast out a fart.
And when the north wind swarms in with snow from Thrace,
I just bury myself in furs and light a fire—
I snap my fingers at the snow.

[SILENUS *yawns.* SATYRS *whisper and fidget*]

Meanwhile the earth, whether it likes it or not,
has to grow the grass that feeds my flocks.
No sacrifices do I celebrate—except to myself:
certainly not to the gods,
only to the greatest god of them all:

[*tapping his tummy*]

the god right here.
To eat and drink from day to day
without a care in the world,
that's the Zeus for any man of sense.
On those who festoon our human life with laws,
I cry down bitter tears.
So I shan't stop pampering myself.
I'm going to eat you . . . However,
as a sop to a guest and to avoid all censure,
you shall have a good hot fire,
some of my father's brine, and of course a cauldron;

which will render you and tender you into a beautiful stew.
Do come inside,
  and gather ye all around this deity of the cave
  who is about to eat . . . and wish him *bon appétit*."

[CYCLOPS *begins to prod* ODYSSEUS *and members of the* CREW
towards the cave]

ODYSSEUS: And to think that I survived the horrors of Troy
  and the perils of the deep only to run aground
  on this obscene creature's whim and lawless heart!

[*Stretching out his arms*]

O Pallas Athena, mistress divine, O daughter of Zeus,
  help me now, help!
This is worse than Troy.
This is rock bottom.
And you, Zeus, patron of travelers,
  throned among the sparkling galaxies,
  look down on what is happening here,
  and if you do not see it,
  Zeus must be someone else and you no god.

[ODYSSEUS *and his* CREW *disappear into the cave, followed by*
SILENUS. *The* CHORUS *of* SATYRS *regroups and chants in a
vividly grim mood*]

SECOND CHORAL LYRIC

STROPHE

CHORUS: Open your big mouth wide, O Cyclops,
  It's "à table" for your dinner of limbs
  Boiled, grilled, hot from the fire.
  So gnaw, tear, champ on the bits
  Of your visitor's parts while you recline
  On your goatskin rug.
  But please do not share it with me.
  Stow it all in your own hold.
  Enjoy yourself in your impious den.

ANTISTROPHE

Enjoy your gluttonous sacrifice,
Your godless eating of your guests.
Cyclops of Etna, bolt them down.
Pitiless the monster who
When helpless travelers come to his home
Butchers them on his own hearth,
Chops them up and chomps them down,
Stewed or grilled over the coals:
Downs them with his dirty teeth.

[ODYSSEUS, *carrying a wineskin slung from his shoulders,
comes out of the cave with members of his* CREW]

SECOND EPISODE

ODYSSEUS: Great Zeus, how can I describe
the nightmare I have seen inside that cave?
Things incredible except in horror tales
outstripping all humanity.
SATYR (leader): What is it, Odysseus?
Don't tell me the sacrilegious Cyclops
has butchered your dear companions?
ODYSSEUS: He has: two of them, the plumpest and most robust.
He weighed them in his two hands.
SATYR: You poor man, how could you bear it?
ODYSSEUS: Once we were inside the rocky cavern,
the first thing he did was to light a fire.
Then, onto the enormous hearth
he threw down a heap of logs from a hefty oak:
a load so large three wagons would hardly have held it.
Then he spread out his pine-needle palliasse beside the fire,
and having milked his young cows
he filled a ninety-gallon butt with their white milk;
next to which he set a bowl with ivy round it . . .
It must have been four feet wide and six deep.
After that, he put a copper cauldron on the fire to boil,
then with an ax he trimmed his blackthorn spits
and brought them to a point within the embers.
Near the axheads were bowls to catch the blood.

* * *

When this hideous cook from hell had made all ready,
   he grabbed two of my men in a single snatch.
Then, in one fluid motion,
   he slammed the first against the copper lips of the cauldron,
                     splitting his throat.
The other he gripped by the heel
   and smashed him against a jut of rock,
   spilling out his brains.
Then with his murderous cleaver
   he sliced off pieces of flesh to roast in the fire
   or flung scraps into the pot to stew.

Meanwhile, I, appalled,
   the tears streaming from my eyes,
   presented myself to the Cyclops.
The others, like frightened birds,
   shrank into the recesses of the rocks,
   all blood drained from their faces.
When he had gorged on my friends enough,
   he staggered backwards, letting out a mighty belch.
It was then an inspiration hit me.
Filling a stoop with Maron's wine,
   I offered it to him, saying:
"Son of the sea god, Cyclops,
   just see what a divine draft full of Dionysiac cheer
   Greece brings you from the grape."
He, bloated with his disgusting meal,
   took it and gulped it down.
Up went his hands in gratitude:
"Wonderful guest,
   you've capped a perfect dinner with a perfect drink."
When I saw how this delighted him,
   I filled his stoop again, knowing full well
   the wine would make him tipsy and give me my chance.
He broke into song
   as I poured him drink after drink
   till his very innards glowed.

* * *

He's there inside,
   singing his head off while my sailors wail.
The din in the cave is deafening.

   [*Turning to the rapt* SATYRS]

I tiptoed out;
   and now I'd like to save myself,
   and you too—if that is what you want.
So tell me yes or no
   whether you want to escape from this loathsome monster
   and live with the nymphs of the fountains
   in the mansions of Bacchus.
Your father inside has already approved
   but he is weak and sozzled with wine.
He sticks to his cups,
   caught in the birdlime like a bird.
But you who are young,
   save yourselves with me and take up again
   your devoted Dionysus, to whom
   the Cyclops can hardly be preferred.
SATYR: Oh what a friend! *That* would be the day!
   Yes, to flee the clutches of this godless Cyclops and

   [*patting his phallus*]

   this poor pipe of mine
   has been useless too long
   with not a thing to hose.
ODYSSEUS: Then listen to my plan.
   It'll finish this unscrupulous savage and free you all from
                        servitude.
SATYR: Speak on. Sweeter than the sound of an Asian lute
   would be the news of the Cyclops' end.
ODYSSEUS: He's so taken with the booze of Bacchus
   he wants to wind his way and whoop it up
   with his Cyclopes pals.
SATYR: I get it. You plan to surprise and kill him in some lonely copse
   or fling him over the cliffs.
ODYSSEUS: Not at all. My scheme's much craftier.

SATYR: I wonder what? I've always heard how clever you are.
ODYSSEUS: I'll discourage his partying:
  say he shouldn't waste such marvelous stuff on Cyclopes
  but keep it all to himself and live it up.
As soon as he succumbs to a sodden Bacchic slumber,
  I'll take that stake of olive wood that's somewhere in the cave
  and with my sword whittle it down to a point.
Then I'll put it in the fire
  and when I see it's well and truly glowing,
  I'll plunge it blazing
  right in the center of the Cyclops' eye
  and singe out his sight.
Just like a shipwright's joiner
  swiveling holes in a beam with his belted drill,
  I'll twirl my firebrand in the Cyclops' pupil
  and sear his eyeball out.
SATYR: Bravo! I'm mad about your plan.
ODYSSEUS: Then I'll put you and your friends,
  and the old man too,
  on board my black galley,
  and with a double row of rowers rowing
  we'll thresh ourselves away from here.
SATYR: Can I have a part in this blessed rite,
  the blotting out of his eye? Hold up the stake perhaps?
This is a job I'd dearly like to share.
ODYSSEUS: You must. The beam is huge. You all must help.
ANOTHER SATYR: I could lift a hundred wagons
  if so it meant the Cyclops died most dreadfully:
  his eye smoked out just like a wasp's nest.

[*The young* SATYRS *gather around* ODYSSEUS, *babbling with excitement*]

ODYSSEUS: Quiet now! You know my gambit.
  When I give the command, trust my generalship.
You see, I'm not out just to save myself,
  abandoning my crew in there;
  although I could escape quite easily
  and get away from this dungeon of a cave.
But it would be disgraceful to desert the friends I came with

just to save myself.

[ODYSSEUS *braces himself and strides into the cave, leaving a chattering bunch of young* SATYRS *outside*]

SATYR: Who is the first, who is the second
   Along the red-hot shaft to twist it
   As we plunge it into the Cyclops' eye
   And sizzle out the light of his vision?

[*The drunken racket of an unmusical chantey issues from the cave*]

A satyr: Quiet! Quiet! here comes the fuddled one
   Weaving out of his rocky den,
Another: Composing ad lib, roaring his head off:
Another: The savagest discord; it makes you weep.
Another: Let's teach him a ditty he hasn't yet heard
   At any carousal.
Another: He's on the point of going blind.

[POLYPHEMUS *emerges from the cave singing, reeling, and belching. He is supported by* ODYSSEUS *and* SILENUS, *holding basins and jugs of wine. The* SATYR CHORUS *clusters around them, dancing and miming*]

SECOND CHORAL LYRIC

STROPHE

CHORUS: Happy the man who lies full length
   Singing his bliss by a fountain of wine,
Carousing away:
   With his arms around a friend or a lovely
   Blonde in bed with him, so sweetly
   Scented and blooming with curls, as he murmurs:
   "Will someone unlock the door for me?"

ANTISTROPHE

CYCLOPS: Whoosh! I'm sluiced with wine and my belly
   Is loaded, I glow with the glut of the feast.
My cargo ship

Is weighted down to my plimsoll line,
While the meadows bid me in early spring
Romp on holiday with my brothers . . .
Reach me, my friend, reach me the flagon.

EPODE*

CHORUS: Lovely the sparkling eye of him
　As lovely the bride steps from her house:
Lover, he loves.
　His lamps are lit, his body tingles
　For his velvety bride in the spongy cave.
　In a moment we shall garland his brow
　With a crown—a crown of a myriad hues.

THIRD EPISODE

ODYSSEUS: Listen, Cyclops, I'm an expert on Bacchus, whose
　　　　　　　　　　　　　　　wine I gave you.
CYCLOPS: Who is this Bacchus? Not a real god, is he?
ODYSSEUS: The greatest life-charmer humans have.
CYCLOPS: [belching] Indeed, every hiccup is a joy.
ODYSSEUS: That's him for sure. Never hurts a soul.
CYCLOPS: But a home in a wineskin? How does a god do that?
ODYSSEUS: He's wherever you put him. And there is bliss.
CYCLOPS: Gods in wineskins! I don't think that's quite right.
ODYSSEUS: What matter, if he's to your taste? Or do you object to
　　　　　　　　　　　　　　　the wineskin?
CYCLOPS: Damn the wineskin! It's the booze I like.
ODYSSEUS: Stay here, then, Cyclops. Drink and be merry.
CYCLOPS: What! Not offer my brothers a sip?
ODYSSEUS: Keep it all for yourself. Drink like a lord.
CYCLOPS: It's more gentlemanly, surely, to share with friends.
ODYSSEUS: But partying ends in brawls and fisticuffs.
CYCLOPS: Well, I'm drunk, but nobody would pick a fight with me.

---

*The entire epode, invoking the imagery of a wedding, is a metaphor for the
destruction of the Cyclops. The joyous anticipation of the bridegroom is the
satyrs' expectation of liberation, the lit lamps are the firebrand, the crown of
a myriad hues is the Cyclops' visage scorched and reddened.

ODYSSEUS: Maybe, my dear sir, but home is the place to be
                                                    tight.

CYCLOPS: What, no fun and games when one's smashed? That's
                                                    silly.

ODYSSEUS: When one's smashed it's wiser to stay at home.

CYCLOPS: [*turning to* SILENUS]
    So, Silenus, what shall we do? D'you think I should stay?

SILENUS: Yes, Cyclops, you should. What do you need other
                                            boozers for?

CYCLOPS: True; and the ground here is carpeted with flowers.

SILENUS: Just the place to carouse in the warmth of the sun.
    So lie you down on your side: stretch out.

[*As the* CYCLOPS *reclines,* SILENUS *slyly sneaks the wine bowl
away from him, but is seen*]

CYCLOPS: Why have you gone off with the wine bowl behind
                                            my back?

SILENUS: I . . . I thought someone passing . . . might knock
                                            it over.

CYCLOPS: You mean, you were trying to snatch a secret swig.
    Put it in the middle.

[*As* SILENUS *puts the wine bowl back where it was, the* CYCLOPS
turns to ODYSSEUS]

And you, stranger, tell me what I should call you.

ODYSSEUS: "Nobody." . . . But don't you have something for
                                            me?

CYCLOPS: Yes, of all your crew I'll eat you last.

SILENUS: [*gulping down a cup of wine*]
    What a lovely present to give a guest!

CYCLOPS: Hey there! What are you up to? Sneaking a swill?

SILENUS: No no—it's my lovely eyes. It had to kiss me.

CYCLOPS: Watch out—flirting with the wine! It's unflirtable.

SILENUS: On the contrary, by Zeus. It finds me irresistible.

CYCLOPS: Here, fill me a bowl and hand it over . . . Just hand it.

[SILENUS *pours out the wine with a little water added and lifts
it to his lips*]

SILENUS: Let me see if the mixture is correct.

[*He takes a gulp*]

CYCLOPS: Damn you! Give it here.
SILENUS: Of course! But first I've got to put a wreath on you
and . . .

[*He grabs a bunch of wildflowers growing near and jams them over the* CYCLOPS' *eye while with his other hand raising his bowl to his lips*]

. . . and have a little taste.
CYCLOPS: What a rascal of a butler you are!
SILENUS: "What a lovely butt of wine!" did you say?
Well now, wipe off your chin before you sip.

[SILENUS *refills the bowl as the* CYCLOPS *wipes his face with the back of his hand*]

CYCLOPS: There, my lips and beard are perfectly clean.
SILENUS: Sò, crook your elbow genteelly—just as you see me
doing—
and drink . . . and . . .

[*He drains the cup*]

as you see, it's gone.
CYCLOPS: Hey, hey! What are you up to?
SILENUS: Drinking deep and sweet.

[*The* CYCLOPS *snatches the bowl away and hands it to* ODYSSEUS]

CYCLOPS: Here, stranger, you pour for me.

[ODYSSEUS *takes charge of the bowl and the wineskin*]

ODYSSEUS: In my hands at least, the grape knows its place.
CYCLOPS: Then pour.
ODYSSEUS: I am pouring. Don't talk so.
CYCLOPS: Not so easy when one's full of wine!

ODYSSEUS: [*handing him a full bowl*]
    There, knock it back. Don't leave a drop.
CYCLOPS: [*draining the bowl*] My! What a clever plant the vine
                                                          is!
ODYSSEUS: What's more, if you deluge a parched stomach after
    a blowout you'll plunge into the sweetest slumber; but leave
                                    a drop and Bacchus will parch *you*.

[ODYSSEUS *pours another bowl for* SILENUS, *who drains it in
one long pull. The* SATYRS *teasingly dance and caper around
him*]

CYCLOPS: [*lurching and swinging*]
    Wow! I can scarcely kick to come to the top. Unmixed bliss!
The whole sky's wheeling . . . into the earth . . . And look, there's
Zeus on his throne and . . . and all the holy heavenly court.

[*An impertinent* SATYR *comes up to him with a mock
invitation*]

No, I'm not going to screw *you*.
Even the Graces are trying to get me.

[*Rolling over and seizing* SILENUS]

I've got my own little Ganymede here . . . He'll do . . .
No disrespect to you Graces . . . with him I'll sleep divinely.
Besides, I like boys more than girls.
SILENUS: [*teasing*] Am I really Zeus's Ganymede, Cyclops?
CYCLOPS: [*squeezing him*]
    By Zeus, you are! I snatched you away from Dardanus.*
SILENUS: Lads, this is the end of me. I'm going to get raped.
CYCLOPS: Tut tut! No blaming your lover just because he's tight!
SILENUS: I know I'm going to be given some terribly sour wine.

[CYCLOPS *reels into the cave, pulling* SILENUS *along with him,
followed by* ODYSSEUS, *who puts the stake in the fire, then
comes out again*]

Dardanus: founder of Troy and father of Ganymede, the beautiful youth
whom Zeus abducted to be his cup-bearer.

ODYSSEUS: [*addressing the* SATYRS]
   Action, my lads, you noble scions of Dionysus!
Soon, up through his disgusting gullet will surge
   a vomit of flesh, and he'll fall asleep.
Our fiery stake is smoking away.
Everything's ready to scorch the Cyclops' eye.
SATYR: We'll be hard as stone, tough as steel . . .
   but quick into the cave with you before our father comes
                                                      to grief.
We'll join you in a trice.
ODYSSEUS: [*lifting his hands in prayer*]
   Come, Hephaestus, lord of Etna,
   once and for all sear the daylights
   from your horrible neighbor's vision.
Get rid of him forever.
And you, Sleep, offspring of pitchy Night,
   descend in full strength upon this god-detested brute.
After all the toils of war and triumph at Troy,
   do not let Odysseus and his sailors be destroyed
   by a creature who cares nothing for man or god;
   or we must think blind Chance governs a god
   and all other gods are governed by blind Chance.

[ODYSSEUS, *watched with wonder by the* CHORUS *of* SATYRS,
strides manfully into the cave]

THIRD CHORAL LYRIC

CHORUS: Tongs like a vise shall grip his gullet,
   This guzzler of guests, the flash of fire
   Shall flush out his sight. Already the firebrand
   Trunk of a tree, deep in the fire,
   Glows red-hot. Go to it, wine—do your stuff!
   Skewer this lunatic Cyclops' eyeball.
   As for me, I long to see
   Our ivy-caparisoned Bacchus again
   And abandon the wasteland of this Cyclops.
   Have we got to the brink of that yet?

[ODYSSEUS *hurries out of the cave, and the* SATYRS *throng around him chattering with excitement. He holds up a hand*]

FOURTH EPISODE

ODYSSEUS: For the gods' sake, you animals, shut up.
  Quiet now! Glue your lips.
  Don't blink, don't cough, don't breathe;
  or you'll wake up the monster and never singe his sight out.
SATYR: [*humbly, as they all fall silent*]
  We won't make a sound, sir, our jaws are clamped.
ODYSSEUS: Into the cave, then. Get hold of the firebrand with
                                                  both hands.
  It's beautifully hot.
SATYR: [*nervously*]
  Sir, settle please who's first in line along the sizzling stake.
  We all want a fair chance of scorching out his eye.
ANOTHER SATYR: We . . . we're too far away from the door
                                          to get the fire-point
  into his eye.
ANOTHER SATYR: And we've just gone a little lame.
ANOTHER SATYR: We have too—isn't it bad luck!—
  We've sprained our ankles standing around. I don't know
                                                          how.
ODYSSEUS: Sprained your ankles, standing still, huh?
SATYR: And now a lot of dust and ashes has got into our eyes—
                                          from somewhere.
ODYSSEUS: You spineless bastards! Cowards all!
SATYR (leader): [*hurt*]
  So . . . because I have some respect for my back and my spine,
  and a disinclination to having my teeth knocked out—I'm a
                                                  coward, am I?
But I do know a magic Orphic chant
  that will propel the firebrand of its own accord
  into the skull of this one-eyed earth-freak
  and char him through and through.
ODYSSEUS: [*with disgust*] I guessed from the first the kind you are
  and now I know it for a fact.
I'll just have to use my own trusted crew;

and if you're too feeble to give a hand,
at least give moral support.
Chant a spell for me and my men to lend us courage.
SATYR: We shall, we shall, we'll be terribly brave out here.
A hundred incantations are as good as a bonfire to burn up the
Cyclops.

[ODYSSEUS *rounds up some of his* CREW *and enters the cave.
The* SATYRS *of the* CHORUS *begin to chant with enthusiasm*]

CHORUS: Go, go, go for it, go!
Ram like a demon, singe his eyebrows off—
This savage eater of guests.
Consume him with fumes, cause him to frizzle,
This ovine herder of Etna.
So go to it: twist, wrench.
But be careful,
His pain will make him mad.

[*An agonized bellow issues from the cave*]

CYCLOPS: Aaaah! My eye is a smoldering cinder.
SATYRS: [*answering*] Whoopie! What music! Croon it, Cyclops,
croon it.

[CYCLOPS, *his face covered in blood, staggers to the threshold
of the cave and stands there roaring as he bars all egress from
the interior*]

CYCLOPS: You, you mobsters, you've done me in.
But you won't get out of these rocks alive to celebrate.
I'll stand here and block the cavern with both hands.

[*As* CYCLOPS *spread-eagles himself across the entrance of the
cave, the* SATYRS *mock him from within*]

A SATYR: What's the matter, Cyclops?
CYCLOPS: I'm wiped out.
ANOTHER: You don't look too good.
CYCLOPS: I'm in agony.
ANOTHER: Did you fall into the fire—smashed?
CYCLOPS: Nobody has destroyed me.

ANOTHER: So no one's hurt you?
CYCLOPS: Yes, Nobody blinded me.
ANOTHER: So you're not blind?
CYCLOPS: I am—damn you!
ANOTHER: But how could nobody blind you?
CYCLOPS: You're jeering at me. Where is Nobody?
SATYR (leader): Nobody's nowhere, Cyclops.
CYCLOPS: Idiot, I mean the stranger, the swine:
    he's finished me. Did it with wine.
SATYR: Ah, wine! One can't wrestle with wine.
CYCLOPS: For the gods' sake tell me, have they got away?
    Or are they still inside?
SATYR: They're standing very still over there,
    underneath a ledge of rock.
CYCLOPS: On which side?
SATYR: To your right.

[CYCLOPS *deserts his post at the entrance of the cave and
starts groping towards the rocks on his right while* ODYSSEUS
and his CREW *slip out of the cave*]

CYCLOPS: Where exactly?
SATYR: Up against that rock. Got it?
CYCLOPS: [*lunging at a rock*]
    Oooh! from bad to worse. I've split my skull.
SATYR: What! did they give you the slip?
CYCLOPS: You said they were here. Nothing!
SATYR: Not here—over there.
CYCLOPS: Where?
SATYR: Turn right round. Over to your left.
CYCLOPS: Curse you! You're laughing—
    making a joke of my misery.
SATYR: Not at all. Nobody's right in front of you.
CYCLOPS: Scoundrel! Where, where?

LYRIC DIALOGUE

ODYSSEUS: [*slipping past with several* SATYRS]
    Well out of reach. I take good care
    to keep Odysseus' person there.

CYCLOPS: Now we're switching names! What for?
ODYSSEUS: Odysseus is the name I got at birth . . .
    I'm punishing you for your unholy dinner.
    It would be outrageous for me, after firing Troy,
    not to be avenged on you for the murder of my crew.
CYCLOPS: Well I never! The oracle of old's proved true,
    which said that on your homeward way from Troy
    I'd be blinded in my eye by you . . .
Ah, but it also said
    that you'd be punished for what you did to me
    and spend an age being tossed upon the sea.
ODYSSEUS: Go on, whine away! What's done is done.
    And now it's down to the shore for me
    to launch my good ship on the open sea,
    bound for my homeland from Sicily.
CYCLOPS: That you shan't.
    I'll tear these rocks apart.
    and smash you with your crew and skiff.
    Blind though I am I'll grope my way between these chasms
    and climb this cliff.

[ODYSSEUS, SILENUS, *and the* CHORUS *of* SATYRS *begin their descent, loaded with cheeses, milk, bleating lambs, and whatever wine is left, leaving* CYCLOPS *bawling at the cliffs as he stumbles among the rocks*]

SATYRS (all): We're off to join the crew of this Odysseus
    and afterwards to serve our own Dionysus.

Glossary of Classical Names

ABAE (ab'ee): a town in Phocis, famed for its oracle of Apollo.

ABSYRTUS (ab sur'tus): brother of Medea, who tore his body to pieces and strewed them in front of her father's pursuing ship when fleeing from Colchis.

ACASTUS (a kas'tus): Argonaut, son of Pelias, brother of Alcestis, killed by Peleus.

ACHAEA (a kē 'a): an ancient province in the Peloponnesus.

ACHAEANS (a kē 'ans): people of the Peloponnesus; eventually, the Greeks.

ACHAEUS (a kē 'us): son of Xuthus and Creusa of Thessaly.

ACHATES (a kay'tees): companion of Aeneas in the flight from Troy.

ACHELOUS (a ke lō'us): son of Oceanus and Gaea. Worshiped as a river god throughout Greece.

ACHERON (ak'e ron): one of the five rivers in Hades: river of woe across which Charon ferried the dead.

ACHILLES (ak kil' ēz): son of Pelius and Thetis. Greatest of the Greek heroes at the siege of Troy. He slew Hector in single combat and dragged him three times round the walls of Troy. Finally killed by Paris, who wounded him in his only vulnerable part—his heel.

ACROPOLIS (a krop' o lis): citadel of Athens, or citadel of any Greek city.

ACTAEON (ak tē 'on): he was changed by Artemis into a stag for having spied on her bathing and was torn to pieces by his own hounds.

ADMETUS (ad mē 'tus): king of Pherae in Thessaly. He was promised by Apollo never to die if he could find someone to die for him. Only his wife, Alcestis, volunteered. He was an Argonaut.

ADONIS (a dō' nis): a youth famous for his beauty. Loved by Aphrodite. He was killed by a wild boar while hunting and from his blood sprang an anemone. Persephone restored him to life on condition that he spend half the year with her in Hades.

ADRASTEIA (ad ras tee' a): Nemesis, goddess of doom. Also a Cretan nymph who nursed the infant Zeus.

AEACUS (ee' a kus): father of Peleus and grandfather of Achilles and of Ajax. He became a judge in the underworld.

AEËTES (ee ee'tees): king of Colchis, father of Medea.

AEGEAN SEA (ee ge'an): an arm of the Mediterranean between Greece and Turkey, bounded on the south by Crete.

AEGEUS (ee'gee us): king of Athens and father of Theseus.

AEGICORES (eege'korez): one of the four sons of Ion.

AEGINA (ee jee'na): daughter of the river god Asopus and Metope.

AEGIS (ee'gis): the shield and breastplate of Pallas Athena. It depicted the head of Medusa twining with serpents. All who looked at it were turned to stone.

AEGISTHUS (ē jis'thus): king of Argos and lover of Clytemnestra. Slain by Electra and her brother Orestes.

AEGYPTUS (ee gip'tus): king of Egypt. Married his fifty sons to his brother's fifty daughters.

AENEAS (ē ñe 'as): Trojan prince, son of Anchises and Aphrodite. After the fall of Troy he was shipwrecked on the shores of Africa, where Dido, Queen of Carthage, fell in love with him, and when he left killed herself. Eventually he reached Rome and became its king. His wanderings are the subject of Vergil's *Aeneid*.

AEOLIA (ē o' li a): home of Aeolus, god of the winds. An island.

AEOLUS (ee'ō lus): god of the winds.

AESCULAPIUS (ees kool lay' pi us): god of medicine and healing. Represented by the caduceus (which see).

AGAMEMNON (ag a mem'non): king of Mycenae and Argos, brother of Menelaus, father of Orestes, Electra, and Iphigenia, husband of Clytemnestra. When he came back to Argos after ten years away at the siege of Troy, Clytemnestra and her lover Aegisthus slew him.

AGAVE (a gā'vē): daughter of Cadmus and Hermione. Mother of Pentheus and sister of Ino and Autonoë, with whom she tore her son to pieces in a Bacchic frenzy.

AGENOR (a jē ' or): king of Phoenicia; father of Cadmus and founder of Thebes.

AGLAIA (ag lay' ar): one of the Graces and sometimes called Pasiphaë but not the same Pasiphaë who fell in love with a bull.

AGLAURUS (a glo'ros): daughter of Cecrops. She was turned into a stone by Hermes.

AGORA (ag'or a): the market place.

AJAX (ā ' jaks): also AIAS, the most famous of the Greek heroes at Troy after Achilles, for the possession of whose armor he quarreled with Odysseus.

ALASTOR (a las'ter): armor bearer of Sarpedon, king of Lycia in Asia Minor. Killed by Odysseus.

ALCESTIS (al ses'tis): wife of Admetus, in whose stead she offered to die. Apollo had promised Admetus that he would never die if he could find someone to die for him.

ALCMENA (alk mee'na): mother of Heracles.

ALEXANDER (al ex zan'der): Paris of Troy.

ALPHEUS (al fē'us): river god and river running past Olympia in Arcadia. He fell in love with Arethusa, and when she fled from him to Sicily, he flowed under the sea to join her.

ALTHAEA (al thee'ar): mother of Meleager. The Fates ordained that his life would last as long as a log of wood thrown by them into the fire burned. But on his slaying his mother's two brothers, Althaea extinguished the fire and thus his life, then killed herself.

AMALTHEA (am al thē'a): the goat that nursed the infant Zeus in a Cretan cave. One of her horns was called "cornucopia" and was filled with whatever its owner desired.

AMAZONS (am'a zonz): tribe of female warriors who cut off their right breasts in order to use the bow more easily: *amazon* means without breast. They had no dealings with men except for breeding, and they reared only their female young.

AMBROSIA (am brō' zhi a): meaning immortal. The food of the gods. Nectar was their drink.

AMMON (am'on): Egyptian god identified with Zeus, whose temple in the Libyan desert was a famous oracle. Alexander the Great consulted it before his conquest of Asia.

AMPHION (am fi'on): son of Zeus and twin brother of Zethus. His music moved the stones of Thebes into place.

AMPHITRITE (am fi try' tay): goddess of the sea, wife of Poseidon and mother of Triton.

AMPHITRYON (am fit' ri on): husband of Alcmena and cuckolded by Zeus. The Roman playwright Plautus wrote a clever comedy called *Amphitryon*.

AMYCLAE (a my' klee): a town in the south of Sparta where Aphrodite was especially honored.

AMYMONE (a mi mowe'nay): one of the fifty daughters of Danaus and Europa. She murdered her husband Enceladus on their wedding night. Also, a fountain in Argos.

ANCHISES (an kī' sēz): so beautiful that Aphrodite seduced him on Mount Ida and became pregnant with Aeneas, who saved his life after the fall of Troy. He came with Aeneas to Italy and died at the age of eighty at Drepanum in Sicily.

ANDROMACHE (an drom' a kē): devoted wife of Hector and chief of the captive Trojan women. She was forced to become the concubine of Neoptolemus, son of Achilles.

ANDROMEDA (an drom' e da): she was chained to a rock to appease Poseidon, who intended her to be eaten by a monster. Perseus saw her, fell in love with her, rescued her, married her, and was always faithful.

ANTAEUS (an tee' us): son of Poseidon and Gaea; giant and

invincible wrestler as long as he touched the earth (his mother, Gaea). Heracles strangled him while holding him off the ground.

ANTILOCHUS (an til' o kus): son of Nestor and friend of Achilles, to whom he reported the death of Patroclus.

APHRODITE (af ro dī' tē or tay): the Roman Venus, daughter of Zeus, goddess of love and one of the twelve Olympians, born out of the foam of the sea (*aphros*=foam) off the island of Cyprus. Paris gave her the prize in the beauty contest between her and Hera and Pallas Athena. Her infidelity was notorious, and her coupling with Ares made her the laughingstock of the gods when she was exposed *in actu* by Hephaestus.

APOLLO (a pol'owe): also Helios, Hyperion, Phoebus; son of Zeus and Leto and one of the twelve Olympians; twin brother of Artemis. Sun god and patron of the arts, medicine, music, and poetry; also god of order. His oracle at Delphi was the most famous in Greece.

ARABIA FELIX (ar'ay bia fayliks): one of the three divisions of Arabia, renowned for its frankincense and aromatic plants.

ARACHNE (a rak' nay): she challenged Pallas Athena to a sewing match and when she lost committed suicide and was changed by Pallas into a spider.

ARCADIA (ar kay' di ar): pastoral region in central Peloponnesus, symbol of quiet happiness. Haunt of the god Pan and birthplace of Pan's father, Hermes.

ARCHELAUS (ar'ke lorz): king of Macedonia who sheltered Euripides in his last years.

ARES (ar'eez): the Roman Mars, god of war, one of the twelve Olympians. Son of Zeus and Hera; illicit lover of Aphrodite; disliked by Apollo. His children were Panic, Fear, Trembling, Strife, and Discord. His favorite animals were the dog and vulture, as scavengers of the battlefield.

ARES' HILL (a'reez): a small eminence near Athens, where the seat of justice called the Areopagus was sited.

ARETHUSA (ar e thuse' ar): wood nymph who accompanied

Artemis when hunting. She fled from the river god Alpheus and was saved from him by Artemis, who changed her into a stream in Sicily.

ARGADES (ar'gad eez): one of the four sons of Ion.

ARGIVES (ar' gīvs): the Greeks of Argos and Argolis in the Peloponnesus, but often used for all the inhabitants of Greece.

ARGOLIS (ar'go lis): a region of the eastern Peloponnesus, between Arcadia and the Aegean Sea. Argos was the chief town.

ARGONAUT (argo'nort): any of those who sailed in the *Argo* to get the Golden Fleece.

ARGOS (ar'gos): capital of Argolis in the Peloponnesus, whose king was Agamemnon.

ARISTAEUS (ar is tee' us): husband of Autonoë and father of Actaeon. He promoted bee-keeping and the culture of olives.

ARTEMIS (ar'te mis): Roman Diana, also called Cynthia, Delia, Hecate, Phoebe, Selene. Daughter of Zeus and Leto; twin sister of Apollo. The moon goddess and patroness of hunting, childbirth, chastity, and unmarried girls. Though reputedly a virgin, she fell in love with the beautiful youth Endymion, who was asleep naked on Mount Latmos, and visited him in his dreams. He prayed to Zeus to let him sleep forever. As Hecate, Artemis was the goddess of witchcraft.

ASCLEPIUS (as' klee pius) sometimes AESCULAPIUS (es kū lay' pi us): god of healing and medicine, son of Apollo.

ASOPUS (a so'pus): a river god, son of Poseidon. Also a river.

ASTYANAX (as ty' a naks): son of Hector and Andromache. Odysseus had him hurled from the walls of Troy.

ATE (ar'tay): also Eris, goddess of strife and discord. When not invited to the wedding of Peleus and Thetis, she rolled the Golden Apple before Hera, Aphrodite and Pallas Athena, saying: "for the fairest," which led to the Judgment of Paris and thus to the Trojan War.

ATHENA (ath'een ar): Pallas, the Roman Minerva, one of the twelve Olympians, born out of the head of Zeus, a virgin. Depicted wearing a helmet and carrying a shield (the Aegis).

ATLAS (at'las): a Titan. He held the heavens on his shoulders.

ATREUS (at' tree us): son of Pelops and Hippodamia, brother of Thyestes and father of Agamemnon and Menelaus—a doomed family. He served up to Thyestes his own sons to eat.

ATRIDES (a trī'dēz): the two descendants of Atreus: Agamemnon and Menelaus.

ATTICA (at'i ka): part of Greece that includes Athens and Eleusis.

AULIS (ow'lis): port in Boeotia from which the Greek armada set sail for Troy.

AURORA (o ro'ra): also called EOS, goddess of dawn.

AUTONOË (o ton'o, or ā): daughter of Cadmus, sister of Agave and Ino; mother of Actaeon.

AXIUS (ax'i us): a river in the valley of Pieria near Olympus.

BACCHAE (bak'ē, or ā): priestesses of Dionysus. They became possessed at his festivals.

BACCHANT, BACCHANTES (bak'us, bak'an tez): female followers and priestesses of Bacchus; also called MAE-NADS, (Meen'adz).

BACCHUS (bak'us): also Dionysus, Bromius. Son of Zeus and Semele. God of wine, mystery, incantation, and the raw potency of nature; reared by the nymphs on Mount Nysa; represented crowned with vine and ivy leaves.

BACTRIA (bak'tree a): an ancient country of southwestern Asia; now part of northern Afghanistan

BISTONIA (bis tō'ni a): a kingdom in Thrace, northeast Greece.

BOEBIA (bee'bi a): a lake in Thessaly, near mount Ossa.

BOREAS (bō're as): the northeast wind, the Roman Aquilo.

BRAURON (brow'ron): a town in Attica where Artemis had a temple. It was there that Iphigenia brought the effigy of Artemis from Taurus.

BROMIUS (brō'mi us): Bacchus.

BYBLUS (bib'lus): a coastal town in Syria where Adonis had a temple.

CADMUS (kad'mus): son of Agenor and Telephassa. The

founder of Thebes, where he overcame a dragon and sowed its teeth on the plain, at which a company of armed men sprang up ready for attack. He was father of Agave, Autonoë, and Ino. He married Harmonia, daughter of Aphrodite.

CADUCEUS (ka du' se us): the wand of Hermes, with which he conducted the souls of the dead across the river Styx and could raise the dead. It was a golden staff entwined with snakes, emblems of healing, and has become the symbol of the medical profession.

CALCHAS (kal'kas): seer attached to the Greek army going to Troy. He predicted that the Greek fleet could not sail without the sacrifice of Iphigenia, and that Troy could not be taken without the help of Achilles, nor without a ten-year siege.

CALLISTO (kal'is to): Arcadian nymph changed by Hera into a bear.

CAPANEUS (ka pa'nay us): one of the Seven against Thebes.

CAPHAREUS (ka far'e us): a mountain and promontory off the coast of Euboea.

CARYSTIAN ROCK (ka'rist i an): a sacred rock on the borders of Attica.

CASSANDRA (ka san' dra): daughter of Priam and Hecuba; the most beautiful of their girls. Apollo gave her the gift of prophecy, but when she refused his advances, ordained that she would never be believed. At the fall of Troy she was dragged from the altar of Athena by Ajax and deflowered. Agamemnon brought her as his concubine to Argos, where Clytemnestra slew them both.

CASTALIA (kas tā'lia): a nymph pursued by Apollo and turned into a spring on Mount Parnassus near Delphi. Those who drank its waters were inspired by the poetic spirit.

CASTOR AND POLYDEUCES (POLLUX) (kas'ter and polly'dū sëz): twin sons of Zeus by Leda. Castor was patron of navigation, Polydeuces of boxing and wrestling.

CECROPS (sē 'krops): son of Gaea and first king of Attica. He had a human torso but from the waist down was a serpent.

When Athena gave Athens the olive tree, he instructed his subjects to cultivate the olive and make her their patroness.

CENTAURS (sen'torz): a race half man, half horse, inhabiting the mountains of Thessaly. The greater part of them were killed by Heracles, the rest driven to Mount Pindus.

CEPHALUS (sef' a lus): faithful husband of Procris, daughter of Erechtheus, king of Athens. He was carried off for his beauty by the goddess Dawn (Eos).

CEPHISUS (se fis'us): the father of Narcissus; also the name of three famous rivers in Greece.

CERBERUS (ser'ber us): the three-headed dog that guarded the entrance to Hades

CHALCEDON (kal'sed on): an ancient city of Bithynia in Asia Minor.

CHALYBIA (kal'ib i a): a region of Asia Minor famous for its iron mines where the workers were naked.

CHARITES (kar' i teez): the three Graces, beautiful attendants of Aphrodite.

CHARYBDIS (ka rib'dis): a monster, the daughter of Poseidon and Gaea. Zeus threw her into the sea where she gulps water eternally and spews it out again. This is the dangerous whirlpool off the coast of Italy opposite the rocky cave where the monster Scylla lived.

CHARON (kā ' ron; kar'ron): minor god in charge of the passage to Hades. For a fee—a coin placed in the mouth of the dead—he would row the souls across the rivers Acheron and Styx to the shores of Hades. Without proper burial, Charon refused to take them and they were condemned to wander for a hundred years.

CHIRON (kī'ron): wisest of the Centaurs and teacher of Achilles.

CIRCE (sur'se): an enchantress celebrated for her knowledge of magic and venomous herbs. She was daughter of the sun god Hyperion.

CITHAERON (si thē'ron): a mountain near Thebes sacred to Zeus; scene of several tragedies.

CLYTEMNESTRA (klī tem nes' tra): daughter of Tyndareus,

king of Sparta, by Leda. Wife of Agamemnon and mother of Orestes, Electra, and Iphigenia. While Agamemnon was away in Troy she took Aegisthus as her lover; when he came back she and Aegisthus murdered him, but were themselves murdered by Orestes and Electra.

COLCHIS (kol'kis): a remote corner of the Black Sea (probably the Crimea); birthplace of Medea; repository of the Golden Fleece.

CORA, KORA (kor'ra): Persephone. "Cora" means maiden.

CORYBANTS, CORYBANTES (kor i'bants, ban'teez): priests of the orgiastic cult of Cybele.

CORYCIA (kor is'ia): a nymph associated with Mount Parnassus.

CRATHIS (kra'this): a river in the Peloponnesus flowing into the bay of Corinth.

CREON (kree'on): king of Corinth.

CREUSA (krū'za): daughter of the king of Corinth.

CURETES (kū rē'tēz): same as Corybantes.

CYBELE (sie'bel ē): the Roman Magna Mater, also Rhea: Titan earth goddess, daughter of Gaea and wife of Cronos.

CYCLADES (sik'la deez): about fifty-three islands in the Aegean Sea roughly circling round the island of Delos.

CYCLOPS (sī'klops) also CYCLOPES (sie'klop ees): one-eyed giants who put together the enormous stones of Mycenae. They were shepherds, and sometimes cannibals.

CYNTHIAN HILL (sin'thian): mount Cynthus where Artemis (Cynthia) was born.

CYPRIS (sī'pris): Aphrodite, born in the sea off Cyprus.

DAEMON (dē'mon): a spirit influencing persons and places; sometimes good, sometimes bad.

DANAANS (dan'a anz) also DANAI (dan'a ee): the Greeks.

DANAË (dan'a ee): Argive princess, raped by Zeus in a shower of gold while she was imprisoned, because an oracle had foretold that her son, Perseus, would cause his father's death. Years later, the father, Acrius, who had fled from Argos for safety, was killed by a discus—thrown by his son.

DANAUS (dan'ar us): twin brother of Aegyptus, whose fifty

sons married his fifty daughters. He became so renowned a king in Argos that later Greeks were often called Danaans.

DARDANUS (dar'da nus): ancestor of the Trojans. He built a city near the foot of Mount Ida in Phrygia which he called Dardania. "Dardanian" became the name for all Trojans.

DAWN: see EOS.

DEÏPHOBUS (de if'o bus): a son of Priam and Hecuba. After the death of Paris, he married Helen by force. He was one of the heroes of the Trojan War.

DELOS (dē' los): smallest island of the Cyclades in the Aegean, birthplace of Apollo and Artemis.

DELPHI (del'fī, del'fē): oracle and shrine of Apollo beneath Mount Parnassus in Phocis. Besides being richly endowed it possessed over three thousand statues. Later plundered by Nero.

DEMETER (de mē' ter): Roman Ceres, one of the twelve Olympians. Goddess of grain, harvest, fruit, flowers and the fertility of the earth. Mother of Persephone, whom she mourned when Persephone was carried down to the underworld by Pluto.

DIOMEDES (di o mee'deez): one of the mightiest champions of the Greeks in the Trojan War, who fed his horses human flesh. Heracles in his eighth labor killed Diomedes and fed him to his horses.

DIONYSUS (dī o nī 'sus): Bacchus.

DIOSCURI (dee os'qu ree): Castor and Pollux (Polydeuces).

DIRCE (dur'sē): wife of Lycus, king of Thebes. She was put to death for maltreating the mother of her two stepsons, who tied her to a bull by her hair and killed Lycus. The gods changed Dirce into a spring.

DITHYRAMBUS (dith i'ram bus): "the twice-born"—another name for Dionysus because he was prematurely born at seven months after Zeus made love to his mother in a stroke of lightning, and then born again out of Zeus's thigh, where he had been secreted to save him from the jealousy of Hera. The dithyramb was also a song and dance in honor of Bacchus.

DORUS (dor'us): a son of Xuthus husband of Creusa.

DRYADS (drī 'adz), also DRYADES (drie'a dees), also HAMADRYADS (hammer'drie adz): nymphs who lived in trees, the equivalent of our tree fairies. They died when their trees were cut down.

DRYAS (drie'as): a son of Lycurgus, driven mad for insulting Dionysus.

DRYOPE (drie'owe pee): a nymph of Arcadia, mother of Pan by Hermes. Also, a nymph ravished by Apollo and changed into a poplar tree. Also, a nymph who fell in love with Hylas and pulled him into the water where she and the other nymphs lived.

ECHINEAN ISLES (ek'in e an): five small islands near Acarnarnia, at the mouth of the river Achelous, which rises in Mount Pindus and falls into the Ionian Sea.

ECHION (e ki' on): father of Pentheus.

EIRENE (ie'ree nee): goddess of peace.

ELECTRA (e lek'tra): daughter of Agamemnon and Clytemnestra, sister of Orestes, whose friend Pylades married her. She murdered her mother.

ELECTRYON (el ek'try on): son of Perseus and Andromeda. Father of Alcmena and therefore grandfather of Heracles. He was accidentally killed by his stepfather Amphitryon.

ELEUSIS (e lū'sis): a town fourteen miles west of Athens, where the Eleusian Mysteries were celebrated.

ELIS (ee'lis): a city and country of the Peloponnesus famous for its horses. Olympia, the site of the Olympic Games, was in Elis.

ENCELADUS (en sel'a dus): a giant buried by Zeus under Mount Etna. When he moves he causes an earthquake.

ENNOSIS ('en noss is): minor deity, spirit of earthquakes.

EOS (ee'os): the Roman Aurora, goddess of dawn. She fell in love with Tithonus, a beautiful youth, and granted him immortality, but he forgot to ask for everlasting vitality and he became a decrepit old man, but still immortal.

EPEIANS (ep'ee ans): a people of the Peloponnesus.

EREBUS (e rin' ēz): a region in the underworld through which souls must pass to reach Hades.

ERECHTHEUS (e rek' the us): sixth king of Athens and father of Cecrops; he introduced the worship of Athena and other cults.

ERIDANUS (e rid' a nus): a river, the modern Po, flowing into the Adriatic.

ERINYES (er in' yez): the Roman Furies: three avenging spirits whose mission was to pursue miscreants; depicted as winged females with serpents twining in their hair and blood dripping from their eyes.

EUBOEA (ū bee'a): the largest island after Crete in the Aegean, running alongside Boeotia.

EUMELUS (yu mee'lus): son of Admetus and Alcestis.

EUMENIDES (ū men' i dēz): a kindlier name for the Furies.

EUPHORION (ū'for ion): a playwright contemporary with Euripides.

EUPHROSYNE (yu fros' i nay): one of the Graces.

EURIPUS (ūr'ip us): a narrow strait separating the island of Euboea from the coast of Boeotia.

EUROPA (ū rō ' pa): sister of Cadmus. Zeus tricked her onto his back by changing himself into a white bull, then swam to Crete, where he ravished her.

EUROTAS (yu'rowe tas): river in Sparta

EURYSTHEUS (yu ris' thee us): king of Argos and Mycenae, cousin of Heracles and his rival. He tried to destroy Heracles by imposing on him a series of impossible tasks known as the Twelve Labors of Heracles. He was killed by Hylus, a son of Heracles.

EURYTUS (ū'ri tus): a captain in the Greek armada setting out for Troy.

EUXINE (ūk'sine): the Black Sea. The word means friendly.

FATES: there were three Fates, daughters of Erebus and Nyx: Atropos, who carried the shears that cut the thread of life; Clotho, who carried the spindle that spun the thread of life; and Lachesis, who carried the scroll that determined the length of the thread of life.

GAEA (jē' a, gaia): Mother Earth, the most ancient divinity; mother of Uranus (the Heavens), with whom she produced the twelve Titans: six males and six females. Also parents of the Cyclops.

GANYMEDE (gan' i mēd): a Trojan boy of such beauty that Zeus carried him off to Olympus on the back of an eagle. He became cupbearer of the gods.

GERAESTUS (ger'ees tus): a port of Euboea.

GERYON (ger'ie on, jer'ie on): a monster with three bodies and three heads that lived in Gades (Cadiz) in Spain. He was a shepherd with a two-headed sheepdog called Orthos.

GOLDEN FLEECE: pelt of the ram Chrysomallus. It hung on a tree on Colchis and was guarded by a dragon. Jason sailed there in the *Argo* and recovered the Fleece with the help of Medea.

GORGONS (gor'gonz): there were three, only one of whom, Medusa, was mortal. They had snakes for hair, claws for hands, and bulging eyes that turned men to stone.

GRACES: see CHARITES.

HADES (hā ' dēz): Pluto, one of the twelve Olympians. Son of Cronos and Rhea, husband of Persephone. The underworld was called after him.

HALCYONE (hal ci' owe nay, or ee): daughter of Aeolus, wife of Ceyx (see'iks). Husband and wife were so devoted to each other that when Ceyx was drowned and his body washed ashore, her grief was so great that she had to be changed into a kingfisher, along with him.

HALIRROTHIUS (hal i'roth i us): a son of Poseidon, who raped Alcippe, daughter of Ares, and was brought to trial at the Areopagus.

HAMADRYADS (hammer'dry adz): see DRYADS.

HARMONIA (har mō ' ni a): daughter of Ares and Aphrodite, wife of Cadmus. They produced Agave, Autonoë, Ino.

HARPIES (har'piz): filthy creatures with the bodies of vultures and the faces of women. They left a stench and snatched food with their clawed feet. They were used by the gods to persecute criminals.

HECATE (hek'a tee): the dark side of Artemis as moon goddess: patroness of magic and spells. Propitiated by the sacrifice of dogs, lambs, and honey.

HECTOR (hek'tor): son of Priam and Hecuba; husband of Andromache and father of Astyanax. The most valiant of the Trojan heroes but finally killed by Achilles, who was furious that he had slain his friend Patroclus.

HECUBA (hek'u ba): wife of Priam and queen of Troy. Mother of fifty sons and twelve daughters, most of whom came to a bad end. After the fall of Troy she was made a slave of Odysseus, and it is said by some that she cast herself into the sea in the voyage to Greece. Vergil in the *Aeneid* says that she changed into a bitch.

HELEN OF TROY (hel'en): most beautiful woman in Greece, daughter of Zeus and Leda, half sister of Clytemnestra. Her abduction by the Trojan prince Paris was the cause of the Trojan War. After which she was brought back to Sparta by her husband, Menelaus, and seems to have wheedled her way back into his affections.

HELIOS (hee'li os): Hyperion, and sometimes Apollo, son of Hyperion. The sun god.

HELLAS (hel'las): the ancient name for Thessaly which came to mean all Greece.

HEPHAESTUS (he fes' tus): the Roman Vulcan, son of Zeus and Hera. He was the smithy of the gods and his most famous forge was under Mount Aetna. When a baby Zeus and Hera kicked him out of Olympus; he broke a leg and became lame. Though unprepossessing he became the father of Eros by Aphrodite.

HERA (hee'ra): Roman Juno, daughter of Cronos and Rhea, wife and sister of Zeus, the Queen of Heaven, patroness of women and childbirth. The most jealous of wives. She spied on Zeus's love affairs, persecuted his mistresses, was vindictive to his children.

HERACLES (her' a klēz): Roman Hercules, son of Zeus and Alcmena; personification of physical strength. At eighteen he killed the lion of Mount Cithaeron. Famous for his

Twelve Labors, which were in punishment for his having killed his own children and those of his brother, though rendered mad by Hera. He died from the poison of one of his own arrows, but was carried to Olympus and endowed with immortality.

HERMES (hur'mēs): Roman Mercury. Son of Zeus and Maia. Patron of the arts and all inventions. As messenger of the gods he sped on winged sandals and wore a winged cap. Patron of travelers, traders, merchants, and robbers. He guided the shades of the dead to the underworld. Was the father of Pan.

HESIONE (hee'sī o nee or nay): daughter of Laomedon, king of Troy. She was rescued from a sea monster by Heracles who gave her to his assistant, Telamon. Telamon took her to Sparta where Priam sent his son Paris to reclaim her, but Paris fell in love with Helen of Sparta and carried her off to Troy, thus causing the Trojan War.

HESPERIDES (hes per'i deez): daughters of Atlas and Hesperis, the daughter of Hesperus. In the Garden of the Hesperides grew a tree with golden apples.

HESPERUS (hes'per us): the Roman Vesper, the brother of Atlas. In English poetry Hesperus is the evening star.

HESTIA (hes'ti a): the Roman Vesta, the daughter of Cronus and Rhea. She was goddess of the hearth and symbol of the home. A virgin, she was the oldest and most sacred of the twelve Olympians.

HIPPODAMIA (hip ŏ day mi a): wife of Pelops and mother of Atreus and Thyestes.

HIPPOLYTUS (hi pol'i tus): son of Theseus and stepson of Phaedra, who fell in love with him. When he refused her advances she killed herself, leaving an incriminating letter which Theseus believed.

HOPLITES (hop'lītes): heavily armed foot soldiers.

HYADES (hī'a deez): the five daughters of Atlas. They wept inconsolably for their brother Hyas who was killed by a wild boar. As a reward for their nursing the infant Bacchus, Zeus placed them among the stars.

HYPERION (hī pēr' i on): see Helios.

IACCHUS (ee' a kus): Bacchus.

ICARUS (ik'a rus): when fleeing from Minos, king of Crete, Daedalus made wings for himself and his son Icarus. The wings were fixed with wax, but Icarus flew too near the sun and the wax melted. He fell headlong into the Icarian Sea.

IDA (ī ' da): a mountain in Asia Minor; site of the Judgment of Paris, abduction of Ganymede, worship of Cybele.

IDAN HILLS (ī'dan): hills in the range of Mount Ida in Phrygia, the source of four famous rivers.

ILIUM (il'i um): citadel of Troy.

INACHUS (in'a kus): river in Argos.

INO (ee'no): daughter of Cadmus and Harmonia; sister of Agave, Autonoë, and Semele. She helped to tear Pentheus to pieces in a Bacchic trance.

IO (ī'o): loved by Zeus and changed by him into a heifer to save her from Hera, who set a gadfly to sting her all over Europe and Asia.

IOLAUS (i ō lay'us): a son of Iphicles, king of Thessaly. He was an accomplice of Heracles.

IOLCOS or US (i ol'kos): the port in Thessaly from which the Argonauts sailed in quest of the Golden Fleece.

ION (i'on, i'own): clandestine son of Apollo and Creusa; abandoned by his mother out of shame; brought up in the temple of Delphi by Apollo; finally discovered and reunited with his mother. Ancestor of the Ionians (Asia Minor).

IONIA (ī ō'ni a): a country in Asia Minor named after Ion.

IPHIGENIA (if i jen' ī a): daughter of Agamemnon and Clytemnestra. After being saved from being sacrificed by her father to get good winds for the Greek armada, she was wafted by Artemis to Taurus, in the wilds of Macedonia, and there became high priestess constrained to carry out human sacrifice. One of the victims was her brother Orestes, with whom she was able to escape back to Argos.

IRENE (ie ree'nee): Eirene, goddess of pearl.

ISMENUS (is'mee nus): river in Thebes.

JASON (jā' sun): leader of the Argonauts in quest of the

Golden Fleece; helped by Medea; married Medea and returned with her to Corinth; had two sons by her, but after ten years of marriage wanted to make a union with the daughter of the king. Medea's outrage is the subject of Euripides' play.

LACONIA (la kō'ni a): a country in the Peloponnesus in southern Greece that comprised Sparta. The Spartans were a people of action and few words; from them we get the word "laconic."

LAERTES (lay ur'teez): father of Odysseus.

LAOMEDON (lay om'e don): king of Troy and father of Priam.

LATONA (la tō'na) also Leto: mother of Apollo and Artemis.

LARISSA (la riss' a): town in Thessaly where Perseus killed his grandfather by mistake.

LEDA (lē'da): wife of Tyndareus, king of Sparta. Zeus, in the form of a swan, seduced her, and she produced two eggs, one of which hatched into Clytemnestra and Helen, and the other into Castor and Pollux.

LEITUS (lay'tus): a commander of the Boeotians at the siege of Troy.

LEMNOS (lem'nos): an island in the Aegean where Hephaestus landed when kicked out of Olympus. Most of its inhabitants were blacksmiths.

LETHE (lē' thē): river of oblivion in Hades.

LETO (lē 'to): mother of Apollo and Artemis.

LEUCOTHEA (lu koth'ee a): a sea goddess who presided over brooks and fountains.

LIGURIA (lig'ū ri a): a region on the west coast of Italy of which the capital was and is Genoa.

LIMNA (lim'na): a stretch of sandy shore near Athens.

LOCRIS (lok'ris): a region in the center of Greece north of the Bay of Corinth.

LOXIAS (lok'si as): Apollo.

LYCAON (lie kay'on): a king of Arcadia noted for his cruelties. To test the divinity of Zeus he cut up his own son and served him to Zeus, who punished him by turning him into a wolf.

LYCIA (lish'i a): a country in Asia Minor whose inhabitants were renowned for their use of the bow.

LYDIA (lid' i a): Phrygia in Asia Minor, whose two most memorable kings were Croesus and Midas.

MAENADS (mē 'nadz): Bacchae, Bacchantes: orgiastic female followers of Bacchus.

MAIA (mī'ya): the mother of Hermes by Zeus. She was the oldest and loveliest of the Pleiades, daughters of Atlas and Pleione.

MALEA (ma'lay a): there were two Maleas: one a promontory of Lesbos, and one in the Peloponnesus south of Laconia.

MARON (mar'on): a high priest of Apollo.

MARSYAS (mar'si as): a satyr who challenged Apollo to a contest on the flute, the loser to be flayed alive. Marsyas lost and was.

MECISTEUS (me'kis tay us): a companion of Ajax.

MEDEA (mē dē'a): barbarian princess and enchantress, daughter of Aetes (ee'ee teez), king of Colchis (on the Black Sea). She helped Jason to acquire the Golden Fleece, fell in love, married him, came with him to Corinth, and lived happily with him for ten years until he announced one day that he was going to marry the king's daughter.

MEDIA (may'di a): a country neighboring Persia whose natives were called Medes.

MEDUSA (me dū' sa, me dū za, mē dū sa): the only one of the three Gorgons that was mortal. Their eyes had the power of killing or turning to stone. When Perseus killed Medusa, he cut off her head and fixed it to the shield of Athena, where it retained its power of petrifying. From the drops of blood sprang the flying horse Pegasus.

MEGES (megg'ez): one of Helen's suitors. He went with forty ships to the Trojan War.

MENELAUS (men e lā' us): brother of Agamemnon, husband of Helen, king of Sparta. After the Trojan War he took Helen back to Sparta.

MOIRA (moy'ra): goddess of Fate, sometimes identified with Anangke, Necessity.

MOIRAI (moy'rie): the Fates: three sisters, grim crones who presided over the birth and life of mankind. Clotho, the youngest, handled the spindle that spun the thread of life, Lachesis the reel that let out the thread, and Atropos the scissors that snipped it.

MERIONES (may ree' ō nez): the charioteer of Idomeneus, king of Crete. He fought with valor at Troy and killed Deïphobus, son of Priam.

MIMAS (mee'mas): a giant whom Zeus destroyed with lightning.

MINOTAUR (min' ō tor): a monster born of Pasiphae, wife of Minos king of Crete. It had the body of a man and head of a bull. It was housed in the labyrinth built by Daedalus, where it was annually fed seven boys and seven girls.

MOLOSSIAN RANGE (mol'oss i an): mountains in Epirus near Dodona in northwest Greece. The region was famous for its dogs.

MUNYCHIA (mū'nee chia): a port of Attica between the Piraeus and promontory of Sunium. Its temple to Artemis was a sanctuary for criminals.

MUSES: the nine daughters of Zeus and Mnemosyne (Memory); patrons of poetry, music, and all the arts.

MYCENAE (mī sē 'nē): ancient capital of Argolis in the Peloponnesus, whose massive walls were built by the Cyclopes. The scene of the tragedies of the house of Atreus.

MYCONUS (mī'kō us): one of the Cyclades islands, for long uninhabited because of its frequent earthquakes.

MYRMIDONS (mur'mi donz): a warrior people of Thessaly who followed their king Achilles in the war against Troy.

NAUPLIA (now'plee a): important naval station of the Argives.

NEMESIS (nem'e sis): daughter of Erebus and Night; goddess of vengeance and destruction.

NEOPTOLEMUS (nay op tol'e mus): a son of Achilles and as brutal as his father. He killed Priam and hurled the infant

Astyanax from the walls of Troy. He forced Andromache to be his concubine.

NEREIDS (neer'iedz): the fifty daughters of Nereus and Doris, who rode the waves.

NEREUS (nee ree'us): amiable sea god who lived in the Aegean surrounded by his fifty daughters, the Nereids, one of whom was Thetis, mother of Achilles.

NIOBE (nī'ō bē): daughter of Tantalus and sister of Pelops. She taunted Leto with having only two children, whereas she had ten sons and ten daughters. She was punished by being turned to stone.

NYMPHS: lesser divinities in the form of lovely maidens who were eternally young and invested trees, lakes, rivers, mountains, seas. The word means bride, and many of them became wedded to gods.

NYSA: a mountain in Thrace (northern Greece) where nymphs cared for the infant Bacchus.

OCEANUS (owe see' a nus): the great body of water that encircled the world.

ODYSSEUS (ō dis' us, o dis' us): Roman Ulysses, married to Penelope, father of Telemachus. King of the small island of Ithaca, west of the Greek mainland, to return to which it took him years of wandering after the fall of Troy—from which we get the word "odyssey." He was the cleverest and most resourceful of all the Greek heroes.

OECHALIA (ee'ka li a): a country and town of the Peloponnesus.

OENOMAUS (ee no may'us): son of Ares and king of Pisa (a city in Greece). He was killed in a chariot race with Pelops, who had bribed his charioteer, Myrtilus.

OENONE (ee nō'nee): a nymph of Mount Ida, married to Paris who deserted her for Helen.

OLYMPIA (o lim'pi a): a constellation of temples, workshops, gymnasiums, and stadia in northwestern Peloponnesus where the Olympic Games originated in 776 B.C. One of the wonders of the world was the giant statue of Zeus fashioned in gold and ivory by Phidias, the most celebrated sculptor of the ancient world. The features of Zeus are thought by many to have been the harbinger of the face of Christ as seen in early mosaics. The statue came into the possession of a Christian in the fifth century but was destroyed by fire.

OLYMPUS (o lim'pus): the highest mountain in Greece, located in Macedonia. The home of the gods and goddesses.

ORESTES (o res'teez): son of Agamemnon and Clytemnestra, brother of Electra. After murdering his mother he was pursued by the Furies (i.e., he went mad) but was cured after visiting Apollo's shrine at Delphi and being acquitted by a court in Athens. He then succeeded to the throne of Argos.

ORION (ō ri'on): a hunter of gigantic stature. He was either the son of Poseidon or, according to some accounts, sprang from the urine of Zeus, Poseidon, and Hermes. He lusted after the Pleiades, who ran and whom he pursued. To save them, Zeus turned them into stars. Three of them had been Zeus's mistresses. Artemis killed him when Eos (Dawn) fell in love with him, and she placed him in the heavens.

ORPHEUS (or' fūs, or' fē us): son of Apollo and Calliope; master of the lyre. All nature was spellbound when Orpheus played: mountains moved, rivers stayed their course, trees listened, animals followed. When his wife, Eurydice, was bitten by a snake and died, he went down to the underworld and so charmed Pluto with his playing that he was allowed to lead her back to the light provided he did not look back. He could not resist looking back to see if she was following him, so lost her.

OSSA (oss'a): a high mountain in Thessaly where the centaurs once lived.

PAEAN (pē 'an): Apollo and Aesculapius as gods of healing. Also, hymn of triumph addressed to Apollo.

PALAMEDES (pal a mee'deez): after fetching Odysseus to serve in the Trojan War, an enmity sprang up between them. At Troy Odysseus falsely accused Palamedes and he was put to death.

PALLAS (pal'as): Athena, virgin goddess of Athens.

PAN: son of Hermes and Dryope; a woodland god who lived in

Arcadia among shepherds and flocks. He had two small horns, pointed ears, and a flat nose, and was a goat from the waist down. A mischievous creature and constantly pursuing nymphs. He invented the panpipe. In remote and desolate places or just before a battle, he could instill a sudden fear, which we call panic.

PANDION (pan di' on): king of Athens and father of Philomela and Procne. He reigned forty years and died of grief when his daughters were turned into swallows.

PARIS: also called Alexander, son of Priam and Hecuba. Though royal he was brought up as a shepherd ·on Mount Ida. He judged Aphrodite the fairest of the three goddesses—Aphrodite, Hera, Athena—at the beauty trial when Eris (Discord) rolled an apple among them with the words "for the fairest." Aphrodite rewarded him by giving him Helen, the cause of the war with Troy.

PARNASSUS (par nass' us): mountain overlooking Delphi, sacred to the Muses, Apollo, and Dionysus.

PASIPHAË (pa sif' ay ee): the wife of Minos, king of Crete. She fell in love with a bull and was able to gratify her passion with help of the arch technician, Daedalus. She produced Ariadne, Androgeus, Phaedra, and the Minotaur.

PEGASUS (peg' a sus): the winged horse that sprang from the blood of Medusa when Perseus cut off her head. He became a symbol of poetic inspiration

PEITHO (pi'tho): daughter of Hermes and Aphrodite; goddess of persuasion.

PELEUS (pe' lūs, pē' lē us): an Argonaut and father, by Thetis, of Achilles. It was at his wedding to Thetis that Eris (Discord) rolled the golden apple, saying, "For the fairest." Peleus lived to a great age.

PELIAS (pē' li as): father of Alcestis and uncle of Jason. He usurped the throne of Neleus, king of Iolcos in Thessaly, but promised to give it to Jason if he fetched the Golden Fleece, hoping thus to destroy him. When he grew infirm his daughters asked Medea to make him well, but she determined to punish him for the way he had treated Jason. She cut an old ram to pieces, threw them into a boiling cauldron, and withdrew a frisky young lamb. She told the daughters that she could do the same for their father, so they cut him into pieces and threw them into a cauldron. Whereat Medea turned her back and walked away.

PELION (pee' li on): a mountain in Thessaly, where Chiron and the other centaurs lived.

PELOPS (pē 'lopz): son of Tantalus, husband of Hippodamia, father of Atreus and Thyestes, grandfather of Agamemnon and Menelaus.

PENEUS (pee nee' us): a river god and father of Daphne, whom he changed into a laurel tree when she was pursued by Apollo.

PENTHEUS (pen'thay ūs or pen'thūs): the subject of Euripides' masterpiece *The Bacchae*. Pentheus, the young king of Thebes, refused to acknowledge the divinity of Dionysus and was torn to pieces on Mount Cithaeron by his mother and two aunts who, in their Bacchic frenzy, took him for a young lion.

PERGAMUM (pur'gam um): the citadel of Troy; also Troy itself.

PERSEPHONE (per sef' ō nē): Roman Proserpina, daughter of Zeus and Demeter, wife of Pluto, queen of Hades. Pluto abducted her while she was picking flowers in the meadows of Enna, Sicily. Demeter threatened to boycott all nature if she was not found. Pluto restored her to earth on condition that she spend six months of every year in Hades. During which time Demeter went into retreat: the winter.

PERSEUS (perz' ūs, per' sé us): son of Zeus and Danae, ruler of Argos and Tiryns. He rescued Andromeda from a monster, married her, and was faithful, a rare occurrence in Greek mythology. He cut off the head of Medusa.

PHAEDRA (fē 'dra, fā 'dra): daughter of Minos and Pasiphaë; sister of Ariadne; wife of Theseus. She fell in love with Hippolytus, her stepson. When he rejected her advances she killed herself, clutching a letter saying that Hippolytus had assaulted her. For the rest see Euripides' play *Hippolytus*.

PHAËTHON (fā' e thon): son of Apollo, who foolishly insisted on driving his father's chariot for one day and was unable to keep the horses on course, thus threatening the world with conflagration.

PHAROS: a small island in the bay of Alexandria later famous for its lighthouse.

PHARSALUS (far'say lus): a town in Thessaly.

PHERAE (fer'ay): a town in Thessaly and home of Alcestis and Admetus.

PHERES (fer'ēz): father of Admetus.

PHINEUS (fi'nus, fin' ee us): a king of Thrace who blinded his children and was himself blinded by the gods. The Harpies polluted his food.

PHLEGRA (fleg'ra): the place in Macedonia where the giants attacked the gods and were defeated by Heracles.

PHOCIS (fo'sis): a region in central Greece of which Parnassus was its celebrated mountain overlooking the oracle at Delphi.

PHOEBE (fee'bee): the name for Artemis as moon goddess.

PHRYGIA (frij'i a): a region of Asia Minor whose most famous town was Troy.

PHTHIA (thē 'a): a town in Thessaly where Achilles was born.

PHYLEUS (fi'lee us): one of the Greek captains at Troy.

PIERIA (pie er'ree a): a spring sacred to the Muses on the slopes of Mount Olympus. A synonym for poetry.

PIRENE (pie ree'nee): a spring at Corinth.

PISA (pee'za): a town of Elis on the river Alpheus in the west of the Peloponnesus.

PITANA or PITANE (pit'a na, or nay): a town of Aeolia in Asia Minor whose inhabitants made bricks that floated on the water.

PITTHEUS (pit'thūs): son of Pelops and Hippodamia; king of Troezen in Argolis; a wise and learned teacher.

PHRYGIA (frig' i a): a region of Asia Minor noted for its civilization. Its last king was Croesus ("as rich as Croesus"), who was defeated by the Persians in 548 B.C. He was a patron of Aesop.

PLEIADES (plī' a dēz): the seven daughters of Atlas. After their death they were placed in the heavens as a constellation. Only six are visible.

PLUTO: see Hades.

PHOCIS (fē 'sis): a region in Greece containing Mount Parnassus and Delphi. Home of King Strophius and Pylades.

POLYPHEMUS (pol i fē 'mus): one-eyed giant, son of Poseidon and chief of the Cyclopes. He lived in a cave near Mount Etna in Sicily. See Euripides' play *The Cyclops*.

POLYXENA (pol ik' sen a): a daughter of Priam and Hecuba. She killed herself, or was sacrificed, at the tomb of Achilles.

POSEIDON (pos ī'don): Roman Neptune, son of Cronos and Thea. One of the twelve Olympians, brother of Zeus and god of the sea. He created the horse, and supported the Trojans in the Trojan War.

PRIAM (prī'am): son of Laomedon and husband of Hecuba, by whom he had fifty sons and twelve daughters, besides at least another forty-two by concubines. He was the last king of Troy and made it the richest and most beautiful city of the ancient world.

PROTESILAUS (prō tes i lā us): a king of Thessaly. He was the first Greek to set foot on Trojan soil and the first to be killed. When his wife, Laodamia, heard of his death she committed suicide.

PROTEUS (prō'tee us): a sea deity to whom Poseidon gave the gift of prophecy and the power to assume different shapes.

PYLADES (pī'lad ēz): son of Strophius, king of Phocis; cousin and bosom friend of Orestes, whom he assisted in the murders of Clytemnestra and Aegisthus. He married Electra, Orestes' sister.

PYTHIA (pith' i a): the priestess of Apollo at Delphi. She sat over a tripod in the center of "the earth's navel" and in a trance delivered the answers of Apollo. The oracle could be consulted only one month in the year, and rich presents were required for Apollo.

PYTHO (pī'thō): the ancient name for Delphi because of the python Apollo killed there.

PYTHON (pie'thon): the large snake killed by Apollo at Delphi.

RHADAMANTHUS (rad a man'thus): a son of Zeus and one of the three judges in Hades.

RHEA (rē 'a): daughter of Uranus and Gaea and mother of the gods.

RHION (ree'on): a promontory at the mouth of the gulf of Corinth.

SALAMIS (sal a mis): an island three miles off the coast of Attica; the scene of a great naval victory of the Athenians over the Persians on October 20th, 480 B.C.

SARONIC SEA (sar'on ik): the Aegean Sea lying south of Attica and north of the Peloponnesus.

SCAMANDER (ska man'der): river in Troy stemming from Mount Ida. Its waters gave a golden tint to human hair. Aphrodite, Athena, and Hera bathed in it before the Judgment of Paris.

SCIRON (sī'ron): a notorious robber in Attica, who threw his victims from the highest rocks into the sea where a giant turtle ate them. Theseus overcame him and he himself became food for the turtle.

SCYROS (sī'ros): a famous island in the Aegean Sea, where Achilles was hidden by his mother to avoid fighting in the Trojan War.

SCYTHIA (si'th ia): an enormous tract of land comprising Russia in Asia, Siberia, Ukraine, Poland, Lithuania, and northern Germany. The Sythians were divided into several nations. They despised money, inured themselves to hunger and fatigue, lived on milk and clothed themselves in the skins of cattle.

SEMELE (sem'e lē): daughter of Cadmus and Harmonia; mother by Zeus of Bacchus. Hera destroyed her out of jealousy, but Zeus restored her and made her divine.

SIDON (sī'don): an ancient city of Phoenicia on the shores of the Mediterranean about fifty miles from Damascus and twenty-four from Tyre. Its people were well known for their skill in arithmetic and astronomy and for having invented glass and linen.

SILENUS (sy'lee nus, si'lay nus): the oldest and wisest of the satyrs. Tutor of Bacchus. An opposite conception of him is of a drunken, rollicking old man crowned with flowers and riding a donkey. He is depicted sometimes with the ears and legs of a goat, and sometimes with the ears and legs of a horse.

SIMOÏS (sim'ō is): river in Troy rising in Mount Ida. It ran through the battleground of Troy.

SINIS (sī'nis): a notorious bandit on the Isthmus of Corinth. He induced travelers to help him bend down a pine tree and then unexpectedly released it so that they were catapulted into the sea. He tried the trick on Theseus, but Theseus released his grasp first and it was Sinis who was catapulted.

SIPYLUS (sip'i lus): one of the seven sons of Niobe, all killed by arrows from Apollo. Sipylus became the name of a mountain in Lydia where there stood a statue of Niobe with tears flowing down her marble cheeks.

SISYPHUS (siz'ifus): king and founder of Corinth, "the craftiest of men" (Homer), with a litany of crimes, for which he was punished in Hades by having to roll a boulder to the top of a hill, and when it rolled down to roll it up again.

SPARTA: a city and country in the peninsula of southern Greece (Peloponnese), also called Laconia, from which we get the word "laconic," because the Spartans (Lacedaemonians) were a people of few words and much action. Sparta was a military state and the age-old enemy of Athens.

STHENELUS (sthen'e lus): son of Capaneus. He went to the Trojan War and was one of those who entered the wooden horse. He was companion and charioteer of Diomedes.

STROPHIUS (stroe' fee us): king of Phocis, married to a sister of Agamemnon and father of Pylades.

STYX (stiks): one of the five rivers of the underworld. It flowed around Hades nine times. Across it Charon ferried the souls of the dead. To swear by the Styx was the most solemn of oaths.

STHENELOS (sthen' los): king of Mycenae and comrade of Heracles.

SUNIUM (sū'ni um): a cape off southeastern Attica, on which stood a gleaming white marble temple dedicated to Poseidon.

SYMPLEGADES (sim pleg'a dees): the Clashing Rocks through which ships had to pass to enter the Black Sea. The Argonauts managed it through the help of Phineus.

TAENARUM (tee'nar um): a promontory off Laconia, the most southerly point in Europe, where Poseidon had a temple. The place had a foul-smelling cave which was said to be the back door to Hades.

TALAUS (tal'a us): one of the Argonauts.

TALTHYBIUS (tal thib' i us): chief herald of Agamemnon, with always something horrendous to announce.

TANAIS (tan'a is): a river separating Argos from Sparta; sometimes confused with a river in Scythia (the Don) separating Europe from Asia.

TANTALUS (tan' tal us): father of Pelops and Niobe, thus ancestor of the doomed house of Atreus. Among his several crimes, he killed his son Pelops and dished him up to the gods for dinner. He was punished by having to stand in water up to his chin. Food and drink would come just within reach, then recede. From which we get the word "tantalize."

TAPHIAN (tay'fee an): of the islands of Taphiae in the Ionian Sea.

TARTARUS (tar'tar us): the lowest region of Hell, where the most wicked are sent.

TAUROPOLIS (tor'o pol is): another name for Taurus (or Tauris) the chief city of Tauria (now the Crimea).

TAURUS (tor'us): mountain range and region of the Caucausus in Asia Minor.

TELAMON (tel'a mon): father of Ajax and Teucer.

THEBES (thēbz): the capital of Boeotia (bee o'sha), founded by Cadmus.

THEMIS (thee'mis or them'is): daughter of Uranus and Gaea; mother of the four Seasons and the three Fates. She had the power of prophecy and was the first goddess to whom temples were built on earth. As a mother-goddess, her temple at Delphi preceded that of Apollo. She was the patroness of justice.

THESEUS (thēs' ē us): an early king of Athens and one of its greatest heroes. Father of Hippolytus.

THESSALY (thes'a li): the largest province of Greece until the expansion of Macedonia under Philip II. Thrace, Macedonia, and Thessaly take in most of northern Greece. Mount Olympus and Mount Ossa are both in Thessaly, which was the home of the Lapiths and the Centaurs. It was from Thessaly that the Argonauts sailed. Its inhabitants were noted for magic and horse breeding.

THESTIUS (thes'ti us): according to Euripides, the father of Leda.

THETIS (thē'tis): a sea goddess, wife of Peleus and mother of Achilles. It was at her wedding that Eris threw the golden apple marked "for the fairest," which eventually led to the Trojan War. She rendered her son invulnerable by plunging him into the waters of the Styx: all but the heel by which she held him, where Paris landed his lethal arrow.

THOAS (thō'as): the Taurian king who would have sacrificed the two young men, Orestes and Pylades, on the altar of Artemis if Iphigenia had not rescued them.

THRONIUM (thrō'ni um): a town in Phocis.

THRACE: an expansive region north of the Aegean, now part of Turkey. The Thracians were barbarous, bellicose, and brave, drank heavily, leched lustily, and sacrificed their enemies to their gods. They were horse breeders and great riders.

THYESTES (thy'es teez): brother of Atreus, father of Aegisthus by his own daughter Pelopia. He seduced his brother's wife, Aerope, and Atreus punished him by tricking him into eating his own children. Thyestes ascended the throne of Mycenae only to be dethroned by his nephews Agamemnon and Menelaus.

THYRSUS (thur'sus): symbol of Dionysus: a staff tipped with pine cones, wreathed in ivy or vine leaves.

TIRESIAS (tī'ree si as): the greatest of the ancient prophets, who lived to a great age spanning several generations. He was blind and twice changed sex.

TIRYNS (tir'inz): nine miles from Mycenae, rising out of the plain of Argolis. Its walls, twenty-five feet thick, are said to have been put together by the Cyclopes. Otherwise who could have lifted such enormous blocks? This was the kingdom of Agamemnon and the site of his murder by Clytemnestra. Schliemann, excavating between 1876 and 1885, unearthed quantities of jewelry, gold masks, and other objects.

TITHONUS (ti thō'nus): son of Laomedon, king of Troy. He was so beautiful that Eos (Dawn) fell in love with him and granted him immortality but forgot to give him eternal youth.

TMOLUS: a mountain in Asia Minor.

TRITON (try'ton): a gigantic sea god, son of Poseidon and Amphitrite. He was half man and half fish. He had power over the sea.

TROEZEN (tree'zen): an ancient city in Argolis in the Peloponnesus, about forty miles from Athens.

TROJAN WAR: traditional dates, 1194–1184 B.C.

TROPHONIUS (trō fō'ni us): a brother of Agamedes, son of Apollo. The brothers became famous as builders of temples, notably the temple of Apollo at Delphi.

TYNDAREUS (tin dā ray us): also Tyndarius; king of Lacedaemon, husband of Leda, by whom he had Castor and Clytemnestra.

URANUS (ou'ran ous): the sky, the heavens: most ancient of the gods.

WHITE RIVIERA: a long stretch of white sand on the coast of Thessaly where Achilles trained his horses.

XUTHUS (zu'thyuss): banished from Thessaly, he fled to Athens and married Creusa, daughter of King Erechtheus. The couple were childless and went to Delphi to seek help. Xuthus was told that the first person he met on leaving the temple would be his son. He met Ion, the secret offspring of Creusa and Apollo. See Euripides' play *Ion*.

ZEPHIR (Zef'eer): also Zephirus, the west wind, whose sweet breath produced flowers and fruits. In his temple at Athens he was represented as a young man with wings on his shoulders and his head crowned with flowers.

ZEUS (zyeus): son of Saturn and Ops. Lord of heaven and father of the gods; nurtured in a cave on Mount Ida. While still a child he vanquished the old order of gods, the Titans. Married to Hera but with six other wives, he spawned a host of offspring out of wedlock. He could change himself into many forms to gratify his passions: a shower of gold for Danaë, a swan for Leda, a white bull for Europa. Hera, wife number one, never ceased to pursue and punish her husband's lovers. His weapon was the thunderbolt, which he would hurl at the slightest provocation.

Classics from
Ancient Greece

.H.D. Rouse
This very readable prose translation tells the tale of
, Agamemnon, Paris, Helen, and all Troy
besieged by the mighty Greeks. It is a tale of glory and
, of pride and pettiness, of friendship and sacrifice,
of anger and revenge. In short, it is the quintessential
n tale of men at war.

.H.D. Rouse
Kept away from his home and family for 20 years by war
and malevolent gods, Odysseus returns to find his house
in disarray. This is the story of his adventurous travels and
his battle to reclaim what is rightfully his.

trans. Patric Dickinson
After the destruction of Troy by the Greeks, Aeneas leads
ojans to Italy where, according to Virgil, he
re-founds the city of Rome and begins a dynasty to last
irgil's greatest triumph, was seen by
many Medieval thinkers as linking Rome's ancient past to

**vailable wherever books are sold or at
signetclassics.com**

SIGNET CLASSICS

LYSISTRATA

by Aristophanes

translated by Douglass Parker

In Aristophanes' most popular play, sex—or lack of it—becomes a powerful agent of reconciliation. As war ravages the mighty city-states of ancient Greece, a band of women, led by Lysistrata of Athens, makes a pact to deny their husbands all sexual favors until they lay aside their weapons. Dismayed and frustrated, the men retaliate, and a battle of the sexes begins...

Written with bawdy abandon and unparalleled wit, *Lysistrata* is at once a powerful indictment of the insanity of war, and a sexual comedy without peer in the history of theater. That it remains both popular and accessible to the contemporary reader proves that the issues and themes that make compelling art never grow outdated.

Douglass Parker's translation presents the play in modern language for the modern audience. As *The New York Times* noted, "[Parker] has a range that can encompass the gravity of Aristophanes as well as the delirious and scabrous wit."

Available wherever books are sold or at signetclassics.com

READ THE TOP 20
SIGNET CLASSICS

SIGNETCLASSICS.COM